MW00583293

How We Forgot the Cold War

How We Forgot the Cold War

A HISTORICAL JOURNEY ACROSS AMERICA

Jon Wiener

UNIVERSITY OF CALIFORNIA PRESS
BERKELEY LOS ANGELES LONDON

University of California Press, one of the most distinguished university presses in the United States, enriches lives around the world by advancing scholarship in the humanities, social sciences, and natural sciences. Its activities are supported by the UC Press Foundation and by philanthropic contributions from individuals and institutions. For more information, visit www.ucpress.edu.

University of California Press
Berkeley and Los Angeles, California

University of California Press, Ltd.
London, England

© 2012 by The Regents of the University of California

Map: Ben Pease, Pease Press Cartography
Index: Sharon Sweeney

Library of Congress Cataloging-in-Publication Data

Wiener, Jon.
How we forgot the Cold War : a historical journey across America / Jon Wiener.
p. cm.
Includes bibliographical references and index.
ISBN 978-0-520-27141-8 (cloth : alk. paper)
1. Politics and culture—United States—History—20th century. 2. Cold War—Historiography. 3. Cold War—Social aspects—United States. 4. Collective memory—United States. 5. World politics—1945-1989. 6. United States—Intellectual life—20th century. 7. Conservatism—United States—History—20th century. I. Title.
E169.12.W486 2012
973.91—dc23 2012011669

Manufactured in the United States of America

21 20 19 18 17 16 15 14 13 12
10 9 8 7 6 5 4 3 2 1

In keeping with a commitment to support environmentally responsible and sustainable printing practices, UC Press has printed this book on Rolland Enviro100, a 100% post-consumer fiber paper that is FSC certified, deinked, processed chlorine-free, and manufactured with renewable biogas energy. It is acid-free and EcoLogo certified.

CONTENTS

ILLUSTRATIONS

MAP

FIGURES

Introduction

FORGETTING THE COLD WAR

In 1991, only a few hours after the USSR collapsed, Congress began making plans for organizing the official memory of the Cold War. The 1991 Defense Appropriations Act included $10 million for the creation of a "Legacy Resource Management Program" that would "inventory, protect and conserve the physical and literary property" of the Cold War so that future generations could understand and appreciate its meaning and significance.[1]

Conservatives dominated the proceedings that followed. Their effort to shape public memory of the Cold War deployed powerful tools of political and cultural persuasion. The ideological apparatus engaged in this effort was famously influential and effective: Fox News, the *Wall Street Journal,* the *National Review,* the *Weekly Standard,* the Heritage Foundation, an endless stream of op-eds and opinion pieces, and of course the voices of leading senators and congressmen as well as that of the Republican president.

Their message: the Cold War was a good war, like World War II. George W. Bush explained it in his 2003 State of the Union address, in which he drew an analogy between defeat of the Soviets and defeat of the Nazis: both the Nazi and Soviet regimes had been led by "small groups of men [who] seized control of great nations, built armies and arsenals, and set out to dominate the weak and intimidate the world. In each case, their ambitions of cruelty and murder had no limit. In each case, the ambitions of Hitlerism, militarism, and communism were defeated by the will of free peoples, by the strength of great alliances, and by the might of the United States of America."[2] The history of the twentieth century is thus a history of the battle between freedom and totalitarianism, good and evil, and it has two chapters: in the first, FDR led the Allies to victory over Nazi Germany; in the second, Reagan led the Free World to victory over the Soviet Union.

Liberals, meanwhile, lacked the conservatives' ideological zeal. Although they had been equal advocates of the Cold War, their priorities did not include claiming victory. Nor did they put forward an alternative interpretation of the meaning and significance of the collapse of the USSR.

This book is about the conservatives' argument—we can call it "the good war framework"—and about the way that argument was presented to the public at historical sites, museums, and monuments. It's also about what happened to that argument: it failed. Despite the immense effort by conservatives to shape public memory of the Cold War, their monuments weren't built, their historical sites have had few visitors, and many of their museums have shifted their focus to other topics. The public did not embrace a heroic story of the triumph of good over evil in the Cold War. The result: what I call "forgetting the Cold War."

What explains this forgetting? How can we understand the complex mixture of public indifference, skepticism, and apparent resistance to what historians have termed "Cold War triumphalism"?[3] And what are the implications for our understanding of the power of official ideology and well-funded media to influence our view of the past? To answer these questions, I examine the conservative efforts to shape public memory.

One thing is clear at the outset: this forgetting the Cold War is not part of a general turn away from recent American history on the part of the public. In fact it coincided with the unprecedented celebration of victory in World War II and of "the greatest generation" that fought it. One and a half million people now visit Pearl Harbor annually and wait in line for hours to see the USS *Arizona* Memorial. Award-winning historical films and TV miniseries on World War II have been seen by millions of Americans.

And it's not just World War II. The country experienced a massive outpouring of public emotion at the unveiling of the Vietnam Veterans Memorial in Washington, D.C., which for more than two decades has been one of the most visited monuments in Washington. And beyond World War II and Vietnam, thousands of new memorials, Erika Doss found, have been created in the past few decades. Andreas Huyssen wrote not long ago that "the notion of the monument as memorial" has "witnessed a triumphal return." History museums in the United States recently reported 100 million annual visitors. And a survey conducted by Roy Rosenzweig and David Thelen found that while the public didn't like the history they had been taught in school, they did like the history they saw in museums. An astounding 57 percent of Americans said they had visited a history museum or historical site in the previous year.[4] So the public's failure to embrace Cold War triumphalism has nothing to do with a dislike of historical sites or museums.

From the beginning of the Cold War until its end, all U.S. presidents, Republican as well as Democratic, had the same policy toward the USSR and China: "containment" and "deterrence." While each described communism as a totalitarian enemy bent on our destruction, all accepted the existence of communist rule within the borders established at the end of World War II, and all were committed to fighting any expansion of communist power beyond those borders—and to threatening nuclear war at moments of crisis.

But conservatives always offered an alternative to this consensus: instead of containment, they said, the United States should seek "rollback"; instead of accepting the status quo of Soviet (and Chinese) power, the United States should pursue victory over communism. This position was argued by Douglas MacArthur at the beginning of the Cold War, by Barry Goldwater in the middle, and by Ronald Reagan near the end.

The Republican right lost all the big policy battles of the Cold War. Republican presidents, as well as Democrats, rejected their arguments. During the Korean War, when MacArthur argued there was "no substitute for victory," Truman fired him and accepted a stalemate. Eisenhower failed to support freedom fighters in Hungary in 1956. Kennedy negotiated an end to the Cuban Missile Crisis that included a pledge not to invade and overthrow Castro. Johnson and Nixon fought another limited war in Vietnam, eventually lost, and then Nixon negotiated détente with the Soviets and the opening to China. The Cold War consensus had been a liberal, "realist" one. Even the fall of the Berlin Wall and the Soviet Union did not bring a rethinking of this history to the mainstream. That made it all the more important for conservatives to make the case retrospectively that they had been right to call for rollback.

Although the Cold War is being forgotten, the country is full of memorial sites of different kinds—museums, monuments, official historic landmarks. But these have received virtually no critical attention. Roy Rosenzweig and Warren Leon ask us to consider, in contrast, the critical attention "lavished on a widely circulated history book on a similar topic." A big Cold War book—John Lewis Gaddis's *The Cold War: A New History*—was the subject of more than a dozen serious and thoughtful reviews, some of them extensive: 1,600 words in the *Washington Post,* more than 5,000 in the *New York*

Review. But as Rozensweig and Leon point out, "a blanket of critical silence has surrounded" history museums and historical sites.[5]

I report here in some depth on almost two dozen Cold War museums, monuments, and historical sites and discuss briefly several dozen more (see map 1). The diversity of sites and objects on display is remarkable: a bomb crater in Nevada that's listed on the National Register of Historic Places; a gigantic mound of radioactive waste, which the public is invited to climb, at a former nuclear weapons plant in Weldon Spring, Missouri; a disarmed ICBM in its silo, open to visitors, permitted under the SALT treaty as a museum exhibit. In what follows I analyze the messages in official tours and the official explanations. Most of these places started out with the conservative interpretation—places like the Nevada Test Site and the Titan Missile Museum in Arizona, which make the case in different ways that nuclear deterrence protected freedom, and the Greenbrier Bunker in West Virginia, which shows how Congress, and thus democracy, would have continued to function after a nuclear war. I also describe the unofficial things that sometimes happened on the official tours—the arguments that broke out, the doubts expressed, and the challenges voiced by ordinary people.

Among the dozens of official Cold War memorial sites in the United States, one type is notably missing: the victory monument. We have such monuments for other wars. Currently the leading example is the World War II Memorial on the Mall in Washington, D.C., dedicated in 2004. "Victory on Land, Victory at Sea, Victory in the Air," it proclaims. It's a vast stone plaza, longer than a football field. Visitors enter through two forty-three-foot-high triumphal arches bearing huge victory wreaths held by gigantic bronze eagles. The text, emblazoned in granite, includes a quote from General George Marshall: "Before the sun sets on this terrible struggle our flag will be recognized throughout the world as a symbol of freedom on the one hand and of overwhelming force on the other."[6]

I found only one Cold War victory monument in the entire country, at the National Museum of the Air Force. This is a granite marker, ten feet high, which bears the legend "Victors in the Cold War," and explains, "The Cold War Didn't Just End... It Was Won" (figure 1). That is precisely the conservative message. A memorial to the Strategic Air Command (SAC), this monument displays a mailed fist holding lightning bolts and an olive branch against a field of clouds on a shield. However, this SAC memorial is not located on the National Mall in Washington, D.C., but rather in the memorial garden at Wright-Patterson Air Force Base, outside Dayton, Ohio. It was

FIGURE 1. Cold War Victors monument: "The Cold War Didn't Just End . . . It Was Won." Wright-Patterson Air Force Base, OH. This 10-foot monument is located not on the National Mall in Washington, D.C., but rather in an Air Force memorial garden outside Dayton, Ohio, and was privately funded by veterans of the Strategic Air Command. It seems to be the only Cold War victory monument in the country. (U.S. Air Force photo)

privately funded by SAC veterans and dedicated at a SAC reunion in May 2008. It is one of more than five hundred memorials in the garden.[7]

The low attendance at this and most of the other memorial sites—what I am calling forgetting the Cold War—has led the people who manage the official memory of the Cold War to make changes of different kinds. The most common change has been to shift the focus of exhibits to more popular topics: the Churchill Memorial in Fulton, Missouri, for example, has moved away from being a museum about Churchill's "Iron Curtain" speech there announcing the beginning of the Cold War; now it is mostly about the blood, sweat, and tears of Britain in World War II. SAC once had a museum, in Nebraska between Lincoln and Omaha, that displayed B-52 bombers and

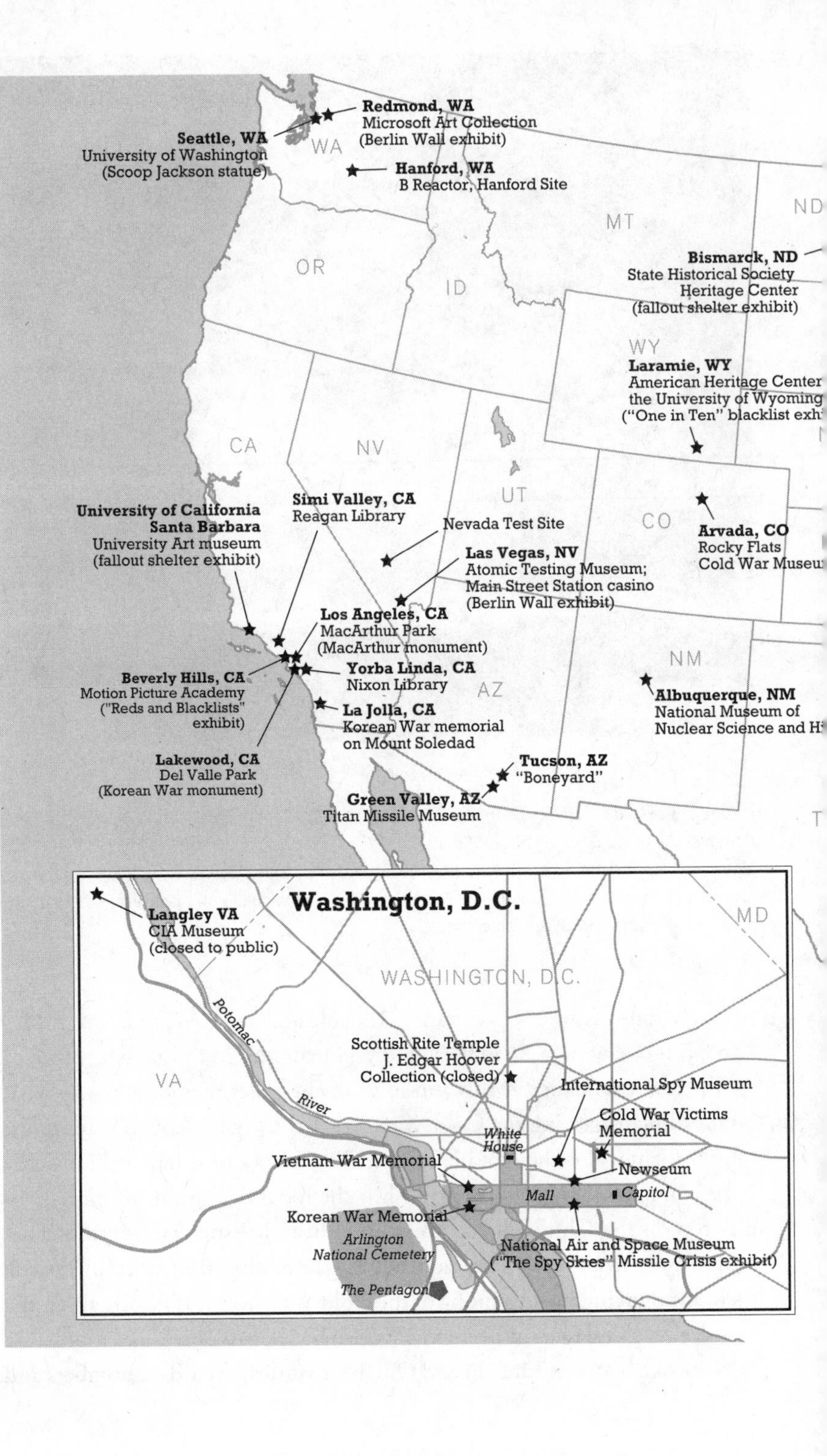
Redmond, WA
Microsoft Art Collection
(Berlin Wall exhibit)
Seattle, WA
University of Washington
(Scoop Jackson statue)
WA
Hanford, WA
B Reactor, Hanford Site
MT
ND
OR
ID
Bismarck, ND
State Historical Society
Heritage Center
(fallout shelter exhibit)
WY
Laramie, WY
American Heritage Center
the University of Wyoming
("One in Ten" blacklist exhi
CA
NV
UT
CO
Simi Valley, CA
Reagan Library
University of California
Santa Barbara
University Art museum
(fallout shelter exhibit)
Nevada Test Site
Las Vegas, NV
Atomic Testing Museum;
Main Street Station casino
(Berlin Wall exhibit)
Arvada, CO
Rocky Flats
Cold War Museu
Los Angeles, CA
MacArthur Park
(MacArthur monument)
NM
Beverly Hills, CA
Motion Picture Academy
("Reds and Blacklists"
exhibit)
Yorba Linda, CA
Nixon Library
AZ
Albuquerque, NM
National Museum of
Nuclear Science and Hi
La Jolla, CA
Korean War memorial
on Mount Soledad
Lakewood, CA
Del Valle Park
(Korean War monument)
Tucson, AZ
"Boneyard"
Green Valley, AZ
Titan Missile Museum
Washington, D.C.
Langley VA
CIA Museum
(closed to public)
MD
WASHINGTON, D.C.
Potomac
River
VA
Scottish Rite Temple
J. Edgar Hoover
Collection (closed)
International Spy Museum
Cold War Victims
Memorial
White
House
Vietnam War Memorial
Newseum
Mall
Capitol
Korean War Memorial
Arlington
National Cemetery
National Air and Space Museum
("The Spy Skies" Missile Crisis exhibit)
The Pentagon

Cold War Museums, Monuments and Memorials

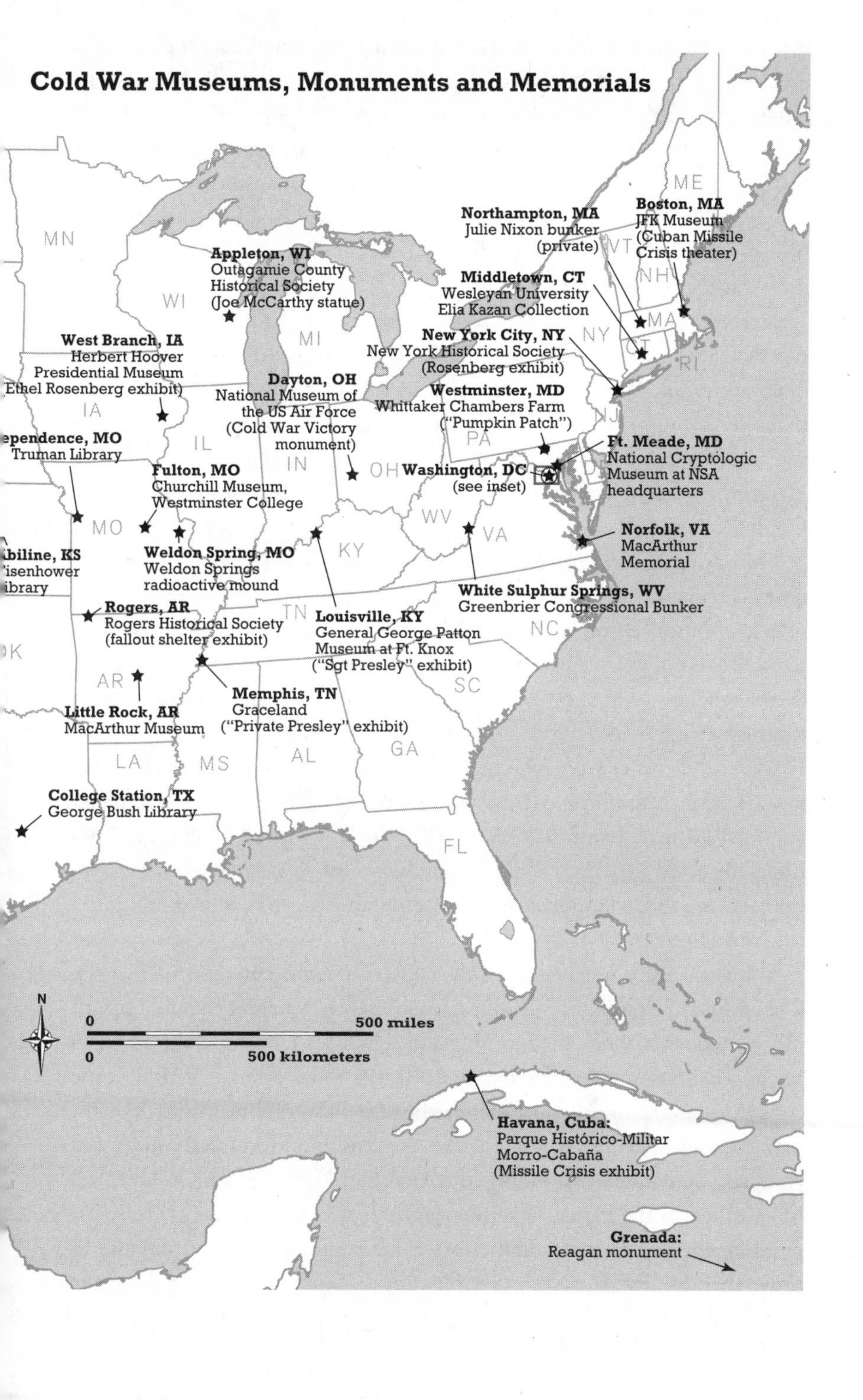

defined its mission as "ensuring the American people remember the vital role SAC played in maintaining world peace" during the Cold War.[8] But that museum was replaced in 1998 by the Strategic Air and Space Museum, which focuses mostly on space travel. Even the Reagan presidential museum in Simi Valley, California, has downplayed Cold War triumphalism with a striking new building displaying Air Force One, the jet used by all presidents from Nixon to George W. Bush, including Carter and Clinton—an apolitical exhibit if there ever was one.

A second change is evident at some of the former nuclear weapons factories that, after the fall of the Soviet Union, initially became official sites for celebrating Cold War victory. Now they operate primarily to reassure visitors that the cleanup of radioactive contamination from weapons production was successful, so you won't get cancer there. That's the point of the tours at Hanford in eastern Washington State and at the Weldon Spring radioactive mound west of St. Louis.

Other sites claiming to be Cold War memorials in fact have other purposes. The San Diego cross, on the highest mountaintop outside the city, is one. Its sponsors describe this forty-foot cross as a Cold War memorial. But that claim is only a legal pretext advanced by Christian activists who want to keep a religious symbol on government property, in violation of the constitutional separation of church and state.

Meanwhile other Cold War memorial sites slumber on unchanged, with low attendance and little energy: the Whittaker Chambers pumpkin patch National Historic Landmark seems to be the least visited of all official national historical sites, even though Chambers remains a hero to conservatives for his claim that communist spies, most notably Alger Hiss, had infiltrated the New Deal.

While the central issue here is the conservative interpretation—that the Cold War was a good war—I found some sites that present the public with other arguments about the meaning and significance of the Cold War. On my travels I found many fascinating and unexpected exhibits critical of the conservative view: in Abilene, Kansas, the Eisenhower Library includes a display about his warning against "the excessive power of the military-industrial complex." In Laramie, Wyoming, the American Heritage Center had an exhibit critical of the House Un-American Activities Committee's (HUAC's) requirement that former communists name names of former comrades to prove their loyalty. The New York Historical Society had a show about the

Rosenberg case that displayed new evidence that Ethel was innocent, along with a real electric chair from Sing Sing, where she was executed.

The two chapters in Part I look at arguments about the end of the Cold War, where the strongest case can be found for the conservatives' "good war" interpretation. Parts II through IV, organized chronologically by decade, discuss specific sites and along the way provide a brief history of the Cold War.

In Part V three alternative approaches to telling the public about the Cold War are presented, each of which offers contending views of the conservatives' good war framework. They demonstrate in different ways what a good museum can accomplish: they all show that the meaning and significance of the Cold War continues to be debated, that historians and journalists and ordinary people disagree over how and why it was fought. Was communism innately militarily aggressive? Was the Soviet Union implacably bent on world domination? Would the Soviets really have attacked us if we hadn't threatened to destroy them? Wouldn't nuclear war have to be waged primarily against civilians—and didn't that make it wrong? Didn't preparing for nuclear war undermine our moral and political values, democracy and respect for human life? Could a simple, dramatic disarmament agreement have changed our expectations and made wider disarmament workable? Wasn't the Cold War a disastrous waste of resources needed for humane projects? The big questions, of course, are whether the Cold War was inevitable and whether it was necessary at all.[9]

The first of the alternative approaches will be found at Rocky Flats outside Denver, where a group of citizens and former workers plan to open (in 2012) a Cold War museum that presents both sides of the debate over the former plutonium weapons factory there. While the federal government has done nothing to commemorate this site, except to open a wildlife refuge on part of the land of the former factory complex, the citizens' group will present the story of America's most dangerous and expensive industrial accident, which occurred in 1979 when Denver was threatened with a Chernobyl-like incident and fifteen thousand demonstrators called for closing the plant. With both sides being presented, visitors will be invited to debate the issues for themselves.

Another approach to this kind of museum-as-debate will be found at the Paley Center for Media in Beverly Hills, in a planned exhibit on the anniversary of CNN's award-winning series *Cold War.* The approach of Ted Turner's documentary team was to give equal time to the Russians—presenting Russian experts and "witnesses" explaining their motives and reasons and their ideas about the Cold War. Again, viewers are invited to decide for themselves which interpretations are more convincing.

And third, the most amazing of all Cold War exhibits is found at the Truman Presidential Library in Independence, Missouri. Whereas most presidential museums argue that their president was right, the Truman museum tells visitors he might have been wrong—about the Soviets' motives and about the kind of challenge posed by the USSR in the years immediately following World War II. The museum explains Truman's position and then declares, with astonishing frankness, that "there are other ways of looking at the subject." Viewers are presented with material critical of the president, written by commentators at the time and more recently by historians—all of whom take up the question, "Was the Cold War necessary?" By inviting visitors to think about alternative interpretations, the Truman Library demonstrates the history museum at its best—a bright light in the often dim world of Cold War commemoration.

PART ONE

The End

ONE

Hippie Day at the Reagan Library

When the Ronald Reagan Presidential Library and Museum in Simi Valley, California, announced it would hold a "hippie contest" one Saturday, I wondered what it would take to win. Dress in tie-dye and refuse to get a job? Put on bell-bottoms, take LSD, and jump out the window? Grow long hair and give the finger to your country, while decent kids were risking their lives defending freedom thousands of miles away?[1]

The hippie contest was part of a daylong "fun-in" (their term) to celebrate the opening of an exhibit titled "Back to the 60s." As visitors went through the library gates that morning into the beautiful tree-lined courtyard, we were greeted by a kindly woman giving out free samples of Ding Dongs (a Twinkie-like confection). Frisbees were also being handed out, bearing the motto "Back to the 60s, Ronald Reagan Presidential Library." Is that really what it was like in the sixties—free frisbees and Ding Dongs for everyone? Handed out by Reagan's people?

According to conservative ideology, victory in the Cold War was the work of one man above all others: Ronald Reagan. Alone among presidents, he refused to accept the continued existence of the USSR. That is the argument John Gaddis makes in *The Cold War,* the definitive statement of the conservative interpretation. Reagan famously described the Soviet Union as an "evil empire." That's why he sought to "hasten [its] disintegration."[2]

The story has been told a thousand times. Indeed, if you Google "Reagan won the Cold War," you get 150,000 results. It was Reagan who stood at the Berlin Wall and proclaimed, "Mr. Gorbachev, tear down this wall!" It was Reagan who funded the mujahadeen to fight the Soviets in Afghanistan, wearing the Red Army down in its own Vietnam-like quagmire. It was Reagan who ordered a massive military buildup, including "Star Wars," that his supporters claim drove the Soviet Union to bankruptcy. And when the Berlin Wall fell, it was Reagan who got the credit.

Margaret Thatcher put it most bluntly: "Ronald Reagan won the Cold War without firing a shot." Bob Dole, running for president in 1996, told the Republican National Convention, "Were it not for President Reagan, the Soviet Union would still be standing today." Dinesh D'Souza summed up the conservative consensus in the *National Review* when Reagan died: "Reagan won and Gorbachev lost.... In the Cold War, Reagan turned out to be our Churchill: it was his vision and leadership that led us to victory."[3]

Thus if Cold War victory were going to be celebrated anywhere, the Reagan Library should be its white-hot heart. But the Reagan Library has never held a "Cold War Victory" festival in its courtyard. Instead, it had Hippie Day.

The library courtyard on Hippie Day was teeming with activity: in one corner, dozens of kids were hard at work tie-dying T-shirts; the results of their labors hung on lines around the courtyard, drying. The tie-dye would be featured in the day's climactic event: the hippie contest.

Onstage in the courtyard, an Ed Sullivan look-alike was introducing a Beatles sound-alike group. They wore the collarless black suits of the early lovable-lads-from-Liverpool period but said nothing about the benefits of LSD or being more popular than Jesus. "The sixties," "Paul" remarked, "when boys liked girls, and girls liked boys, and the only one swinging both ways was Tarzan."

While the group played "She Loves You," the photo studio under the arcade offered visitors two different ways to have their pictures taken. You could put on combat fatigues (which they provided) and pose in front of a Vietnam battlefield mural, or you could put on hippie garb (of which they had an impressive assortment) and pose with life-size standup figures of the Beatles in their Sgt. Pepper outfits. The action was with the Beatles; all the kids wanted to be hippies, not soldiers. What would Nancy Reagan say about that?

Reagan's political ascent, as the museum exhibits explain, began during the 1964 presidential campaign, when he gave a half-hour TV speech supporting Goldwater. His message was apocalyptic: "We are faced with the most evil enemy mankind has known in his long climb from the swamp to the stars." "Freedom" was fighting a worldwide battle to the death against "the ant heap of totalitarianism." If we lost this battle, "a thousand years of darkness" would follow.[4]

Reagan was so much more effective than Goldwater at delivering the message that, as Rick Perlstein has shown, a group of party leaders decided that night he would make a better candidate.[5] They started him on the road to the White House with a campaign for governor two years later. Any serious exhibit about Reagan and the sixties would put "the speech" at its center, on a big screen in a darkened theater, where visitors could savor that historic night.

Instead, on Hippie Day, Reagan's speech ran on a small TV set in a museum gallery dominated by a VW Beetle painted pink and decorated with yellow flowers and butterflies, surrounded by life-size white plaster figures wearing hippie garb, posed working on signs for a demonstration. The signs read, "Vets for Peace in Vietnam," "Hey Hey LBJ—how many kids did you kill today?," "We shall overcome," and "Tyranny is always dependent on a silent majority"—the latter a response to Nixon's speech proclaiming himself spokesman for the silent majority. Reagan built his political career by attacking the people who carried these signs, which made this part of the exhibit incredible.

The TV set playing Reagan's historic 1964 convention speech was set up in a replica of a middle-class sixties living room, with modern furniture and posters on the walls that said "Surfing Party," "Hootenanny," and "Sock It to Me." I don't know of any families that had a "Sock It to Me" poster in the living room.

The problem that seems to face museums like the Reagan Library is that few people will visit if all they're going to get is right-wing ideology about Cold War victory. To attract visitors, they need to find something people will drive twenty or thirty miles to see—something like Hippie Day. The folks at the Reagan Library seemed to think people were still interested in the Beatles but not in Reagan's role in defeating communism. Of course, the version of the sixties on display here lacked the confrontational edge of the original, and it was nothing like the way Reagan portrayed the decade, nor did it have anything in common with Republican ideology that sees Reagan's role in history as equivalent to FDR's in leading the free world to defeat the totalitarian enemy.

Later in the day, the hippie contest began. The entrants were a dozen sweet kids, virtually all girls and all around ten years old. They came onstage, happy and excited, wearing their newly tie-dyed T-shirts and bell-bottoms, sandals, headbands, and beads. One by one they walked across the stage, flashed the peace sign, and shouted "Peace!" Nobody seemed to remember that Nancy had denounced her daughter Patti Davis as "nothing but a damn hippie."[6]

"Let's hear it for these wonderful kids in their hippie outfits," the announcer shouted. "Everybody here is a winner!"

It's not that the Reagan Library neglects Reagan's claims regarding the fall of the Soviet Union. The story is there, with a big multiscreen video history of the entire Cold War narrated by Reagan—among the new exhibits introduced in 2011. And of course the Reagan Library exhibits feature the Berlin Wall, which the *National Review* called "the most visible, stark symbol of the Cold War divide, a gray, cold tombstone to human freedom."[7]

It's not just the right that found the Berlin Wall a potent symbol of an abhorrent system. John Le Carré wrote in 1989 about standing at the wall "as soon as it started going up" and staring at "the weasel faces of the brainwashed little thugs who guarded the Kremlin's latest battlement." "I felt nothing but disgust and terror," he continued, "which was exactly what I was supposed to feel: the Wall was perfect theatre as well as a perfect symbol of the monstrosity of ideology gone mad." And Chalmers Johnson described the fall of the Berlin Wall as "one of the grandest developments in modern history."[8]

The Reagan Library is the nation's central place for commemorating the fall of the Berlin Wall. The museum has no fewer than three displays about it. A segment of the "real" wall, three and a half feet wide and ten feet high, weighing six thousand pounds, is displayed outdoors on a terrace (figure 2). The marker doesn't tell you much about the wall, but it does say the display of the segment of it here was "made possible through the generosity of Carl and Margaret Karcher." Carl was the founder of Carl's Jr., a member of the John Birch Society, and the biggest funder of California's Briggs Initiative, the 1978 proposition that would have required firing all gays and lesbians from employment as public school teachers. Even Reagan opposed it, and it didn't pass.

At the library's dedication in 1991, two years after the fall of the Berlin Wall, Reagan highlighted the segment on display. Before an audience that included Bob Hope, Arnold Schwarzenegger, and Jimmy Stewart, Reagan said, "Visitors to this mountaintop will see a great jagged chunk of that Berlin Wall, . . . hated symbol of, yes, an evil empire, that spied on and lied to its citizens, denying them their freedom, their bread, even their faith. Well,

FIGURE 2. Tourists at the Berlin Wall exhibit, Reagan Library, Simi Valley, California. (photo by David Weiner)

today that will all exist only in museums, souvenir collections and the memories of a people no longer oppressed."[9]

A second Berlin Wall exhibit at the Reagan Library is part of a replica of Checkpoint Charlie in Berlin, with a mannequin of a "resolute" U.S. Army MP on one side, standing in front of a huge American flag and a sign that reads, "Achtung! You are leaving the American sector." On the other side of the gate is a gigantic Soviet flag; "an East German border guard stands menacingly," the pocket guide declares.[10] It's a popular background for photos of family members—some of which are posted online at personal websites.[11] When I was visiting, the only comment I heard on this exhibit was a woman complaining to her husband, "They said the wall here was real, but it's a fake!" (I explained that the "real" one is outside in back.) As for the East German border guard, when I asked a couple of teenagers whether he looked "menacing" to them, they told me, "Not really." Raised on horror movies and violent video games, they are used to much more demonic villains.

The wall text here declares, "From 1961 to 1989, the Soviet goal was clear: to 'bury' the decent and free democracies of the West in the name of Communism. The crimes of Communist regimes against civilians resulted in the deaths of 100 million people. President Reagan identified this as the essence of an 'evil empire,' yielding nothing but death and destruction where it comes to power. The Cold War ended when the Soviet Union finally heeded Ronald Reagan's demand to 'tear down this wall.'" That's the message in a nutshell: Reagan told them to do it, and they did.

After Checkpoint Charlie comes a side gallery on the Cold War featuring a video in which Reagan says, "At my first presidential press conference, I said, 'They reserve unto themselves the right to commit any crime.'" The Soviet goal, according to Reagan, was "a one-world Soviet state." To put a stop to this, Reagan says, "I decided we had to send a strong message"—so we invaded Grenada! Not only did this help prevent a one-world Soviet state; within a couple of years the Soviet Union itself collapsed. No less than Margaret Thatcher provides the conclusion to the video: "In ending the Cold War, Ronald Reagan deserves the most credit." I'm furiously taking notes, then look around to find myself alone in an empty room.

Grenada gets its own very small display at the library. The wall text reads, "US rescues 800 US medical students," next to a button labeled "Press button to learn more." In Grenada, on the other hand, a big monument commemorating Reagan's invasion can be found outside the airport (figure 3). It was dedicated in 1986 by Reagan himself. The monument reads, "This plaque expresses the gratitude of the Grenadan people to the Forces from the United States of America and the Caribbean who sacrificed their lives in liberating Grenada in October 1983." However, the monument was erected not by the people of Grenada but by the Veterans of Foreign Wars of the United States.[12]

The Cold War room at the Reagan Library is mostly empty because it's a side gallery on the walkway to what the library rightly bills as its biggest attraction, literally and figuratively: the Air Force One exhibit, the "Flying White House" that went on display in 2005. The signs on the freeway say, "Ronald Reagan Presidential Library & Air Force One." They do not say, "Reagan Library and Berlin Wall Exhibit." Here, Reagan's "dream" is described not as tearing down the Berlin Wall but as having "this magnificent aircraft here at his Library"—and that dream, the library declares, "has finally come true. We are privileged to have this national treasure and honored by the trust the United States Air Force has placed in us to share it with the American people."[13]

The Air Force One exhibit is completely apolitical. Conservative ideology is nowhere to be found in the 90,000-square-foot, $30 million display. Reagan's "Flying White House," visitors learn, was used by every president

FIGURE 3. Invasion of Grenada monument in Grenada. The marker reads, "This plaque expresses the gratitude of the Grenadan people to the Forces from the USA . . . who sacrificed their lives in liberating Grenada in October 1983." It was erected not by the people of Grenada but rather by the Veterans of Foreign Wars of the United States. (photo by Robert Kitay)

from Nixon to George W. Bush, including Carter and Clinton—and thus is hardly a monument to Reagan's unique role in winning the Cold War, which is not mentioned. Instead, visitors learn that Reagan flew more miles in this plane than any other president and that it was in this plane that he "officially started the Daytona Beach, Florida, NASCAR race via phone." He is quoted as saying, from Air Force One, "Start your engines, Daytona."[14]

As for souvenirs of the Berlin Wall, the gift shop sells a paperweight with the inscription, "Mr. Gorbachev, tear down this wall!" It's $49. But it's only one of thirty-three "desk items" for sale. Other paperweights are inscribed with other quotations from the president, including one for $39 that says, "There is nothing as good for the inside of a man as the outside of a horse."[15]

Does Reagan really deserve credit for the collapse of the Soviet Union? It's true that there's "Mr. Gorbachev, tear down this wall!," which is featured prominently, and appropriately, at the library. An uncompromising voice of freedom spoke—and totalitarianism crumbled. But what happened in

Berlin in fact was something quite different. Michael Meyer was *Newsweek*'s bureau chief in Germany and Eastern Europe in 1989 and wrote about it in his book *The Year That Changed the World.* Chance, he says, played a huge part in bringing down the Berlin Wall; what happened was mostly an accident. It began when Hungary decided to open its border with Austria. East Germans thus for the first time had an exit route to the West, and tens of thousands departed every day. East German leader Egon Krenz decided he had to do something to stem the tide; he concluded that, if travel to the West was not banned, East Germans would return after visiting. So he announced freedom of travel, to begin "immediately"—by which he meant the next day, with some kind of "appropriate" controls.

But on November 9, 1989, as soon as the announcement was made, East Germans headed for Checkpoint Charlie, where a border guard decided to open the gate. What happened next is what we call "the fall of the Berlin Wall." As the historian Gerard DeGroot explained, "History pivoted on the misinterpretation of a word. Krenz called it a 'botch.'"[16]

Conservative writers claim that the fall of the wall was the result of a longer-term process, also instigated by Reagan: a massive military buildup by the United States that set off a new round of the arms race that bankrupted the USSR. But these claims, as Sean Wilentz writes in *The Age of Reagan,* have "little credible evidence" to back them up. "New expenditures by the Soviet Union in the face of Reagan's buildup were not especially heavy in the 1980s," he writes, "and certainly were not enough to cause major damage to its already wracked economy." Scholars examining the Soviet archives that were opened in the nineties found no evidence of any "panicky response to the Reagan rearmament that led to Soviet economic or political depletion."[17]

Moreover, the skyrocketing defense budget of the Reagan White House was based on "manifestly exaggerated estimates of the Soviet Union's military superiority," Wilentz writes, "which were later proved wrong." A sizable portion of the Reagan defense increase was "consumed by fraud, waste, and mismanagement." Meanwhile the weapons Reagan so passionately promised—the $15 billion MX missile system and the $26 billion Star Wars program—were never deployed.[18]

The claim that Reagan's aggressive military budget and bellicose rhetoric forced Kremlin leaders to come to the bargaining table is equally unsupported by evidence. The change was the work of Gorbachev, who came to power in March 1985. "Without Gorbachev," Wilentz writes, "it is conceivable that the Soviet Union might have carried on for decades, its nuclear deterrent strong enough to ward off threats from the West, its conventional forces powerful enough to contain rising discontent within its own satellites in eastern and central Europe."[19]

George H. W. Bush said pretty much the same thing on the tenth anniversary of the fall of the Berlin Wall. Instead of praising Reagan, he gave credit to the Soviet leader. "We can never repay the debt we owe Mikhail Gorbachev," Bush declared at a ceremony in Berlin in 1999. "History still hasn't given him the credit he deserves, but it will."[20]

One more thing: when Reagan proposed the Star Wars missile defense system in 1983—also featured at the library—he did not say his goal was "to hasten the disintegration" of the USSR (John Gaddis's words). He said his goal was "introducing greater stability" in the relationship between the United States and the Soviet Union. He said, "We seek neither military superiority nor political advantage."[21] Those quotes are not displayed on the wall at the Reagan Library.

In private communications with Soviet leaders Reagan was even clearer. He wrote Gorbachev's predecessor, Konstatin Chernenko, in 1984, "I have no higher goal than the establishment of a relationship between our two great nations characterized by constructive cooperation. Differences in our political beliefs and in our perspectives on international problems should not be an obstacle to efforts aimed at strengthening peace and building a productive working relationship."[22] You might call that policy "détente."

As for the "Reagan Doctrine"—U.S. military aid to anticommunist forces around the world seeking the "rollback" rather than the "containment" of communism—visitors to the library are told that Reagan's "unshakeable lifelong opposition to communism . . . helped to free hundreds of millions of people around the globe." But the Reagan Doctrine's role in hastening the demise of the Soviet Union is exaggerated at the library and by conservative writers.[23] In Nicaragua, U.S. support for the Contras led to perhaps 200,000 deaths but didn't hurt the Soviet Union and was abandoned at the insistence of Congress. In the meantime the Reagan White House sent arms to the Contras, paid for with the proceeds from selling weapons to Iran in exchange for the release of hostages—the "Iran-Contra Affair"—which did a lot more damage to the Reagan administration than it did to the USSR. (The library display on Iran-Contra says only that it happened "without his knowledge.") In another prong of the so-called Reagan Doctrine, the United States supported the anticommunist rebels in Angola led by Jonas Savimbi, but that also had virtually no effect on the Soviet Union.

The strongest case for the Reagan Doctrine leading to the collapse of the Soviet Union can be found in U.S. support for the mujahadeen in Afghanistan, which of course is emphasized in the exhibits at the Reagan Library. But even with that argument, two major problems arise. First, support for the mujahadeen began before Reagan. It was started by the Carter administration—although the Jimmy Carter Library in Atlanta doesn't mention that.[24] Second, and more important, that support wasn't significantly increased until 1986, a year after Gorbachev had come to power and was already reversing Soviet policy and beginning withdrawal from Afghanistan.

And the official premise of the Reagan Doctrine turned out to be faulty. In its original formulation, antidemocratic left-wing regimes were described as incapable of change and thus required force to overthrow them, while antidemocratic right-wing regimes were described as open to peaceful transformation. But support for the right in Afghanistan led to a vicious civil war, the triumph of the Taliban, and the rise of Bin Laden, and the notion that regimes on the left could be changed only by military force was definitively disproven—by the case of the Soviet Union.

The greatest weakness at the Reagan Library concerns Reagan's meeting with Gorbachev in 1986 at Reykjavik, where the president proposed phasing out all "offensive" missiles. The exhibit in Simi Valley doesn't give the president the credit he deserves. Something monumental almost happened at Reykjavik. Reagan sincerely dreamed of a world without nuclear weapons. Eric Hobsbawm, perhaps the greatest left-wing historian of the twentieth century, writes that, at Reykjavik, Reagan's "simple-minded idealism broke through the unusually dense screen of ideologists, fanatics, careerists, desperados and professional warriors around him." The president "let himself be convinced" by Gorbachev that the two superpowers could live in peace. For practical purposes, Hobsbawm concludes, the Cold War ended at Reykjavik—and we should not "underestimate the contribution of President Reagan."[25]

More than thirty places in the United States in addition to the Reagan Library display segments of the Berlin Wall, and these displays present a stunningly wide range of interpretations: one treats its graffiti as art; another treats the whole thing as a joke. And size matters: there are competing claims over who in the United States has the biggest section of the Berlin Wall. The Newseum in Washington, D.C., says it does; the Wende Museum in L.A.

says it does. L.A. wins, with ten segments compared to the Newseum's eight. However, the Newseum claims it has the largest section of "unaltered" wall segments, as well as a real East German guard tower.[26]

The Kennedy Library in Boston has a segment of the Berlin Wall, because Kennedy went to the wall just after it was built and said, "Ich bin ein Berliner." When the wall went up, Kennedy and the other Western leaders said they were outraged, but, as Tony Judt explains, "behind the scenes many Western leaders were secretly relieved." Berlin had been the focus of official anxiety and unsuccessful diplomacy for three years. Now "Western leaders privately agreed that a wall across Berlin was a far better outcome than a war"—because "whatever was said in public, few Western politicians could seriously imagine asking their soldiers to 'die for Berlin.'" Dean Rusk explained simply and clearly that the wall was not a bad thing for the West: "the probability is that in realistic terms it would make a Berlin settlement easier."[27] And Kennedy himself said in private, "A wall is a hell of a lot better than a war."[28] That fact is missing from every exhibit on the Berlin Wall.

There's another segment of the Berlin Wall at the Nixon Library in Yorba Linda, but according to the Reaganites, Nixon doesn't merit any credit because he pursued détente with the Soviets rather than victory over them. There's a segment of the Berlin Wall at Westminster College in Fulton, Missouri, where Churchill gave his "Iron Curtain" speech—but that was fifteen years before the wall was built.[29]

The George H. W. Bush Library in College Station, Texas, has outdone all of them. The entrance displays a monumental bronze statue of five horses jumping over the rubble of the Berlin Wall (figure 4). The entire sculpture is thirty feet long and weighs seven tons. The sculptor explains, "The horses simply represent humanity and the sculpture represents a victory of the human spirit." He also says the sculpture received the CIA's Agency Seal Medallion for "Best Artistic Expression of the end of the Cold War."[30]

Bush of course was president when the wall fell. The text here claims that he "was very instrumental in . . . the coming down of the Berlin Wall." But in fact he was completely surprised by the events in Berlin.[31] The website www.berlin-wall.net sells a photo titled "Presenting the Berlin Wall to Vice President Dan Quayle." It's actually just a small piece, but that piece is not on display at the Dan Quayle Museum in Huntington, Indiana. In his now-forgotten 2000 presidential campaign, Quayle did claim to have "participated in winning the cold war" as vice president.[32]

FIGURE 4. "The Day the Wall Came Down," sculpture at the George Bush Library, College Station, Texas. It's thirty feet long and weighs seven tons. The sculptor says, "The horses simply represent humanity and the sculpture represents a victory of the human spirit." It received the CIA's Agency Seal Medallion for "Best Artistic Expression of the end of the Cold War." (photo courtesy of George Bush Presidential Library and Museum)

Microsoft has a segment of the wall in its art collection at its Redmond, Washington, campus, outside of Seattle (figure 5). That wall segment, and the rest of the collection here, can be seen by the public by appointment only, and tours are offered one Thursday per month. Visitors learn that the official Microsoft collection includes, in addition to the Berlin Wall section, 4,500 works of art hanging in more than one hundred Microsoft buildings around the world, where they are "displayed for the benefit and enjoyment of Microsoft employees, their guests and our customers." Visitors also learn that the Microsoft Art Collection, including the Berlin Wall section, "represents an important aspect of the culture at Microsoft." That's because, "in partnership with artists and the business community, the Collection takes a leadership role in shaping culture."

And there's more: Microsoft believes that art in the work environment, including its chunk of the Berlin Wall, "enhances employee morale, leads to networking opportunities, reduces stress, increases creativity and productivity, broadens employee appreciation of diversity, encourages discussions and

FIGURE 5. Berlin Wall segment in the Microsoft Art Collection, Redmond, Washington. Wall text reads, "Is this Art?" Answer: yes. It contains "a richly colored, energetic and tightly-composed abstraction." Ronald Reagan is not mentioned. (photo courtesy of Microsoft Art Collection, Accession Number 1996274)

expression of opinions," and "evidences the company's interest in improving quality of life in and outside of the company."[33] So the Berlin Wall section on display here helps make the eighty thousand Microsoft employees happier, more productive workers.

Microsoft's 12-foot-high, 4-foot-wide, 3.5-ton section of the Berlin Wall was a gift from Daimler-Benz AG of Germany, presented to Bill Gates when he visited the Mercedes corporate headquarters in Berlin. The German company "wanted to establish a long-term strategic partnership involving software technology . . . for future in-car computers."[34] Of course it didn't require the fall of the wall for Mercedes to do business with Microsoft, but the 3.5-ton gift does symbolize the victory of capitalism in a big way.

This segment of the wall, like the others, is covered with graffiti. The Microsoft exhibit guide opens with the question, "Is this Art?," pointing out that many people "customarily think of graffiti as little more than urban vandalism." Microsoft wants viewers to know that "the Wall attracted artists—unknown and well-known— . . . whose efforts ranged from scribbled words to complex compositions." This particular chunk contains "a richly colored, energetic and tightly-composed abstraction—a collage of urban graphic gestures."[35] So it belongs in an art collection. Ronald Reagan, however, is not mentioned in Microsoft's exhibit text.

At the other end of the spectrum of cultural capital, another graffiti-covered piece of the Berlin Wall is on display in Las Vegas, at the Main Street Station casino, in the men's room. It's behind a row of three urinals. "Of all the Berlin Wall chunks in museums and memorials across America, we think this one is the most fun," declared the guidebook *Roadside America,* which bills itself as "a caramel-coated-nutbag-full of odd and hilarious travel destinations." Their piece was titled "Pee at the Berlin Wall."[36]

This site was named "Las Vegas' number two historic bathroom" by the Travel Channel in its *Las Vegas Top 10 Bathrooms* documentary and is featured at the Cheapo Las Vegas website.[37] To get there you leave the glitter and crowds on the strip and head downtown—and downscale—to what is politely termed the "budget" area of the city's tourist attractions. Main Street Station has a Victorian/Gay Nineties décor and offers rooms "at the mid-range of the low end" of downtown Las Vegas, as one gambler there explained it to me. The hotel for some reason is a favorite of visiting Hawaiians and of serious gamblers who come for what I was told was one of the most liberal craps games in town.

On the way to the men's room you pass the quarter slots and video poker and $5 blackjack tables. The piece of the Berlin Wall in the men's room is about four feet high and six feet long. You're not really supposed to urinate on the wall but rather in the standard urinals attached to it. Above the wall and the row of urinals is a plaque reading, "Gentlemen: The Berlin Wall . . . over 100 people were killed trying to escape to freedom." The plaque does not mention Reagan. The hotel says that women who want to see the wall can ask a security guard to make sure the coast is clear. The urinal/Berlin Wall is featured at the website Urinal.net, "the best place to piss away your time on the internet."[38]

In 2009, on the twentieth anniversary of the fall of the wall, a commemorative "art event" was held in Los Angeles, not far from the Reagan Library. Described as "the most ambitious commemoration of the 20th anniversary of the fall of the Berlin Wall outside of Germany," the event was staged across the street from LACMA, the Los Angeles County Museum of Art, by the Wende Museum, a wonderful Culver City repository of artifacts of Cold War life in Eastern Europe and the Soviet Union.[39] The event was in two parts: "The Wall Along Wilshire," segments of the real wall billed as "the longest stretch of the Berlin Wall in the world outside of Berlin," on display across the street from LACMA, indefinitely; and "The Wall Across Wilshire," a three-hour event at which "60 feet of specially-constructed material" were erected blocking the street, "bringing traffic to a stop for three hours on one of the busiest and most important thoroughfares in Los Angeles" (figure 6). At midnight on November 8, 2009, "select segments of the Wall" were "destroyed by invited dignitaries" and by a wild crowd.[40] A street party followed. The twelve-hundred-word press release didn't mention Ronald Reagan.

The art part of the project consisted of commissions to artists to paint the two "Berlin Walls" with images expressing "their creative response to the Walls in our lives." Among the artists selected were Shepard Fairey, who did the iconic Obama "Hope" poster, and a French muralist named Thierry Noir. In interviews with the *Los Angeles Times,* Fairey said his painting on the wall in L.A. was an "antiwar, anti-containment piece" that "makes a parallel to the Wall of Palestine." Noir said his painting would draw an analogy between the Berlin Wall and the border wall between the United States and Mexico—the point being that "every wall is not built forever."[41]

FIGURE 6. The Wende Museum's "Wall Across Wilshire" event to commemorate the twentieth anniversary of the fall of the Berlin Wall, Los Angeles, November 9, 2009. The artists said the wall that separated East and West Berlin is like the walls today separating Israel and Palestine and the United States and Mexico. (photo by Antoine Themistocleous/The Wende Museum)

So the wall separating East and West Berlin, communism and freedom, is like the wall separating Israel and Palestine and the one separating the United States and Mexico. The Berlin Wall prevented victims of communism from reaching freedom in the West, the way the Israeli wall prevents victims of Zionism from returning to their homes in Palestine, the way the U.S. border wall prevents Mexicans from entering their historic territory. That's the meaning of the fall of the Berlin Wall "in our lives" today, according to "the most ambitious commemoration of the 20th anniversary of the fall of the Berlin Wall outside of Germany." Back at the Reagan Library in Simi Valley, one can only imagine the dismay at the range and diversity of public commemorations of the Berlin Wall and the end of the Cold War.

TWO

The Victims of Communism Museum

A STUDY IN FAILURE

It was supposed to be like the Holocaust Museum: a $100 million Victims of Communism Museum, built on public land in Washington, D.C., and paid for with private money. It was to commemorate those who died in the "unprecedented imperial communist holocaust" that we call the Cold War.[1] The number of victims was said to be one hundred million, quite a bit more than the six million memorialized at the Holocaust Museum. The plans called for a re-creation of the Gulag, a hall of infamy, and a hall of heroes with statues of anticommunists like Ronald Reagan and Margaret Thatcher. It was supposed to have a big courtyard with a 200-foot-high statue of the Goddess of Democracy, modeled on a 33-foot-high version that was displayed in Tienanmen Square during the 1989 protests. Congress passed legislation authorizing the victims memorial in 1993, and President Bill Clinton signed it.[2]

But today there is no Victims of Communism Museum in Washington. The story of what happened to the planned $100 million building is another part of the larger phenomenon of forgetting the Cold War.

The proposal to commemorate the victims of communism came from the right, but it's not as if writers on the left have ignored the toll of Stalinism or Maoism or Pol Pot. Noam Chomsky objects to the "vision of our own magnificence alongside the incomprehensible monstrosity of the enemy" but writes that the Chinese famine of 1958–61 was a "terrible atrocity" that "fully merits the harsh condemnation it has received for many years" and that "it is, furthermore, proper to attribute the famine to Communism."[3] Perry Anderson writes that Stalin's regime in the 1930s "launched an all-out war on the peasantry, in which mass deportations and famine cost perhaps 6 million lives, reducing it to a sullen, broken force from which Russian agriculture has never recovered." In China, he writes, the policies of the Great Leap Forward resulted in 1958–61 in "the worst famine of the century, in which at least 15 and perhaps 30 million died."[4] Even Eric Hobsbawm, often denounced for never having quit the British Communist Party, condemned the "brutal and dictatorial" Soviet system and the "murderous absurdity" of Stalin's policies in his history of the twentieth century.[5]

But the launch of the Victims of Communism Memorial project was something else. It came with all the trappings of official Cold War ideology, starting with bipartisan support in Congress and approval by a Democratic president. The initial proposal, of course, came from the heart of the Reagan right. In the Senate the bill was introduced by Jesse Helms. In the House it was introduced by Dana Rohrabacher, a Republican from Orange County, California. He had started out as a speechwriter for President Reagan and won election to the House in 1988 with the help of his friend Oliver North. His right-wing credentials remain impeccable: a supporter of the Iraq war and the torture of suspected terrorists, fiercely anti-immigrant, and a man who does not believe global warming is caused by human activity. He's famous for suggesting, at a congressional hearing in 2007, that global warming in a previous era might have been caused by "dinosaur flatulence."[6] And although he wrote the legislation creating the Victims of Communism Memorial, his website in 2008 did not mention his role in establishing it or his attendance at the groundbreaking.[7] Apparently by 2008 even the author of the idea was letting it fall away.

The roots of the victims of communism project lie deep in the fifties. It was conceived by the founders of Captive Nations Week, which began in 1959 as an expression of the ethnic politics of Eastern European immigrants. Congress gave the job of creating and operating the victims memorial to the National Captive Nations Committee, Inc., which set up a nonprofit foundation to raise the funds. It seemed to have a promising start, with George H. W. Bush agreeing to serve as honorary chairman.

It should have worked. Memorialization of victims is an increasingly powerful theme in public commemoration, as Erika Doss showed in *Memorial Mania* and Kirk Savage in *Monument Wars*. "Victim monuments" find their template in the Holocaust Museum, but we also have memorials to the victims of terrorism, of lynching, of slavery, of the internment of Japanese Americans, and of the Irish potato famine (the Irish Hunger Memorial, a "huge monument" unveiled in 2002 "on a prime piece of real estate in lower Manhattan").[8] In 2003, when a competition was held for a monument to the victims of the 9/11 attack, more than five thousand entries were submitted. "Much of today's memorial making is excessive, frenzied, [and] extreme," Doss writes.[9] So the sponsors of a memorial to the victims of communism had good reason to think their project would succeed.

The plan was greeted enthusiastically by the right. The day before Clinton signed the bill, it was welcomed by *Boston Herald* columnist Don Feder, author of *A Jewish Conservative Looks at Pagan America.* He suggested that the memorial's Hall of Heroes should include, in addition to the Contras and the Cuban exiles who failed at the Bay of Pigs, the Afghan mujahadeen (he didn't mention the problem that they included Osama Bin Laden). He suggested that the memorial should also include a "Hall of Useful Idiots, to document the delusions of the appeasers, detenteniks, apologists and peace marchers." The "Useful Idiots" on his list included, in addition to the inevitable Jane Fonda, some more puzzling names, including Anthony Lewis of the *New York Times* and Senator Lowell Weicker.[10] Nixon was not mentioned in this context, although he was certainly America's number one detentenik.

But skepticism about the memorial began to surface even before Clinton signed the bill. An article in the *Washington Post* described the problem of too many monuments in the nation's capital, noting that more than ninety had been proposed. A National Park Service official said, "One memorial seems to breed another. . . . Someone goes to the Vietnam Veterans Memorial and says, 'This is important, but I'm not recognized here.'" The paper listed the Victims of Communism Memorial as an example, alongside a proposed monument to "scout dogs in Vietnam."[11]

Another kind of skepticism about the proposed monument was expressed by historians and journalists who had long criticized the conservative argument about the Cold War. The Cold War, they argued, should not be seen as a struggle between good and evil but rather as a more ordinary conflict between states with particular interests that they worked to defend and advance; this was the "realist" view. Realists emphasized the USSR's interest in maintaining a defensive buffer zone in Eastern Europe to slow or prevent another German invasion—understandable in view of their experience during World War II of the loss of twenty million people to German attack. While this buffer zone of satellite states was bad news for the Eastern Europeans, it wasn't a direct threat to the people of the United States.

Realists argued also that the United States did not represent "good" but rather pursued resources and markets around the world like other powerful countries and that competition with the Soviets often led the United States to support antidemocratic dictators who served as our allies. Thus the claims that the United States represented "freedom" everywhere were hollow. Radical historians added to the realist view that the interests the United States pursued around the world were primarily the interests of corporations pursuing private profit rather than public good. Of course, neither the realist nor the radical case was part of the argument the Victims of Communism Memorial planned to make.

The case for a Cold War memorial was argued anew in 1997 by the conservative columnist Charles Krauthammer, who called on President Clinton to establish one. Apparently he was unaware that something similar had already been approved four years earlier. Krauthammer, restating the conservatives' argument, called the Cold War a "struggle, no less momentous, no less victorious than World War II." He thought liberals like Clinton would "welcome a monument to an enterprise that, after all, was launched by Harry Truman and so resoundingly reaffirmed by John Kennedy," which was true enough; indeed, they already had welcomed such a monument. Krauthammer thought a monument should include a "gallery of heroes"—his list consisted of Truman, Marshall, Churchill, and Reagan—and a "hall of the fallen," featuring "the secret agents who died in anonymity." And he wanted what he called "a display of confusion: the great Western intellectuals who, from Sartre on down, professed to see no difference between the two sides." The Cold War, he concluded, "is the story of how, as soon as we disposed of one inhuman ideology, we turned to defeat another. And did, gloriously."[12] The fact that a leading voice of the right didn't seem to know about the $100 million plan voted into law four years earlier suggests how quickly this idea was being forgotten.

During the decade when the fund-raising was languishing, the Victims of Communism Memorial Foundation produced a number of "papers and studies." A notable one was published in 2002, nine months after 9/11, titled "International Terrorism: The Communist Connection Revisited: Archives show Islamist terrorism linkages to Soviet Cold War intelligence." The author, J. Michael Waller, reported that Reagan's CIA director, William J. Casey, had found that "there is virtually no terrorist operation or guerrilla movement anywhere in the world today . . . with which communists of one sort or another have not been involved." It's hard to imagine a more harebrained understanding of Osama Bin Laden, whose anticommunist credentials were, to say the least, impeccable. And yet the foundation still carries that paper on its website.[13]

Fund-raising failures led the foundation to scale back its plans in a series of stages. In 2003 a new plan called for a $25 million building with the goddess statue plus the Hall of Heroes (Reagan et al.), the Hall of Infamy, a section of the Berlin Wall, and then "a Soviet Gulag barracks, a torture room from the 'Hanoi Hilton,' a cell from Castro's infamous Isle of Pines," and, according to Jay Katzen, president of the foundation, a "Roll Call of Victims—the names, photos, and where possible, personal testimony of victims of Communism." With one hundred million victims, this section would have to be quite large. Katzen thanked a bipartisan group of politicians who backed the creation of a memorial. "Sen. Joseph Lieberman has been very helpful," he said. "So has Sen. Joe Biden."[14]

The plans were scaled back further in 2004. The *Wall Street Journal* reported that the memorial would consist not of a building but instead of the statue of the goddess along with "an eternal flame" in front of it, and, "on either side, bronze tablets . . . display[ing] quotations from the likes of Presidents Truman, Kennedy and Reagan, as well as Pope John Paul II, Vaclav Havel and Lech Walesa."[15]

The search for a site for the memorial continued. The foundation declared it wanted its memorial on Capitol Hill within view of the Capitol, across the street from the Japanese American Memorial, but that proposal was turned down by the National Capital Planning Commission. Next the foundation went after an available site near the Supreme Court, but it was turned down for that one too. In July 2004 the National Capital Memorial Commission finally approved a site for the memorial in a neighborhood park in Northeast Washington opposite the Veterans of Foreign Wars headquarters (at Third and Maryland).

Then came the lowest point in the history of the Victims of Communism Memorial: in December 2004 neighborhood residents rejected the plan to erect it in their park. Washington, D.C., has Advisory Neighborhood Commissions, and the commission for District 6C, which had two thousand constituents, argued that the memorial "has nothing to do with our neighborhood." The local commissioner said the neighbors were "worried about losing two large, 50-year-old oak trees on the site . . . and about the loss of green space to concrete." She explained that the neighbors "resent having their public space taken away. They've used it for many years. . . . There's too little green space in our area, and we don't need a statue there."[16] The chair of the Victims of Communism Memorial Foundation, Lee Edwards, replied, "With regard to the trees, of course those trees are beautiful," but one of the trees "is already showing some signs of distress. We will either save the tree or . . . we will substitute and put in two new trees."

The Stanton Park Neighborhood Association newsletter reported what happened next: Advisory Neighborhood Commission 6C "voted against the location of the monument . . . unanimously."[17] One blogger wrote that the neighborhood vote was "just one more way the political left infects our culture. The Holocaust, which killed 10 million, gets its own museum here in D.C. (and deservedly so). Communism, which killed in the vicinity of 100 million (and still counting if you count North Korea and Cuba), well, you have to bend over backwards to get a mere statue."[18] He had a point; convincing people to accept the conservative interpretation of Cold War victory was turning out to be extremely difficult.

The next step downhill, as explained by the foundation's president, Jay Katzen, came when it "decided to proceed with an online virtual museum, rather than a bricks-and-mortar facility at this time." He promised "exhibits which will feature the testimony of survivors of communism, documentation of communism's crimes against humanity, and tributes to those who helped win the Cold War." Katzen declared, "I'm proud of our economies and our decision to go for the present with an online museum."[19]

The search for a site to replace the park continued until 2005, when the foundation received approval for a statue at the intersection of Massachusetts and New Jersey Avenues, near the National Guard Memorial Museum. Foundation chair Lee Edwards called the National Guard Memorial Museum an "important connection."[20] Almost thirteen years after the president and Congress authorized the memorial, in November 2006, a groundbreaking ceremony was held. That might seem like a long time, but "it took the U.S. Holocaust Memorial Museum 14 years," Edwards declared in the *Washington Times,* "so we are just about even"—except that the Holocaust Museum ended up after that period with a lot more than a ten-foot statue on Massachusetts Avenue.[21]

The groundbreaking was attended by only fifty people. Instead of the big names of the right who had initially made the case for its significance, the memorial's groundbreaking had the same lineup as the old Captive Nations Week: representatives of Bulgaria, Estonia, Lithuania, Latvia, Moldova, Poland, the Czech Republic, Slovakia, Ukraine, Georgia, and Romania, along with the Republic of China (Taiwan). Among those invited who did not attend were Vaclav Havel, Lech Walesa, Bill Clinton, Nancy Pelosi, and, most notably, Honorary Chairman George H. W. Bush.

The Victims of Communism Memorial, a ten-foot-high replica of the thirty-foot-high Goddess of Democracy from Tienanmen Square, was finally dedicated on June 12, 2007, the twentieth anniversary of Reagan's "Tear down this wall" speech in Berlin and seventeen years after the memorial had first been proposed. Four hundred people attended the ceremony on Mass. Ave. (In contrast, when the monument to the African American educator Mary McLeod Bethune was dedicated in Lincoln Park in 1974, twenty thousand people attended.)[22] President George W. Bush said, "In this hallowed place we recall the great lessons of the Cold War: that freedom is precious and cannot be taken for granted; that evil is real and must be confronted; and that given the chance, men commanded by harsh and hateful ideologies will commit unspeakable crimes and take the lives of millions" (figure 7).[23]

However, Bush failed to make the conservative argument equating Cold War victory with victory over fascism in World War II. Instead he drew another parallel, as the *Washington Post* reported: the president "equated the Sept. 11, 2001, attacks . . . with the tyrannical rule imposed on residents of countries like China, North Korea and the former Soviet Union." The *Post* quoted Bush as saying, "Like the communists, the terrorists and radicals who have attacked our nation are followers of a murderous ideology that despises freedom, crushes all dissent, has expansionist ambitions and pursues totalitarian aims."[24]

Despite the participation of the president, the event got little media attention, except for the *Post,* which ran a story on page one of its "Style" section. Most of the coverage was limited to the *American Spectator,* the *National Review,* and the *Washington Times*—a fact cited as evidence of the left-wing bias of the mainstream press. "You'd think a memorial dedication to the 100 million victims of the greatest evil in modern times would get a little more attention from the dominant liberal media," one right-wing media watch website declared, "but perhaps the 'victim' Paris Hilton is more important to them."[25]

Bush's speech at the dedication did get some attention from the liberal media. At the *Huffington Post,* Chris Kelley wrote, "There are some people who might think Bush cheapens everything he touches, and that using Stalin and Mao's dead millions as a way to plug the occupation of Iraq is sort of loathsome, but . . . if you go to a George Bush show, you're going to hear about the time he let 19 guys fly four planes into three buildings and a field.

FIGURE 7. George W. Bush at the dedication of the Victims of Communism Memorial, Washington, D.C., June 12, 2007. Shaking hands with Bush is Rep. Tom Lantos (D–CA); at left is Victims of Communism Memorial Foundation chairman Lee Edwards. (AP Photo/ Charles Dharapak)

And how, since then, to put an end to murder, we've killed and killed and killed and killed."[26]

Kelley had a point. Although no one at the Victims of Communism Memorial Foundation was going to say it, Bush's global war on terror was not part of their agenda. Instead, they want the battle against communism to be pursued to total victory, the way World War II brought total victory over all the fascist governments. Apparently they take seriously the conservative analogy between World War II and the Cold War. Because communism survives in Cuba, North Korea, and China, their website declares, "Cold War victory remains incomplete."

It's an important argument, developed with characteristic brilliance by Chalmers Johnson. The notion that "the Cold War is over," he noted, ignores the continuation of "the simultaneous Cold Wars in East Asia and Latin America," which "continue unabated" because of their "different ideological and material foundations."[27]

The Victims of Communism Memorial leaders argue that "a free society must not allow itself to be content" until we can celebrate victory over communism in Cuba, North Korea, and China.[28] Many regard the collapse of

Communist China as unlikely—but, the foundation argues, who thought the USSR would disappear so quickly?

But Bush at the dedication of the memorial did not call for the overthrow of the People's Republic of China—even though the memorial reproduces a pro-democracy statue from China. No doubt he had been told that would offend the Chinese, to whom we were in debt in many ways.[29] So even George W. Bush, the most conservative and ideological president in decades, strayed from the conservative message about the meaning of the Cold War that had been proclaimed a decade earlier by Fox News, the Heritage Foundation, the *National Review,* the *Weekly Standard,* and the rest of the right-wing ideological apparatus. Even George W. Bush.

One other key element was missing from Bush's speech at the dedication: he spoke of "millions" of victims of communism, which of course is very different from the hundred million claimed by the Victims of Communism Memorial Foundation. The figure one hundred million comes from *The Black Book of Communism,* a massive (850-page) book published first in France in 1997 and then in English in 1999 by Harvard University Press.[30] The volume contains essays on different countries by different French scholars and was edited by Stéphane Courtois, who announced the thesis of the book in his introduction: communism represents a greater evil than Nazism. Courtois got to 100 million victims by estimating 65 million deaths caused by communism in China, 20 million in the former Soviet Union, 2 million in Cambodia and North Korea each, 1.7 million in Africa, and one million in Vietnam and Eastern Europe each. Courtois said the Nazi death total, in contrast, was only 15 million. Moreover, he declared, "the methods introduced by Lenin and perfected by Stalin and their like not only recall the Nazi methods, they often predate them."[31]

Of course the book received both praise and criticism. Notable among the critics were two important contributors to the volume who publicly rejected its thesis: Nicolas Werth, who wrote the key chapter on the Soviet Union, and Jean-Louis Margolin, who wrote the other key chapter, on China, Vietnam, and Cambodia. After seeing the introduction, the two "consulted a lawyer to see if they could withdraw their respective contributions from the book. They were advised they could not."[32]

So Werth and Margolin took their criticism to *Le Monde,* writing that Courtois was obsessed with reaching a total of one hundred million victims despite the best evidence showing a lower total. Werth also insisted Nazism and communism were qualitatively different. "Death camps did not exist in the Soviet Union," he told *Le Monde,* and "the more you compare communism and Nazism, the more the differences are obvious."[33] The book was especially controversial in France because it was published during the 1997 trial of Nazi collaborator Maurice Papon for crimes against humanity for his role in the deportation of Jews from Bordeaux to Hitler's death camps. Papon's lawyers introduced the book as evidence for the defense.[34]

Those who have challenged the hundred million figure point out that more than half of that number consists of deaths by famine and that famines in the USSR and China should not be put in the same category of crime as intentional mass murder by shooting—the work of the Nazi Einsatzgruppen—or gassing—at Auschwitz and Treblinka. The UCLA historian J. Arch Getty argued in the *Atlantic* that the Soviet famines of the 1930s were caused by the "stupidity or incompetence of the regime"[35] and should not be equated with genocide, which is precisely the equation Courtois had made.

The millions of Ukranians who died of starvation in 1932–33 rightly appear on the list of victims of communism, but recent scholarship has established another equally significant event on the other side of the capitalist–communist divide: the 1943 Bengali famine, in which at least 1.5 million died while British authorities continued to export Indian grain. Churchill's role in the Bengal famine seems similar to Stalin's role in the Ukrainian famine.[36]

And a significant proportion of the hundred million figure cited by the Victims of Communism Memorial Foundation comes from what demographers call "excess mortality" due to poor nutrition and inadequate medical care—in the Gulag, in particular. However if "excess mortality" is the standard, then a significantly higher death rate can be found in capitalist India than in Communist China over the past fifty years, despite the Chinese famines of 1958–61, as Amartya Sen has shown. Sen estimates the excess of mortality in India over China to be close to four million a year: "India seems to manage to fill its cupboard with more skeletons every eight years than China put there in its years of shame [1958–61]."[37] And even the conservative American Enterprise Institute agrees that "excess mortality" has been greater in capitalist Russia since the fall of communism than it was during the decades before.[38]

Other reviewers objected to the way *The Black Book* lumped together vastly different societies on the sole grounds that their leaders claimed to be Marxist-Leninists. Tony Judt, who gave the book a rave review in the *New*

York Times, nevertheless conceded that "in practice the Cambodian massacres, to take just one case, have more in common with the horrors of Rwanda and Bosnia than with Stalin's secretive, paranoid, targeted purges."[39]

The Black Book's argument had a larger problem. Courtois's purpose, as Richard J. Goslan pointed out, was not purely "remembering Communism's victims"—ostensibly the purpose of the memorial in Washington. Rather, as the Holocaust historian Annette Wieviorka argued, Courtois was "attempting to substitute the memory of Communism's crimes for the memory of Nazi crimes."[40] Even worse, Courtois, in his argument for the hundred million figure, was explicitly attacking what he called the "international Jewish community" for emphasizing the crimes of Hitler in a way that displaced the much greater crimes of communism. Blame the Jews: that argument leaves *The Black Book* tainted.

While the book nevertheless received an enthusiastic reception in the United States, the assessment in the *Journal of American History* was reasonable: "*The Black Book* fails to provide the reader with a sense of how communism captured the popular support of millions of people around the world. . . . It may be most useful as a historical artifact of the immediate post–Cold War era when blanket condemnations of communism that equated the Soviet Union and Nazi Germany . . . came back into vogue. But, with the fading ardor of Cold War triumphalism, a more balanced assessment of the rise and fall of international communism that neither whitewashes its crimes nor suppresses its periods of mass popularity remains to be written."[41] Maybe that's why George Bush did not use the claim of one hundred million victims when he dedicated the memorial.

On a recent visit to Washington, I asked the hotel concierge if he knew where to find the Victims of Communism Memorial. "Is that a memorial to us taxpayers?" he quipped. "Just kidding," he added. He had never heard of the memorial.

I got the address from the website and took a taxi to the memorial. Feigning ignorance, I asked a dozen people walking by, "What is this statue?" "I don't know," was the most common answer. One young person explained patiently, "There are statues everywhere in Washington." (He was echoing the *Washington Post*'s declaration in 1891, "Washington is a city of statues.")[42] Another looked at it for a moment and then commented, "Kind of random." Another, apparently a tourist herself, pulled out a "Points of Interest" map,

FIGURE 8. Day of remembrance for the thirty-fifth anniversary of the fall of Saigon, April 30, 2010, Victims of Communism Memorial, Washington, D.C. (photo © 2011 Victims of Communism Memorial Foundation)

studied it for a minute, and said, "Daniel Webster?" (She was close; there is a Daniel Webster statue on Mass. Ave., a few blocks farther up.)

The Victims of Communism Memorial today is not a popular center for celebration of the Cold War as a good war. Instead the statue at the intersection of Massachusetts and New Jersey Avenues functions as a place for an occasional wreath-laying ceremony for events like the anniversary of the fall of Saigon (figure 8)—while twenty thousand cars drive past every day. The millions of victims of Stalin's Gulag, the millions who starved to death during Mao's Great Leap Forward, and all the rest deserve better than this lifeless exercise in ideology.

PART TWO

The Beginning: 1946–1949

THREE

Getting Started

THE CHURCHILL MEMORIAL IN MISSOURI

"From Stettin in the Baltic to Trieste in the Adriatic, an Iron Curtain has descended across the continent"—those famous words, declaring the start of the Cold War, were spoken by Winston Churchill in 1946 in an unlikely setting: Fulton, Missouri. Westminster College, where he gave that speech, established the Churchill Memorial in 1969 to commemorate it. Since then, the world's leading conservatives have come here to declare, again and again, that the Cold War, like World War II, was a good war, a war to defeat totalitarianism, and that victory in the Cold War was equal in significance to the defeat of Hitler. The list includes Presidents Reagan, Ford, and the first President Bush, as well as British Prime Minister Margaret Thatcher and Polish President Lech Walesa. It's hard to think of a figure other than Churchill who provides such a clear link between victory over fascism and victory over communism: Churchill led the Allies in defeating the first totalitarian enemy, and he was the first to sound the alarm that would lead to defeating the second. He opposed the appeasement of Hitler, then alerted the West to the coming struggle against Stalin.

But today at the Churchill Memorial, the "Iron Curtain" speech has receded in significance. The commemoration here now is centered on the blood, sweat, and tears of the struggle against Hitler. What began as a monument to the birth of the Cold War has become one more place to celebrate World War II's Greatest Generation.

If the site for this celebration is an unlikely one, the structure commemorating Churchill's Iron Curtain speech is even more unlikely: the Church of St. Mary the Virgin, Aldermanbury, a twelfth-century church moved to Missouri from London. Destroyed in the Great Fire of 1666, it was redesigned by Christopher Wren in 1677 and turned into rubble by the Luftwaffe during the blitz, after which the Brits never repaired it. Then in the mid-sixties the people at Westminster College arranged to have all the bricks collected and shipped to Fulton, Missouri, to restore the church—sort of the way London Bridge was moved to Lake Havasu, Arizona (figure 9). One problem is that Churchill himself never attended this church when it was in London (but they say Shakespeare might have).

Tom DeLay, the House Majority Leader for the Republicans under George Bush, gave a speech at the Churchill Memorial in 2002 in which he presented the right-wing interpretation: "The history of modern man has been framed largely by the struggle between these incompatible forces: Freedom and tyranny, good and evil, . . . Nazism and Communism." DeLay connected Churchill's statement at the dawn of the Cold War with Reagan's stance near its end: "President Reagan challenged us to acknowledge what we knew to be true. He defined the Soviet Union as an evil empire." DeLay said we needed to "strive boldly to spread our democratic principles" and "liberate millions of men and women from the grip of tyranny."[1]

Margaret Thatcher spoke at the Churchill Memorial on the fiftieth anniversary of Churchill's speech. She offered the requisite praise for Churchill having provided "the first serious warning of what was afoot, . . . [which] helped to wake up the entire West." "That speech," she said, "bore rich fruit in the new institutions forged to strengthen the West against Stalin's assault." The Marshall Plan, the Truman Doctrine, and the formation of NATO, she said, "helped to usher in what the Marxist historian, Eric Hobsbawm, has ruefully christened the 'Golden Age of Capitalism.'" Who knew that Margaret Thatcher read Eric Hobsbawm? In the end, of course, "the communist system was forced into, first reform, then surrender, and finally liquidation." But "none of this . . . was pre-ordained. It happened in large part because of what Churchill said here fifty years ago." If that claim seemed dubious, it was followed by an even more unlikely one: "it was his speech, not the 'force' celebrated by Marx, which turned out to be the midwife of history."[2]

Stalin the equivalent of Hitler; Reagan the equivalent of Churchill; both Churchill and Reagan promising "no compromise with evil" and pledging to "force" the "surrender" of the USSR: speakers at the memorial have agreed that that's the message of Churchill's "Iron Curtain" speech.

When we arrived at the Winston Churchill Memorial one Saturday afternoon, we opened the door to be greeted by a video of Churchill saying, "I

FIGURE 9. Winston Churchill Memorial, Westminster College, Fulton, Missouri. In an effort to attract visitors to a museum commemorating Churchill's "Iron Curtain" speech, delivered here in 1946, Westminster College moved a seventeenth-century Christopher Wren church from London to this site. The Churchill part is now in the basement of the church. (photo by Judy Fiskin)

have nothing to offer but blood, toil, tears, and sweat." The museum's focus is clear from the start, and it's not the Iron Curtain and the Cold War. The first clip was followed by another of Churchill saying, "If the British Empire lasts a thousand years, men will say this was their finest hour"—"this," of course being the Battle of Britain. Being reminded about the glories of the British Empire in a small town in Missouri was a strange experience. And of course the British Empire didn't last a thousand years after 1940; it only lasted about twenty (unless you count the Falklands War of 1982 as the end point).

We headed straight to the museum's "Sinews of Peace" room, where the video of Churchill's Iron Curtain speech is played. The room has four benches seating a total of sixteen people, but only one other person was in the room, and he was standing in the back, reading the wall text. We pressed the button to start the video and found that the Churchill speech has been cut to six minutes—the original was forty-four. The younger generation of course finds even six minutes oppressive; but we did get "From Stettin in the Baltic . . ."

Listening to the speech today, what is striking is the way Churchill repeatedly contrasted the "tyranny" of the USSR with the "liberties" enjoyed not just in the United States and Britain but also "throughout the British Empire." Empire was very much on Churchill's mind as he invoked the "special relationship" of the United States to Britain and her Empire (always capitalized in his text) in the new postwar geopolitical context. The danger, he argued, lay not just behind the Iron Curtain but also in Italy and France, and in Asia as well. In fact, communist parties "constitute a growing challenge and peril to Christian civilization" everywhere "except in the British Commonwealth and in the United States." But, he concluded, "let no man underrate the abiding power of the British Empire." In Churchill's view, then, the opponent of Soviet communism was not the "free world" but rather the United States, Britain, and the British Empire. The speech was understood by many at the time to amount to a proposal that the United States oppose the decolonization movement that, as Churchill spoke in Fulton, was spreading from India to Burma, Ceylon, Malaya, and Singapore—and eventually all Britain's colonies in Africa.

But the exhibits at the Churchill museum in the "Sinews of Peace" gallery provide virtually no historical or geopolitical context for the speech. On the sides of the video room are some of the homemade banners that greeted Churchill and Truman as their motorcade rode down Fulton's Main Street in 1946 and photos of the motorcade, along with a few quotations from locals who were there: "'The program was one of the greatest thrills I've had since the invention of radio!'—Marjorie Doyle, Osceola, Ark., March 8, 1946."

Outside the "Sinews of Peace" room is a small video station titled "Cold Warriors." It has a touch screen that lets you choose between speeches about

Churchill by Reagan, Gorbachev, and Margaret Thatcher. We picked Reagan, who said, "His Fulton speech was a firebell in the night." But this bracing declaration of American Cold War triumph had no audience here in Fulton, at least on that Saturday afternoon. Only three other people were at the "Cold Warriors" exhibit.

The other galleries, "The Formative Years," "The Wilderness Years," "The Gathering Storm," the RAF display, and the biggest, "World War II," have more visitors. The last is featured in the list of official "highlights" of the memorial: "See and hear the effects of a London air raid at the height of 'The Blitz' as you are placed in the midst of a dazzling light and sound show." From there you go to "Watch Churchill lead Britain through World War II in the stirring film 'Churchill's Finest Hour,' narrated by the world-renowned newsman Walter Cronkite." After that, "Become a spy—deciphering World War II secret codes or finding clues from the secrets locked in a Cold War briefcase."[3] Last comes the "Wit and Wisdom" room, where you are invited to "sit back in an overstuffed chair surrounded by the ambiance of an English Gentleman's Club and laugh while listening to Churchill's 'wit and wisdom.'" And in "The Private Side" gallery, a few more people were looking at the exhibition of Churchill's paintings. The official "highlights" do not include "From Stettin in the Baltic . . . "

The speakers program at the Churchill Memorial has the same focus as the exhibit highlights. Speakers' topics recently included "Friendship between Winston Churchill and Franklin Roosevelt during WWII," "Churchill and France during the Second World War," and Martin Gilbert on "Churchill's War Leadership."[4] The gift shop recently featured the book *Wartime Letters from a Londoner to Her American Pen Pal,* and the newsletter highlighted newly discovered video of Churchill and Eisenhower visiting the U.S. 101st Airborne Division training for D day.[5] (One unexpected item was a month-long temporary exhibition, *Women in the Military: A Jewish Perspective,* from the National Museum of American Jewish Military History, "from the Civil War to the Gulf War.")

Back at the ticket counter, Cathy, who was on duty, conceded, "It's pretty quiet here on weekends. But it's busier during the week, when we get school groups and Red Hat ladies."

Red Hat ladies?

"You know, they wear red hats with black tassels, and they go places together."[6]

The restored Wren church upstairs has nothing to do with the Iron Curtain speech Churchill gave here, but it is breathtaking, with huge windows and gleaming white everywhere.

Conservatives could use Churchill's Iron Curtain speech to emphasize how the left was blind to the threat posed by Stalin. That could make for an interesting museum display. Churchill's speech was understood across the political spectrum as a call to break up the Allies of World War II in favor of an Anglo-American military alliance against the Soviet Union. In *The Nation,* for example, I. F. Stone criticized "the incredible naïveté and clumsiness of the President in involving himself with the Churchill Speech," which he argued was based on "the assumption that war [with the USSR] must come sooner or later"—which would mean "war with the atomic bomb."[7]

When Churchill arrived in New York City in 1946 after his speech in Fulton, his parade met with loud left-wing protests, and the official dinner at the Waldorf Astoria was ringed by a thousand pickets organized by the CIO, faced by five hundred New York City policemen and one hundred detectives. The pickets chanted, "G.I. Joe, home to stay/Winnie, Winnie, go away!" and "The English people turned him down/so do we, so do we" (Churchill had lost the recent election in Britain)—as reported on page one of the *New York Times* the next morning.[8] And at Columbia University, where Churchill was awarded an honorary degree, 1,700 students met to hear his Fulton speech denounced by Adam Clayton Powell, Howard Fast, and Michael Straight of the *New Republic.*[9] A few weeks later Vice President Henry Wallace gave a speech declaring that "aside from our common language and common literary tradition, we have no more in common with Imperialistic England than with Communist Russia."[10]

But it wasn't just the fellow-traveling left that denounced Churchill's speech; neo-isolationists, mainstream liberals, and "realists" came to a similar conclusion. The *Wall Street Journal* responded to Churchill by declaring that "the United States wants no alliance, or anything that resembles an alliance, with any other nation."[11] The *Chicago Sun,* a liberal tabloid owned by Marshall Field III, called Churchill's speech "an address of threat and menace" that sought "world domination, through arms, by the United States and the British Empire."[12] The *Boston Globe* warned that Churchill was proposing to make the United States "heir to the evils of a collapsing colonialism."[13] Eleanor Roosevelt told an audience of a thousand that Churchill was wrong to think that the United States and Britain could get their way in the world "without the far greater number of people who are not English-speaking."[14]

Eleanor Roosevelt was responding to the conclusion of Churchill's speech, where he said, "Let no man underrate the abiding power of the British Empire"—especially if it was backed by American military and economic might. The natives were restless across Asia; Britain was already involved in a confrontation with Russia in Iran, which had been occupied jointly by the two countries at the end of the war. And of course there was China.

Walter Lippmann was one of many who warned that Churchill's speech sought to recruit the United States to defend British imperialism. Immediately after Churchill's speech, he wrote a column declaring that "the line of British imperial interest and the line of American vital interest are not to be regarded as identical." He warned against forming a new "alliance which is avowedly anti-Soviet." In private, his biographer Ronald Steel reports, "he was a good deal harsher. 'I deplored Churchill's speech,'" Lippman wrote a colleague, "'because he presented this necessary and desirable objective'"—U.S. support for Britain in the Middle East—"'in the one way most calculated to make it dangerous and impossible to achieve—namely as a combination against the Soviet Union . . . accompanied by a directed incitement to a preventive war within the next five years.'" Lippmann concluded that Churchill's "Iron Curtain" speech was an "almost catastrophic blunder."[15]

In subsequent weeks Lippmann wrote widely read columns criticizing Britain's "secretly keeping intact Wehrmacht units" as part of a plan to create "a powerful centralized Germany . . . as a bulwark against the Russians." Lippmann's three-part series on this issue "created a sensation," Steel reports, "and was reprinted in every important paper in the United States and Western Europe."[16]

Many elected officials believed along with Lippmann that Churchill had been wrong and that a peaceful settlement with Stalin was still possible. "Congress Splits on Churchill Plea," declared the page one headline in the *New York Times* two days after the speech. Three senators issued a joint statement declaring that "Mr. Churchill's proposal . . . would destroy the unity of the Big Three, without which the war could not have been won." They said it was "shocking" to see Churchill aligning himself with "Tories who strengthened the Nazis as part of their anti-Soviet crusade."[17]

"Washington Splits over Churchill," another *New York Times* headline read; the story reported that the negative reaction in the capital had forced President Truman to deny he had had advance knowledge of what Churchill would say—despite the fact that everyone knew Truman accompanied him to Missouri and sat next to him on the podium in Fulton, smiling and nodding in agreement. In an effort to further distance the administration from Churchill's proposals, Dean Acheson, undersecretary of state, "abruptly canceled" his plans to attend the dinner welcoming Churchill to New York City after his Fulton speech, where he had been scheduled to give the official administration greeting; other members of the administration, including of course Henry Wallace, were openly critical of Churchill.[18]

So conservatives today could use Churchill's speech to argue that liberals had been wrong about the threat posed by Stalin and that they had been right. But that argument raises a fundamental question: what kind of a threat did Stalin pose to the United States and "the West" in 1946? How much of the Cold War was necessary? It would be hard to raise these questions in a museum exhibit but not impossible. As I. F. Stone wrote, with characteristic brilliance, after Churchill's speech, "The United States cannot . . . give in to unlimited expansionist demands by the Soviet Union. But the question to be answered is whether they are unlimited, and where to draw the limit."[19]

And at the end of the Cold War, Eric Hobsbawm looked back at its beginning. "On any rational assessment," he wrote, "the USSR presented no immediate danger to anyone outside the reach of the Red Army's occupation forces. It emerged from war in ruins, drained and exhausted, its peacetime economy in shreds." And "nobody knew better than Stalin how weak a hand he had to play." While the American right warned about the danger of Soviet world supremacy sometime in the future, "Moscow was worried about the actual hegemony of the USA now, over all parts of the globe not occupied by the Red Army."[20]

Back in the museum, the exhibit "The Cold War Defined" gives a strikingly different interpretation of the significance of Churchill's speech from the one declared by the site's conservative speakers. Instead of saying that Churchill linked the two totalitarian enemies of freedom in the twentieth century, that Churchill taught us there is no compromise with evil, it says that "Churchill's perspective" was to combine "Military Strength" and "Dialogue with Russia to prevent antagonism from becoming war." It says Churchill's approach was "managing Cold War tensions with a view toward mutual resolution."

It shows that when Churchill announced the beginning of the Cold War, he never called for victory over Stalin or forcing the surrender of the USSR.

Indeed the video here concludes with his discussion of the Soviet Union: "I repulse the idea that a new war is inevitable; still more that it is imminent. . . . What is needed is a settlement, and the longer this is delayed, the more difficult it will be and the greater our dangers will become." This is not exactly a call to defeat the evil empire.

He didn't call for freeing Eastern Europe from Soviet domination either. On the contrary, his speech called for peaceful coexistence. "I have a strong admiration and regard for the valiant Russian people and for my wartime comrade, Marshal Stalin," Churchill declared. "We understand the Russian need to be secure on her western frontiers by the removal of all possibility of German aggression. We welcome Russia to her rightful place among the leading nations of the world." That's not exactly a precursor to Reagan and Thatcher.

Churchill did describe the absence of free elections and freedom of speech in Poland as something to be lamented. He warned about communism in Italy and France. But, he declared, the United States and Britain must reach "a good understanding on all points with Russia under the general authority of the United Nations Organization. . . . There is the solution which I respectfully offer to you in this Address to which I have given the title 'The Sinews of Peace.'"[21] The point then was precisely not to define the USSR as an evil empire that should be defeated; the point was rather for the United States and Britain to form a military alliance that could prevent what Churchill called "the indefinite expansion" of Soviet power. This was something like the goal of the containment doctrine that George Kennan had proposed to President Truman in his "Long Telegram" just two weeks earlier.

Churchill's most dramatic turn came in May 1953, two months after the death of Stalin. Once again he was prime minister, and in a major speech to the House of Commons, he declared that "Russia has the right to feel assured that, so far as human arrangements can run, the terrible events of the Hitler invasion will never be repeated." That meant, he said, that Russia had a right to be assured "that Poland will remain a friendly Power and a buffer, though not, I trust, a puppet, State." He urged "the NATO Powers" not to do anything that might "supersede or take the emphasis out of what may be a profound movement of Russian feeling," a "spontaneous and healthy evolution" following the death of Stalin. I. F. Stone noticed; he wrote a piece headlined "Churchill Abandons the Cold War." Recalling Churchill's early years, he wrote, "the man who wanted to strangle bolshevism in its cradle had suddenly announced that he was prepared to live with it in its prime."

The man who had announced the establishment of the Iron Curtain, Stone wrote, was now "calling off the cold war."[22]

At the Churchill Museum in Fulton, the wall text spells out the massive difference that arose at that point between Churchill's approach to the Cold War and the Americans': "The US took a more confrontational stance, threatening 'massive retaliation' with nuclear weapons and adopting a policy of Mutual Assured Destruction. The U.S. sought to win the Cold War; Churchill sought to overcome it." Next: "Of the U.S. policy, Churchill remarked, 'if you go on with this nuclear arms race, all you are going to do is make the rubble bounce.'"

Then comes the kicker, the final panel, "The Cold War resolved": the way the Cold War ended proves "Churchill was indeed the one 'who knew the right way home.'"

So the memorial in Fulton doesn't say Churchill sounded the warning about not compromising with evil. It says Churchill opposed U.S. policy for being too confrontational, for pursuing an arms race that threatened destruction of everyone, and for failing to seek a settlement. And it says Churchill was right and the Americans were wrong. That's the concluding message of America's Churchill Memorial.[23]

FOUR

Searching for the Pumpkin Patch

THE WHITTAKER CHAMBERS NATIONAL HISTORIC LANDMARK

The most popular National Park Service site is the Blue Ridge Parkway in Virginia, which has around 17 million visitors a year; the least popular seems to be the Whittaker Chambers pumpkin patch National Historic Landmark, near Baltimore, which has around two visitors a year. I was one of them.[1]

One windy fall day I set out from Baltimore with friends, searching for the pumpkin patch. The Reagan administration designated it a National Historic Landmark (officially called "Whittaker Chambers Farm") in 1988 over the unanimous objection of the National Park Service Advisory Board.[2] The site, outside Westminster, Maryland, commemorates the spot where, in 1947, Whittaker Chambers reached into a hollowed-out pumpkin and pulled out some 35mm film. He said it showed that Alger Hiss, a pillar of the New Deal, had been a Soviet spy.

The "pumpkin papers" helped convict Hiss of perjury in 1950, which transformed public opinion, convincing Americans for the first time that communism posed a real danger to the country. The obscure congressman named Nixon who pushed the Hiss case won a Senate seat the year Hiss was convicted, and got the vice presidential nomination in 1952; a month after Hiss's conviction, Senator Joseph McCarthy gave the speech in Wheeling, West Virginia, that launched his career and gave the new, virulent anticommunism its name. For the next forty-five years, the Cold War served as the iron cage of American politics.

Conservatives had hoped this site would provide a place where the public could be told that the Communist Party did not just defend a totalitarian regime; it also recruited its members to spy on that regime's behalf. Thus the hunt for communist spies was not "McCarthyism"; it was a noble cause.

But, like the other Cold War commemorative efforts, the pumpkin patch National Historic Landmark is remarkable primarily as a failure.

In Westminster, outside the Carroll County courthouse, we stopped to ask a cop in a squad car if he could tell us where the Whittaker Chambers pumpkin patch National Historic Landmark was. "Never heard of it," he said definitively—even though it turned out we were less than two miles away. If we were looking for a pumpkin patch, his advice was "go to the Farm Museum."

Munch's Smoke-Free Cafe is in the middle of town, on Main Street; we asked the man behind the counter if he knew where the pumpkin patch National Historic Landmark was. "Never heard of that one," he said. But another patron at the counter, obviously a local, said, "Isn't that where the spies hid the microfilm in World War II?" Conversation ensued. Somebody else said, "That Alger Hiss deal"; another chimed in, "Yeah, that's the guy"; and then the man behind the counter said, "I never knew that was in Carroll County." Of course it wasn't World War II that was commemorated at the landmark; it was supposed to be the Cold War. The locals' confusion on this point suggested that the conservative campaign had been a complete failure. They suggested we ask for directions at the tourist center in town.

At the Carroll County Visitor Center on Main Street we found a variety of brochures, including "Ghost Walk in Carroll County," which said the countryside here had drawn "opportunists"—was this a reference to Whittaker Chambers? It continued, "Seldom has one area played host to such a diverse and interesting array of local ghosts and specters." Hadn't Karl Marx himself said that communism was a specter haunting bourgeois society? But the ghost of Whittaker Chambers was not listed here.

We asked the volunteer on duty at the Visitor Center about the Whittaker Chambers pumpkin patch; she offered to direct us to places where we could pick pumpkins. When we said no, we're interested in the National Historic Landmark, she started telling us instead about Civil War battles. Since no battles were actually fought in Westminster, her presentation focused on battles that should have been fought here—in particular, the Battle of Gettysburg. (Gettysburg is forty miles to the north.) She seemed disappointed and actually somewhat bitter about this situation. She even had a map that showed where the battle should have been fought, between Westminster and Taneytown, "if Meade hadn't run into the troops up there in Gettysburg." This little lecture was interrupted by a phone caller asking where he could find the all-you-can-eat pancake breakfast.

When we brought the conversation back to Whittaker Chambers, she agreed to draw us a map, remarking quietly that "about two people a year go up there." A National Historic Landmark with two visitors a year? That must be some kind of a record—and makes you wonder how this site got established in the first place.

In the last days of the Reagan administration, conservative true believers finally succeeded in persuading Secretary of the Interior Donald P. Hodel—one of their own—to overrule the National Park Service Advisory Board and declare the pumpkin patch an official National Historic Landmark. For them, only the Berlin Wall provided a more vivid site where the Cold War could be commemorated.

The landmark designation was announced by Hodel not in a public ceremony, which might have seemed the appropriate occasion, but rather in a media event at the Heritage Foundation. There Hodel called Chambers "a figure of transcendent importance in the nation's history." Chambers, he said, saw the Cold War as a "conflict of two irreconcilable faiths—Godless Communism versus the freedom of Divinely created and inspired Man."[3]

Reagan himself, the audience was reminded, had posthumously awarded Chambers the Presidential Medal of Freedom a few years earlier. Reagan had declared that "at a critical moment in our Nation's history, Whittaker Chambers stood alone against the brooding terrors of our age." Reagan had described Chambers as a "consummate intellectual, writer of moving, majestic prose, and witness to the truth," and said Chambers's testimony against Hiss "symbolized our century's epic struggle between freedom and totalitarianism, a controversy in which the solitary figure of Whittaker Chambers personified the mystery of human redemption in the face of evil and suffering." Reagan had concluded that "as long as humanity speaks of virtue and dreams of freedom, the life and writings of Whittaker Chambers will ennoble and inspire."[4]

Witness, published by Chambers in 1952, four years after his HUAC testimony, was a best-seller. In the book Chambers described why he left the communist underground: he said he had been reading a book about the Gulag and concluded, "This is evil, absolute evil. Of this evil I am a part." Then "a voice said with perfect distinctness: 'If you will fight for freedom, all will be well with you.'" Chambers understood this as the voice of God: "There tore through me a transformation with the force of a river." And so he became a Christian and an anticommunist. *Witness* described the Cold War as a battle in which it would be "decided for generations whether all mankind is to become Communist, whether the whole world is to become free, or whether, in the struggle, civilization as we know it is to be completely destroyed." The Cold War was not just a superpower conflict but a battle to the end between "irreconcilable opposites—God or Man, Soul or Mind, Freedom or Communism."[5]

Hodel reminded the Heritage Foundation audience about *Witness* and then said, "My staff informs me that certain persons or organizations appear to be engaged in an effort to prevent designation of the Whittaker Chambers Farm as a National Historic Landmark. . . . If there be objection by some as to this designation, or if there is controversy, so be it. When we consider Mr. Chambers' observation that one must be 'willing to die that your faith may live,' it seems to me that mere controversy is not sufficient reason to walk away from the opportunity to do what is right."[6]

Hodel later presented the bronze plaque intended to mark the site to Chambers's son John. John Chambers told the *Washington Post,* "For all of his life, Donald Hodel will be welcome at Pipe Creek Farm."[7] But what about the rest of us?

The *New York Times* and the *Washington Post,* along with other publications, criticized the designation, siding with the Park Service Advisory Board in arguing that the site failed to meet the criterion of historic significance. The official History Division of the National Park Service pointed out that "the pumpkin patch was gone. The area where the famous pumpkin once grew had been partially paved over, and what remained was no longer a garden, but rather a grassy patch with a large evergreen tree growing in it." Thus from a landmarks point of view the site raised "a very considerable issue of integrity."[8]

But the real objections concerned the politics behind the designation. The *New York Times* in an editorial called the designation "a low-water mark in landmarking."[9] An op-ed in the *Washington Post* called the designation "a rush to judgment by an influential group of arch-conservatives who wish to see Chambers appropriately 'honored.' . . . The fact is that neither Chambers nor his farm possesses 'transcendent national significance,' as Hodel proclaimed."[10]

Then the *Washington Post* ran a follow-up column asking "where this landmark business would stop, if it really got rolling." Some of their suggestions:

"the place in the Tidal Basin where that stripper, Fanne Foxe, leaped after bailing out of Wilbur Mills' car"; "the spot where George Bush's father disciplined him with a squash racket"; and "the radio station where Ronald Reagan broadcast the fictitious baseball game after communications with the ballpark broke down." "So much history," the piece concluded; "so few plaques."[11]

Meanwhile, back in the Westminster Visitor Center, the woman behind the counter dug out a one-page typewritten sheet titled "The Pumpkin Patch Papers." It started out with the fact that Alger Hiss "was a native of Baltimore"—obviously the local angle is everything here. Chambers's real name, it reported, was "Jay Vivian Chambers," but he changed it to Whittaker "so not to be ridiculed by his classmates." Chambers's farm, it said, "is well known for the microfilm hidden in a hollowed out pumpkin, and sometimes referred to as the Pumpkin Patch Papers" (well, not exactly). The information sheet said the site "will have a bronze plaque erected." The fact sheet also said that in 1925 Chambers "left college disillusioned and joined the communist party" and then "worked alongside Alger Hiss in the Communist underground"—something that Hiss denied for fifty years, to his dying day.

There's another big museum with an exhibit about the pumpkin patch: the Nixon Library in Yorba Linda. Garry Wills once wrote, "Richard Nixon: Hiss is your life."[12] Nixon, a member of Congress and of HUAC in 1947, pursued Whittaker Chambers's espionage charge against Hiss; Hiss's conviction for perjury propelled the formerly unknown Nixon into national prominence. The Nixon Library has one display case about Chambers and Hiss, which includes a plastic pumpkin and vines (figure 10). There's also a Woodstock manual typewriter. Visitors at the museum are told that Hiss's Woodstock typewriter convicted him when samples typed on it were found to match documents Chambers said Hiss had given him to transmit to the Soviets. The typewriter in the display case is a replica of Hiss's Woodstock, and library officials told the *L.A. Times* that the original Hiss typewriter is kept in a vault in the library basement.[13]

Could it be true that Nixon himself had the Hiss typewriter? Most of the artifacts in the library are on loan from the National Archives; I asked Archives spokeswoman Susan Cooper about the typewriter in the Nixon Library vault. "It's not ours," she said, "not the National Archives'." It turns

FIGURE 10. Pumpkin patch exhibit, Nixon Library, Yorba Linda, California. (photo by Pamla Eisenberg/The Richard Nixon Presidential Library & Museum)

out it isn't Hiss's either; that typewriter was returned to Hiss after his trial, and at the time the Nixon Library opened, in 1990, it was in the attic of the documentary filmmaker John Lowenthal.

The claim that Nixon has Hiss's typewriter in a vault in the library basement added another bizarre chapter to a forty-year saga. At the time Chambers charged Hiss with espionage, the typewriter on which Hiss was said to have typed the documents was missing; Hiss claimed it would prove him innocent. Despite a massive FBI effort to locate the typewriter, the Hiss defense found it and presented it triumphantly to the court, only to learn that it matched the Chambers documents. Ever since that time the Hiss defense claimed that the typewriter was used to frame him, that the FBI manufactured a phony duplicate Woodstock to match the Chambers documents and left it for Hiss to find—a type of fabrication that even the Hiss critic Allen Weinstein acknowledged "had become standard procedure in the repertoire of espionage agencies by the time of the Second World War."[14]

Although the "forgery by typewriter" theory seems unlikely, evidence keeps cropping up suggesting that it's true. In Nixon's book *Six Crises,* published in 1962, he wrote that the FBI had the typewriter four months before Hiss's attorneys found what they thought was the right Woodstock. That fit Hiss's "forgery by typewriter" theory. After a period of embarrassed silence, Nixon put out a press release saying this had been a researcher's error; subsequent editions of the book said the FBI never had the typewriter. Eleven years later, during the Watergate crisis, John Dean, counsel to President Nixon, recalled Nixon telling him, "The typewriters are always the key. We built one in the Hiss case." Nixon's edition of the White House tape transcripts confirmed Dean's account, quoting Nixon as saying, "We got the typewriter, we got the Pumpkin Papers. We got all of that ourselves."[15] The debate for fifty years focused on the authenticity of the typewriter Hiss introduced at the trial; now it seems that the Nixon Library vault holds a second phony Woodstock.

Needless to say, the "forgery by typewriter" theory is not presented in the Nixon Library display. One visitor standing next to me at the display commented, "Isn't that something! I remember hearing about the Pumpkin deal, but I never understood what it was about."

The Nixon Library, and the "fact sheet" on the Whittaker Chambers pumpkin patch, could have said the evidence on which Hiss was convicted of perjury had not been very convincing. The first trial resulted in a hung jury. A second trial was held four months later; during the interval, the Soviets exploded their first atomic bomb, and the communists won power in China, intensifying Cold War hysteria in the United States over communist espionage. The fact that Hiss was convicted in this overheated atmosphere created a cloud of doubt about the verdict that has never dissipated.

The doubts were renewed when the Pumpkin Papers themselves were released in 1975 in response to Hiss's own Freedom of Information lawsuit. What Chambers had pulled out of the pumpkin that night in 1948 included some unreadable film and some innocuous Navy Department documents dealing with life rafts and fire extinguishers (they said they should be painted red). The documents were unrestricted at the time and obviously distributed widely—to everyone in the navy with jurisdiction over fire extinguishers. If these pages of the Pumpkin Papers had been made public at the time of the trial, the prosecution would have been laughed out of court.[16]

The rest of the fifty-five images are of State Department documents that had been introduced at the two Hiss trials. All dated from 1938. At the time, government prosecutors—and Richard Nixon—described them as classified national security documents. But the topics seem routine—trade relations with Germany, developments in Japanese-occupied Manchuria—and many people other than Hiss had access to them.[17] In the Rosenberg case, the prosecution said its evidence included a drawing revealing the secret of the A-bomb; the Pumpkin Papers contained nothing remotely like that. But you wouldn't learn that at the Nixon Library, or at the pumpkin patch National Historic Landmark.

The opening of the Soviet archives after 1991 led conservative historians to look forward to the discovery of proof that Hiss was guilty, but in 1992 General Dmitri A. Volkogonov, chairman of the Russian government's military intelligence archives, conducted a search and reported that "not a single document substantiates the allegation that Mr. A. Hiss collaborated with the intelligence services of the Soviet Union.... If he was a spy then I believe positively I would have found a reflection in various files."[18] None have been found there since. (Volkogonov subsequently qualified his remarks, noting that evidence implicating Hiss could be in archives he hadn't consulted.)

But the efforts to prove Hiss guilty continued. The most important attempt focused on the Venona documents, released in 1996 by the National Security Agency (NSA), Soviet messages from and about their spies decoded by the United States. At the time *New York Post* editor, Eric Breindel, wrote in the *New Republic* that one of the Venona documents, purportedly sent by a Soviet spy in Washington to his superiors in Moscow in 1945, proves "beyond doubt" that Hiss "was still a Soviet agent in 1945."[19] Many others agreed.

The Venona page released by the NSA, dated March 30, 1945, reports that "ALES has been working with the NEIGHBORS continuously since 1935"—"neighbors" was the code word for Soviet military intelligence—"working on obtaining military information only." It also reports that "after the Yalta Conference, when he had gone on to Moscow, a Soviet personage in a very responsible position ... allegedly got in touch with ALES and at the behest of the Military NEIGHBORS passed on him their gratitude and so on."[20]

At the bottom of that page a note declares, "ALES: probably Alger Hiss." But that statement does not come from the Soviet document. Instead it appears in a separate section at the bottom of the page titled "Comments," written by an unknown NSA functionary and dated August 8, 1969—twenty-four years after the original cable. Crucially, the identification of "Ales" as Hiss is not supported by any evidence from the Soviet archives.[21]

It is true that Hiss attended the Yalta conference and then went on to Moscow. But in 2007 the historian Kai Bird made headlines with new evidence that "Hiss was not Ales." In a lengthy article in the *American Scholar,* Bird, a Pulitzer Prize–winning biographer of J. Robert Oppenheimer, and his coauthor, Svetlana Chervonnaya, showed that Ales's travels did not match Hiss's: Hiss was in Washington when Ales, according to his Soviet handlers, was in Mexico City. Through painstaking research Bird and Chervonnaya were able to identify another State Department official whose travel matched Ales's, who had gone to Yalta and then Moscow, and who had also been in Mexico City at the crucial time: a man named Wilder Foote. The FBI had suspected him of espionage, and the FBI file documenting their investigation of Foote is large. But Foote was never indicted. Instead, because of Whittaker Chambers, and the Pumpkin Papers, they went after Hiss.[22]

Back in Westminster, Maryland, searching for the Whittaker Chambers pumpkin patch National Historic Landmark, we left the Visitor Center, heading out of town with directions and a map called "Carroll County Roads to Gettysburg Driving Tour," but it contained nothing about the National Historic Landmark. Another map, the "Carroll County/Classic Country/Bicycle Friendly Bicycle Tour," also "highlights historical attractions"—but that map doesn't show the pumpkin patch National Historic Landmark either. The road itself is marked "scenic route," and indeed it is, with beautiful rolling hills and farms and forests gleaming this day in their full fall colors.

At the corner of Bachman's Valley Road and Saw Mill Road, where the landmark was supposed to be, we saw nothing but a field with a few horses in it. The bronze plaque displayed at the Heritage Foundation back in 1988—the one that was supposed to mark this spot—was nowhere to be seen.

Off Saw Mill Road was a handsome brick gate. I had an old article from the *Washington Post* that said the pumpkin patch was "in back of the barn." We could see the barn; we were almost there. We drove through the gate and headed up the tree-lined driveway—but were confronted by a sign reading,

"No Trespassing, hunting or fishing/Violators will be prosecuted to the full extent of the law."

Prosecuted for visiting a National Historic Landmark?

Surely the taxpayers—who paid for the plaque—deserved better than this. I went home and sent an e-mail, as any concerned citizen would, to the National Park Service; Barry Mackintosh replied. He said he had asked John Chambers—at that point a staff member at the Joint Congressional Committee on Printing—what happened and was told that he kept the plaque "inside one of the houses on the property," because he "feared the plaque might be a target for thieves" if it were displayed outside. "I fully appreciate his concern," Mackintosh wrote.

Then I got a second e-mail, from Robbie Lange of the National Park Service. Government regulations, he wrote, "clearly indicate that the government provides NHL [National Historic Landmark] plaques for the purpose of public display. A National Historic Landmark not providing some degree of public access does not meet the requirements for the receipt of a plaque at government expense. Thank you for bringing this matter to our attention."[23]

Thus the pumpkin patch National Historic Landmark is evidence not of conservatives' success in honoring one of their heroes but rather of their failure. How many tourists are interested in being told that HUAC's hunt for communist spies was not "McCarthyism" but rather a noble cause? "About two people a year."

FIVE

Naming Names, from Laramie to Beverly Hills

The American Heritage Center at the University of Wyoming in Laramie recently had an exhibit titled "One in Ten: Adrian Scott." The meaning of the title may not be immediately apparent, especially in Laramie. The "ten" in question were the Hollywood Ten: actors, directors, writers, and producers who refused to cooperate with HUAC's investigation of communism in Hollywood in 1947 and after. Adrian Scott, one of the Hollywood Ten, had produced several noteworthy films in the 1940s, including *Murder My Sweet,* a classic film noir featuring Dick Powell as Raymond Chandler's hero, Philip Marlowe, and *Crossfire,* a noir about anti-Semitism starring Robert Mitchum, Robert Young, Robert Ryan, and Gloria Grahame that received five Academy Award nominations. As the Wyoming exhibit explains, Scott was "convicted of contempt of Congress, fined $1,000 and jailed for one year at the federal prison in Ashland, Kentucky. Upon his conviction RKO fired him, claiming violation of the morals clause in his contract."[1]

Scott's crime, as the "One in Ten" exhibit explains, was that he refused to name names. Naming names was one of the central features of Cold War America, and even today looms large in the memories of those required to participate. Here I explore the public commemorations that inform the public about this history, and the explanations they offer.

HUAC and other governmental bodies claimed to be searching for security risks and seeking to investigate communist infiltration of the film industry, universities, unions, and other institutions, but as Victor Navasky pointed out in his book on the subject, the committees already had the names. The public hearings, where witnesses were required to appear, were in fact what Navasky termed "degradation ceremonies," an opportunity offered to former leftists to denounce their former comrades, renounce their past commitments, and participate in a public ritual of political purification.

The hearings were carefully staged. Witnesses were always asked the same questions: first, the most famous question of the fifties, "Are you now or have you ever been a member of the Communist Party?" And if you answered that question "Yes," you were then required to answer a second, asking for the names of others who were also Communists.

The problem with the second question, the demand to name names, was that it went against a deep-seated cultural value in America. As Navasky explains, those who name names are considered "rats," "finks," "stool pigeons," and—deeper and more powerful in a Christian country—"Judases." If a witness named names, those names would be published in the newspapers, and those people would be required to appear and submit to the same rituals.

If you didn't want to name names—or if you objected to the first question—you had three choices, all carefully choreographed. You could refuse, in which case you would be found guilty of contempt of Congress and sentenced to a prison term. This was the route taken by the Hollywood Ten in 1947, including Adrian Scott. Or you could "plead the Fifth": you could respond that you refused to answer under the privilege granted by the Fifth Amendment, the constitutional prohibition on self-incrimination. In that case you would not go to prison but you would be fired and blacklisted—prohibited from working in Hollywood, or the universities and public schools, or the unions.

Or you could name names. The ritual required one final statement by those who named names: in order to be "cleared" to return to work, you had to thank the committee. You had to say something like, "I am grateful for the opportunity to set the record straight." You had to acknowledge the legitimacy of the committee and tell the world that what the committee had done to you was the right thing.

These hearings were not a search for spies. Those subpoenaed were not accused of espionage or sabotage; they were not charged with violating any laws. These hearings instead inquired about past and present political affiliations and beliefs.

Most of the public commemorations of the blacklist over the past thirty years have honored those who resisted and condemned those who named names. Most of these commemorations have focused on Hollywood, where the high profiles of some of those blacklisted made them public figures, unlike union officials or public school teachers. Many books and several films have examined the subject, and a couple of museums have mounted exhibits that tell the story of the blacklist to the public.[2]

The exhibit at the American Heritage Center in Laramie featured the letter Adrian Scott received from the president of RKO pictures firing him, which makes for interesting reading: because he "refused to answer certain questions propounded . . . by a committee of the House of Representatives," he had brought himself into "disrepute," "offended the community," and "prejudiced this corporation as your employer." The Wyoming exhibit also included transcripts of the hearings, photos and film posters, contracts for film and TV scripts written by Adrian Scott under pseudonyms—a way blacklisted writers could work—and information about the other members of the Ten. The entire exhibit is now online. If you already know about the blacklist, it provides some fascinating details. But if you don't, it doesn't really dramatize the issues in a compelling way.

The mother of all blacklist exhibits was the one at the Motion Picture Academy in Beverly Hills—the people who run the Oscars. "Reds and Blacklists in Hollywood," on exhibit in 2002, made headlines for its frank and unqualified admission that the Academy had joined with HUAC and the studios "in destroying or damaging the careers of hundreds." It was a big exhibit—more than two hundred items in fourteen "visual areas," including film clips, posters, photos, audio- and videotape, and documents, along with wall text and an audio tour narrated by the actor Peter Coyote and a series of film screenings.[3]

The key document: a page, prominently displayed, revising the bylaws of the Academy, stating that anyone who admitted membership in the Communist Party "or who refuses to testify before a 'duly constituted Federal legislative committee or body' . . . shall be ineligible for any Academy Award."[4] That's what the show was apologizing for.

The audio tour, written by Larry Ceplair, exhibit curator, explained that "for the first time in the history of the U.S., a large group of artists and craftspeople, perhaps as many as 500, were denied employment solely because they refused to reveal to the HUAC their political beliefs and activities and act as informers."[5]

The titles given to sections of the exhibit suggest its political spirit. The first section focused on the 1930s, when "class conflict erupts in Hollywood," and it went on to "anticommunist witch-hunt begins in Hollywood," which described how Walt Disney and Hedda Hopper played key roles. Then came "Un-American Activities Committee launches era of trial by congressional committee and stool pigeon," followed by "movie industry capitulates to communist witch-hunt." After that visitors saw "the blacklisted fight blacklisting" and finally "the battles continue"—a section on the protests over the Academy giving friendly witness Elia Kazan an honorary Oscar in 1999 for "lifetime achievement."[6]

Only one voice was raised in protest against the Academy's mea culpa. The *Los Angeles Times* ran an opinion piece by Roy Brewer, who had been head of the stagehands' union, IATSE, and a militant anticommunist and fierce advocate of the blacklist. In his piece Brewer said communism had been a real threat, and he also said there had been no blacklist. "Contrary to popular myth," he wrote, "no such single document of names ever existed." What happened was that "studio executives were businessmen, and they knew that communism was bad for box office."[7]

One museum brings the larger issues surrounding naming names to life forcefully and successfully: the Truman Library in Independence, Missouri. The museum at the Truman Library features a "Decision Theater" titled "Spies in Government: How far do you go to find them?" Visitors here are confronted with the conflict between the freedom guaranteed by the Bill of Rights and the restrictions imposed in the name of "national security." The theater's design and content, Benjamin Hufbauer reports, were completed before the 9/11 attacks and have gained relevance since then.

At other museums, visitors typically look at objects and wall text. In this exhibit, visitors are instructed to sit on wooden chairs and answer questions in a space the online guide describes as "a loyalty review interrogation room" or "a setting that resembles a congressional hearing room" for HUAC or Joe McCarthy. Visitors face a glass wall behind which they see various objects, including a table from a congressional hearing with a microphone on it. Each visitor has a keypad to be used to answer questions.

The exhibit begins with the voice of an interviewer: "Welcome! I'd like to thank you for coming here today. Now that you are seated, we would like to begin with a few brief questions about basic American rights. Do you agree that freedom of speech is a basic constitutional right that must be protected? Please press blue for yes or red for no.

"The majority of you agree that freedom of speech is essential.

"But, do you think that, during a war, the media should be permitted to broadcast military information, such as the location of troops and ships? Press blue for yes or red for no."

Then: "Do you agree that you also have the constitutional right to be safe in your home against unreasonable search and seizure? Please vote. . . . But do you think that the government should be permitted to wiretap the home of anyone they suspect might be a terrorist or a spy? Please vote."

Then a radio plays highlights of Winston Churchill's "Iron Curtain" speech, and a narrator says, "Republicans accuse the Truman administration of being 'soft on Communism'; and call for the president to purge the government of communists. . . . In response, President Truman issued an Executive Order, in March 1947, creating the first peacetime loyalty program in the history of the United States. The program required security checks for every government employee. . . . In early 1947, Loyalty Review Boards, in cooperation with the FBI, began interviewing government employees."

Suddenly a camera flashes in the faces of the seated visitors, who now see their own shocked reflections in the glass. As Hufbauer explains, "Audience members, perhaps having voted for security measures even if this meant curtailing liberties, suddenly face the result of their choice as they are interrogated."

Now an interrogator says, "Thank you for coming before this board. We appreciate your cooperation. We would like to ask you a few simple questions." But these new questions are not about opinions on the conflict between freedom and security; instead they focus directly on the actions and associations of the person in the witness chair:

"Are you a citizen of the United States?

"Do you attend church? Do you attend regularly?

"Have you or any member of your family ever belonged to an organization suspected of disloyalty to the United States?"

And then comes the big question, the question about naming names: "Have you ever suspected any of your friends, neighbors, or coworkers of disloyalty to the United States? Would you be willing to share those suspicions with members of this board?"

Visitors still have their keypads; again they can press blue for yes or red for no. It's an incredible moment, and a unique one in museums of the Cold War.

The program comes to a quick end as a narrator poses the underlying issue: "How should a president balance individual rights and national security issues? Even if the question is tough, it must be asked."[8]

Of course there's a different way to remember naming names: the right might erect some sort of monument to the friendly witness. The most prominent of the latter was the director Elia Kazan. Wesleyan University, where Kazan deposited his archives, celebrated the centennial of his birth in 2009 with an exhibit about his life and work—an appropriate place to make the case that HUAC's leading man did the right thing when he ratted on his friends.

Kazan was at the peak of his career when he got his HUAC subpoena in 1952. He had revolutionized theater with his smash hits on Broadway, *All My Sons* (1947) and *Death of a Salesman* (1949), and had already made several striking Hollywood films. At his first HUAC appearance, in January 1952, he answered the questions about himself but refused to talk about others.

The film historian David Thomson explained what happened next: "People in power in the picture business told him his career was in jeopardy. He went back and named names."[9] He named eight members of his Group Theatre company from the mid-1930s.

Lots of people named names, but Kazan went further than any of them, when, two days later, he took out an ad in the *New York Times* explaining his reasons for naming names and urging others to follow his example. "We must never let the Communists get away with the pretense that they stand for the very things which they kill in their own countries," he wrote. "I am talking about free speech."[10] But cooperating with HUAC was not a good way to defend freedom of speech or to fight communism, because HUAC was an enemy of free speech. If Kazan had really wanted to defend free speech, he could have published a statement in the *New York Times* criticizing communism without giving the committee what it wanted. Instead he contributed to HUAC's legitimacy and supported the committee's claim that it was America's greatest weapon for defending freedom.

The right hailed Kazan as a patriot; many liberals praised him for making a difficult decision; and the left forever after regarded him as "the ultimate betrayer." "If Kazan had refused to cooperate," a blacklisted director later said, "he might well have broken the blacklist. He was too important to be ignored." Navasky comments, "Probably no single individual could have broken the blacklist in 1952, and yet no person was in a better strategic position to try than Kazan, by virtue of his prestige and economic invulnerability, to mount a symbolic campaign against it, and by this example inspire hundreds of fence sitters to come over to the opposition."[11]

Kazan refused to speak to Navasky about naming names in the late seventies, and the subject was still a problem for him when he published his autobiography in 1988. On his book publicity tour, he did a memorable interview with Susan Stamberg on NPR's *All Things Considered*—worth quoting at length. She opened the interview by declaring, "I would like to get the HUAC business out of the way first."

KAZAN: "Oh no. Let's not start with that!"

STAMBERG: "I'd like to."

KAZAN: *(annoyed, loud)* "In every interview it comes out that that's the most important thing, and I'm tired of it! . . . Start with something else."

STAMBERG: "No, I'd like to start with it, to get it out of the way."

KAZAN: "No! You're not going to get me to talk!"

That's not what he told HUAC.

STAMBERG: *(softly)* "So reluctant to discuss this?"

KAZAN: "No, I'm not a bit reluctant. . . . But as soon as you start with it, it makes it the most important thing. It's not the most important thing in *my* life."

Stamberg relented and asked him about working with Marlon Brando, which of course he was delighted to discuss. A few minutes later, she said, "Now we get to HUAC. . . . You could choose NOT to appear. You could choose TO appear and refuse to speak on the grounds that it might incriminate you. You could choose to appear and speak only about yourself. Or you could name names. Your choice was the last. Why?"

KAZAN: *(says each word as if it were a separate sentence)* "When I faced that choice, I wavered. . . . Something not nice about naming names. . . . I felt that there's no use ruining my career for something I didn't believe in at all. I had a violent antipathy towards it. . . . You ask me if I LIKED doing it? I did not."

STAMBERG: "Basically you wanted to keep working in film, and you believed that your film career would be jeopardized if you kept quiet."

KAZAN: "I ASSURE you that had very little to do with it, because I had a good career in the theater."

But just a moment earlier he had said resisting the committee would have meant "ruining my career."

STAMBERG: "Mr. Kazan, I can understand not liking what the Communists were doing in the United States. The hard part is understanding how that dislike can translate into action which then can ruin the lives of others."

KAZAN: "It didn't ruin their lives at all . . . because they all had the same choice I did."[12]

When Kazan died in 2003, naming names was featured prominently in his obituaries, though it had been more than fifty years since he testified. His obituary in the *New York Times* reported that "his naming of names prompted many people in the arts, including those who had never been Communists, to excoriate him for decades." The *Times* reminded readers that in 1997 the American Film Institute had refused to give him a lifetime achievement award "because of his decision half a century earlier to inform on others." The Motion Picture Academy had given him a lifetime award two years later, which, the *Times* said, revived much of the debate over his 1952 action. The obit quoted Arthur Schlesinger Jr. saying at the time, "If the Academy's occasion calls for apologies, let Mr. Kazan's denouncers apologize for the aid and comfort they gave to Stalinism."[13]

The "Elia Kazan Centennial" exhibit at Wesleyan University's Rick Nicita Gallery in 1999 featured "rare photos, clippings, scripts, posters, private notebooks, personal and professional correspondence, and more."[14] But what about his HUAC testimony? What about his ad in the *New York Times*? What place did they have in this celebration? Joan Miller, head archivist of the Wesleyan Cinema Archives, told me that "the exhibit did not contain any information about Kazan's HUAC testimony."

Commemoration of the blacklist could take another form: telling the story from the standpoint of HUAC and the FBI and Joe McCarthy. I searched for a HUAC museum or memorial but couldn't find one anywhere in the

United States. (I had hoped for a monument to J. Parnell Thomas, chairman of HUAC when it came to Hollywood in 1947, who was convicted of fraud the next year and sentenced to eighteen months in Danbury federal prison in Connecticut, where Lester Cole and Ring Lardner Jr., members of the Hollywood Ten, were serving their sentences for contempt of HUAC. But there's no historical marker at Danbury—or in his hometown, Jersey City.)[15]

I found a museum exhibit about Joe McCarthy—only one, despite the recent effort by Ann Coulter to rehabilitate him—in his hometown, Appleton, Wisconsin, at the Outagamie County Historical Society. It ran from January 2002 to January 2004 and was titled "Joe McCarthy: A Modern Tragedy." The text in the online version is written at the sixth-grade level: "McCarthy looked for Communists in government. Other senators became dissatisfied with what they considered McCarthy's crude tactics and reckless accusations. In 1954, his colleagues censured him for disregarding Senate customs. Three years later, while still in office, McCarthy died of acute hepatitis at the age of 48."[16]

The Outagamie County Courthouse in Appleton had unveiled a bronze bust of McCarthy in 1959, two years after his death—the only Joe McCarthy memorial in the country. A photo displayed at the "Tragedy" exhibit shows a Marine honor guard at the unveiling and a crowd of a few dozen people (figure 11). In the 1980s county supervisors began "pushing for its removal," and the bust was donated to the local museum in 2001. It is now reportedly "in inventory."[17]

If it's hard to find museums of HUAC or Joe McCarthy, the FBI does have its museums—and as Ellen Schrecker showed in her book *Many Are the Crimes,* the FBI worked closely with HUAC in the hunt for communists and former communists.[18] For decades the tour of the FBI building in Washington, D.C., was a major attraction for tourists, but it was closed after 9/11, and, according to the FBI website, "no date has been set for its reopening."[19] I still have my 1960 children's book about the museum tour, *Let's Go to the FBI* (figure 12),[20] and still remember vividly the exhibition of target shooting at the firing range in the basement and the stories about the legendary gangsters of the thirties, Machine Gun Kelley, Pretty Boy Floyd, and the Barker-Karpis gang, all of whom had been brought down by G-men. That tour described the FBI as a scientific body that analyzed fingerprints, fibers, paper, and ballistics to solve crimes and displayed wanted posters. Exposing communists in Hollywood went unmentioned in the old FBI tour; not even spies got much attention.

FIGURE 11. Joe McCarthy Memorial dedication, Outagamie County Courthouse, Appleton, Wisconsin, in 1959, two years after his death. The only Joe McCarthy memorial in the United States, the bust was removed in 2001. (photo courtesy of *Appleton Post-Crescent*)

The current FBI web page reporting that the tour "is presently closed" recommends visiting the FBI exhibit at the Newseum in Washington, "G-Men and Journalists"—an excellent topic, especially since the news media were a crucial component of the blacklist. Although the Newseum is privately run, the exhibit is described as "A collaboration between the FBI and the Newseum" and the FBI's website devotes a page to it. Cathy Trost, the Newseum's director of exhibit development, said, "It's been an incredibly popular attraction since the day it opened." According to Trost, the idea came from the FBI, and Bureau employees around the country "opened their desk drawers, their storage closets, and their file cabinets and found some amazing things" to "help bring the exhibit to life."[21]

The Newseum, which opened in 2008, describes itself as "not a dusty, musty museum with tiny words on the wall. The Newseum is alive with energy—big screens, games, videos and interactives. . . . This is an experience,

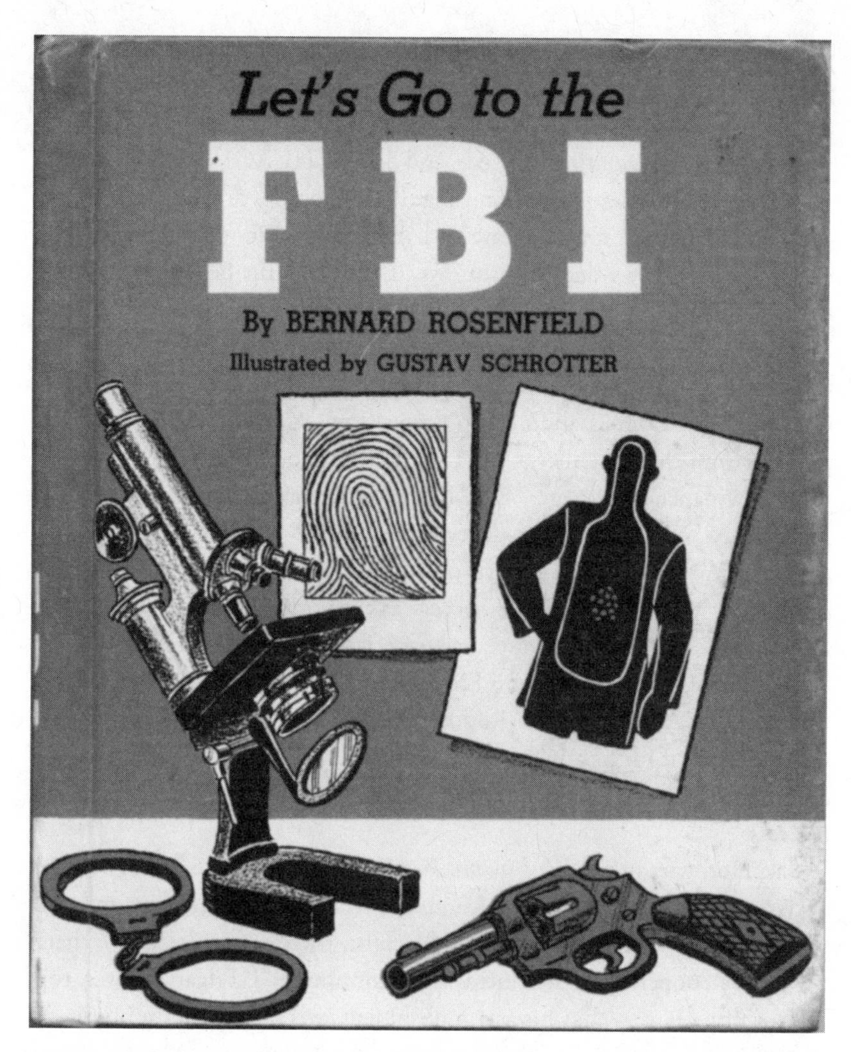

FIGURE 12. *Let's Go to the FBI*, published in 1960. The FBI tour was canceled after 9/11. (© G.P. Putnam's Sons, 1960; illustration by Gustav Schrotter)

filled with stories that help you recall the memorial times of your life." Indeed, this museum has some great stuff: the actual Idaho cabin of Ted Kaczynski, the Unabomber; pieces of the rental truck Timothy McVeigh used to blow up the Oklahoma City federal building in 1995; the coat and gun used by Patty Hearst, aka "Tania," during her bank robberies with the Symbionese Liberation Army in the mid-1970s; and, most important, "the desk, chair, and office accessories used by Director J. Edgar Hoover." The three photos on the FBI website are of Ted Kaczynski's cabin, Patty Hearst's gun, and J. Edgar Hoover's desk.

But what about hunting for Reds, and helping HUAC?

The opening display is not promising: Pretty Boy Floyd, the Barker-Karpis gang, and Machine Gun Kelley are back, this time not in wanted posters but in news stories. The video narrator says, "Go behind the headlines and find out what really happened!"

After "Bank Robbers and Kidnappers, Gangsters and Mobsters" comes "Spies and Terrorists." The entire exhibit was packed on the Saturday I visited, and people were standing two deep at the section titled "Fighting Espionage from the Rosenbergs to Hansen." The top of the wall displayed a giant newspaper front page, "EXTRA: Rosenbergs Die"—from the *Call-Bulletin,* a San Francisco newspaper—appropriate in a news museum. The exhibit features newspaper reports on "Ike's Last Words on Spies." The wall text reads, "Counter-espionage success after World War II enhanced the FBI's image. The Bureau was seen as America's protector, ferreting out the likes of A-bomb spies Julius and Ethel Rosenberg and elusive Soviet operative Rudolph Abel." A bit on Rudolph Abel, something on Robert Hanssen, and that's it for fighting communists in the United States. This exhibit cosponsored by the FBI has nothing about its work repressing domestic radicals.

Sari Horowitz of the *Washington Post* is next on the introductory video, declaring, "There's a natural tension between law enforcement and the press." In fact, when it came to the blacklist, there was no tension; there was happy cooperation. The intro video continues: "J. Edgar Hoover, top cop for fifty years, . . . but his accomplishments were tarnished by abuses of power."

What were these abuses? Photos at this point in the video show Martin Luther King Jr. and antiwar demonstrators in Grant Park in Chicago in 1968.[22] For more, we go to the "video blog," which focuses on a wax effigy of Hoover—on loan from Madame Tussaud's, we are told—and standing next to him (it?) is Patty Ruhle, Newseum projects editor. She says, "He kind of leaves a mixed legacy. . . . He had problems with communism, and that obsession led to him sort of overstepping the bounds of power. He also didn't like people like Martin Luther King Jr., and did a lot of dirty tricks to sort of undermine his rising power in the civil rights movement, and he also did a bit to dispel the power of the anti-war movement. So he leaves a mixed legacy, but he's here because he's such a powerful force on what made the FBI what it is today."[23]

You might think that a museum of the news media would want presentations that were grammatical and perhaps even literate rather than something that would earn a C- in a high school history class. You might think a museum of news would focus more on the news media. In fact, there's an important story to be told here about the news media, the FBI, and Martin Luther King: in 1963 Hoover persuaded Attorney General Robert Kennedy to let him wiretap King. The taps turned up evidence of King's extramarital sex life. The FBI sent what it said were King sex tapes to newsmen it considered friendly, but none of them would report on the tapes. The Newseum might highlight this story as an example of the independence and judgment of the media, but instead we get only that vague remark from the Newseum project director about J. Edgar Hoover's "dirty tricks to sort of undermine" the "rising power" of Martin Luther King.

There's more. J. Edgar Hoover's desk is featured in an online exhibit: click on items on the desk to learn more about them. Among the items: a letter—from Joe Kennedy, father of Jack and Bobby and Ted, in 1955, proposing that if Hoover would run for president, "that would be the most wonderful thing for the United States, and I would guarantee you the largest contribution that you would ever get from anybody."[24] Was there something in particular that Joe wanted from J. Edgar in 1955? Or was he just keeping the lines open and friendly?

That exhibit also includes a photo—of Walter Winchell. The caption explains that he was "one of a select group of favored journalists to whom Hoover gave inside information on FBI cases." This is promising, since in his column Winchell "regularly offered up names" to HUAC "with the suggestion that they should be added to the blacklist."[25] Winchell's syndicated column reportedly appeared in something like two thousand newspapers, and he claimed to be read by fifty million people a day at his height in the 1940s and 1950s. Notably he named Lucille Ball in a 1953 column; in fact she had registered as a communist in the 1936 election. Nevertheless she was too powerful for HUAC and emerged from her private session as one of the few to keep working. That story is told not in the Newseum but rather at the Chicago Museum of Broadcast Communications website.[26] (Other columnists who participated in the same practice included Hedda Hopper, Victor

Riesel, and George Sokolsky.) But all that is missing from the Newseum exhibit of the photos behind J. Edgar Hoover's desk.

Washington had another FBI exhibit—or rather another J. Edgar Hoover exhibit: the little-known J. Edgar Hoover Collection at the Scottish Rite Temple. Hoover was a Mason—or as the exhibit described him, "America's No. 1 crime fighter and one of Freemasonry's most renowned Brothers." "In 1955," the exhibit said, "he was coroneted a Thirty-third Degree Inspector General Honorary and awarded the Scottish Rite's highest recognition, the Grand Cross of Honour, in 1965."[27]

This exhibit was short on text and featured instead objects in Hoover's office: bookcases, display cases, and, once again, Hoover's desk. A collection of photos hung on one wall, including Hoover with Deanna Durbin in 1941—she was a singer in popular Hollywood musicals and in 1945 and 1947 reportedly the top-salaried woman in the United States; Hoover with Lana Turner in 1941; and Hoover with Dorothy Lamour in 1951—according to one Hoover biographer, he "pursued Lamour romantically, but she was initially interested only in friendship with him," and the two "remained close friends to the end of Hoover's life."[28] There's also a "personally autographed photo of Sophie Tucker" from 1946; she was a superstar of the vaudeville stage, one of the most successful Jewish celebrities, and at her peak "one of the few women in entertainment to make more than men doing the same job."[29] Tucker also was active in efforts to unionize professional actors and in 1938 had been elected president of the American Federation of Actors. None of the women in the pictures on Hoover's wall had been subpoenaed by HUAC.

On another wall visitors saw posters of films about the FBI: Charles Bronson in *Machine Gun Kelly* (1958); Warren Oates in *Dillinger* (1973). At least four portraits of Hoover were also on display, painted in oil, along with a bronze bust of his head "commissioned by Society of Former Special Agents of the FBI Inc." and presented to Hoover in 1964. A framed news clipping from 1937 was displayed, with a photo captioned, "Head G-Man J. Edgar Hoover, with his right-hand man, Clyde A. Tolson."[30] Hoover often described Tolson as his alter ego. The two rode to work together in the same bulletproof car, ate lunch and dinner together every day at the same restaurant, went to nightclubs together, and vacationed together. Tolson was

Hoover's heir and moved into Hoover's house when he died, and the two are buried in adjacent plots.[31] The exhibit doesn't mention any of that.

The Hoover Collection here displayed one additional object, an incredible one: J. Edgar Hoover's Masonic cap, "as a 33° Inspector General Honorary, Grand Cross." It's white silk with a velvet purple band and gold piping and an elaborate gold cross on the front.[32] But the exhibit had nothing about Hoover's fight against communists.

The Scottish Rite website says, "Tours begin every fifteen minutes beginning at 10:00 am." But the website of the J. Edgar Hoover Foundation says something quite different: "In November 2008 the J. Edgar Hoover Center for Law Enforcement ended its relationship with the Supreme Council of the Scottish Rite Freemasons in Washington, DC. The J. Edgar Hoover Collection ... is currently located at Ely Corporation, one of the premier fine arts storage facilities in the Washington, DC, area."[33]

I asked Jason Van Dyke of the Media Relations Office of the Supreme Council of the Scottish Rite about this in 2010, and he explained, "The Hoover Collection was part of our rotating collections in partnership with the Hoover Center for Law Enforcement, and indeed it has been removed to make way for a new exhibit. Sorry for the confusion."

Thus there seems to be nowhere in America where a history museum defends the blacklist or presents HUAC in a positive light. Most of what the public is told at museums honors those who resisted and condemns those who named names. The other museums, the ones that might defend HUAC—like the FBI exhibit at the Newseum—avoid the topic. Meanwhile the Truman Museum shows it is possible to convey in a powerful and effective way the larger issues raised by the HUAC hearings—the threat to individual freedoms that arise out of "national security" issues—and also dramatize the tension and anxiety the hearings created. It's worth a trip to Independence to see how they do it.

SIX

Secrets on Display

THE CIA MUSEUM AND THE NSA MUSEUM

The two most secret government spy agencies during the Cold War were the CIA and the NSA, the National Security Agency, which specialized in decrypting foreign communications. Each has a museum. The CIA Museum at the Agency headquarters in Langley, Virginia, according to the CIA website, "is the preeminent national archive for the collection, preservation, documentation and exhibition of intelligence artifacts, culture, and history." It's big, with five galleries taking up 11,000 square feet. The mission of the museum is clearly stated: it "supports the Agency's operational, recruitment, and training missions." As the museum's curator, Toni Hiley, explained in an interview with *USA Today,* "All new CIA officers get a tour on their first day, and seasoned veterans also stroll in often. . . . I've had officers tell me that they walk potential recruits through the museum, and they often find that that person will sign on the dotted line after seeing the stories and the artifacts."[1]

There's only one problem: "because the Museum is located on the CIA compound, it is not open to the public."[2] However the Agency has created an online virtual tour of the museum (figure 13). In principle, there's nothing wrong with that; many museums have online tours, some of them excellent. So we took the virtual tour.

The tour opens at the entrance to a room with six display cases, three on each side of a central isle, three shelves in each case, each shelf displaying objects and text. The visitor can navigate onscreen down the aisle, turn to the left and right, and examine each item on display by clicking on it to see a close-up view along with the accompanying wall text. Some of the objects can be manipulated: in the "Communication" case, for example, a fake silver

FIGURE 13. CIA Museum Virtual Tour. Most of the exhibits here are about World War II, before the CIA existed, rather than the Cold War. (courtesy Central Intelligence Agency, www.CIA.gov)

dollar is displayed; a click of the mouse opens it up to reveal a secret compartment for concealing messages.

But the exhibits here are mostly about World War II—before the CIA existed—rather than the Cold War. The first two cases contain items from the CIA's World War II predecessor, the OSS: a "fighting knife," a matchbox camera, and a device used to take letters from their envelopes without opening the seals. Also: OSS insignia for a shoulder patch designed by "Wild Bill" Donovan, head of the OSS, but rejected by the Joint Chiefs of Staff. It's the kind of stuff that used to come in cereal boxes for kids—the Captain Midnight decoder ring and that X-ray viewer.

When we get to the Cold War era, we find nothing about the big events in the early history of the CIA—covert action, the Agency-sponsored coups that put the shah in power in Iran in 1953 and the one that threw Arbenz out of office in Guatemala in 1954. Arbenz had been elected in 1951, and after the CIA coup Guatemala had decades of civil war in which hundreds of thousands died. The history of Iran after the shah is well known. Instead the

1950s at the CIA are represented by a shovel, the one used in the ceremonial groundbreaking for the new headquarters building in 1959. Another display features a pneumatic tube from the Original Headquarters Building—the "OHB." But didn't lots of office buildings use pneumatic tubes, going back to the late nineteenth century?

Another key chapter in the history of the CIA is also missing: its secret funding of the cultural cold war, which enlisted prestigious intellectuals and artists to combat Marxist and communist ideas, especially in Europe. The key here was the CIA's creation of the Congress of Cultural Freedom in 1950.[3] It recruited Bertrand Russell, John Dewey, Arthur Koestler, Raymond Aron, Stephen Spender, Ignazio Silone, and Sidney Hook to do battle with Jean-Paul Sartre, Simone de Beauvoir, Bertolt Brecht, Louis Aragon, and Pablo Picasso. Not one of these names appears in the CIA's museum.

The museum does display volume 1, number 1, of the CIA's in-house journal, *Studies in Intelligence,* from 1955—dedicated to the principles of "intellectual rigor," "a willingness to hear other opinions," and "a candid admission of shortcomings." These are excellent principles. At the top of the list of what you might call "shortcomings" of the CIA is the 1961 Bay of Pigs invasion. There, the brigade the CIA trained and sent to Cuba had 1,189 members captured and 114 killed, along with 10 pilots killed—6 Cuban exiles and 4 Americans. Afterwards, Kennedy "wanted to destroy the CIA," according to Tim Weiner, but decided instead to put his brother Robert in charge. "For the next nineteen years, no president would place his full faith and trust in the Central Intelligence Agency."[4] But the Bay of Pigs is not mentioned in the CIA Museum.

To find a memorial commemorating the Bay of Pigs, you have to go to Miami. The city has a monument to the anti-Castro "martyrs" of the Bay of Pigs in the Little Havana district, dedicated in 1972—a six-sided marble column with a plaque displaying the coat of arms of the "brigade," a Cuban flag wrapped around a cross.[5] On top is an "eternal flame," but when the *Guardian*'s Ed Wilkington visited in 2008, he found only "a soot-blackened wick," he reported. "The eternal flame has gone out."[6] There's also a new memorial to the pilots who died in the failed invasion. It's at the Wings Over Miami Air Museum, located at the private Kendall-Tamiami Executive Airport on the outskirts of Miami. It features a Douglas B-26 Invader "as it might have looked on that day almost 50 years ago"—that is, without identifiable U.S. markings. It went on display in 2009, but the site seems to lack information for visitors about the plane or its role in the failed invasion—as does the semiofficial website, which concludes, "For great footage of this aircraft in low level hazardous forest fire fighting flight, I would recommend the 1989 movie, *Always*—with Holly Hunter, Richard Dreyfuss and John Goodman."[7]

The next chapter in the CIA's history is the Cuban Missile Crisis. The conventional view is that the CIA's discovery of the missile sites using aerial photography from a U-2 spy plane was a triumph of technical intelligence that led to a historic victory over the Soviets. But that's not the story told in the museum. The U-2 display at the CIA Museum is about the Soviets shooting down the U-2 piloted by Francis Gary Powers in 1960. The museum exhibits the U-2 model displayed by Powers during his 1962 Senate Armed Services Committee testimony about the downing of his aircraft. The wings and tail of the model in the exhibit "are detachable to show the aircraft's breakup after the shootdown." (To see a real U-2, you can go to the National Air and Space Museum on the Mall in Washington or the National Museum of the U.S. Air Force at Wright-Patterson Air Force Base outside Dayton, Ohio, where a U-2 sits in a gigantic "Cold War Gallery" along with sixty other planes.)[8]

The downing of the U-2 over the USSR was a huge event in the history of the CIA and of the Cold War. Khrushchev and Eisenhower had agreed to hold a summit meeting in Paris to establish a nuclear test ban treaty and begin a process of disarmament. But two weeks before the scheduled Paris summit, Powers and his U-2 were shot down. Eisenhower had wanted to stop the provocative flights but acceded to CIA demands to continue them in exchange for CIA willingness to support a test ban treaty. For the Soviets, the U-2 flights were almost an act of war; they feared a U-2 could drop an atomic bomb on Moscow. So Khrushchev canceled the summit. The summit would not have brought an end to the Cold War, but both leaders had hoped it would provide a way to break the spiral of the nuclear arms race.[9] They don't say anything about that at the CIA Museum.

The CIA's U-2 photos discovered Soviet missiles in Cuba—one of the greatest success stories in the history of the CIA, especially in view of the failure of the NSA to provide advance warning that the missiles were on their way to Cuba. But the CIA's online museum barely mentions this triumph. The only reference to the U-2 photos of missiles in Cuba is a brief note in the wall text: "For more information on the U-2 program: SEE '*Politics and Intelligence:* The "Photo Gap" That Delayed Discovery of Missiles in Cuba,' by Max Holland—published in CIA *Studies in Intelligence*." There's no link in the virtual tour, but with a little work the article can be found elsewhere on the CIA website. It's a twenty-five-page piece with more than one hundred footnotes, and even if it's not really part of the virtual museum, it's a fascinating document. And it is about a "shortcoming": it explains why it was not the CIA's fault that it missed the Soviet introduction of missiles in Cuba.

A month before the Missile Crisis, film from a U-2 flight over Cuba revealed a surface-to-air missile (SAM) site (which is not a missile that could reach the U.S. mainland). It was the same missile that had shot down Powers's U-2 over Russia, which had led Eisenhower to promise to end the flights. The same day the SAM was photographed in Cuba, the Soviets caught another U-2 violating its airspace, and a week later yet another U-2 was shot down over China. The Pentagon and the State Department demanded that the CIA stop its U-2 flights, and Kennedy agreed, ordering the CIA to end aerial surveillance over Cuba. That was four days before the arrival of the Soviet ship carrying the first missiles that could reach the United States from Cuba. John A. McCone, new director of Central Intelligence and the hero of the story referred to in the CIA Museum, demanded the flights be restored, and Kennedy soon agreed.

What happened next, when new U-2 photos arrived, is a story that belongs in the CIA Museum. "The CIA's analysts gazed upon images of the biggest communist weapons they had ever seen," Tim Weiner writes. "All day long on October 15, they compared the U-2 shots to photos taken of the Soviet missiles paraded through the streets of Moscow every May Day." The analysts concluded that "they were looking at the SS-4 medium range ballistic missiles capable of carrying a one-megaton warhead from western Cuba to Washington."[10]

The missiles were a "near-total intelligence surprise," according to the president's Foreign Intelligence Advisory Board, reviewing the situation a few months later. The president had been "ill-served" by the CIA, which had "failed." This failure, the foreign intelligence board concluded, was the result of "inadequate" human intelligence from inside Cuba, as well as the failure to analyze properly the results of aerial photographic surveillance.[11]

So the CIA's Virtual Museum wants visitors to know the CIA's side of the story of its "shortcoming" in the Missile Crisis.

People think of the CIA as America's spy agency, but the CIA Museum has virtually no information about American spies inside the USSR. There's a reason for that: while the Soviets had dozens of spies highly placed in the

United States, the CIA, according to Michael D. Gordin, "had exactly zero human informants in the Soviet Union." The United States "never managed to develop a reliable information network of human informants" within the Soviet nuclear weapons industry.[12] "Over the entire course of the cold war," Tim Weiner found, "the CIA had controlled precisely three agents who were able to provide secrets of lasting value on the Soviet military threat, and all of them were arrested and executed."[13]

In the absence of spies who could provide information about Soviet leaders and their intentions, the CIA relied on technical means of gathering information: tapping phones, intercepting cables, decrypting messages, and sampling of airborne radiation to detect weapons tests. The CIA Museum thus has to emphasize the technical side of intelligence gathering. And it does.

The goal of intelligence is to find out what the other side is doing, and to avoid surprises. The surprises for the United States were many during the Cold War, and Cuba provided only some of them. In Vietnam, the Tet Offensive of January 1968, when 400,000 Viet Cong simultaneously attacked every major city and army garrison in South Vietnam, was the most successful surprise attack on the U.S. military since Pearl Harbor. Obviously hundreds of thousands of Vietnamese knew about the plans for the attack; why didn't the CIA? Director Richard Helms concluded that the CIA "could not have predicted the Tet offensive," Tim Weiner reports, "because it had next to no intelligence on the enemy's intent."[14] But that's not in the museum.

The CIA has claimed a major success in Vietnam: its Phoenix program, which identified leaders of the National Liberation Front (NLF) who provided "civilian infrastructure" for the Viet Cong. The goal of the Phoenix program was to capture, interrogate, torture, and/or assassinate them. The program was run by William Colby, who later became CIA director. (Weiner describes it as a precursor to the CIA's torture program during the Bush-Cheney years.)[15] The CIA claimed its Phoenix program succeeded in killing more than twenty thousand people, but of course the program did not prevent the Communists from defeating the Saigon government. Congress held investigations of the Phoenix program in 1971, and critics pointed out many problems in the CIA effort. Some supporters of the Saigon government reported their political rivals were NLF civilian leaders in order to get the CIA to kill them. In other cases, corrupt local Saigon officials accepted bribes not to pursue CIA targets. The CIA countered by setting monthly quotas for targeted assassinations of civilians, but these sometimes led to the killing of personal enemies rather than NLF officials.[16] The Phoenix program is not mentioned in the CIA Museum's Vietnam exhibit.

The only mention of Vietnam in the CIA Museum is the text accompanying an Air America cap. "During the Vietnam War," the exhibit explains, "Air America, a CIA proprietary airline, flew a variety of missions in the Far East. These missions ranged from undercover CIA operations to overt air transportation. The Republic of Vietnam and various US government agencies contracted with Air America. Because of the tropical climate, Air America pilots favored comfortable attire—shorts and a baseball cap—rather than their official uniforms." Not mentioned: Air America's best-known operation, the evacuation of Americans fleeing Vietnam after the defeat of the United States. The iconic photograph of the defeat of the United States in Vietnam, the one on every front page in America, showed the last Americans fleeing the country by boarding a helicopter on the roof of the "U.S. Embassy." This was in fact an Air America helicopter. (And it was the roof, not of the embassy, but of an apartment building used by CIA employees.) But the Air America exhibit at the CIA Museum doesn't include that photo or that story.

Eighteen years before the Tet Offensive, the United States had also been surprised—when North Korea attacked South Korea in June 1950. "The agency failed on all fronts in Korea," Weiner found. "It failed in providing warning [and] in providing analysis," and "a great deal of Korean War intelligence was false or fabricated." An investigator from the State Department reported at that time that "our intelligence is so bad that it approaches malfeasance in office."[17] The Korean War is not mentioned in the CIA Museum.

One more big issue in the history of the CIA: the Agency failed to predict the fall of the Berlin Wall, or the collapse of the Soviet Union. The chief of the CIA's Soviet division, Tim Weiner reports, learned about the fall of the wall from CNN. That night, "the White House was on the line: What's happening in Moscow? What are our spies telling us? It was hard to confess that there were no Soviet spies worth a damn—they all had been rounded up and killed, and no one at the CIA knew why."[18]

The CIA Museum does include an exhibit about Afghanistan. But it's not about the CIA's support during the Reagan years for the mujahadeen resistance to the Red Army—the effort that made Osama Bin Laden a hero for parts of the Islamic world. Instead the CIA's Afghanistan exhibit focuses on its role in the post-9/11 Afghan war. The virtual tour includes a few key items recovered from Al Qaeda sites—a training manual, a gas mask—but in 2008 the Agency permitted the Voice of America to shoot a video report about the real Afghan exhibit in the real museum, which is now posted on YouTube. The theme of the exhibit in the real museum: the resemblance of today's Afghan campaign not to the Cold War battles in that country but rather to—yes—World War II. Curator Toni Hiley says, "The exhibit was designed to show how today's CIA officers operating in Afghanistan are much like their World War II predecessors of the OSS." The officers who went into Afghanistan after 9/11 told her, she says, that "they felt just like their World War II predecessors. . . . [T]hat gave us the idea to position the exhibit with a comparison between our World War II predecessors and our officers in Afghanistan."[19]

The history of the CIA includes at least one positive chapter. In 1967, as the antiwar movement grew in strength and numbers, Lyndon Johnson became convinced it was financed and controlled by the Soviets and the Chinese. He asked the CIA to investigate. Director Richard Helms "reminded the president that the CIA was barred from spying on Americans," Weiner writes. LBJ wanted him to go ahead anyway, so eleven CIA officers "grew long hair" and set off to infiltrate the antiwar movement. The program was called CHAOS, and it was exposed in the 1974 Senate Church Committee hearings. In violation of its charter, the CIA compiled a computer index of 300,000 names of Americans and assembled detailed files on 7,200 Americans. The result: nothing. Not a shred of evidence indicated that the antiwar movement was controlled or financed by the Soviets or the Chinese. The positive note: Helms told LBJ the truth about antiwar Americans. The CIA had found no evidence "that they acted under any direction other than their own."[20] That story also is missing from the CIA Museum.

Some museums have comment books for visitors, and some websites invite comments. The CIA Museum doesn't do either, but comments from the public have been posted at USAToday.com, which ran a feature story in 2008 about the virtual museum. The comments are ranked by popularity, and the most popular comment was brief: "A museum for the few paid for by the many." Most of the other comments were along the same lines but more vociferous: "The fact that this is a museum for apparently very few people . . . is unaccountable and undescribable *[sic]* stupidity and/or absurdity"; "What a waste of tax money. . . . Central Intelligence Agency? Central Idiotic Agency. . . . What a stinking joke! Museum is a public relations campaign for another failed bureaucracy."[21]

The museum—and the CIA—had only two defenders among *USA Today* readers. One addressed the critics who had posted: "If you have ever been outside of Bubba's trailer (the double wide) and had a chance to see this museum you might recognize that it is actually pretty cool. . . . Bubba2—not to worry, nobody is going to take away your precious NASCAR museum—yeeha." The second defender wrote, "Funny, all the negative comments. When most have no actual knowledge of what the CIA really does. . . . Well in fact your *[sic]* very wrong. Some of the most proven techniques and people are at work for them. If you only knew." To which another reader replied, "Please, enlighten me then." No response was posted.[22]

So what does the CIA want the public to learn from its online museum about its history and "the contributions it makes to national security"? Despite the embrace of "intellectual rigor," "a willingness to hear other opinions," and "a candid admission of shortcomings" in its official journal, its museum displays are limited mostly to some neat stuff from the heroic days of World War II spies—before the CIA existed; plus some fun facts, like Air America pilots in Vietnam favoring "shorts and a baseball cap—rather than their official uniforms"—and also some items from the recent efforts of the CIA in pursuit of Al Qaeda in Afghanistan. Missing: Cold War covert action; the cultural Cold War; and the CIA's role in Korea, Cuba, and Vietnam.

The National Security Agency is more secretive than the CIA. For a long time insiders said the initials stood for "no such agency," or perhaps "never say anything." It was founded after World War II to "prevent another Pearl Harbor." Its mission is to intercept and decode foreign communications—intelligence gathering via electronic surveillance, including code breaking.[23] Despite its legendary secrecy, the NSA has a museum that is open to the public. The National Cryptologic Museum is at NSA headquarters at Fort Meade, Maryland, southwest of Baltimore, in its own building, outside the NSA security perimeter. The museum's official mission statement is amazing: to "give employees a place to reflect on past successes and failures."[24] Note the term *failures.* Museums are usually places of celebration and commemoration.

The National Cryptologic Museum casts its net broadly. The displays cover not only the NSA and its immediate predecessor but also earlier periods and other kinds of secret codes, including "Hobo Communication in the Depression" (a chalk-mark drawing of a top hat outside a house means "a wealthy man lives here"). It also features exhibits on "Women in American

Cryptology," "highlighting twenty-four women who have helped create cryptologic history," starting with "a member of the Culper Spy Ring during the American Revolution who used her laundry as a secret code." And if your museum has women, you will also have "The African-American Experience," an exhibit that reports that by the end of World War II "a segregated office of thirty African-Americans was engaged in researching messages encrypted in unknown systems, analyzing them, and producing translations."[25] This is an impressive effort, especially in contrast to the CIA Museum, which doesn't even try.

On my visit I joined a guided tour for a group of college students from Baltimore who arrived on a bus at 9 A.M. Tour guide Jennifer spent a majority of the time in the World War II galleries, first explaining how the Enigma machine worked. She asked whether the group had seen the Kate Winslet film *Enigma* (written by Tom Stoppard, directed by Michael Apted, and produced by Mick Jagger). None of them had. Nevertheless she described the ways it was inaccurate.

Next came the exhibit about World War II Navajo code talkers. Jennifer asked whether the students had seen the movie *Windtalkers* (a John Woo film starring Nicholas Cage). None of them had. Nevertheless she described the ways it was inaccurate.

Then we headed into the "Cold War" room, for what I thought would be the climax of the tour, and the greatest triumph of the NSA in its history, the Venona Project—the decrypting of World War II–era Soviet coded cables, previously considered an impossible task. When Venona decryptions were made public by the NSA in 1995, they made headlines around the world, especially for documenting the way the USSR had used the Communist Party of the United States as a recruiting ground for spies during World War II—notably the "atom spy" case that concluded with the execution of Julius and Ethel Rosenberg. But Jennifer walked past the Venona display without saying a word.

Instead she stopped in front of the "Computers" exhibit. The NSA is reputed to run the biggest computers in the world. She asked whether the students had seen the Matthew Broderick film *War Games,* about a teenage computer geek who accidentally hacks into the Pentagon computer and, thinking it's an online game, nearly starts World War III. None of the students had seen the film. Nevertheless she described the ways it was inaccurate.

Maybe if there had been a film about Venona, Jennifer would have stopped at that exhibit. But if you're not going to talk about Venona on the tour of the

NSA museum's Cold War exhibits, what are you going to do? Jennifer led the group to what she called the "most entertaining story in this gallery," right behind the Venona exhibit: a wooden great seal of the United States given to the American ambassador in Moscow in 1952 by Russian schoolchildren who had carved it. The ambassador hung the seal in his office. It turned out that a microphone was hidden inside, and not discovered for years. This object, she says, is a copy; the original is in the director's office.

The story of the U-2 came next. Jennifer explained how the Soviets shot down Francis Gary Powers in 1960. She explained that the National Cryptologic Museum has the only piece of Powers's U-2 in the United States. Originally the pieces had been removed from the site of the shoot-down outside Sverdlovsk to Moscow and put on display there in the Armed Forces Central Museum. This display case at Fort Meade includes an "Official Letter of Transfer" and a "Certificate of Authenticity." Also in the same display case: a small piece of the Berlin Wall, a Soviet army hat, and a lock labeled "Soviet Nuclear Weapons Bunker Lock from 1995." That made me worry: has that bunker been unlocked since 1995? None of these objects has anything to do with the NSA; the U-2 program was run by the CIA.

While Jennifer led the tour into the next room, the "Information Assurance" gallery, I stayed behind at the Venona exhibit: two modest cases displaying photos, documents, and text—not much for such an important chapter in the NSA's history (figure 14). The main case has photos of Stalin and secret police chief Lavrenti Beria on one side and Julius and Ethel Rosenberg on the other—although the two couples are not really equivalent. The text here doesn't explain what Venona was, or how the code was broken. Instead, the exhibit describes—briefly—the success of Venona in identifying Klaus Fuchs, Harry Gold, David Greenglass, the Rosenbergs, and also, it says, Alger Hiss.

The case displays five pages of Venona decryptions. Strangely, three of them are about Max Elitcher, a minor figure whose only role was to testify against Morton Sobell in the Rosenberg trial. The other Venona transcripts here, however, contain some wonderfully evocative spy talk: "In the development of new people LIBERAL recommends the wife of his wife's brother, RUTH GREENGLASS, . . . she is a TOWNSWOMAN and a GYMNAST"; her husband "is now working at the ENORMOUS plant in Santa Fe." ("Enormous" of course was the excellent Soviet code word for the

FIGURE 14. Venona exhibit, National Cryptologic Museum, National Security Agency, Fort Meade, Maryland. The NSA's greatest triumph gets only one small display case. (photo by author)

Manhattan Project; a "townswoman" was a U.S. citizen, and a "gymnast" was a member of the Young Communist League. "Liberal" was the apparently ironic code name for Julius Rosenberg. Also, San Francisco was "Babylon," and Washington, D.C., was "Carthage.")

The NSA museum displays without comment the only Venona decryption mentioning Ethel Rosenberg, dated November 27, 1944: "LIBERAL's wife, surname that of her husband, first name ETHEL, 29 years old. Finished secondary school. A FELLOW COUNTRYMAN since 1938. Sufficiently well developed politically. Knows about her husband's work." The last five words have been quoted often by conservative historians defending the death sentence for Ethel. But in the United States, wives are not executed for knowing that their husbands are engaged in espionage—except for Ethel Rosenberg. (See chapter 10.)

One crucial item is missing from the exhibit of Venona decryptions: the November 12, 1944, message reporting the recruitment of "TEODOR KhOLL." In 1950, when the code breakers gave that name to the FBI, they easily identified Theodore Hall.[26] Though the Soviet bomb had already been tested, the NSA's identification of Hall as a spy at Los Alamos is one of the greatest achievements of code breaking, because he's the one who gave the Soviets the key information they needed to speed their bomb project—not the Rosenbergs. But the FBI decided to pursue Julius Rosenberg and let Hall go. Theodore Hall is not mentioned at the NSA museum.[27]

The museum does highlight the identification and subsequent prosecution (by the British) of Klaus Fuchs, the other great success of Venona. However, linking Fuchs to the Rosenbergs, as this exhibit does, following the prosecution case in the Rosenberg trial, minimizes Fuchs's contributions to the Soviet bomb and greatly exaggerates the significance of the Rosenbergs for the Soviet project.

The cell phone audio guide does a much better job than the wall text or the tour guide of explaining what the Venona project was and how it succeeded. During World War II, it says, Soviet diplomats communicated by enciphered telegrams using a system called the one-time pad. "Pads containing unique sets of keys were manufactured in pairs. For each message, the sender had one pad, the receiver had the other, and no other copies existed. Used correctly, a one-time pad system cannot be cracked." But in 1943 a cryptanalyst analyzing coded telegrams discovered a manufacturing error: a Soviet factory "had produced 40,000 pages for which there were two extra copies.... [A]nd the top secret Venona project was born." Two years later the linguist Meredith Gardner was able to "assign meanings to code groups"—"an amazing intellectual achievement." The Venona project looked at 750,000 Soviet diplomatic telegrams and successfully decoded 2,200, mostly from 1943 and 1944. They identified 130 Americans as spies for the USSR during World War II. One hundred cover names—77 percent—are still unsolved today.[28]

What happened to Venona? When and why did it stop? Any museum of cryptology needs to answer that question, but here the NSA museum fails. In 1948, at the very beginning of the Cold War, the Soviets abandoned the codes the Venona project was starting to break. On what went down in NSA history as "Black Friday"—October 29, 1948—the Soviets "flipped a switch and instantly converted to new, virtually unbreakable encryption systems and from vulnerable radio signals to buried cables." James Bamford, author of the classic history of the NSA, *The Puzzle Palace,* writes that, on that day, "in the war between spies and machines, the spies won."[29]

The Soviets defeated the Venona code breakers because they had a spy inside the American code-breaking effort: William Weisband, a Russian linguist working for the U.S. Army, who told the Soviets about the weaknesses in their cryptology that the Americans had exploited. "It was a blow from which the code breakers would never recover," Bamford writes, calling it "perhaps the most significant intelligence loss in U.S. history."[30] That ought to go on the list of "failures" about which Agency staffers might "reflect"—but it's not in the museum.

Venona was indeed a stunning achievement, yet its value turned out to be purely retrospective. The mission of the NSA was to prevent another Pearl Harbor, to provide information about our enemies' plans for the future. The code breakers were supposed to help stop our enemies from getting our secrets—to prevent the Russians from using espionage at Los Alamos to develop their own atomic bomb. At this task, Venona was obviously a failure. Virtually all the Venona decryptions date from the period after the Soviet bomb had already been tested in 1949.

Moreover, virtually all the successful decryption work was done after the Soviets abandoned the system in October 1948, and virtually all of it dealt with messages sent between 1943 and 1945, when the flaws in the one-time pads existed. Between December 1948 and June 1950, Meredith Gardner's work led the FBI to uncover the Soviet spy ring that had operated five years earlier, during World War II. The Venona decryptions released by the NSA in its official volume end on September 17, 1945, two weeks after V-J day, when the United States and the USSR were still allies.[31]

The public unveiling of Venona in 1995, which proved that the Soviets had used the Communist Party in the United States as a recruiting ground for spies, also indicated that Venona's information had been limited to the years of World War II. More shocking was the information that most of the spies identified by the Venona project were never prosecuted. As Matthew Aid reports in his definitive history, *The Secret Sentry: The Untold History of the National Security Agency,* Venona "turned out to be an intelligence asset that could not be used."[32] Venona led the FBI to identify 206 Soviet agents, but only 15 were ever prosecuted—mostly because the government didn't want to reveal the existence of Venona in a public trial. "As a result," Aid writes, "most of the 'big fish' who spied for the Russians got away." Most galling to many in the NSA: the man who betrayed Venona, William Weisband, was never prosecuted for espionage. He was charged only with contempt of court in 1950 for refusing to testify before a federal grand jury. He served a year in prison in 1950, then "worked for the rest of his life as an insurance salesman in northern Virginia" and died at home from a heart attack in 1967, seventeen years after he got out of prison.[33]

One other astounding fact is missing from the NSA's Venona display: President Harry Truman was never told about the decryptions. Senator Daniel Patrick Moynihan reported this discovery in 1998 when the Commission on Government Secrecy, which he headed, obtained Top Secret FBI files. The decision not to tell Truman was made, Moynihan learned, not by J. Edgar Hoover but by Omar Bradley, chairman of the Joint Chiefs of Staff. In Moynihan's 1998 report on excessive secrecy he pointed to this decision as highlighting the problem of "government secrecy in its essence: Departments and agencies hoard information, and the government becomes a kind of market. Secrets become organizational assets, never to be shared save in exchange for another organization's assets."[34]

The result, Moynihan concluded, was that "all Truman ever 'learned' about Communist espionage came from the hearings of the House Un-American Activities Committee, the speeches of Senator Joseph R. McCarthy, and the like."[35] He argued that if Truman had been told about Venona he would have taken the initiative in searching for real Soviet spies rather than allow HUAC and then McCarthy to launch their own witch-hunts.

The 1948 end to Venona's decrypted Soviet messages led to a series of disastrous intelligence failures. When one hundred thousand North Korean troops invaded South Korea in 1950, the NSA's predecessor hadn't had a clue; they weren't covering North Korea, and, according to Matthew Aid, it didn't even have a Korean-language dictionary. The NSA museum has one panel on the Korean War, but it doesn't mention this failure.

The next big moment in Cold War history of course was the Soviets' movement of missiles into Cuba in 1962. Wall text at the NSA museum says one of the Agency's "brightest moments", came from "the intelligence provided during the Cuban Missile Crisis." The key word here is *during,* which is not the same as *before.* In fact the NSA failed to decipher messages that would have led them to report that Soviet missiles and nuclear warheads and the people trained to fire them had moved to Cuba. The NSA never figured that out; the CIA did, using aerial photos taken by U-2 planes. The NSA's own internal history concluded that the Cuban Missile Crisis "marked the most significant failure of SIGINT [signals intelligence] to warn national leaders since World War II."[36]

As for the Vietnam War, the NSA museum describes it as another success story for the cryptologists. The Vietnam exhibit is in a separate room decorated as a bunker, with sand bags and camouflage netting. "At the height of the Vietnam War, there were more than 10,000 cryptologists supporting the war effort in SE Asia," visitors are told. "These cryptologists served everywhere—in large field stations like Phu Bai, in field support campaigns with combat units, . . . and in small boats plying the steamy estuaries of the Mekong Delta. . . . [M]any would be wounded and some would die." And: "While the US was involved in VN . . . NSA provided warnings of enemy action to those in combat."

One key episode of the NSA's work in Vietnam is missing here: the Agency provided the Johnson administration with misleading data that provided the justification for the major escalation of the war, the 1964 Tonkin Gulf Resolution. Congress and ordinary Americans were told that the North Vietnamese had attacked two U.S. Navy destroyers, which in fact were part of a secret NSA eavesdropping mission. But a top secret NSA analysis of the incident, completed in 2000, cited by Matthew Aid, concluded that the second attack never took place—and that was the one LBJ relied on for justification for the war. "Instead," Aid writes, "NSA officials deliberately withheld 90 percent of the intelligence on the attacks and told the White House only what it wanted to hear."[37] Of course you won't find out about the NSA's role in the Tonkin Gulf Resolution at the NSA museum.

And of course the most important warning for the United States during the entire Vietnam War would have alerted the Americans, and the Saigon government, to the plans for the Tet Offensive. Here the NSA museum could claim considerable success for the Agency. The ten thousand NSA cryptologists, Aid reports, never broke the codes of either the North Vietnamese or the Viet Cong, although the big NSA listening post at Phu Bai was able to monitor and measure the volume and source of enemy radio traffic. On that basis, the NSA did provide a warning on January 25, five days before the Tet Offensive, of an imminent coordinated attack. But they said the targets would be the western highlands and Khe Sanh and Hue.

The NSA warning was ignored or rejected by the CIA and the White House. General Westmoreland, commander of U.S. forces in Vietnam, believed the real North Vietnamese objective was the conquest of the marine base at Khe Sanh. When the Tet attack came, it targeted Saigon and every other city, town, and major military base in the country, including thirty-eight of the Saigon government's forty-four provincial capitals and seventy district capitals.

In the official postmortem of U.S. intelligence leading up to Tet, the NSA conceded that it had been "unable to provide advance warning of the true nature, size, and targets of the coming offensive." But the CIA praised the

NSA, declaring that "the National Security Agency stood alone in issuing the kinds of warnings the US Intelligence Community was designed to provide."[38] That story about one of the near-successes of the NSA is missing from the museum's Vietnam exhibit.

Instead, the centerpiece of the Vietnam display at the National Cryptologic Museum is a North Vietnamese military motorcycle with a sidecar. Wall text says this is a BMW design from 1939 copied by Stalin and widely used by the Red Army in World War II, that at least three thousand World War II Red Army motorcycles were given to the North Vietnamese and used on the Ho Chi Minh trail, and that "hundreds were used in the Tet Offensive buildup." The motorcycle has nothing to do with cryptanalysis, but it is a great object to put on display.

After several post–Cold War exhibits, visitors arrive at the inevitable museum shop. Along with the usual caps and T-shirts, this one sells NSA golf balls, NSA lip balm, and NSA beer steins.

The NSA gets credit for opening its museum to the public. It also deserves credit for not doing what many other museums have done: deemphasize the Cold War in favor of World War II. In these areas it is miles ahead of the CIA Museum. But the NSA's Cold War exhibit mostly skims the surface and tells well-known stories about the Rosenbergs and Alger Hiss, and about Vietnam. In the end, the NSA museum is a disappointment. It ought to claim credit for the Agency's Tet Offensive warning and acknowledge its failures in anticipating the Cuban Missile Crisis. And the code breakers' most important achievement during the Cold War, the decrypting of Soviet cables from World War II, does not get the attention it deserves. Venona deserves better.

SEVEN

Cold War Cleanup

THE HANFORD TOUR

It's not easy to get to America's newest National Historic Landmark, the Hanford B Reactor, which produced plutonium for nuclear weapons during the Cold War (and World War II). The 586 square miles of the Hanford Site, located in the remote desert of southeastern Washington State, remains a restricted area because of the radiation hazard. You can get to B Reactor only on an official tour, and the official Hanford tour is one of America's toughest tickets. Only 2,544 seats were available for all of 2009; advance reservations are required; all the tickets for the coming year are released on one day; and in a recent year, all seats for all sixty tours were taken by 11:30 the morning they became available.[1]

The 2008 announcement of the reactor's Landmark designation was made with considerable fanfare by officials of the Departments of Energy and the Interior. "B Reactor has a special feeling and association—as a landmark should," Deputy Secretary of the Interior Lynn Scarlett said. Her announcement included a promise of "a new public access program to enable American citizens to visit," so that tourists could learn how, in the words of Acting Deputy Secretary of Energy Jeffrey F. Kupfer, "the men and women who worked on the B Reactor made their mark on history with an extraordinary technological and human achievement."[2]

The official announcement did not make the conservative argument that the plutonium manufactured here protected American freedom from Soviet aggression, and that this deterrent ultimately led to victory over totalitarianism. "Hanford was the battleground of the Cold War," in the words of the site's official historian, Michele Gerber; she wrote the book about Hanford and also works as spokesperson for cleanup contractor Fluor Hanford Inc.[3] But that's pretty much it for Cold War commemoration here.

Many of the men and women who worked on or near B Reactor see Hanford neither as a site for celebration of Cold War victory nor as a place to honor "the power of human ingenuity and enterprise." Rather they see it as a monument to the government's failure to protect its weapons production workers from deadly radiation. That's why 2,300 of them have sued Hanford contractors, claiming they got cancer and other diseases from radiation released here.[4] Far from "serving as inspiration to others," B Reactor and the rest of Hanford serve today as a warning to others—because Hanford is the nation's most contaminated nuclear site, the most poisoned place in the Americas.[5]

B Reactor produced the first plutonium for weapons in 1944, starting with the atomic bomb tested at Alamogordo and the one dropped on Nagasaki in 1945. In explaining the reasons for designating the reactor as a National Historic Landmark, the Department of the Interior explained that it "provides a physical link to both the end of World War II and the start of the Cold War."[6] It produced plutonium for Cold War weapons until 1968, when technological changes made it obsolete.

But the tour seems to have a different purpose from the one officially announced in the Landmark designation. While the tour does point to "the power of human ingenuity and enterprise," it features repeated official reassurances that the radiation danger from this site is under control and that former workers and residents should feel safe and satisfied with the decontamination work under way. Hour after hour, for five hours, this tour focuses on the current cleanup effort rather than the historical significance of Cold War nuclear weapons production in America's victory over communism.

When you make your reservation for this tour—online—you are told that tours are "subject to immediate cancellation" any time the "SECON level" is raised above 3. "SECON" is "Security Condition," set by the Department of Homeland Security. Those with reservations are also told that "in the unlikely event of an emergency or other unforeseeable situation, the tour bus may be required to remain on the Hanford Site for longer than scheduled." Those with reservations must comply with the "prohibited articles" list: no cell phones, cameras, or laptop computers; iPods, MP3 players, Palm Pilots, and audio and video recording equipment are also prohibited.[7]

The first tour of the day starts at 7:30 A.M., and those with reservations are instructed to meet north of Richland, Washington, at "Volpentest HAMMER." It's the beginning of a long day of acronyms: "HAMMER" stands for "Hazardous Materials Management and Emergency Response."

This is a training facility to "secure the United States from terrorist attacks or threats." "Volpentest," however, is not an acronym or an abbreviation; it is the last name of HAMMER's founder, Sam Volpentest.[8]

The forty-five people lucky enough to get on the bus include many retired Hanford employees; others are enthusiasts on the national nuclear weapons trail who have already been to the Nevada Test Site and the Trinity Site and Oak Ridge. The tour has high security—guards check IDs, guard dogs sniff backpacks; those who are not U.S. citizens are not allowed on the bus. Those with reservations who present the appropriate photo IDs and are in compliance with the prohibited articles list are issued visitor badges, which must be displayed "in plain sight above your waist." The badges show a sun rising over green hills, and bear the motto "Hanford: Environmental Excellence"[9]—not "Hanford: Cold War Victory through Plutonium."

The tour starts with what the guide calls "a security briefing," although what he says is, "I will not be discussing or answering questions regarding Hanford Site security." What kind of security briefing is that? He adds, "You can be assured that the Hanford Site has a well-trained and equipped security force with the ability to respond as the need requires" (figure 15).[10]

The first official stop is Volpentest HAMMER, where a private corporation, Fluor Hanford, runs a practice area for terrorist fighting. There's nothing historic here; it's all about threats in the here and now. The tour guide explains that it features "a three-story burn building with propane-fueled fires, a two-story search and rescue building with reconfigurable mazes ... and smoke generators," "a propane-fueled fuel truck fire, a rail car with a simulated vapor leak, and an overturned tanker with a simulated liquid leak." Finally there's "a port-of-entry prop constructed by the U.S. Department of State" for training border guards. The guide explains HAMMER's motto: "The Training at HAMMER Is as Real as It Gets!"

The bus passes some low, abandoned factory buildings undergoing demolition. This is the fuel fabrication plant, which made twenty million pieces of uranium fuel, the first step in the manufacture of plutonium for weapons. Each piece, the guide explains, looked like "a roll of quarters." But quarters never gave anybody cancer.

The tour has had some skeptics, like James Long, who wrote for the Portland *Oregonian* for more than forty years. As his bus headed out, he wrote, the view out the big windows "looks more like a national park than a nuclear wasteland.... There's the occasional ugly building, of course. But no bubbling pools of waste. Nothing that glows. The damage isn't easy to see." Long

FIGURE 15. Hanford bus tour, Hanford Nuclear Reservation, Washington. Hanford produced plutonium for nuclear weapons until 1968 and is now the most contaminated radioactive site in the western hemisphere. The bus tour offers official reassurance about the decontamination work under way. (AP photo/Ted S. Warren)

remembered "a Hanford old-timer," Ralph Wahlen, whom he interviewed in the 1990s, fifty years after Wahlen went to work in the fuel fabrication plant. "They didn't tell us it was uranium," Wahlen told him. "They didn't tell us anything."[11]

At this point in the tour, the guide explains that the laboratories in this area did research during the Cold War not only to "improve the efficiency of weapons production" but also "to immobilize or dispose of radioactive waste." So it wasn't just weapons: "Over the years," scientists here "have conducted research in life sciences, analytical chemistry, bioremediation, robotics, and waste-treatment methods such as the ceramic melter," which was "the world's first large-scale system for transforming high-level radioactive waste into a stable, glasslike product suitable for long-term disposal." That's reassuring.

Next the bus rolls by the TEDF—the Treated Effluent Disposal Facility—which "represents a major achievement, by ending a half-century practice of discharging liquids into the ground." "The permit that regulates the quality of the water being discharged is the strictest in Washington State," the guide says. This leads him to a general presentation on the cleanup: "The Hanford

Site is now engaged in the world's largest project to clean up the legacy of radioactive and hazardous wastes that resulted from plutonium production."

That's only the beginning: "The U.S. EPA and the Washington State Department of Ecology regulate Hanford's cleanup program under a long-term compliance agreement called the Hanford Federal Facility Agreement and Consent Order (better known as the Tri-Party Agreement, or the TPA). This agreement sets the framework and time lines on the cleanup work to bring Hanford into compliance with environmental standards."

The guide doesn't say that the state of Washington went to court in December 2008, arguing that "the federal government has failed to meet its commitment to clean up Hanford" as "required by federal and state law" and by that Tri-Party Agreement. "This cleanup project is already 20 years behind schedule," the governor declared. If the state of Washington does not prevail, he said, "the completion of cleanup will likely extend into the next century." The governor also said he hoped the new administration in Washington would do a better job than the Bush people had.[12]

The people on the bus are told that the Hanford cleanup is "focused on three outcomes": first, "restoring the Columbia River Corridor or shoreline"; they built reactors along this river because they needed millions of gallons of water to cool the reactors. The second goal is "transitioning the Central Plateau to long-term waste treatment and storage"—that's the empty desert area—and the third, "preparing for the future." That indeed is the central theme of the tour.

Next the bus passes an abandoned school. This is all that's left of the old town of Hanford, where three hundred people lived until 1943, when the army moved them out—and brought in fifty thousand construction workers. "Do we have anybody who worked here?" the guide asks the people on the bus. During his tour, Long reported, "a tiny lady with short gray hair" raised her hand—Betty Breitenfeldt, who was eighty-five at the time. She told Long she was "teaching in a one-room school in Iowa" when she and a girlfriend "heard about Hanford." They drove out together in 1943. "I wanted to work in a laboratory," she said, "but the only thing they offered me was waitress."

The bus goes through a security gate and stops at B Reactor (figure 16). It is "perhaps the ultimate atomic icon," said Tonia Steed, who visited with a group from the Seattle Center on Contemporary Art and the L.A.-based Center for Land Use Interpretation. "I expected maybe a giant industrial

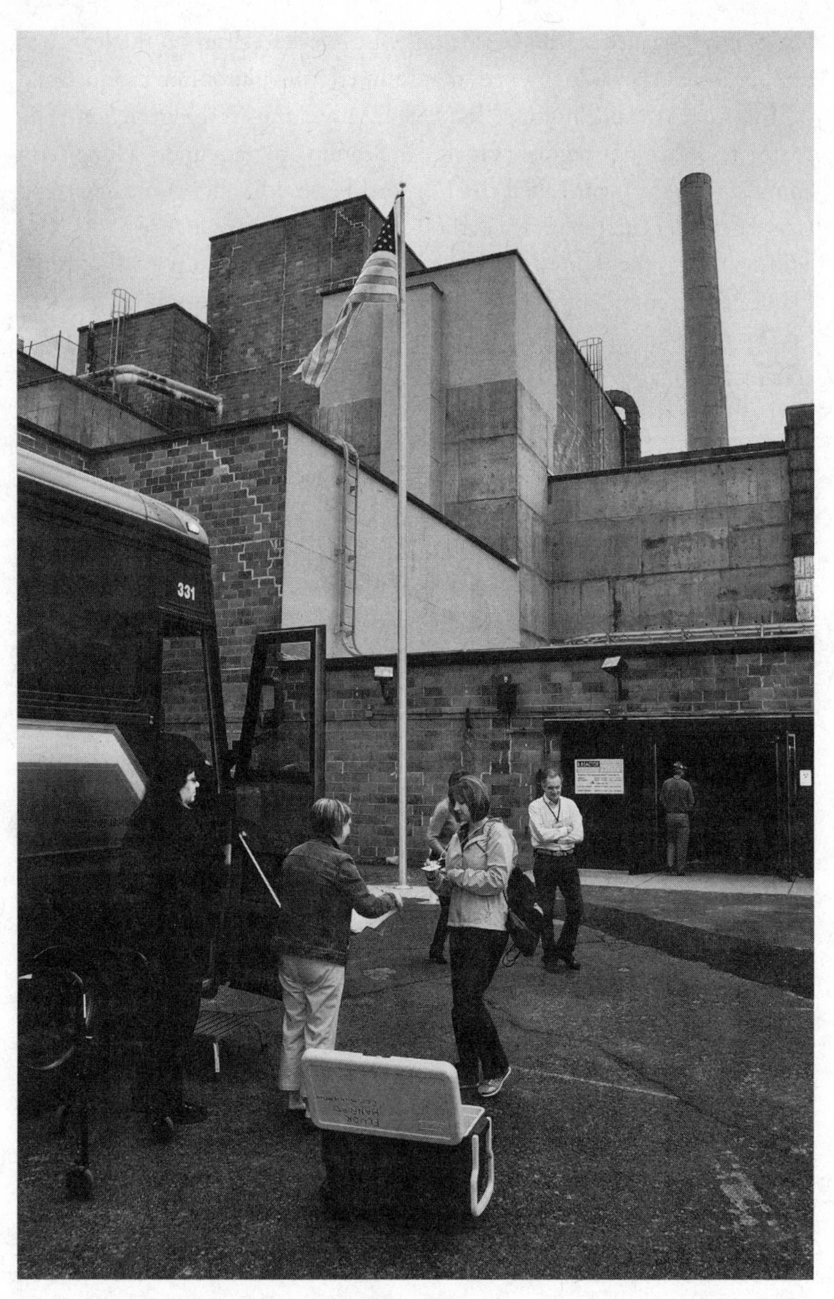

FIGURE 16. Public tour, Hanford B Reactor, America's newest National Historic Landmark. It manufactured plutonium 239, the most dangerous substance on earth. One millionth of a gram—basically a speck of dust—is known to cause cancer if ingested by animals, and thus almost certainly in humans. They don't tell you that on the tour. (photo courtesy U.S. Department of Energy)

gorgon still belching radioactive smoke," she wrote. "But the B Reactor is just another isolated concrete husk, trimmed with pink asbestos pipes and ringed with barbed wire." It "sits on a flat, nearly featureless desert plain, in what feels like the middle of no place at all."[13]

The tour group goes inside. As Long described it, it looks like "any small factory," "buffed-concrete floors, white-over-green walls, a pegboard with a sign-in sheet, a water cooler, a building floor plan with instructions on what to do if an alarm goes off." The group heads down a long corridor into a huge room four stories high.

Here the group learns how B Reactor worked. Long explained it best: "B Reactor was in the alchemy business, the old human dream of turning one element into another. Except B Reactor didn't turn iron into gold; it turned uranium into plutonium." Uranium 238, when bombarded in the reactor by neutrons, became radioactive plutonium 239—the most dangerous substance on earth. "A piece the size of a cue ball and weighing maybe 10 pounds could level a fair-sized city," Long explained. That's what happened at Nagasaki, with plutonium manufactured right here in B Reactor. And plutonium 239—with a radioactive half-life of 24,100 years—is "toxic beyond human experience," according to Dr. Donald P. Geesaman, a health physicist formerly with Lawrence Livermore Laboratory. "It is demonstrably carcinogenic to animals in microgram quantities." That means one millionth of a gram—basically a speck of dust—is known to cause cancer if ingested by animals—and thus almost certainly in people.[14] They don't tell you that on the tour. If you knew that, you might not take the tour.

The most striking feature of B Reactor is a gigantic chimney towering over the building. Now we know that fission products went up the chimney, especially radioactive iodine 131, and drifted downwind to nearby ranchland. "There," Long wrote, "cows ate tainted grass and passed along the radioactivity, in their milk, to people." They don't tell you that on the tour either.

Then it's back on the bus, where the Seattle group was told about a group from Nagasaki that visited B Reactor. Steed quoted the guide as saying, "They were very nice. They took a lot of pictures."[15]

B Reactor is being preserved as a historic landmark, but the other reactors in the area are being "cocooned." The guide explains: "Eighty percent of the reactor building is demolished down to the four-foot-thick solid concrete walls surrounding the reactor core. All remaining openings—except for one door—are sealed with cement or steel plate. . . . The single remaining door is welded shut and opened once every five years [for inspection]."

Opening the door once every five years "reduces the risks to people and the environment." The reactors will remain in their cocooned state for seventy-five years, during which "government regulators" will have "time to determine an ultimate disposal option"—that is to say, figure out what to do with these reactors. The guide concludes, "Cocooning produces a much smaller, safer facility"—more good news about the cleanup, and once again nothing about Cold War achievements.

Next on the tour come the "separation plants," where the radiation hazard was immense. Here, slugs of radioactive metal were dissolved in hot nitric acid to extract the plutonium. Long explained the problem: here, "a screaming-hot radioactive stew" of waste was discarded into underground tanks; here, 53 million gallons of radiochemical waste were stored in 177 giant underground tanks. "A vast potpourri of chemical unpleasantness," in the words of David Fishlock of the British journal *New Scientist.* "Cauldrons of highly radioactive soup bump and burp, belching flammable gases. Subterranean plumes of carbon tetrachloride, chromium salts, radionuclides and other poisons inch their way through the soil towards the Columbia River."[16]

The "burping tanks," as Fishlock described them, are "huge sealed stainless vessels," each holding a million gallons or more, "into which chemical and radioactive wastes were dumped indiscriminately by the contractors who ran Hanford. The tanks boiled for years with the heat of their own radioactivity—intense enough, it was believed, to destroy the 'organics' like rubber, plastics and oils that were dumped in too." He called the tanks "chemical reactors . . . generating hydrogen and various toxic gases such as oxides of nitrogen and organic vapors. The contents now are highly stratified: viscous at the bottom, then more liquid, and topped by a semisolid crust. And still highly radioactive."[17]

Hanford had 177 such tanks, and 18 of them burped: for example, tank 241-SY-101, which had been "eructating regularly every four months." The soup in that tank is thirty-three feet deep, and the gases released "build up enough pressure to burst through the crust in a mighty belch." If you Google "Hanford Tank 241-SY-101," you get more than three thousand results. There's an entire book about it: *Hanford's Battle with Nuclear Waste Tank SY-101: Bubbles, Toils, and Troubles,* by Chuck Stewart, published in 2006. Amazon sells the book. But tank SY-101 is not mentioned on the tour.

The problem with the tanks is not just the belching. Less dramatic but more significant is the leaking. At least sixty-seven tanks have leaked. That's not in the official tour script either—but it was big news when the hot radioactive sludge from leaking tank C-106 was pumped into a more secure double-hulled tank. The local Bush administration cleanup officials issued a press release that declared, "In completing this project, Hanford will demonstrate national leadership in the movement to reinvent government by proceeding based on local approval authority. Previously, the ability to proceed with this project would have been controlled by DOE Headquarters in Washington, D.C."[18] Local officials were able to act without approval from those bureaucrats in Washington because they got a FONSI—Finding of No Significant Impact—in their EASER—Environmental Assessment and Safety Evaluation Report—a report on pumping the radioactive sludge into a tank that didn't leak.[19] Half the radioactivity at Hanford is in these tanks. But from the bus you don't see any boiling or belching or leaking tanks, only gravel-covered areas with pipes and access panels surrounded by chain-link fence.

There's more: some radioactive waste wasn't deposited in the tanks; it was simply poured on the ground. For decades. Eighty square miles of Hanford are now contaminated with radioactive iodine 129, strontium 90, technetium 99, tritium, and uranium, along with such hazardous chemicals as carbon tetrachloride and chromium. "The Energy Department acknowledges that some has trickled into the Columbia River," Long wrote. The tour guide concedes that "past disposal practices across the Hanford Site pose potential risks to the Columbia River" and that "about 80 square miles of Hanford's groundwater is contaminated at levels above the Federal Drinking Water Standard."

This problem, people on the bus are told, is being addressed by the GRP—the Groundwater Remediation Project—which has a "pump-and-treat" system that moves contaminants out of the groundwater. GRP had pumped-and-treated 2.7 billion gallons of contaminated groundwater as of 2007. That seems like a lot of water, but what the tour guide doesn't say is that it represented less than one percent of the 440 billion gallons that were contaminated.[20]

The contaminants removed from the water are then deposited, along with the contaminated soil from the area, at the ERDF—the Environmental Restoration and Disposal Facility—which "serves an extremely important role in Hanford's cleanup." The ERDF is basically a series of extremely impressive holes in the ground—cells, each of which is "500 feet wide at the bottom, 70 feet deep, and over 1000 feet wide at the surface." ERDF has a liner intended "to prevent migration of contaminants to the soil and groundwater."

ERDF, the guide explains, currently receives about 3,000 tons per day and now holds more than 7 million tons. It has room for another 3 million tons, "which is equal to the amount of contaminated soil we expect to clean up at Hanford," the tour guide says.

Another thing they don't tell you on the tour: the EPA announced in 2007 that it was fining the Department of Energy $1 million for violations here at ERDF. The contractor, according to the EPA, failed to conduct required regular tests of the long-term structural stability of waste disposed in the landfill. The required tests were not performed between June 2005 and January 2007.[21]

"Some things are too dicey even to put in this pit," Long wrote—the material contaminated with plutonium, mostly from the Plutonium Finishing Plant. This is not one building; this site originally had sixty-three buildings spread over fourteen acres that contained about twenty tons of plutonium-contaminated trash. The ductwork alone, Long wrote, contained perhaps one and a half tons of plutonium—enough "to give some country a significant nuclear arsenal." They don't tell you that on the tour, but if you ask, you will learn that "all salvageable plutonium" has been "retrieved and placed under high security."

The tour stops at PUREX—the Plutonium-Uranium Extraction Plant. The guide says that "PUREX operated between 1956–72 and between 1983–88." The dates go by pretty fast, and it's late in the tour, but they hint at some genuinely significant facts. Nixon shut down America's plutonium weapons plant in 1972, as part of détente with the Soviet Union. Reagan restarted plutonium weapons production in 1983 after declaring in 1982 that the USSR was "the evil empire." Then Reagan shut the PUREX plutonium weapons factory down at the end of his second term, after he tried to negotiate the abolition of all nuclear weapons with Gorbachev at Reykjavik in 1986 and signed the intermediate range nuclear forces treaty in 1987. PUREX at Hanford enables us to date the "second Cold War": 1983–88, following a decade of détente.

The tour ends with some good news: because the high security prevented almost all human activity at most of the Hanford site for the past seventy years, Hanford's 586 square miles of high desert are teeming with wildlife: "mule deer, elk, coyotes, badgers, rabbits, skunks, bald and golden eagles, herons, ducks, ground squirrels, several species of mice, lizards and three species of snakes." The Nature Conservancy of Washington has found "56 new populations of rare plants . . . [and] 205 species of birds," including "72 species considered rare." In addition, "close to 1,000 insect species also were documented, including 19 species new to science and 200 species new to Washington State."

And the public can visit the wildlife: in 2000 President Clinton created the Hanford Reach National Monument, a corridor along the banks of "the last stretch of free-flowing water in the Columbia River." It's a kind of paradise: "more Chinook salmon spawn in this 51-mile stretch than in any other river in the U.S. outside of Alaska." The Reach is also home to "sturgeon up to 12 feet in length," as well as steelhead trout, an endangered species. Soon there will be "boat launches and campgrounds" at Hanford Reach National Monument, along with "historical displays and kiosks," and maybe even "horseback riding." So much good news![22]

The official tour doesn't mention another side of the wildlife here: the radioactive wasps and the gophers digging radioactive dirt. But James Long does. "Burrowing animals insist on bringing radioactive dirt to the surface," he wrote, "while fruit flies have proved to be fond of special paint used to immobilize radioactive contaminants in walls." When workers were demolishing some random auxiliary buildings at one of the reactors, they "discovered that mud dauber wasps had been using radioactive mud to build nests." And some of the ants, as well as some of the birds, are radioactive.

But the tour ends with the good news about the wildlife. The last line from the official guide is, "We're glad you came and were able to see first-hand the progress being made at the Site." Note that the guide did not say, "We're glad you were able to see first-hand how America's freedom was protected by the heroism and dedication of the people who worked here." Instead, the people on the bus are told at the end of the tour, "You can be involved in Hanford cleanup activities and decisions"—just "visit the website at www.hanford.gov."

Going back over the tour script, I see that while the theme ought to be that the plutonium produced here kept Americans safe during the Cold War, the fact is that during the entire five hours the words *Cold War* were mentioned only three times.[23] And none of those three times presented the conservative interpretation that Cold War victory was achieved in part by nuclear deterrence. The first mention came in the 300 Area, where "during the Cold War . . . laboratories performed research to expand and improve the efficiency of weapons production." That's it. The second mention came at H

Reactor, which "was built as part of Hanford's first Cold War expansion." Period. The third came at N Reactor: "With the end of the Cold War, there was no longer a need for plutonium production, and N Reactor was never restarted." End of story.

If the Cold War was mentioned only three times on the five-hour tour, "cleanup" was mentioned twenty-one times. Example: "Cleanup of waste sites and burial grounds is underway at most of the reactor sites and is scheduled to be completed in 2013." "Safety" was mentioned twelve times: for example, Hanford's twenty-eight underground, double-shell tanks, each holding one million gallons of radioactive waste, have a second shell as "a safety feature to prevent leaks."

But "radioactivity" and "cancer" were barely mentioned. "Radioactivity" appears twice in the script: "waste contaminated with radioactivity has been packaged or boxed and buried in trenches at Hanford since World War II"—and is now part of the "cleanup." "Cancer" was mentioned only once, and in the most benign context: Hanford considered producing "medical isotopes for treating cancer." You'd never know from the tour that Hanford workers or residents had any concerns about cancer caused by exposure to plutonium.

While "cancer" is mentioned only once on the Hanford tour, if you Google "Hanford" and "cancer" you get 1.4 million hits, starting with the 2005 news report in the *Seattle Times* that "a federal jury yesterday found that the Hanford factories that produced plutonium for the nation's nuclear arsenal probably caused cancer." Also near the top of the Google list: the Hanford Health Network site of the state of Washington: "Established in 1943, Hanford released radioactive materials into the air, water and soil.... The basic assumption of radiation protection is that any dose of radiation poses a health risk [of cancer]."[24]

And you'd never know from the tour about those 2,300 locals who sued former Hanford contractors, arguing that accidental and intentional releases of radioactive iodine 131 from bomb-making operations made them ill. According to the Associated Press, "Both sides in the case agree that at least 740,000 curies of radioactivity were released from Hanford during the years in question.... The plaintiffs contend that no amount of radiation is safe; the defense contends that amount is equivalent in damage to about a dozen chest X-rays."[25]

The first trial in this lawsuit—also not mentioned on the tour—concluded in May 2005. One headline read, "Hanford Likely Caused Cancer

Downwind, Jury Decides," and the article stated, "The decision by the jury in Spokane is a historic first for those who have accused the federal government and contractors of sickening people by secretly releasing radiation.... A jury has never before said a U.S. nuclear-bomb plant sickened citizens living downwind. The 12-member jury found that thyroid cancer suffered by two plaintiffs more likely than not came from radiation that Hanford released, exposing them as children in the 1940s and early '50s."[26]

Michele Gerber has spent more time thinking and writing about Hanford than anyone else. She concludes her history on a note that is decidedly unheroic. "At Hanford," she writes, "the bellicose speeches of the Cold War delivered in distant Washington, D.C., or in Moscow were made real in concrete, steel, lead, uranium, and in men's and women's daily lives." It happened at Hanford, because "in the grand tradition of the American frontier, the 'dirty jobs' were sent 'out West.'" Historians say the Cold War ended not with a bang but rather with silence. "But Hanford is not silent," Gerber writes. "Echoes of the Cold War can be heard in the busy machinery of the cleanup."[27]

How successful can the cleanup be? The National Research Council concluded in 2000 that hazardous radioactive waste at Hanford "will remain, posing risks to humans and the environment, for tens or even hundreds of thousands of years."[28] That's because of our newest national monument, Hanford's B Reactor. Before B Reactor, Gerber writes, "four one-millionths of one pound of plutonium had been produced in the laboratory in all of world history. Once B Reactor began operating, tons of the deadly and powerful substance became available."[29] There's no sense of triumph or victory in this account.

The people on the bus from the Seattle Center on Contemporary Art ended up in a sober mood, thinking less about the cleanup and more about the original purpose of the site. One guy called B Reactor "a black box—this unassuming building in the desert that changed history.... It reminds us that we were on the brink of destroying ourselves." A person from the museum was struck by the desolate quality of the site: "The whole place is dead; the B Reactor is absolute wreckage." Another said it reminded him of his visit to Dachau: "I was looking at a gigantic factory complex devoted to death."[30]

James Long ended his tour in a different frame of mind. After he got off the bus, he drove into Richland, remembering that 10 percent of the city's drinking water comes "from the same Hanford aquifer that contains, upstream, radioactive tritium, good for making hydrogen bombs." He knew the city tests the water all the time—but still. As he told the story:

> My favorite Mexican restaurant, 3 Margaritas, is on Jadwin Avenue. The waiter puts down a bowl of salsa and chips.
>
> "Corona?"
>
> "Si, señor."
>
> The waiter nods and comes back with the frosty beer and a glass of water. I look at the water. I drink the beer.[31]

PART THREE

The 1950s

EIGHT

Test Site Tourism in Nevada

The bus tour of the Nevada Test Site, where the United States tested nuclear weapons from 1951 to 1992, leaves from the Atomic Testing Museum not far from the Hard Rock casino in Las Vegas. Once a month, several dozen people get a free, all-day trip to the most bombed place on earth, a place where a thousand nuclear weapons were exploded, a hundred in the open air, many of which exposed Americans to radiation comparable to that from Chernobyl. I signed up to see how this part of Cold War history was being turned into a tourist attraction.[1]

According to the conservatives' "good war" framework, the United States was able to prevail in the Cold War first of all because American nuclear weapons deterred the Soviets from attacking the United States and then because the Soviet Union was bankrupted by a renewed arms race in the Reagan years—which included nuclear weapons testing. Soviet leaders in the mid-1980s were terrified that Reagan would launch a nuclear attack on their country, and, according to this theory, they plunged ahead toward expensive new deterrents that in the end they couldn't afford. American testing continued right through to the last days of the Soviet Union in 1991 (when the United States conducted seven nuclear tests at the Nevada Test Site).[2] Thus the Nevada Test Site ought to provide a place to tell the story of how active testing of nuclear weapons, the weapons that defined the Cold War, guaranteed America's freedom and then brought America's eventual victory in a fifty-year struggle to defeat an enemy that was as significant, and as evil, as Hitler.

The day I went on the tour the bus was full, with forty on board. Two types of people were on the bus: those taking notes and the rest. The rest were mostly retired sunbirds and vacationing families. Those taking notes were mostly young men interested in "Area 51," widely known among *X-Files* types as the secret CIA airstrip adjacent to the Test Site. The UFO folks think the government has used Area 51 to make contact with aliens. Two young guys on the bus wore baseball caps that said "Area 51: Top Secret Research Facility." "We got 'em at a comic book convention," one of them explained. They said that they planned to stay that night near Area 51 at the A-Lee-Inn.[3]

When we arrived at the Test Site, it was a beautiful cloudy day, with immense vistas of dry basins and bare mountains—an awesome desert landscape that looked like Death Valley (which would have been an appropriate name for this place). The bus reached the crest of a low mountain, and below us lay Yucca Flat, the site of eighty-six aboveground nuclear explosions. This hilltop, dubbed "News Nob," was the place the Atomic Energy Commission's (AEC's) PR people would bring VIPs and reporters to watch atmospheric tests; it was the first tourist site here, part of the Cold War ideological machine. The bleachers were still standing. When our bus stopped and we got out, the desert was breathtakingly quiet.

Our guide, a retired sixty-ish former engineer who had worked here, introduced himself as Drew. He was crew-cut, tan, fit, and enthusiastic. He explained that "VIPs would sit right here and watch, back in the fifties and sixties. The wind blew the fallout in the other direction. Still, now we think, 'you don't wanna do that stuff.'" He continued: "Of course military personnel would be much closer, in trenches. Soldiers were given the order to advance toward the mushroom cloud . . . " His sentence trailed off.

Drew didn't tell us what it was like for those soldiers, but a few of them have described it. Robert Merron was a twenty-year-old soldier at the time. He told Carole Gallagher, author of *American Ground Zero,* about it: "The fireball is every color of the rainbow, green, blue, red . . . *directly* above us. It obliterated entirely the sky. . . . I don't know how long we stood there, and I was just sobbing and weeping, with no shame at all, as was every single guy there."[4]

Robert Carter was also in that exercise. He was only seventeen at the time. He told Gallagher that, standing under the mushroom cloud, "I understood evil and was never the same. I was sick inside and it stayed with me for a year after. I seen how the world can end."[5]

The men interviewed in *American Ground Zero* were part of Troop Test Smoky, documented in the film *The Atomic Café.* It contains official army footage, starting with the briefing of the troops. "You are here to participate in an atomic maneuver," the briefing officer tells several hundred soldiers.

> This is not a haphazard maneuver.... Watched from a safe distance, this explosion is one of the most beautiful sights ever seen by man. You're probably saying, "So it's beautiful—what makes it so dangerous?"
>
> Basically there are only three things to think about—blast, heat, and radiation. Radiation—that is the one new effect obtained by the use of an atomic weapon. Truthfully, it's the least important of the three effects as far as the soldier on the ground is concerned.... Film badges and dosimeters issued to you enable the radiological safety monitor in your unit to read the amount of your exposure.... If you follow orders you'll be moved out in time to avoid sickness.
>
> Finally, if you receive enough gamma radiation to cause sterility or severe sickness, you'll be killed by blast, flying debris or heat anyway.
>
> Well, that's the story. Don't worry about yourselves. As far as the test is concerned, you'll be okay.

Then we see part of an army training film where the narrator declares, "You cannot sense the presence of nuclear radiation effects. Alpha and beta particles, because of their low penetrating power, are stopped by most surfaces. Even a soldier's skin. They are a hazard only when material emitting these particles get into the body through breaks in the skin or through the nose or mouth."[6]

Then comes live newsreel footage of soldiers climbing into foxholes, and then the bomb goes off, the shock wave rattles the camera as a dust cloud roars by, and the soldiers climb out of their foxholes and walk across the desert floor directly under the mushroom cloud, under a downpour of dust and dirt that we know is radioactive. It is a horrifying sequence, and it was shot live.

Next comes a newsreel shot of an interview with a soldier. The interviewer asks, "Did you keep your mouth shut, or did you get a mouthful of dirt?" The answer: "I got a mouthful and a face full of dirt."

Interviewer: "We see pinned on your laps here this white badge.... They can tell from that if you've received a lethal dose?" Answer: "That's right. They can."[7]

Back on the tour bus, Drew seemed defensive about those orders given to American boys forty years ago to march under the mushroom cloud. "They had state-of-the-art equipment," he told us. "Keep that in mind." Gilbert Fraga was an AEC radiation monitor at the Nevada Test Site who distributed and collected the radiation film badges intended to determine which people at the site had reached the permissible limits of exposure. "The truth of the story is, hundreds and hundreds [of radiation badges] got thrown in the pail because we didn't have time to read them all, no better than 40–50 percent," he told Carole Gallagher. "I had my own badge. It didn't work well enough. They were worthless."[8]

Somebody in the front of our bus asked whether this area was still radioactive. Drew said, "Where we're going is basically background radiation, and there is no threat to anyone here." At that moment we drove past a sign that read, "Radiation Hazard—touching or removing scrap objects is prohibited" (figure 17).

As the bus rolled across the desert floor, Drew said, "I was asked about Area 51. There is no Area 51 at the Nevada Test Site." A young guy next to me, one of the note-takers, murmured, "You're lyin.'"

The guy across the aisle from me, "John," had a compass, which he used to follow our route and plot our progress on his map. He was another one who had no interest in the role of atomic testing in winning the Cold War. He came out here, he told me, because he was interested in Area 51: "Spent a night on a nearby mountaintop last year watching it, while the sheriffs watched us all night. We were just desert rattin' around." An aerospace guy from Ontario, California, he wanted to see the secret jets that use the CIA airstrip. He said his son, a member of the Coast Guard, was sent to Johnson Atoll west of Hawaii. "They say it's a bird sanctuary, but it's where they test chemical and biological weapons. You'll be shot on sight if you go there." Drew listened and then explained why that was necessary: "The public isn't used to discipline."

Every historic site needs some explanation, but our guide was strangely inarticulate about the meaning and significance of what went on here. "The tests here were all coordinated with Civil Defense activities," Drew explained. "Those who are a little older will remember, we just knew we were gonna be attacked by Russia. Well, they discovered out here that the biggest casualties from bombs dropped on downtown L.A. or New York or Washington would be from glass—glass would be the most crippling projectile. Their work here led to the conclusion that people should open their windows when the warning sirens went off to equalize the air pressure from the blast and prevent broken glass from becoming a projectile." End of speech.

That's it? The significance of the Nevada Test Site is that it showed that people should open their windows just before the Soviet bombs fell? He should have been telling us that atomic testing here was crucial to preserving

FIGURE 17. Nevada Test Site. (photo by Center for Land Use Interpretation)

our freedom in the face of aggressive communism; that atomic testing was necessary to deter a Soviet nuclear attack; that because weapons were tested here, we never had to open those windows.

What really moved Drew was not the role of this place in the Cold War but rather what's happened here since its end. Like so many other people in America today, he worried about jobs. "We had ten thousand employees at the Site in its heyday," he said, "but it looks like a ghost town now. And the jobs being lost are not $4.50 an hour burger flippers. These are men with their doctorates. Building weapons is the only thing they know."

When we rolled through Mercury, the Test Site town, it was indeed ghostly: dormitories for a thousand people, empty; a movie theater, a bowling alley, and a swimming pool—Drew called them "facilities so people wouldn't go nuts out here"—all closed. Nobody wants their town to lose its industry and turn itself into a tourist attraction—not even if your town is Mercury.

Like all the other deindustrialized areas in the United States, the Nevada Test Site is dreaming of luring industry back. That became clear at our next stop, where we got out of the bus at a building called CP-1, Control Point 1, the mountaintop control center for the nuclear tests performed here. Inside we sat at the control panels and were shown two videos: first, one Drew called "the sales tape," made by the Department of Energy to persuade private corporations to rent parts of the Test Site for their own work with toxic or radioactive materials. Over stirring music, the video announcer described the Test Site as "a secure area the size of Rhode Island," where "ample office space is available," where employees can "relax at a bowling alley and swimming pool." The official website adds that prospective employers will benefit from "Nevada's favorable tax structure with no corporate income tax, no personal income tax, no franchise tax, no inventory tax, no admissions tax, no unitary tax, no inheritance tax, and no capital stock tax."[9]

Drew told a story about an underground test during which he was working in CP-1: "I was watching on the live video, and a coyote chased a rabbit onto ground zero just at zero time. The ground shook, both animals fell down, the rabbit got up first and ran for his life, the coyote got up, looked around, and trotted away. At least we saved something out here—we saved that rabbit's life."

But the story is supposed to be that here is where we saved American freedom.

A different rabbit story was told to Carole Gallagher by Ken Case, the "atomic cowboy" who herded cattle on the Nevada Test Site as part of the AEC animal experimentation program. At ground zero at zero time on an atmospheric test, the target area would burst into flames. "All the weeds and grass, and if there were trees, they would be on fire too. Rabbits would run across there and they would be on fire. It was something."[10] (Case had eleven surgeries for tumors and died in 1985 with cancer in most of the organs of his body.)

The rest of the tour consisted of riding around and looking at the remains of objects built or brought here for the sole purpose of blowing them up. Especially noteworthy was a bank vault: after a nuclear war, "they knew people would survive," Drew explained; "we would therefore need to have money. So a bank vault was tested. They didn't put money in it, just papers—I understand they survived." Some on the bus nodded with satisfaction; others rolled their eyes, murmuring about "insanity."

The bus rumbled across the desert floor, and we learned here they planted a pine tree forest; it was vaporized. Here they built a parking lot to see what cars would do in a blast; the cars became projectiles. Here they built a railroad trestle bridge to see how the rail network would stand up; the steel I-beams were bent by the blast into crescents. Here they built a little suburban town with nineteen buildings—a school, a fire station, a library; suburban houses that were fully furnished, with food on the kitchen tables. It was all blown

FIGURE 18. Nevada Test Site, Sedan Crater. (photo by Center for Land Use Interpretation)

away, except for the blasted shell of one of the "typical American homes" that remains standing today.

The National Register of Historic Places is the official mark of tourist significance, and those who seek to increase tourism here want to get several locations at the Test Site listed on the Register. One has made it: the only official Historic Place here is Sedan Crater.[11] Our bus stopped at the overlook platform at the crater's edge (figure 18). It was an incredible sight: a quarter of a mile wide and 320 feet deep. The explosion here, in 1962, was part of a project seeking peaceful uses of nuclear weapons. The nuclear people knew that big bombs could be used to move large quantities of earth; they said they had in mind digging a new Panama Canal. The Sedan blast was five times more powerful than the bomb dropped on Nagasaki. It was a success at digging a big hole, and, as Drew explained, the crater "would have been much bigger, but a lot of the 12 million tons of earth blown into the sky by the blast fell back into the crater." He added, "There was one problem: radiation. So they didn't use nuclear explosions to build a new Panama Canal."

The immense crater was still completely barren of visible life except for a few desolate tumbleweeds. Drew found this significant. "See the tumbleweeds growing over there? Life starts over," he said. "It's beautiful." Drop a bomb like this on Las Vegas, and thirty-five years later you'll have a few tumbleweeds sprouting out of the radioactive sand.

Next came Bilby Crater, eighty feet deep. The bus drove down into it. The Bilby shot, in 1963, was pure Dr. Strangelove: this bomb was exploded in the underground water table, just to see what would happen to the groundwater—on which Las Vegas depends. Drew explained that Bilby showed that "the recoil sucked most of the radioactivity back to ground zero, and the soil pulled the radioactivity out of the water—everything except tritium." Radioactive tritium remained in the groundwater, and it's still there. We were assured that "there is no chance radioactive water will ever leave the Test Site." Of course earthquakes could change the structure of the water table and move the radioactive water to Las Vegas some time in the future.

Over the years the site had a different kind of visitor, in addition to the VIPs and newsmen brought here to spread the word of the successes of American nuclear weapons: the peaceniks, the demonstrators, the no-nuke activists. During the 1980s they were arrested here by the thousands, the largest demonstrations of civil disobedience in U.S. history. They left their mark on the architecture of the Test Site: the first structure inside the perimeter on Highway 95, which we saw on our way out, was "The Pen," a large chain-link prison yard where arrested demonstrators were held while waiting to be "processed." And across the highway from the front gate we saw the remains of "peace camp," where as many as three thousand people spent the night before the big demonstrations. Any serious tour of this site today needs to tell their story, and Drew told a little bit of it: "Easter Sunday protests started in this area. I remember a protester jumping in front of an employees' bus, crawled underneath it and handcuffed himself to the rear axle. These were highly motivated individuals."

Rebecca Solnit was one of those highly motivated individuals. "I came to the Test Site four springs in a row," she wrote in *Savage Dreams*. "My second year I went in with a bunch of anarchist women from San Francisco and Seattle." The action that year was called "Reclaim the Test Site," so they walked in pairs across the "Forbidden Line," and got a quarter of a mile into the Test Site before the helicopters found them and two security guards handcuffed them. The other woman went limp and refused to walk, so the guards dragged her by the arms, "through thorn bushes and over cacti. . . . Finally she gave up and, near tears, asked them to stop. She began to walk . . . to where a big van was waiting for us. The van was there to take us to the huge holding pens the Department of Energy had built a year or so before, next to the main gate."[12] That was the pen where our tour bus stopped.

"There's something profoundly American about getting arrested at the Nevada Test Site," Solnit wrote.

> To start the day in the deadly cold of a desert morning, sitting on rocks and drinking coffee, to fill one's water bottle and mill around with friends and acquaintances as the day gradually creeps toward hotness, to sit through a sometimes stirring and often dull rally of speeches and music, folk to punk and back again, to commit the fairly abstract act of climbing under a wire fence that separates the rocky expanse of cactus and creosote bushes from the rocky expanse of creosote bushes and cactus, to be confronted by hired help in the wrong-colored camouflage, as though they, not we, had a use for stealth, to go through numerous pairs of disposable plastic handcuffs as we captives were rearranged, to idle in a sort of cattle pen built just for us, to be escorted after many hours in the sun into a special luxury bus and be given a tour of scenic Highway 95, to be interrogated by hard-faced sheriffettes with piles of teased hair who are irritated by anyone who wants to give a more complicated name than Jane Doe or Shoshone Guest, to be tossed out into a small town, to catch up on one's friends' well-being and head for fast food and ice cream in the middle of the night, . . . to retrace the pointless route as the liberated activists get driven back to the camp, to wander back through the rocks and thorns in the dark to a sleeping bag on hard, uneven ground under a sky more full of stars than almost anyplace else in the world—could anything be more redolent of life, liberty, and the pursuit of happiness?[13]

The tour I was on reflected something different: a political calculus at work. Conservatives were trying to find ways to commemorate victory in the Cold War. They hoped to bring coherence to their cause by enshrining nuclear weapons in an honored place in American history. The weapons opposed by the peaceniks and pacifists ought to provide a key ideological battle ground, and the Nevada Test Site ought to be the place where the no-nukes people are categorically refuted. But the people on the tour weren't interested, and even the tour guide seemed to lack the heart to make that case.

In addition, the DOE has economic reasons for running this tour. The plans to use the Nevada Test Site for storing high-level radioactive waste have faltered. The notion of developing a high-tech research center there, a Nevada-style Silicon Valley, has gone nowhere, stymied perhaps by the 115 degree temperatures. But Las Vegas, only an hour away, is one of America's great vacation destinations, and there isn't a whole lot to do there outside the casinos and shows—so the DOE sees an opportunity to turn an expensive liability into a commercial as well as an ideological asset.

The dream for the Nevada Test Site tours is privatization. The DOE tours have only nine thousand people a year, according to Test Site spokesman Derek Scammell. "We think there's a bigger market for it," he said, "and private enterprise could probably make this into quite a profitable business." Instead of one bus a month, the spokesman said, a private company running four buses a day could take fifty thousand people a year.

But what about the radioactivity? Matthew Coolidge of the Center for Land Use Interpretation, which published the authoritative book *The Nevada Test Site: A Guide to America's Nuclear Proving Ground,* said their studies found little radioactivity at ground level anywhere on the tour.

Jonathan Parfrey, who was executive director of Los Angeles Physicians for Social Responsibility, had a different view. "On the tour, Helen Caldicott has pointed out, you could inhale microscopic specks of plutonium," he told me; "one-millionth of a gram of plutonium inhaled into the lung gives a 100 percent probability of lung cancer." Staying on the bus with the windows closed reduces that risk. Aside from lung cancer, the greatest risk of radioactivity is birth defects. Parfrey's advice for women was to take the tour only if they're not planning to have (more) children.[14] Indeed the tour website now says, "Pregnant women are discouraged from participating in test site tours," but explains that that's not because of the radiation danger but rather "because of the long bus ride and uneven terrain."[15]

"You don't have to wander into the radioactive desert to find out about the tests," as the *Orange County Register* reported;[16] you can stay in Las Vegas and go to the Atomic Testing Museum. It's a private institution, which opened in 2005 and is run by the Nevada Test Site Historical Foundation, with half the funding for design and construction coming from private firms currently involved in military contracting—Lockheed Martin, Bechtel, Wackenut—and half coming from federal money obtained by Nevada Senator Harry Reid. You would expect that kind of money would produce a museum that put forward the conservative interpretation of the Cold War—and this one does.

At the opening ceremonies, the main speaker was Linton F. Brooks, Bush's undersecretary of energy for nuclear security. He said the work of the Nevada Test Site had been "integral to America's nuclear deterrent." He said that because of nuclear testing here, "the apocalypse never came." The museum, he concluded, "helps us celebrate victory in America's longest war."[17]

In this museum, the history of testing, in the words of Edward Rothstein of the *New York Times,* "is largely the history of its justification."[18] That's not clear from the beginning, however. Visitors buy tickets at a restored Wackenut guard shack. The central exhibit is "Ground Zero Theater," where visitors sit on benches in something like the inside of an observation bunker. The exhibit has a video screen acting as the window that overlooks the desert flats. There's the inevitable countdown, then video of the mushroom cloud rising over the desert. But visitors here get some additional theme-park special effects: blasts from hidden air cannons imitate the bomb's shock wave, while subwoofers roar at a frequency that you feel in your gut. For a brief moment, it's a little scary. When it's over, you can watch a video in which a "witness" says, "There was never a detonation when you weren't scared."

But aside from that moment, the rest of the museum works hard to "strip the bombs of the fear and awe they inspired," as Rothstein reported, "to make them seem like ordinary weapons that could be tactically used on the battlefield."[19] The most unintentionally horrifying images are of soldiers near ground zero after a blast—this must have been Troop Test Smoky—using brooms to brush radioactive dust off each other's uniforms; one exhibit displays a helmet and goggles worn by a soldier who was ordered to march to a spot 2,500 yards from an explosion while the mushroom cloud rose overhead. The museum doesn't tell you that many of these soldiers eventually died of leukemia and that their families received compensation from Congress. To its credit, the museum does cite a comment made in 1948 by one military official, who said that if atomic testing was not conducted in the United States, the lack of direct American experience would result in an "unhealthy, dangerous and unjustified fear of atomic detonations."

The Atomic Testing Museum, with its message that testing nuclear bombs helped bring American victory in the Cold War, has not been very successful. It's true that Teller of Penn and Teller listed it among "Things I love about Las Vegas"—along with the Liberace Museum and Hoover Dam—asking, "How many other cities in the world offer you the chance to relive the good old days when you could watch nuclear weapons in action from your hotel-room window?"[20]

But the consensus view was summed up in a headline in the *Boston Herald:* "Dull Atomic Museum Not Much of a Blast."[21] TripAdvisor.com posts comments from visitors, some of which are remarkable; for example, "I understand the rationale for dropping the bombs and for developing nuclear weaponry over the years to help ensure peace, but to not include the story of the first victims of the bombs when talking about the impact of the atomic bomb is incredibly sad. The atomic bomb may be a necessary tool, but it is a terrible tool. I am a Caucasian American who served in the military, so I don't have an axe to grind. I just find the absence of more information about the hundreds of thousands of victims of the two bombs dropped in Japan to be a travesty."[22]

Another visitor wrote, "There are some shocking videos of U.S. troops being ordered to march into ground zero of an above ground test and a display and artifacts related to the disastrous 1954 'Castle Bravo' test in the Pacific that irradiated innocent islanders and a Japanese fishing boat. My take away from the visit is that atomic testing is even more dangerous than I thought. . . . I thought there is a little too much praise put on the bomb testers. . . . The museum is worth a visit, but afterwards you'll want to return to The Strip for a stiff drink."

"I highly recommend a visit to this museum," still another wrote. "You should plan to spend at least 3–4 hours here to get through everything. . . . There is a small section regarding the people, animals and plants that were/are native to the test site area, however, the museum doesn't comment on their fate and the tone of the museum is definitely pro-nuclear."[23]

And finally: "Absolutely would recommend this place to anyone who has a car and wants to do something besides doubling down."[24]

Attendance has been disappointing: fewer than 1,000 people a week visit the Atomic Testing Museum, for a total of 50,000 a year. That's not because everyone visiting Las Vegas spends all their time in casinos. The figures for other museums in Las Vegas are instructive: twice as many people go to see the Picassos at the Bellagio Art Gallery; 470,000 people a year go to the Howard W. Cannon Aviation Museum, a bunch of old planes perched on a walkway above the baggage claim area at McCarran International Airport; Madame Tussaud's Wax Museum draws 530,000; and number one on the list is the Shark Reef Aquarium at the Mandalay Bay hotel, with one million visitors annually. Even the Liberace Museum—which closed in 2010 because of low attendance—had more visitors than the Atomic Testing Museum.[25]

If you want to see the real thing, the schedule for the bus tours of the Test Site remains one tour per month. Instead of the hoped-for fifty thousand people learning about the Test Site, fewer than five hundred take the trip annually. Since 9/11, the DOE has established "Security Requirements" and mandates that prospective tourists fill out a "Badging Form" to provide a record of their identity. Applicants are advised to apply six weeks in advance of their requested tour dates. And new rules have been imposed for those on the bus: "Visitors are not permitted to bring cameras, binoculars, telescopes, or tape recorders on the tour. Cell phones are not permitted." Also on the "Prohibited" list are "Privately-owned Laptop Computers."[26] It's almost as if they want to discourage people from documenting their visit.

All that remains here of conservative claims regarding Cold War victory is a single sentence at the web site: the Nevada Test Site "helped maintain world peace, and the national security of the United States."[27]

NINE

Memorial Day in Lakewood and La Jolla

KOREAN WAR MONUMENTS OF CALIFORNIA

The Memorial Day ceremony in Lakewood, California, adjacent to Long Beach, is always held in the city park, and the speakers always stand in front of the Korean War memorial (figure 19). The memorial is a Douglas F-3D Skyknight, a fighter plane flown by the Marines in combat in Korea, painted gray and white to look like a shark. It was donated to Lakewood by the Marine Corps in 1956 and has been in the park ever since. I went one Memorial Day, and was shown around by D. J. Waldie, city manager of Lakewood, who is also the author of the wonderful memoir *Holy Land,* a book about growing up in Lakewood in the fifties. He told me that "in the mid-1950s, the Marine Corps donated gutted fighters to cities if they would haul one away to a public place and have the plane repainted at regular intervals." Douglas Aircraft had a big plant nearby, so Lakewood was delighted to take one of the planes, put it in the park, and declare it their Korean War memorial.[1]

The Marines gave the city the jet fighter "as a pure husk," Waldie writes, "as a toy. And it was, for a time." When the jet arrived in Lakewood, it had no landing gear, so the city laid it flat on the ground in the park. Children climbed on it. But "almost at once," Waldie says, "the F-3D began to hurt children, who broke arms and legs jumping from its wings."[2]

Of course the city's lawyers said the children had to be protected, so Lakewood put the Skyknight on a twelve-foot-high concrete pylon. "The county construction crew fixed the plane in a gentle climb," Waldie said, so that now it looked like "a mid-1950s hood ornament."[3] Since this was the city's Korean War monument, they put a plaque on the pylon, dedicating it to the city's Korean War dead. But for some reason the only names that appear on the plaque are the members of the city council, none of whom served in Korea.

FIGURE 19. Memorial Day observance in Lakewood, California. The jet was declared a Korean War memorial, but the names on the plaque are not Korean War dead. Instead they are the members of the city council, none of whom served in Korea. (photo by D. J. Waldie/City of Lakewood)

"The memory of war," Susan Sontag wrote, "is mostly local," and Korean War memorials provide some fascinating examples of that notion.[4] The Korean War provided an intense and ominous opening to the Cold War. In 1950, when the North Korean army crossed the 38th parallel, the line the UN had established in 1945 to separate the two sides in a Korean civil war, it was only five years after World War II had ended. For Americans, John Gaddis wrote, the attack "was almost as great a shock as Pearl Harbor."[5] Korea made it clear that our new rivalry with the Soviet Union was not going to be peaceful. The war made people afraid of communism, and that fear was exploited by McCarthyism.

The war also took a terrible toll in American lives: 54,000 dead, plus 92,000 wounded and more than 8,000 missing in action.[6] Most alarming of all, this tremendous sacrifice had brought no victory. Unlike World War II, in Korea the United States was unable to force the enemy to accept surrender. The war ended with Korea divided almost exactly the way it had been at the start.

Korea was thus the first war in history that the United States did not win—a fact that made the Cold War, just beginning, especially frightening.

In conservative ideology during the 1950s, the Korean War had special significance: it demonstrated how implacable and aggressive our communist enemy was; how easily the free world perimeter could be penetrated; how much vigilance and military might were required to defend that perimeter. And it also showed that a strong president was one who would fight communism and not seek accommodation with the Soviets and their puppets.

You might think the scale of losses and their ominous significance would lead to widespread commemoration of the Korean War dead—the first sacrifices in what conservatives would regard as a fifty-year struggle to defend freedom from its enemies, sacrifices that were made at a time when the ultimate victory was by no means certain. You might think nothing makes the case more strongly for the essential goodness of the American side in the Cold War, and the essential evil of the enemy, than the contrast today between South Korea and North Korea.

But Korean War commemoration has never been very popular or very big. Resentful veterans and their supporters called it "the forgotten war." For forty years after its conclusion, no federal monument honored Korean War veterans; instead, commemoration was left to cities and towns—places in California like Lakewood and La Jolla.[7]

So every Memorial Day, a ceremony is held in Lakewood at the Korean War monument in the park. Led by elected officials and veterans' groups, the attendance has been steady, around 150 people. The day I went, the fighter jet I had read about in Don Waldie's book was now surrounded by towering trees—after all, they had had fifty years to grow. The ceremony opened with the presentation of the flag by the Lakewood High School Naval ROTC, which turned out to be four African American girls in crisp black and white dress uniforms. The commander of the local American Legion post brought out the black POW/MIA flag and set it down next to the American flag. The pledge of allegiance was recited, a chaplain gave an invocation, and the mayor provided a few words of welcome.

Then came the speakers. The first was introduced as the official historian of the local state senate district—a position I hadn't heard of before this. He started at the appropriate point: "History teaches us we won the Cold War." But, he said, it wasn't over yet: Castro and Red China had survived. He said the "stock market had soared"—which was true at the time—"making it easy to believe the sacrifice honored today was unnecessary." He said that belief was wrong.

Then he brought up some new topics. He said, "We must pass legislation to protect the American flag from desecration." He said, "May 6 was VE day, but I didn't see anything about it in the papers." Then he said, "Thank you," and sat down. It seemed like he had a few too many complaints and not enough to say about the sacrifices that were supposed to be remembered that day.

The second speaker was the woman who represented the area in the state assembly in Sacramento. She took a completely different tack: she recited the Gettysburg Address. She said, "The world will little note what we said here, but it will never forget what they did here." Here in Lakewood?

Then a woman on the school board gave a short speech, most of which was about the trip she had taken the previous year to Normandy. "Let me tell you, the place is absolutely beautiful," she said.

Waldie wrote in *Holy Land* that the ceremony always ended with the reading of the names of young men from Lakewood who had died in Vietnam. "It is always the same list of thirty-two names," he said. Indeed that's what happened next.

But that wasn't the end. Then the speaker read the names of members of the local American Legion and Veterans of Foreign Wars and the Disabled American Veterans posts who had died—not in Korea, or in Vietnam, but in Lakewood during the past year. It was a long list. I had thought Memorial Day was the day to honor those who died while they were "in service to their country."

Then the Lakewood High School band played Taps, and the ceremony was over.

So the plaque at the Korean War memorial in Lakewood lists the names of the city council members who presided when it was constructed but doesn't list the names of those who died in Korea. And at the Memorial Day service at the memorial, the speeches barely mentioned the Cold War; they read the names of people who died in the previous year but again nothing about people who fought or died in Korea. It seemed as if Cold War commemoration had almost been forgotten.

The official Korean War Veterans Memorial in Washington, D.C., is located across the mall from the Vietnam Memorial. It was dedicated in 1995 by President Clinton after a decade of wrangling over the design. The memorial features nineteen stainless steel figures of combat soldiers on patrol. Why nineteen? The official text explains, "The original design of the memorial was to have 38 statues to represent the 38th parallel. Most of the fighting occurred along this line but due to space limitations the number of statues had to be cut in half."[8]

That's the kind of complaint that dominated discussion of the Korean War Memorial from its inception. The biggest problem for the activist vets of the Korean War was always the Vietnam Veterans Memorial: it got all the attention, leaving them unrecognized. The Korean vets wanted something equivalent in size and significance, but they definitely did not want something abstract and funereal; they wanted something "realistic" and heroic. Congress and President Reagan authorized a memorial in 1986 but specified that the funding had to be private—an early source of bitterness, and of delay.

The moment of takeoff for the Washington Korean War Memorial came when "Dear Abby" published a letter on Memorial Day in 1988. It was one long complaint: "There has been much publicity about the Vietnam Memorial, but the military personnel who fought to secure the freedom of South Korea have only the TV series *M*A*S*H* to remind people that we were there." And *M*A*S*H* of course was an antiwar black comedy. The writer said her husband had been killed flying his first combat mission over North Korea. She asked, "Who will remember: 1. That when they returned, there were no welcoming parades—only apathy? 2. That in 1953 they had to live with their own silent hell of wartime memories, as 'post-traumatic stress disorder' was unknown then? 3. That their feats were chronicled in only a few paragraphs in history books, and they have all but been ignored by the media?" She asked if Abby would help raise money.[9] Abby did, and the contributions poured in.

But the complaints didn't stop. Veterans' groups bitterly protested that the design did not include a wall with the names of all Korean War casualties, like the one that was so moving at the Vietnam memorial. The American Battle Monuments Commission rejected that kind of wall; instead Korean vets got a "kiosk" listing the names on an "honor roll." The architects who won the award for the design argued they were being ignored, and eventually they sued the Army Corps of Engineers, the American Battle Monuments Commission, the Korean War Veterans Memorial Board, the organization that ran the design competition, and the Washington firm that was commissioned to build the memorial.[10]

At the completed monument, the complaints continue. The official National Park Service text declares that the Korean War "is not thought of as significant, and often not even mentioned. However, if one compares the statistics of the Korean War (54,246) to those of Vietnam (58,226) which lasted over sixteen years, by ratio the Korean War was far bloodier than Vietnam."[11] That's a telling statistic, but it's not the kind of thing that really belongs at a memorial to the fallen.

What are the lessons of the Korean War? What should we remember about it today? Almost 54,000 Americans were killed, along with something like 900,000 Korean and Chinese soldiers and two million more Korean civilians.[12] But the war nevertheless concluded with a stalemate that amounted to a barely disguised defeat of the most powerful country in the world by an insignificant power. The obvious question is, how could this have happened? It was asked at the time, and is still being asked.[13]

The official memorial on the Mall avoids that question, but it does make one positive claim: the lesson of the Korean War, visitors are told in big letters inscribed in a central space, is "freedom is not free." But that is a generic motto that has been applied to virtually every American war, from 1776 to Iraq; and although South Korea today has a lot of political freedom, it certainly didn't in 1950 or 1953.

A more specific claim for the historical significance of the Korean War appears at the official website of the Army Corps of Engineers, which declares that the war "set the course of World history"—because "prior to the conflict America was disarming from World War II, ignoring the communist threat. After the North Korean invasion, President Truman set the doctrine that no country would fall to communism. It marked the beginning of the end of the Soviet Union and established our industrial base for the next 50 years."[14] That claim, that the Korean War "marked the beginning of the end of the Soviet Union," expresses the conservative ideology of Cold War victory in an original and interesting way: in the darkest hour of "the forgotten war," when so many died in what seemed at the time like an ominous stalemate, the triumphant end of the world conflict could now be seen. On the other hand, the idea that the Korean War set the course of history by making our industrial base dependent on military spending is usually part of the left's interpretation of the Cold War rather than that of the right.

While the conservative understanding of the Korean War has not changed much since the 1950s, a "revisionist" school of interpretation arose along with the Vietnam War. Instead of viewing Korea as a case of aggression against the "free world" orchestrated in Moscow as part of a global campaign to expand communist domination, historians now see Korea as something like Vietnam: both countries were occupied by Japan in World War II; both countries had wartime liberation movements dominated by communists; both countries were divided at the end of the war between Soviet- and U.S.-dominated regions; both countries faced civil war as World War II ended; both countries were the sites of massive U.S. military intervention to prevent communist victory in a civil war.

This interpretation emphasizes the local origins of the war and describes it as a dispute originally between Koreans, one in which the Korean communists won support primarily with a nationalist appeal rather than as representatives of global communism. And although the North Koreans were eager for Soviet and Chinese help, they also had their own goals independent of Soviet and Chinese strategy. Meanwhile South Korea was hardly an outpost of "freedom" or democracy; it was a dictatorship dependent on U.S. military backing.

The destructive force employed by the United States to prevent communist victory in Korea was appalling: in a country of 30 million people, almost one million Korean soldiers died, along with two million Korean civilians—many of them victims of starvation after the United States bombed the irrigation canals on which rice cultivation depended.[15] The American "capacity to inflict largely uncontested damage on Korea was almost without parallel," Tom Engelhardt writes. "The air force dropped World War II levels of explosives on the peninsula, leaving hardly a building standing in the northern and central part of the country. . . . [N]aval ships prowled the waters off North Korea, untouchable, bombarding coastal areas with unprecedented ordnance." The city of Wosun, for example, was bombarded around the clock from the sea for forty-one days and nights—"'the longest sustained naval or air bombardment of a city in history,' according to Rear Admiral Allan F. Smith."[16] But as America learned in Vietnam, massive conventional warfare could not bring victory in this new kind of war. And the American public didn't support this new kind of war. In 1951, before the first year of the war had ended, only 39 percent of Americans supported it. And that figure kept dropping.

Of course conservatives at the time advocated an alternative to the stalemate: an attack on China with atomic bombs. The war with Japan had ended just five years earlier after the atomic bombing of that country; the war with North Korea and its Red Chinese allies could end the same way—that was

General Douglas MacArthur's proposal. "I would have dropped between thirty and fifty atomic bombs," he said in an interview published posthumously, "strung out across the neck of Manchuria."[17] Of course Truman rejected MacArthur's A-bomb proposal and removed him as supreme allied commander.

At the time even liberal critics of the Korean War were challenging conservative ideology and anticipating the revisionist school. George Kennan, who had enunciated the doctrine of containment in the famous Long Telegram, criticized Cold War strategy for its Manichean view of a worldwide struggle between good and evil. His view was that American interests in various world hotspots needed to be considered on a case-by-case basis and that the doctrine of containment had made that impossible.[18]

The same kind of argument was made by the columnist Walter Lippmann, who called the doctrine of containment a "strategic monstrosity" and argued that viewing every crisis as part of the same ideological crusade would lead to U.S. support for "an array of satellites, clients, depends and puppets," requiring a series of interventions in countries like Korea where the issue was not freedom versus slavery.[19] But there are no monuments to the revisionist interpretation of the Korean War.

Another Korean War monument, another memorial ceremony, another case where Korean War commemoration seemed not very important: Veterans Day in 2003, at San Diego's Korean War memorial, where a ceremony commemorated the fiftieth anniversary of the signing of the armistice at Panmunjom (figure 20). Several hundred people attended the event at Mount Soledad, above La Jolla. One speaker, a seventy-two-year-old retired colonel who had been named "San Diego County Veteran of the Year" in 2000, raised the question of whether the Korean War was justified. He described visiting South Korea the previous year, and said he had met "smiling" people who "kissed him and thanked him for fighting for their country." "'Was our intervention worth it?' he asked. 'In my heart, I totally think so.'"[20] Next came a tribute to Bob Hope, who had entertained the troops in Korea and elsewhere and had died a few months earlier. The owner of the San Diego Chargers presented a plaque to two of Hope's children. It read, "Thanks for the Memories."

San Diego Mayor Dick Murphy then "presented a proclamation honoring the Mount Soledad memorial," and, according to the *Union-Tribune,* "made

FIGURE 20. San Diego cross, Mount Soledad. The sponsors call it a Korean War memorial. Atheists—and the ACLU—say its presence on public land violates the separation of church and state. (AP Photo/Denis Poroy)

a brief reference to the legal controversy that began in 1989 when a self-described atheist filed a federal lawsuit challenging the cross on the land."[21]

If you Google "San Diego," "Korean War," and "Cross," you get more than a million hits. That's because San Diego's Korean War monument has been the subject of twenty years of contentious litigation, which has ranged from the city council to the U.S. Senate to the Bush White House. The battle has raised several questions: should the service of veterans in the Korean War be commemorated with a cross, or does that violate the separation of church and state? And if a cross is permissible, should it be a twenty-ton cross that is forty-three feet high and placed on the highest hilltop along the San Diego coast? Is it okay that Jews, Buddhists, Muslims, agnostics, and atheists driving by on Interstate 5 may feel excluded from commemorating the Korean War dead here?

The story of the Mount Soledad cross starts in 1954, when the American Legion dedicated a forty-three-foot concrete cross in the city park on the mountain. They said it was a monument to Korean War veterans. But in San Diego the cross was known as the place for Easter morning services. For the next thirty-five years, services were held at the cross every Easter at dawn, and nobody complained.

The second act of the story started in 1989, when Philip Paulson, an atheist and Vietnam War veteran, sued the city of San Diego, which owned the Mount Soledad property, arguing that the cross should be removed because it violated the establishment-of-religion clause in the Bill of Rights. He and the American Civil Liberties Union (ACLU) said the cross was not an appropriate memorial to Korean War veterans, that a memorial should not be religious but rather display secular symbolism, such as the flag.

Supporters of the cross replied that this cross had nothing to do with religion but instead was simply a Korean War memorial. They said it "salutes veterans, not religion." They said the fact that it had been a war memorial since 1954 meant that this particular cross had been "de-sacralized." And in general, "the cross is the quintessential symbol of fallen soldiers in Western civilization," said Phil Thalheimer, who headed a private group called San Diegans for the Mount Soledad National War Memorial. "No one is being coerced to participate in any religious activity," he said. The *San Diego Union-Tribune* added that Thalheimer "makes a point of saying he is Jewish."[22]

The third act came in 2006, after the federal courts ordered the city to remove the cross, when Congress passed a law taking the Korean War memorial, including the cross and the land on which it stood, and making it federal property. The argument was not that San Diego was unable to operate a Korean War memorial but rather that the rules governing religious monuments on federal property were not as strict as California law regarding municipal property. That meant the San Diego cross could be "saved" from "judicial activism"—President Bush's words.[23]

All this made it seem that Korean War commemoration provided only a legal cover for keeping the cross—that honoring Korean War veterans was never the primary purpose of this site. Instead, Korean War commemoration supplied the necessary legal pretext to continue what had originally been a religious purpose.[24] Paulson, the original plaintiff, and the ACLU provided some compelling evidence for that argument. First, the marker: the site has a plaque stating that the cross was dedicated in 1954 as a Korean War memorial. However, the plaque was not installed until 1992, almost three years after the lawsuit was filed. The site had no marker declaring it a Korean War memorial for its first thirty-eight years.

Then the ACLU looked at old maps—the Thomas Brothers maps, which are the semiofficial ones, reissued annually. Every San Diego map starting in 1954, when the monument was dedicated, to 1989, when the lawsuit was filed, had a label for the site in question, and the label was not "Korean War Memorial." It was "Mt. Soledad Easter Cross." On every map after 1989, after the lawsuit was filed, the name of the site has been "Mt. Soledad Memorial."

Every Easter sunrise since 1954 a Christian worship service had been held at the cross. At the service Jesus was described as the savior of mankind who died on the cross for our sins, who was resurrected, and belief in whom brings eternal life. Nothing specifically about Korean War veterans was included in the Easter sunrise service.[25]

The main argument made by the defenders of the site pointed to the memorial section around the cross: concentric brick walls with 3,200 black granite plaques, privately purchased, displaying the names and photos of war veterans. A typical plaque reads, "Arthur J. Leonard, Master Sergeant, Marine Corps . . . assault and seizure of Inchon; Capture and Securing of Seoul; Chosin Campaign. Till the end of time/Je T'Aimerai/Bernadette, Mike and Christine."[26] Some of the individual plaques contain religious symbols that aren't crosses; those who counted found twenty Jewish stars. Thus, defenders of the site argued, the cross was not the only religious symbol at the site. However, these other symbols are a few inches tall, nothing like the forty-three-foot height of the cross. But that isn't the key fact. The key fact is that the entire section of individual plaques under the cross was constructed after a court noted that nothing at the site indicated that the cross was dedicated to Korean War veterans. That was one reason why the court ordered the cross removed.

In 1994, after the federal court ruled that the cross had to be removed from city land, the city came up with the solution of selling the land under the cross to a private party—a fifteen-foot square of land that included the base of the cross and the iron fence surrounding it. The notice soliciting bids was explicit that the sale was "for the purpose of maintaining a historic war memorial." The city accepted the bid of the Mount Soledad Association, which had maintained the cross and run the Easter sunrise services for the previous thirty years. But the Ninth Circuit, sitting en banc, found that the sale "was structured to provide a direct, immediate, and substantial financial advantage to bidders who had the sectarian purpose of preserving the Cross" and that the sale was therefore invalid.

One memorable moment came in 1996 when Peter Irons, the attorney and political science professor at UC San Diego who represented the original plaintiffs, discovered that the group that ran the Easter Sunday service at the cross had somehow failed to get the required permit. "So I got one," he told me. "You have to have an organizational sponsor, so I got the Atheist Coalition. The next morning the headline in the *San Diego Union-Tribune* was as big as the one that said 'World War II Ended'—this one said 'Atheists Take Over Easter Cross.'"[27]

On that Easter Sunday, the head of the Atheist Coalition gave a speech at the cross describing it as "a clear message that, in the eyes of the City of San Diego, Christians are to be preferred." As he was speaking, Irons reported, "a group of Bible-waving protesters pushed their way through the crowd, loudly singing hymns to drown him out." The *Union-Tribune* reported that "there were hell-fire shouters and . . . men in white robes carry staffs. . . . A man, naked except for a loincloth, carried a cross." Also present was Tom Metzger, national leader of the White Aryan Resistance; Irons described him as "San Diego's most notorious racist and anti-Semite." He kept quiet. Nobody on that Easter Sunday said anything about Korean War veterans.[28]

The ACLU proposed in 2004 that the cross should be moved to the grounds of a nearby church and replaced by "a nonsectarian symbol," thus preserving what the city claimed was the original intent of the site, a Korean War memorial. The local American Legion post unanimously supported the settlement, but the city council and the mayor put an initiative on the ballot to keep the cross at the site. Defenders of the cross denounced their opponents for their "shameless betrayal" of veterans who had "sacrificed their lives" in Korea and other wars.[29] But the voters rejected the initiative, and the city prepared to move the cross.

At the last minute, San Diego congressman Randy "Duke" Cunningham, at the time a powerful member of the House Appropriations Committee, introduced a bill in Congress to have the federal government take over the site and "designate the Mt. Soledad Veterans Memorial a national veterans memorial," to be maintained and administered by the National Park Service. He didn't say his goal was to do a better job commemorating Korean War veterans; he said his goal was to "save the cross." An ACLU press release pointed out that at the same time Cunningham was saving the cross, "he was abusing his political office by accepting bribes. Cunningham subsequently pled guilty to this crime and is now serving time in a Federal penitentiary."[30]

At the end of 2004, President Bush signed Randy Cunningham's bill into law. After some foot-dragging by the city, new legislation was introduced in Congress, calling for the federal government to seize the site under its power of eminent domain. The Senate bill, which passed by "unanimous consent," was sponsored by Dianne Feinstein and supported by Barbara Boxer. President Bush signed the new bill in 2006 at an Oval Office signing ceremony, which the *Washington Post* reported was "attended by cross supporters and Republican House members who sponsored the bill."[31] Note: not by Korean War veterans or their representatives.

Now the cross stood on federal land, which raised a new set of legal issues. The ACLU filed a new suit on behalf of the national Jewish War Veterans organization, arguing, among other things, that "the federal taking of the cross brought . . . government endorsement of the Christian doctrine."[32] In August 2008 a new federal judge ruled that the cross could stay. "The court finds the memorial at Mt. Soledad, including its Latin cross, communicates the primarily nonreligious messages of military service, death and sacrifice," wrote U.S. District Judge Larry Alan Burns. "As such, despite its location on public land, the memorial is constitutional."[33]

Of course the ACLU appealed, and in January 2011 a three-judge panel reversed that ruling and declared the cross was an unconstitutional "government endorsement of religion." But that panel did not order the cross removed. Instead, it sent the case back to the trial judge for "further proceedings" to determine whether the cross could be modified to "pass constitutional muster" as a war memorial.[34]

Meanwhile back in San Diego, the alternative press took up the issue of the Mount Soledad Korean War memorial. Edwin Decker, columnist at *San Diego CityBeat,* stated his argument in the persona of "Arnold Solomon, a private in the United States Army." "I'm dead now," "Solomon" wrote. "I was 20 years old when my ass got shot off in South Korea on July 16, 1950. . . . I was posthumously awarded the Purple Heart and a whole lotta other medals. Oh, and, also, I am a Jew." And "as a Jew, I'm especially offended. The crucifix isn't a unifier. It is the thing that separates Christians from Jews. It is the symbol of our differences." He suggested instead "a real war memorial. You know, like a statue of soldiers raising a flag on some war torn Hell-hill, or maybe a great general sitting in his battle chair. Jesus, even a bronze depiction of a sailor cruising hookers in Kwangju would be a more inclusive memorial than that wretched cross."[35]

Another alternative press writer took up the notion of a Korean War memorial: D. A. Kolodenko, also writing in *San Diego CityBeat.* He noted that the highest peak inside the city of San Diego is not Mount Soledad; it is Cowles Mountain. He proposed a second Korean War memorial be built on top of Cowles Mountain, arguing, "If you think one Korean War memorial is enough, you should take a cold, hard look in the mirror and ask yourself why you don't support our troops."

His proposed design was for "a massive, six-pointed star, like two triangles performing the 69 sex position—a shape that some are bound to call a 'Star of David' or 'Jewish star,' even though the Cowles Mountain Star will be a historical war memorial rather than a primarily religious symbol."

His proposed monument was 150 feet tall, and included a "kosher snack bar/deli inside the memorial" that would offer "all your favorite traditional trail fare, as well as an array of noshes, like rugalach, macaroons and the best damn bagels this side of Manhattan." While the Korean War memorial on Mount Soledad is the site of Easter Sunday services for Christians, on Mount Cowles "the giant Star of David will encourage Jews to establish an annual Cowles Mountain Passover seder."

Kolodenko recalled that he "grew up Jewish and under anti-Semitic siege in the late 1970s, in the neighborhood right between Cowles Mountain and 'Jew Hill.' Now they'll both be called Jew Hill. And why would a Star of David war memorial on top of Cowles Mountain guarantee it the name 'Jew Hill' when nobody calls Mount Soledad 'Christian Hill?' Prejudice? Tyranny? The deli, of course."[36]

Thus at Korean War memorials, what is often at issue is not the memory of that war but rather other issues: the use of public land for religious purposes in La Jolla, the recent deaths of VFW members in Long Beach. Even at the official memorial in Washington, D.C., resentment over the priority given to Vietnam veterans seems as significant as the "lessons" of Korea. At these sites, Cold War commemoration once again has faltered.

TEN

Code Name "Ethel"

THE ROSENBERGS IN THE MUSEUMS

If Whittaker Chambers gets a national monument for fingering a Red spy, shouldn't David Greenglass? He not only named names in court, like Chambers did; his testimony sent two people to the electric chair. Of course this is the Rosenberg atom spy case, in which Julius and Ethel Rosenberg were executed in 1953 because, Americans were told, they stole the secret of the atomic bomb and gave it to the Soviets. But while conservatives have created a National Historic Landmark to honor the man whose testimony sent Alger Hiss to prison, they have built no monument to the man whose testimony won the death penalty for the prosecution in the Rosenberg case. The David Greenglass National Monument? It has been hard for conservatives to make a hero out of the man who sent his sister to the electric chair.

And it has been a lot harder since 2001, when Greenglass admitted that his testimony against his sister was false. After his arrest in 1950, he implicated his brother-in-law, Julius Rosenberg, and his own wife, Ruth. But then in 1951, a week before the trial was to start, prosecutors reminded Ruth that her husband had not yet been sentenced and that she was still subject to indictment. At that point, Ruth declared for the first time that Ethel had typed David's notes for the Soviets six years earlier. Then Greenglass changed his testimony to agree with his wife's. He testified in the 1951 trial that the notes he took for the Soviets had been typed by his sister. Greenglass's testimony got him two things: a reduced sentence for himself—ten years, instead of the death penalty—and no charges against his wife.[1]

But fifty years later, when he appeared on *60 Minutes II* as part of the publicity tour for his just-published biography, *The Brother*, by the *New York Times* reporter Sam Roberts, David Greenglass admitted he had lied in the trial about the most important evidence against Ethel. Asked whether he remembered that his sister did the typing, he told his biographer, "I frankly think my wife did the typing"—as Sam Roberts reported in *The Brother*. "So what am I gonna do, call my wife a liar? My wife is my wife," he told Roberts. "I mean, I don't sleep with my sister, you know."[2]

There is no David Greenglass National Monument, but there are a couple of museums that include displays about the Rosenberg case. The one with the most visitors—700,000 a year—is the International Spy Museum in Washington, D.C., a private operation rather than an official congressionally supported site. It promises in its publicity that the stories of "the great spies of history from Mata Hari to Julius and Ethel Rosenberg . . . are all in the museum."[3]

The Spy Museum presents the prosecution view of the Rosenbergs. A big wall text display reads, "'The Rosenbergs provided very significant help in accelerating the production of our atomic bomb.'—Nikita Khrushchev, in his memoirs."[4] This claim is a problem for conservatives today, because almost nobody believes David Greenglass's sketch helped the Russian bomb builders. The facts were presented decades ago by Dr. Phillip Morrison, co-holder of a patent on the atomic bomb, who said, "The entire testimony of Greenglass concerning the bomb is confused and imprecise[;] . . . he had neither the scientific background . . . nor was he closely associated with the technical aspects of the project." As for the sketch Greenglass said he gave to Julius to transmit to the Soviets, Morrison said it was "so rough, and contained so many errors that it could have been of no use to the Russians."[5] Other leading atomic scientists, including Harold Urey and J. Robert Oppenheimer, said the same thing.[6]

Of course the Soviets spied on the United States—and the United States spied on the Soviets. The Soviets did learn key atomic secrets from two highly placed spies inside the Manhattan Project—much higher than David Greenglass, a lowly machinist. At the time the Rosenbergs were indicted, a real atomic scientist was also tried—by the British—and convicted: Klaus Fuchs, who was sentenced to fourteen years in Britain and served ten. And there was one spy who was never prosecuted, an American physicist who worked at Los Alamos who really did give vital information about the A-bomb to the Soviets: Theodore Hall.

So Julius was a spy, but he didn't give the Soviets the secret of the atom bomb; Ethel was innocent, but she was framed by her brother. The FBI never caught the spy who really did give A-bomb secrets to the Soviets. You won't learn any of that at the International Spy Museum.

The dramatic centerpiece of the International Spy Museum "Spies Among Us" exhibit, the one people remember best, is a dark room with one wall displaying several backlit panels of text, accompanied by a solemn voice-over, which traces the government's chain of evidence against the Rosenbergs. Then the final panel flashes a headline: "Reds Have Atom Bomb." At this point the PA system overhead broadcasts the voice of the narrator saying one word, "Outcome?" Then a countdown begins, starting in English and finishing in Russian. Then flashing strobe lights illuminate the darkened room, the floor trembles, and the sound track plays something that sounds sort of like a bomb going off. Visitors look at each other nervously, wondering if the noise is going to get louder and the shaking floor worse. No doubt the prosecution would have loved to give this experience to the jury (although when I visited, after the shaking floor stopped and the roaring noise ended, a sarcastic teenager in the room told his younger sister, "That wasn't so bad").

"Spies Among Us" does express a certain uneasiness at least over the prosecution of Ethel Rosenberg. One panel of wall text—small and in a back corner—reads, "When Julius was caught and refused to talk, the FBI arrested Ethel too, in the hopes of breaking her husband. Amid widespread sympathy and doubt, both were found guilty and sentenced to die in the electric chair." Careful readers will note the absence of any claim that Ethel was guilty.

Here the museum seems to be referring to the history recounted by Sam Roberts of the *New York Times,* who in 2008 interviewed William P. Rogers, deputy attorney general at the time of the execution. Roberts asked whether the prosecution goal was to execute the Rosenbergs. No, Rogers replied, "the goal wasn't to kill the couple. The strategy was to leverage the death sentence imposed on Ethel to wring a full confession from Julius—in hopes that Ethel's motherly instincts would trump unconditional loyalty to a noble but discredited cause."

Roberts then asked, "What went wrong?" He writes, "Rogers's explanation still haunts me. 'She called our bluff,' he said."[7] That's the most chilling sentence in the entire history of the case.

Another panel in another area of the Spy Museum takes up the issue: "Even after their conviction, many people believed the Rosenbergs and others were innocent. Top secret Soviet diplomatic cables proved otherwise. The intercepted cables—the Venona papers—named Soviet spies Julius Rosenberg and Alger Hiss. Public doubt was removed." Again, the careful reader will note the absence of Ethel from the "proof."

The exhibits include a reproduction of the cut Jell-O box the prosecution said David Greenglass used for identification when he met Harry Gold, who was to serve as courier of the secret of the atomic bomb. The Jell-O box was not exactly proof that the Rosenbergs were atom spies, but it did provide a memorable object for the jury and also later a museum display. In a memorable line at the trial, Greenglass said that when he met Gold, Gold presented a cut Jell-O box and uttered the prearranged secret phrase, "I come from Julius." Greenglass had the other half, which he said Julius had given him. When the two halves matched, that, Greenglass said, confirmed the identity of each for the other.

Critics of the government case pointed out it was unlikely that the spies' secret password would include the actual name of another member of the spy ring. Indeed when the FBI released some documents from their Rosenberg case file in the 1970s, they showed that Greenglass's original statement was that Gold had identified himself as "Dave from Pittsburgh," while in Gold's original statement, according to former FBI agent Richard Brennan, he said he had used the phrase "Benny sent me." Prosecutors put their two witnesses together before the trial, and they then agreed to testify the phrase was actually "I come from Julius."[8]

The Jell-O box was the key piece of evidence tying the Rosenbergs to atomic espionage. Irving Saypol, the prosecutor, told the jury that the Jello-O box "forged the necessary link in the chain that points indisputably to the guilt of the Rosenbergs."[9]

Of course the prosecution did not present the "real" Jell-O box from Albuquerque as evidence at the trial. Instead the prosecutors displayed to the jury a replica that they said was like the one Greenglass and Gold had carried. The Rosenbergs of course denied they had anything to do with any Jell-O box. The cut Jell-O box at the International Spy Museum is part of the "Design for Disguise" section of the "Student Spy Guide" and is displayed in the museum's "Red Alley."[10] They say it's like the Jell-O box that the prosecution said was like the one used by the spies. It's a copy of a copy.

The "Student Guide" for the Spy Museum has "Spy for a Day" projects for young visitors. One project is about Ethel Rosenberg. It says, "although there was much controversy over Ethel's involvement in actual spying, decryptions of Soviet messages reveal that Ethel was indeed a Soviet spy." Then it says, "Your Mission: pretend you are this person and imagine that you have been assigned the following: you must pick up intelligence at a dead drop site located on the corner of Fifth and Vine[,] ... decode the message ... [and] use another dead drop site to pass this information to your Soviet handler."[11]

But of course the prosecution never said Ethel picked up intelligence at a dead drop site, or passed information to a Soviet handler. And the decryptions of Soviet messages—the Venona decryptions—actually suggested Ethel was not a spy (see chapter 6). But apparently the education department of the Spy Museum thinks it will be fun for kids to pretend they are Ethel Rosenberg.

The Spy Museum also features one entire wall covered with the code names found in the Venona decryptions. Apparently a key feature of spying is having a code name. Ethel isn't there. And in the room where the strobes go off and the floor shakes, the members of the atom spy ring are all introduced by their code names. We hear, "Harry Gold, code name 'Goose'"; "David Greenglass, code name 'Caliber'"; "Julius Rosenberg, code name 'Liberal'"; and then "Ethel Rosenberg, code name 'Ethel.'"

But "Ethel" is not a code name. It was her real name. The fact that she did not have a code name is pretty good evidence that Ethel was not a spy.

After "Ethel Rosenberg, code name 'Ethel,'" visitors hear one more name in the "Spies Among Us" exhibit: "Theodore Hall—code name 'Mlad,' which means Youth. Graduate of Harvard. Leaked atomic secrets to the Soviets." That takes twelve seconds. The International Spy Museum has nothing more about Theodore Hall. In fact he did more to help the Soviets build their A-bomb than anyone else. How Ted Hall stole the secret of the A-bomb, and how the FBI failed to catch him, is a story that belongs in any decent museum of spying. We know the story, because he told it after his name appeared in the Venona transcripts released by the National Security Agency in 1995—in a book by Joseph Albright and Marcia Kunstel titled *Bombshell: The Secret Story of America's Unknown Atomic Spy Conspiracy.*[12]

Hall had been questioned by the FBI in 1950 but never arrested. He moved to England in 1962 to take up a research position at Cambridge University, where his work with electron microscopes in biological X-rays won wide acclaim. He lived a long life as a distinguished scientist in Britain until his death in 1999 at the age of seventy-four.

Hall explained his motivation for helping the Soviets in a statement he wrote for the book about his case: "During 1944 I was worried about the dangers of an American monopoly of atomic weapons if there should be a postwar depression." He contacted the Soviets "to help prevent that monopoly." But what about the fact that he was helping Stalin, who had killed millions in the purges and the gulags? "In 1944 I did not realize the nature and scale of the atrocities perpetrated in the Soviet Union during and after the 1930s," Hall said. "Many reports about these things had been proved false, and they seemed incompatible with the obvious dedication of the Soviet Army and people during the war. If I had seen the whole picture in focus, I feel quite convinced that I would have acted differently. . . . On reflection, I think my emotional revulsion against Stalin's terror would have stopped me in my tracks. Simple as that."[13]

But he also felt breaking the American monopoly on the bomb may have had positive effects: "For example, the bomb might have been dropped on China in 1949 or the early fifties. Well, if I helped to prevent that, I accept the charge. But such talk is purely hypothetical."[14]

How important was Ted Hall? The Moscow correspondents for Cox newspapers who wrote his story, Joseph Albright and Marcia Kunstel, conclude that while the Soviets would have developed their bomb without him, it would have taken them "until the mid-1950s at the earliest," instead of 1949. Here's the key: "Without details from a second source like Hall, the suspicious [Lavrenti] Beria [head of Soviet atomic espionage] would have had information only from one scientist named Fuchs, who had the drawback of being German. The material from Greenglass was too naïve and garbled to substitute for Ted Hall's scientific formulations." And Hall is "the only American scientist known to have given the Soviet Union details on the design of an atomic bomb."[15]

Hall was the youngest physicist at Los Alamos, joining the bomb project after he graduated from Harvard at eighteen. "He was at the center of the scientific pioneering that made the bomb happen: he handled implosion experiments for Fat Man, the plutonium bomb dropped on Nagasaki," which the Soviets copied. Hall also "helped determine the critical mass of uranium for the Hiroshima bomb."[16]

If there was "a secret" of the A-bomb, it was implosion—"one of the seminal inventions of the twentieth century." That's the idea that plutonium could be brought to critical mass, and an explosive chain reaction created, by squeezing a sphere of it to increase its density. The squeezing was accomplished by simultaneous conventional explosions. The sketch David Greenglass gave Harry Gold, the centerpiece of the Rosenberg trial, featured a mold for a high-explosive lens designed to focus the explosions on the nuclear core, but Greenglass "had only the dimmest understanding of it. Betraying his confusion, he erroneously told Harry Gold the purpose of the implosion experiment was to determine the critical mass of uranium," whereas implosion required plutonium. And evidence from the Soviet archives "virtually rules out Fuchs—and strongly points to Hall—as Moscow's first source on the implosion principle."[17]

Hall's help for the Soviet bomb project ranks "among the more remarkable intelligence feats of World War II," Albright and Kunstel conclude. "Despite all the resources of Nazi intelligence, Reichsführer Heinrich Himmler never came close to piercing General Groves' security [at Los Alamos], nor did Japanese Prime Minister Koiso Kuniaki. Yet the Soviets knew all the main elements of America's secret weapon five months before it was tried out at Alamogordo—thanks in no small measure to Theodore Hall's decision to volunteer."[18]

The Soviets surprised the United States by exploding an atomic bomb in August 1949, and a few days later Hall informed the Soviets that his espionage work for them was finished. He decided to abandon nuclear physics, switch fields to biophysics, and enter a Ph.D. program at the University of Chicago that fall, where he and his new wife became Progressive political activists.

The news of Klaus Fuchs's confession to the British authorities made headlines in the United States in February 1950, along with the conviction of Alger Hiss in his second trial for perjury. The same month, Senator Joe McCarthy gave a speech in Wheeling, West Virginia: "I have here in my hand a list of 205 people that were known to the Secretary of State as being members of the Communist Party . . . "

At about the same time, the Venona project succeeded in breaking the Soviet code. In 1950 the code breakers came up with the name that led the FBI to Theodore Hall, and they found him in Chicago. The FBI put a dozen agents on morning-to-night coverage of the graduate student and his wife in Hyde Park. The FBI agent in charge reported, "Their actions on behalf of the Progressive Party and the Chicago Tenant's *[sic]* Action Council have revealed a disregard for adverse publicity and there appears to be nothing of a covert nature in their current activity." The report concluded that Hall "is not presently engaged in surreptitious espionage work."[19]

A few days later Harry Gold named David Greenglass as his Los Alamos source, and Greenglass confessed and named his wife and his brother-in-law, Julius Rosenberg, as the people who recruited him. Greenglass's wife, Ruth, then named her husband's sister, Ethel Rosenberg. Hoover now had the evidence for a trial of "the crime of the century," and they gave up on prosecuting Ted Hall. He and his wife went on to become activists opposing the Korean War and circulating the Stockholm Peace Petition urging the United States not to use the atomic bomb again. The FBI agent in charge of the Hall investigation told Albright and Kunstel that they stopped suspecting Hall of spying because "it was never the policy of the Soviet Union to allow their undercover agents to blow their cover by attracting attention to themselves by having connections with public Soviet front organizations," and the FBI considered the Stockholm petition that kind of Soviet front.[20] The FBI interrogated Hall during the Rosenberg trial, but in 1951 the Bureau decided not to prosecute him.

In 1953, when Eisenhower denied clemency to the Rosenbergs, Ted Hall "was gripped by guilt" and "made a poignant offer to his Soviet control officer," according to his biographers. He proposed giving himself up, saying, "Don't pin it all on the Rosenbergs because I was more responsible than they were." Later he told a friend, "I meant it. I would have done it. I felt that strongly about it." Why didn't he? Because his Soviet controller "felt it wasn't a good idea at all."[21] Hall went on to work in cancer research at Sloan-Kettering before moving to England in 1962 and becoming well known for his pioneering research in the use of electron microscopes in biological X-ray microanalysis.[22]

Stealing the secret of the A-bomb was "the crime of the century" in J. Edgar Hoover's view; in the view of President Eisenhower and others, it gave Stalin the confidence to start the Korean War. Historians agree that it was one of the most successful acts of espionage in modern history. But you won't find out about it at the International Spy Museum.

The Eisenhower Presidential Library and Museum in Abilene, Kansas, has an exhibit about the Rosenberg case, because the Rosenbergs appealed for clemency from Eisenhower, for a commutation of their death sentences to life in prison, and Ike refused to prevent their executions. In Abilene the display is in a section named "Personal Liberties." One side is Joe McCarthy; the other is the Rosenbergs, and is titled "American Spies?" Note the question mark.

The museum run by the National Archives of the United States, the official museum of the president who presided over the executions, has a question mark heading its exhibit about the Rosenbergs.

Under the question mark, the wall text begins, "In 1951, Julius and Ethel Rosenberg were convicted of giving atomic bomb secrets to the Soviet Union and sentenced to death. The case outraged many who doubted their guilt or deemed the penalty too severe." That's a pretty good start. It goes on to say that Ike denied the appeal to commute the sentences to life in prison and quotes from his "later writing": "the nature of the crime . . . involves the deliberate betrayal of the entire nation and could very well result in the death of many, many thousands of innocent citizens."

The next panel in Abilene is "The Venona Intercepts." It reads, "The Venona messages reveal that Rosenberg headed a spy ring," and concludes, "Documents refer to Ethel Rosenberg as supportive, but they also state that 'she does not work.'" A Venona "comment" page explains that "work" in this context means "conspiratorial work in the interests of the USSR."[23] So the Eisenhower Museum displays evidence that Ethel was not guilty—although they do not state that explicitly.

The next case displays three items. The first is a leaflet headlined, "Parents to Die on Wedding Anniversary; Rosenberg Children Plead with President." The leaflet has a photo of the two boys, captioned "Robert and Michael Rosenberg"—they were six and nine years old in this 1953 photo. The leaflet also displays Michael's letter to President Eisenhower, written in careful boyish script: "Please let my mommy and daddy go and not let anything happen to them. If they come home Robbie and I will be very happy and will thank you very much." It is signed, "Very Truly Yours, Michael Rosenberg." You'd have to have a heart of stone not to be moved by that letter.[24] But it turns out that a lot of people had hearts of stone in 1953.

Next to that poster in the same display case, Ethel's handwritten letter to Eisenhower requesting clemency is displayed. The caption reads, "She appealed to his sense of mercy and asked him to consult with Mamie rather than his political advisors."

Next to that is the official "Appeal for Executive Clemency," with the handwritten note "Application Denied. D.E."—terse, yet eloquent.[25] It's an emotionally potent and moving exhibit, surprisingly so for a presidential museum. As for the question mark in the exhibit title, it would not be hard to conclude from the Eisenhower museum exhibit that Julius was guilty but Ethel was not.

The Newseum in Washington, D.C., has a small but potent display about the Rosenberg case. This is the big, beautiful new museum of the history of the news media, across the street from the National Gallery, run privately by the First Amendment Foundation, which is sponsored by the big media corporations and foundations—Annenberg, the New York Times, Bloomberg, Hearst, and Rupert Murdoch's News Corp. A long, long gallery upstairs displays front pages for key stories for most years of the twentieth century. For 1953, the museum exhibits three front pages: "Korea Truce Signed," "Royal Coronation," and "Rosenbergs Executed."

For the "Rosenbergs Executed" story, the Newseum displays the front page not of the *New York Times* or the *Washington Post* but rather the *National Guardian*—the left-wing weekly that argued the Rosenbergs were not guilty. "Eisenhower Refuses Clemency in Face of a Horrified World" is the subhead you read at the Newseum; "13,000 picket White House in clemency vigil."[26] Another story describes ten-year-old Michael delivering a second appeal to Eisenhower to the guard at the White House gate. Michael is quoted as saying he hopes the president got his first letter. The Newseum's decision to display the *National Guardian* to tell the story of the Rosenbergs' execution is stunning.[27]

There's another museum exhibit about Ethel Rosenberg: it's at the Herbert Hoover Library—not the Hoover Institution at Stanford but the Herbert Hoover Presidential Museum, run by the National Archives, in West Branch, Iowa, the president's birthplace, east of Iowa City. In 2000 the library put up an exhibit, which is still running on the official website: "American Women! A Celebration of Our History" (exclamation mark theirs). It's organized chronologically, and the section "From Fifties to Feminism, 1950–1990: Baby Boomers Expand the Boundaries" features four women who, they say, exemplify the postwar era: Rosa Parks, Rachel Carson, Lucille Ball—and Ethel Rosenberg.[28]

Each is identified by one quotation. For Rosa Parks, it's "The only tired I was, was tired of giving in." For Rachel Carson, "The human race is challenged more than ever before to demonstrate our mastery—not over nature but of ourselves." For Lucy, "Knowing what you cannot do is more important than knowing what you can do. In fact, that's good taste." And for Ethel Rosenberg: "'Always remember that we were innocent...'—written in a final letter to her sons."

It sort of takes your breath away. So does the exhibit text, which says the Rosenbergs were convicted at a time when "the 1950s Cold War made a fair trial impossible." The judge, visitors learn, declared that Julius was a spymaster and that Ethel was "a full-fledged partner in his crime," but "numerous appeals—including those from Ethel herself, from the Pope and from the Rosenbergs' two sons—were written to President Eisenhower to commute their death sentence." The text concludes with a report that the Venona documents showed Ethel was "little more than a witness."

The exhibit at the Herbert Hoover Presidential Library included several artifacts: Ethel's letter to President Eisenhower requesting clemency; the poster showing the two Rosenberg children with Michael's letter to Eisenhower; and a poster declaring, "The Electric Chair Can't Kill the Doubts in the Rosenberg Case."[29]

The most thorough and authoritative museum exhibit on the Rosenberg case opened at the New York Historical Society on October 2, 2001, and ran for almost six months. The opening came four weeks after the 9/11 attacks, so the exhibit never got the attention it deserved. "The Rosenbergs Reconsidered: The Death Penalty in the Cold War Era" offered a "reexamination" of the case, which "American society is still debating." The problem, according to the introductory text, was that "the Cold War anti-Communist crusade fueled demands for the couple's death sentence—making the process of justice vulnerable to the passions of the moment."

What made the exhibit a powerful one was, first of all, a display of original evidence that was unprecedented, and second the presentation of evidence from two important books on the case that had just been published—Sam Roberts's biography of David Greenglass, *The Brother,* and the memoirs of Alexander Feklisov, the retired KGB officer who supervised Julius's intelligence work in 1940s New York. Roberts, who also served as historical consultant for the exhibit, quoted Greenglass admitting he had lied in the testimony that sent Ethel to the electric chair; Feklisov's coauthor said the purpose of their book was "to prove that Ethel is completely innocent."[30]

Museum exhibits need objects, and the centerpiece of this exhibit was a stunning one: an electric chair from Sing Sing, where the Rosenbergs had been executed (figure 21). The wall label followed the standard museum format: object name, date, materials, and source: "*Electric Chair,* c. 1890. Oak, leather, metal. Courtesy of New York State Department of Corrections Training Academy." The wall text explains how the electric chair was invented and reports that this one "was first used in Clinton Prison, Dannemora, New

FIGURE 21. New York Historical Society exhibit, "The Rosenbergs Reconsidered: The Death Penalty in the Cold War Era." Life-size mug shots on the wall behind the real Sing Sing electric chair. (photo by Miguel Colon/New York Historical Society)

York in 1892. A total of 26 prisoners were executed in it. . . . It dates from the same period as the Sing-Sing Prison electric chair used to execute Julius and Ethel Rosenberg."

Curator Kathleen Hulser told me that as they were putting the show together on September 11, 2001, she got a voice mail message: "Lady, this is the trucker with your electric chair, and I can't get into Manhattan because all the bridges are closed. What do you want me to do?"

The first item greeting visitors at the exhibit was the painting that appeared on the cover of *Collier's* magazine in August 1950: "Atom Bomb Hits New York."[31] It's a view from the harbor looking toward Lower Manhattan with a fireball rising above Midtown. The wall text explains that this issue "appeared just as the Rosenbergs' arrest dominated the headlines. It captures the apocalyptic mood of the 1950s, as people imagined an imminent worldwide nuclear catastrophe. This nuclear fear helps to explain why much of the American public was eager to see the Rosenbergs executed. They could be blamed for giving Russia the bomb and making the end of civilization a near possibility."

The heart of the exhibit consisted of the actual Greenglass drawings presented by the prosecution as evidence in the trial—and, crucially, wall text explaining the debate over their significance. Visitors saw "Government. Exhibit 2, David Greenglass (b. 1924), *High Explosive Lens Mold*, 1950. Pencil drawing. Courtesy of NARA—Northeast Region (New York City), *U.S. v. Rosenberg* (S.D.N.Y. 1951)"—along with wall text that read:

> David Greenglass quickly crumbled under FBI questioning. In what he called an effort to save his own wife, (who, in fact, he had unwittingly implicated) he confessed to passing atomic secrets during his army tour at Los Alamos. He drew these sketches of bomb parts from memory for the prosecution to use in the trial. When introduced as evidence, they were termed "like the drawings" he gave to Harry Gold and his handler, Julius Rosenberg.
>
> [Because the Rosenbergs' attorney didn't challenge Greenglass's sketches,] the jury never saw them at all. This legal maneuver has been criticized as a serious defense error because it allowed the jury to assume that the sketches were in fact "the vital secret of the atom bomb." Although the prosecution had listed many prominent scientists as potential witnesses for the case, none actually appeared on the stand to certify that the drawings were accurate and important.

For "Government exhibit 6," another Greenglass pencil drawing of a lens mold, the wall text read:

> The idea of using a lens to shape the explosive charges that could detonate a nuclear reaction was a novel idea in 1944/45. When Dr. Harold Urey, a Nobel laureate from the Manhattan Project and Philip Morrison, holder of a patent on the atomic bomb, saw the sketches in 1966 they thought them crude and inaccurate. Based on such appraisals critics say Greenglass failed to tell the Soviets anything valuable. Unlike the physicist Klaus Fuchs, Greenglass worked as a low-level machinist, removed from the most sophisticated experiments on atomic explosions at Los Alamos.

This section ended with one more Greenglass pencil drawing, "Sketch of Cross-Section of A-Bomb, 1950," and beside it, providing a stunning contrast, visitors saw actual blueprints of "Manhattan Project, *Atom Bomb, 1 & 2*, 1945, Declassified 1995." Of course the blueprints are dense and complex, and the Greenglass sketch is simple. The conclusion is inescapable: the government lied about the value for the Soviets of the Greenglass drawings.[32]

At the Historical Society's panel discussion of the exhibit, Ronald Radosh spoke from the floor during the question period. "As for the scientific evidence" of the usefulness of the Greenglass sketches, he said, Greenglass and Rosenberg "would have given everything possible to the Soviets if they could have."[33] But of course you don't usually get the death penalty for crimes you "would have" committed if you "could have."

The next section of the exhibit was titled "Lower East Side 'Commies'" and described the political context in which the Rosenbergs, the Greenglasses, and many others came to embrace "left-wing activism in the 1930s." The exhibit explains, "The Rosenbergs and their friends found much to admire in the Russian Revolution":

> Immigrant workers in factories pulled no punches in their denunciations of capitalism, as the Depression threw thousands of Americans out of work. Many New Yorkers spoke out for both workers' rights and the socialist experiment. Already as a teenager, David Greenglass delivered the *Daily Worker,* a communist paper. Ethel Greenglass (who married Julius) organized strikes and sang at political rallies and benefits.
>
> Many City College students joined the Young Communist League and hotly disputed how to fight fascism in the tumult of the 1930s. For example, Julius Rosenberg joined the YCL and the Steinmetz Society, where he debated politics with Morton Sobell, William Perl, Max Elitcher, Joel Barr and others. All were investigated in the 1940s and 1950s, as communist sympathies became a mark of suspicion in Cold War America.

This section concluded, "Russian sources now confirm that these men did work to pass industrial and military secrets to the Soviet Union in the 1940s." Photos of the central figures before they were arrested were displayed, along with more objects from the trial.

Then came a section titled "Death Penalty Doubts," where the wall text declared that "many New Yorkers" questioned the sentence on the basis of "the sparse and questionable evidence in the trial, the climate of red baiting, the seemingly biased rulings of Judge Irving Kaufman, and the many unsuccessful appeals to win a hearing on new evidence." The wall text reports that critics of the verdicts

> focused particularly on Ethel's death sentence. Government documents declassified in the 1970s show that the authorities hoped that the capital sentence for Ethel would pressure Julius to confess and implicate more spies. Observers noted that if the ultimate goal was more information about Russian intelligence operations, it made no sense to kill the people who might

eventually talk. No American woman had been put to death for anything less than homicide, since the 1865 execution of an accomplice in President Lincoln's assassination. The British courts only meted out a fourteen-year prison term to Klaus Fuchs who had actually confessed to giving precious atomic research to the Russians.

After a section on Morton Sobell's trial and on Feklisov's spying operation, the exhibit closed with two more objects. The first was an item introduced as evidence in the trial: a collection can found by the FBI in the Rosenbergs' apartment labeled "Save a Spanish Republican Child," from the period following the Spanish Civil War. The wall text explains, "The prosecution introduced it as 'proof' that the Rosenbergs were communists."

The final item in the New York Historical Society exhibit was a Remington portable typewriter similar to one Ethel had owned. The wall text reads, "Her brother David Greenglass testified at the trial that Ethel had typed his notes on the Los Alamos atomic bomb at her apartment. But in his latest statements to author Sam Roberts in *The Brother,* Greenglass said he does not remember her typing at all. The typing incident was the only overt act that linked Ethel to the spy work of her husband. Many analysts of the trial believe that without the typing testimony, Ethel would not have been convicted and sentenced to death."

The *New York Times* barely mentioned the New York Historical Society exhibit on the Rosenberg case (it published a 24-word listing after it opened), although it did run an 1,100-word review of another New York Historical Society show that opened at the same time, about panoramas of Manhattan.

Thus the Rosenberg case, which constituted a key episode of the Cold War, has been treated by museums in conflicting ways. Although there is no memorial honoring David Greenglass, who provided the key testimony that sent his sister to the electric chair—testimony he later admitted was false—the International Spy Museum in Washington, D.C., a popular private institution, presents the prosecution's view of the case. But it has been possible to organize and display a historically responsible and truthful exhibit, as the New York Historical Society demonstrated. It had the bad luck to open shortly after the 9/11 attack, and as a result got virtually no attention.

One more thing: how much did the Soviet spy ring help the USSR build its bomb? The most authoritative answer comes from Senator Daniel Patrick

Moynihan, vice-chairman of the Senate Select Committee on Intelligence: in 1945. Hans Bethe estimated that the Soviets would be able to build their own bomb in five years. "Thanks to information provided by their agents," Moynihan concluded, "they did it in four. That was the edge that espionage gave them: one year."[34] That fact belongs in any museum about spying.

ELEVEN

Mound Builders of Missouri

NUCLEAR WASTE AT WELDON SPRING

The greatest pre-Columbian archaeological sites in North America are the mounds built by ancestors of Native Americans a thousand years ago. UNESCO has declared one of them a World Heritage Site: Cahokia Mounds in southern Illinois, a few miles east of St. Louis. The biggest, Monks Mound, was apparently a ceremonial site with a large temple on top. It's the largest pre-Columbian earthwork in America north of Mexico—92 feet high and almost 1,000 feet long, roughly the same size at its base as the Great Pyramid of Giza and larger than the Pyramid of the Sun at Teotihuacán.[1]

Recently a similar mound was constructed on the other side of St. Louis, about forty miles west of Monks Mound: the Weldon Spring Mound, 75 feet high and 1,600 feet long. The difference, aside from the time of construction, is that the Weldon Spring Mound is not a ceremonial site; it's an official Energy Department "disposal cell" for radioactive waste products from Cold War nuclear weapons manufacturing. The radioactive material came from the plant that operated here in the fifties and sixties.

The site includes a million-dollar, 9,000-square-foot visitor center that opened in 2002, along with a hiking and biking trail and an eight-acre area of restored prairie featuring eighty species of native grasses. Visitors are encouraged to "go to the top of the 75-foot-high disposal cell to view the prairie in bloom."[2] Of course when they do that they are standing on 1.5 million cubic yards of contaminated material, including uranium and radioactive thorium.[3]

At Weldon Spring, federal officials have gone further than any other Cold War radioactive weapons facility to open the place to the public. Rocky Flats is completely closed to the public; at Hanford and the Nevada Test Site, only a few hundred people a year are allowed to visit; Wackenut guards on twenty-four-hour duty keep everybody else out. Weldon Spring is the opposite. They want everybody to come in.

Department of Energy officials described it as an experiment to see if openness worked better than secrecy to reduce public skepticism about the radiation danger from former nuclear weapons plants. "You don't tell people they're safe by putting a fence around something. Fences communicate a very negative barrier," said Pam Thompson, the Department of Energy's project manager at Weldon Spring, on opening day in 2002. "The quickest way to make sure people doubt you or question you or fear you is to lock people out."[4]

The new concept represents "a turnaround from the department's tradition of secrecy," according to Art Kleinrath, manager of the Department of Energy's long-term surveillance program in Grand Junction, Colorado. "There will always be people who don't trust us," said Jessie Roberson, the Energy Department's assistant secretary for environmental management. "We just have to keep providing them with information to make them feel comfortable." Opening day in 2002 was considered a great success. More than two hundred visitors "swarmed a new museum-like interpretive center," the *St. Louis Post-Dispatch* reported, and "dignitaries climbed on top of the gigantic covered mound."[5]

But anxieties remain among locals about site safety. The *Post-Dispatch* story about opening day was headlined "Radioactive Site Is Opened to Tourists"—even though the official message is that the site is not radioactive, that all radioactive material is buried underneath eight feet of clay, sand, and rock, that testing proves "the site is safe."[6]

When we arrived at the Weldon Spring Interpretive Center one hot Saturday morning, two docents were on duty—Karl and his wife, Shirley. The volunteer docents aren't supervised by the Department of Energy but rather by the private company that did the environmental remediation work here and now maintains the site, the S. M. Stoller Corporation.[7] That tells you something about the kind of information the docents provide. The only other people in the Interpretive Center were two parents with three kids. Shirley was taking them around.

Karl was waiting at the door and pounced on us when we entered. "I talk a lot, so tell me when to stop," he said, and led us over to the big map on the floor in the center of the room (figure 22). A lot of his spiel was about the

FIGURE 22. Tour group, Interpretive Center, Weldon Spring Site, St. Charles, Missouri. Instead of telling visitors about how the uranium factory here contributed to Cold War victory, the message is one of reassurance about the decontamination process. (photo by Center for Land Use Interpretation)

World War II TNT factory on this site; he barely mentioned the uranium factory or the radiation hazard it caused. We asked about his background, and he said, proudly, "I worked for ten years on the cleanup of the TNT factory." We asked about the monitoring for radioactivity, and he answered briefly that they monitor the groundwater.

Karl didn't really fulfill the mission of the visitor center, which is reassurance about the radiation danger that stems from Cold War uranium processing here. One display hints at the problem: at the panel "Weldon Spring Site through the 20th Century," the section on the Cold War is, to put it mildly, brief. In its entirety, the "Cold War" section reads:

> *1955:* As the U.S. involvement in the Cold War with the former Soviet Union intensified, the U.S. Atomic Energy Commission (AEC), a predecessor to the U.S. Department of Energy, constructed the Uranium Feed Materials Plant on 205 acres acquired from the U.S. Department of the Army [here at Weldon Spring].

1957–1966: Mallinckrodt Chemical Works, contractor to AEC, operated the Uranium Feed Materials Plant. The plant was a uranium processing facility, which assayed "yellow cake" (uranium ore concentrate), converted it into uranium metal, and/or shipped it off for further processing at other sites. The uranium processed at the Weldon Spring plant was ultimately used in both the nuclear weapons and nuclear fuels cycle processes. In December 1966, AEC ceased operations at the plant.[8]

That's not only brief; it's also not heroic. There's nothing about the conservatives' "good war" framework for the Cold War, about the sacrifices made by workers here that preserved our freedom.

How dangerous was the uranium processing to the people who worked here? Is there any danger at this site today? When you walk in the front door, on your left is a big display, "The Fundamentals of Radiation." It is relentlessly reassuring.[9]

The display begins, "What Is Radiation?" The answer: "Radiation is in every part of our lives. It occurs naturally in the earth and can reach us through cosmic rays from outer space. Radiation may also occur naturally in the water we drink or the soils in our backyard. It even exists in food, building materials, and in our own human bodies."[10] It's not only natural, and everywhere, it's also good: "Radiation is used for scientific purposes, medical reasons, and to power some submarines."

So far, there's nothing about the danger to humans from radiation. The next section is "Radiation and the Human Body." It says, "Eighty percent of human exposure comes from natural sources: radon gas, the human body, outer space, and rocks and soil. The remaining twenty percent comes from man-made radiation sources, primarily medical X-rays."

Still nothing about the fact that radiation causes cancer. But the next panel implies that possibility: "How does one protect oneself from radiation?" There are three ways, it says: "Time, Distance, & Shielding." Time: "If you decrease the amount of time you spend near the source of radiation, you decrease the amount of radiation exposure you receive. To imagine this, think of a trip to the beach as a comparison. If you spend a lot of time on the beach, you will be exposed to the sun, and, ultimately, get a sunburn. . . . This is similar to the way radiation exposure works."

But a single brief dose of radiation can kill you if it's big enough. The sun can't do that. Death from radiation poisoning has occurred quickly not only in Hiroshima and Nagasaki but also at Chernobyl (thirty-one died), at other nuclear reactor accidents, and from improper handling of radioactive and nuclear materials and ingestion or inhalation of radioactive material.[11] None of that is in the "Radiation and the Human Body" display at Weldon Spring.

The second way you protect yourself from radiation, the display says, is distance: "The farther away you are from a radiation source, the less exposure you will receive. Compare this to an outdoor concert. You can sit directly in front of a speaker or 50 yards from the stage or on the grass in the park across the street. If you sit in front of the speaker, you will probably suffer some damage to your hearing. Radiation exposure is similar." Yes, but if you knew that going to an outdoor concert could give you cancer, you might not go at all.

Third is shielding: "If you increase the shielding around a radiation source, it will decrease your exposure. For example, if you stand out in the rain without an umbrella, you will get wet. But, if you use an umbrella to shield you from the rain, you will remain dry and protected. This is similar to the idea of shielding in radiation protection." Yes, but rain can't kill you.

The word *cancer* has still not appeared. The next section, however, does raise the issue of "biological effects resulting from exposure to radiation." There are four possibilities, and of course we start with the good news. First, "Cells are undamaged by the dose . . . no negative effect." Second possibility: "Cells are damaged, repair the damage and operate normally." Third: "Cells are damaged, repair the damage and operate abnormally. . . . Such cells can be the underlying causes of cancers." At last, the word we have been looking for!

And there is one more possibility: "Cells die as a result of the damage." But "cells die" is not quite the same as a person dying.

Then comes the real question this site has been designed to answer: "How much radiation am I receiving at the WSSRAP?" (Actually no one asks about "WSSRAP," the Weldon Spring Site Remedial Action Project; the question should have been worded, "How much radiation am I receiving right here, from the mound?")

The answer is that the radioactive materials in the mound are "naturally occurring"—which suggests they are not the result of the manufacturing activities here. It's true that the radioactive materials at the site, including uranium, radium, and thorium, can also be found in nature.

Finally, how much radiation are you exposed to here at Weldon Spring? This is the point of the entire interpretive center, indeed the mission of the entire Weldon Spring site: "Walking to the top of the disposal cell and standing on the platform at the peak you will receive less exposure to radiation than you would receive standing in your own backyard." That's because of the clay, the sand, the crushed limestone, and the "geosynthetic liners," all of which act as a shield.

Final question: "What was the highest external dose received by a worker at the WSSRAP?" We've already been told in this display that the average American receives 360 millirem of radiation per year. The answer to the question: "The WSSRAP has had only a few worker radiation doses above 100 mrem/year, the highest of which was a total effective radiation dose of 192 mrem/year in 1996 during Raffinate Pit 4 debris consolidation." That's only half of what the average American receives, so the news is good.

That last section is misleading—in fact deeply dishonest. This information is only about workers' exposure during the cleanup. But what about workers' exposure during the operation of the uranium factory? Did any uranium workers here get cancer? Did any die?

The Rev. Gerald J. Kleba, a Catholic priest who has been a leading critic of the cleanup, called the safety claims made here "ludicrous." Kleba, whose church is in South St. Louis, wrote in his parish newsletter column at the end of 2005, "I was involved in the blessing of the monument to remember the people who died working for the government processing the uranium for the Atomic Bomb. Sadly, some of them died of the same rare dreaded cancer that killed Japanese victims." He went on, "In my prayer I mentioned the 'lies and cover-ups of our government.' Rep. Kenny Holshoff and Senator Talent referred to my prayer in their speeches. Two Republicans agreed with me in a ten minute period."[12]

So people died as a result of their work at Weldon Spring. That takes us to the "Tribute to the Uranium Workers," one of the thirty-one displays in the Interpretive Center. It's a wall of text behind a ten-foot-high replica of the St. Louis Arch. When we arrived, three cute kids were standing under the arch, smiling for photos being taken by their proud parents, oblivious to the panel behind them.

The "Tribute" display includes one large panel, a "Timeline of the Nuclear Age," starting in 1938 with the first demonstration of nuclear fission. Most of the events listed involve peaceful uses of nuclear energy for "medical diagnosis and treatment" and nuclear power plants, although it does mention Khrushchev's "We will bury you" speech, the failed Bay of Pigs invasion, the Berlin Wall, and the Cuban Missile Crisis—all reported telegraphically as facts without any argument about a struggle between freedom and communism for the fate of the world. Strangely, the Weldon Spring site is mentioned only twice in the "Tribute to Uranium Workers": "1957, operations begin" and "1966, operations end."

Visitors do read telegraphic entries regarding Three Mile Island and then Chernobyl, where "massive quantities of radioactive material are released."[13] The careful reader of the time line will find clues that Three Mile Island and Chernobyl weren't the only problems:

> 1999 July: The DOE and Secretary of Energy Bill Richardson acknowledge that nuclear weapons workers placed in harms way should be compensated for suffering occupational illnesses as a result of exposure to the unique hazards in building the Nation's nuclear defense.
>
> 2000 July: RECA Amendments pass and added two new claimant categories (uranium mill workers and ore transporters), provided additional compensable illnesses, lowered the radiation exposure threshold for uranium miners, included above-ground uranium miners, modified medical documentation requirements, and removed certain lifestyle restrictions.
>
> October: The Energy Employees Occupational Illness Compensation Program Act (EEOICPA) passes. This act provides a $150,000 lump sum payment and related medical expenses to workers who contracted certain diseases as a result of exposure to beryllium, silica or radiation while working for the DOE, its contractors or subcontractors in the nuclear weapons industry. Under the EEOICPA, benefits are also paid to qualified survivors of deceased employees and uranium employees previously compensated under the RECA.
>
> 2005 February: Special Exposure Cohort status is given to Mallinckrodt Destrehan Street workers (1942–1948). This status allows eligible employees with any of 22 specified cancers to be compensated without determination of radiation dose and causation.[14]

Twenty-two cancers? There's nothing else anywhere in the Interpretive Center that says the people who worked in the uranium factory got twenty-two kinds of cancer.

The "Tribute to Uranium Workers" includes an extremely brief history of nuclear weapons: with the beginning of the Cold War, "it fell to Mallinckrodt to apply the accumulated experience, that of others as well as their own, to the development and integration of processes for producing pure metal from ores. . . . In cooperation with Mallinckrodt chemists and engineers, and under the sponsorship first of the Army, later of the Atomic Energy Commission, new facilities were designed and built—facilities that have been the prototypes for others subsequently built. This is an important part of America's atomic energy story, and the story of a Mallinckrodt assignment."

That's the end of the "Tribute to Uranium Workers." There's no information at all about how many workers here got cancer, died from cancer, or received compensation from the government for exposure to radiation.

And the workers weren't the only ones who got cancer. People who lived near the uranium factory also had unusual problems, as Father Kleba discovered when he was assigned to work as a pastor in this distant suburb of St. Louis. "What he saw shocked him," the alternative weekly *Riverfront Times* reported in 2001. Kleba said, "This parish has more sick and dying children than I have ever experienced in my 35 years as a priest."

"Older parishioners described the thick yellow smoke that burned their eyes when the Atomic Energy Commission took over Weldon Spring to purify uranium for the Cold War," the *Riverfront Times* reported. "One woman remembered her aunt hanging diapers on the clothesline and furiously brushing away gray ash from the site's incinerator. The baby who wore those diapers, she added, got cancer in her 30s." Father Kleba found that "*everybody* said there was more cancer out here—also more miscarriages, birth defects, neurological problems, autism, ADD. . . . [P]eople used to joke that you'd glow if you drank from the water fountains at Francis Howell High School, just a quarter-mile to the north of the plant."[15] Kleba organized a parish group to campaign for an epidemiological study and to monitor the cleanup. Their passion explains a lot of the effort at reassurance on view at the Interpretive Center.

We stepped outside the back door to gaze at the mound. Shirley was there to tell us about the prairie restoration project. She started by asking, "Do you really want somebody cutting the grass out here for the next thousand years?" We tried to explain that we were in favor of the prairie restoration project, but she didn't stop: "The prairie should be restored to what it was before the white man arrived and screwed everything up." We were tempted to ask whether "screwing everything up" included the radioactive contamination at this site, but she moved on quickly to tell us some of the highlights of climbing the mound. "We had a guy in training who came out here and would run up and down the steps," she said.

FIGURE 23. Weldon Spring Site, path to the top of the radioactive mound. According to historian Jason Krupar, it "serves as an unofficial monument to the billions spent building and maintaining the country's atomic arsenal" and "a permanent reminder" of the "environmental harm, health risks, and the politics of the arms race." (photo by Center for Land Use Interpretation)

It was already in the upper eighties, and humid, but we could see tiny figures laboring up the mound. "That's the Cub Scouts," Shirley said. "They didn't spend much time with the exhibits. They wanted to start climbing." The wildflower garden, planted by a local garden club, was beautiful; the spring grasses waving in the warm breeze were wonderful.

The Energy Department emphasizes the wildflowers and the hiking and biking across the restored prairie—but there's another way to look at it. The mound "serves as an unofficial monument to the billions spent building and maintaining the country's atomic arsenal"—that's what the historian Jason Krupar says. It serves as a "permanent reminder" of the "environmental harm, health risks, and the politics of the arms race," as well as the secrecy that prevented the public from finding out about the work being carried out here—and the damage done to the people who worked here.[16] But you would never know about any of that from the Interpretive Center.

How do the modern-day mound builders attract the public to this Cold War weapons site? When it opened, Energy Department officials told the *Post-Dispatch* that the facility would "serve as a memorial to the nation's defense" during the Cold War. Department spokesman Kleinrath said Weldon Spring "gives you a place, a striking place, to talk about the history of the Cold War."[17]

But the exhibits here barely mention the sacrifices made here that conservatives say helped to keep America free in the fifties. Instead, they want people to come here to hike, ride bikes, and look at the wildflowers. It's like beating your swords into ploughshares but not mentioning the swords.

In the end, Weldon Spring is not a memorial to those whose sacrifices here helped bring victory in the Cold War. Instead, it's a monument to the cleanup. The message is that whatever happened here is over now; whatever danger existed in the past has been removed. We can forget about the Cold War, and instead enjoy the flowers. The view, they say, is best from the top of the radioactive mound (figure 23).

TWELVE

Cold War Elvis

SGT. PRESLEY AT THE GENERAL GEORGE PATTON MUSEUM

Elvis is America's most famous Cold War veteran. That's the message of the exhibit "Sgt. Elvis Presley" at the General George Patton Museum of Cavalry and Armor at Fort Knox outside Louisville, Kentucky (figure 24).[1] Elvis was drafted in March 1958, assigned to a tank division—the one formerly headed by Patton, hence the exhibit at the Patton Museum—and sent to Germany in October 1958. American tanks were there—thousands of American tanks—to stop thousands of Russian tanks from pouring through the famed Fulda Gap, a flat corridor between mountain ranges at the border between East and West Germany. Hannibal had invaded through the Fulda Gap. Napoleon and Patton had taken the same route. American strategists said the Red Army could do it too, coming through the Fulda Gap to take Frankfurt, the financial capital of West Germany, then the big NATO airfield outside of Frankfurt, then the rest of West Germany, and then all of Western Europe. As one tank commander explained, "We stop 'em here or not at all."[2] Stopping them was Elvis's mission.

The Patton Museum bills itself as "America's Premier Armor Museum," and Fort Knox was the home of the Third Armored Division—Elvis's unit—for ten years before it was sent to Germany in 1958. The message of the Patton Museum exhibit might have been that Elvis helped protect America from a Soviet threat to our allies in Western Europe. At the time, that's what Elvis himself said, sort of: he told the press he felt "sincere gratitude" for "what this country has given me. And now I'm ready to return a little. It's the only adult way to look at it."[3] America gave Elvis the freedom to become a rock 'n' roll star; and now it was time for him to help protect that freedom.

In fact the theme of the exhibit at Fort Knox was something less than that: Elvis, it said, was "the serious Soldier who did his duty." He could have spent

FIGURE 24. "Sgt. Presley: Citizen Soldier" exhibit entrance, General George Patton Museum of Cavalry and Armor at Fort Knox, outside Louisville. Elvis is America's most famous Cold War veteran. (photo by Vic Damon of 3AD.com staff)

his army stint in a special services unit, traveling around the globe to entertain troops. "But Presley didn't want it that way," the exhibit explains. "Instead, he spent much of his duty in a jeep as part of a reconnaissance platoon." Museum director Frank Jardim concluded, "He could have had a cushy life as a superstar, but instead, as a matter of his dignity, he just (wanted) to do his part like everyone else."[4]

The exhibit opened under a banner reading "Sgt. Presley: Citizen Soldier." At the left stood a big placard on an easel displaying a headshot of Elvis in uniform, the insignia of the division, and a poem, "Legendary Soldier," written by "Elvis's #1 Fan, Patti A. Tucker":

> A legendary soldier remembered by all
> Stood up and answered the call.
> A king, as he was known by his fans,

Now addressed as Pvt. Presley, a military man.
An oath he took one March day
To defend, protect, and diligently obey. . . .

That indeed was the official argument: the army sent Elvis and hundreds of thousands of other U.S. soldiers to Germany to "defend" and "protect" American freedom from Soviet attack.

The display features Elvis's uniforms, photos of Elvis on duty, and "examples of weapons and equipment Elvis would have used during his time in service," including a rifle, a helmet, a mess kit, and a serving of C rations—emblems, indeed icons, of the life of the ordinary soldier. One of the photos shows Elvis on a training maneuver with the Third Armored Division in Grafenwöhr in November 1958. The monthlong exercises Elvis participated in there required living in the rough and facing live fire, sort of like what they would experience if those Red Army tanks came pouring through the Fulda Gap.

But the Elvis exhibit at the Third Armored Museum at Fort Knox was not all military stuff. One big case displayed Elvis-in-the-army collectibles (an Elvis doll in uniform, an Elvis-in-uniform lunchbox), another featured the records and publicity released by RCA while Elvis was in the army, and a third dealt with the film *G.I. Blues,* a lighthearted musical about Elvis in a tank company in Germany, shot after he ended his tour of duty. Another case contained sympathy cards Elvis received after his mother died (he had been in training at Fort Hood, Texas, at the time). It was a pretty basic exhibit that included nothing about why he was there—no claim that he helped keep Germany, or America, free from Soviet attack—except for that one line in the poem from Elvis Fan #1.

A second exhibit about Elvis's Cold War opened at Graceland in March 2008 on the fiftieth anniversary of Elvis's induction into the army. (Graceland itself had been declared a National Historic Landmark in March 2006 by Bush's secretary of the interior, Gale Norton. "Graceland is one of the five most visited home museums in the United States," Norton said in announcing the designation, "and the most recognizable residence in the nation after The White House.")[5] The Graceland exhibit, "Private Presley," was similar to the one at Fort Hood, featuring army fatigues, dress uniforms, and photos, starting with Elvis's army induction, and then an exhibit about the death of his mother. His army footlocker was displayed, and also a shirt he wore in the film *King Creole,* directed by Michael Curtiz and based on a novel by

Harold Robbins, which was released while he was in Germany. (The shirt was red, but the film was shot in black-and-white.) The exhibit (which closed in 2010) also focused on Elvis meeting Priscilla in Germany, where her father served in the air force. The Graceland exhibit featured a set of bongo drums she gave him for Christmas there, and an army jacket he gave her before he left Germany.[6] Not mentioned: the fact that at the time they met, she was fourteen years old.

Neither museum exhibit explains why Elvis and the rest of the U.S. Army were in Germany in the late 1950s, what they were supposed to be doing there, or how "the Berlin Crisis" filled headlines in the United States during those years—the "context" beloved by historians. In November 1958, while Elvis was on maneuvers in Grafenwöhr, Khrushchev issued an ultimatum giving the United States six months to agree to withdraw from Berlin. What followed was "the Berlin Crisis."

But Elvis himself, and his fellow GIs in the tank corps, had some questions about all this—at least that's what one of his officers reports. William J. Taylor Jr. was Elvis's lieutenant and wrote a book about it, *Elvis in the Army.* Taylor is no ordinary fan-book author. He has a Ph.D. in international relations from American University and today serves as a senior adviser in the National Security Program of the Center for Strategic and International Studies in Washington. His bio says he has "appeared on major television and radio networks worldwide more than 1,200 times" and that he has published "more than 500 articles in major newspapers internationally"—as an authority on national security, not an Elvis expert.[7] He has published a total of seventeen books, including *American National Security: Policy and Process,* now in its sixth revised edition from Johns Hopkins University Press.

The officers, he writes, understood the importance of the unfolding Berlin Crisis for the American tanks in southern Germany. Elvis's unit, the 32nd Tank Battalion, "would be among the first units to take on a Soviet attack," Taylor writes, "and test our resolve for victory or death." The maneuvers in Grafenwöhr practicing for that invasion were massive—Elvis was one of sixty thousand U.S. soldiers who participated in Operation Winter Shield in January 1960. Taylor describes in detail the war games at Grafenwöhr a year earlier in which he and Elvis participated: they were "a graded test of our capabilities to operate in combat," in which another U.S. Army unit played the role of the "aggressor force," that is, the Red Army tank corps. "We were in full tactical," he writes, "meaning that we had to do everything the way we would do it in combat." And "the specter of Soviet battlefield tactical nuclear and chemical weapons worried me as much as anyone."[8] They also knew the Soviet tank force was considerably bigger than the American one.

But the enlisted men, poorly educated working-class guys, didn't understand that strategic situation. As Taylor tells the story, during a break in the war games, Elvis posed the big question: "Lootenet, what's goin' on in the world?"

"The minute he asked that," Taylor writes, "two or three other guys nearby overheard and walked over."[9]

"Well guys, things are mixed up right now," Taylor recalls telling them. "The Berlin crisis is not over, and our butts could be ordered into combat at any minute." But, he said, Germany was not really a Russian target. The Soviets' "main moves will be to force or convince people in parts of the world that are poor and backward to become communists and work with the USSR against American national security interests." He was thinking about where the next Korean War would be, and he didn't think it would be at the Fulda Gap. That meant the U.S. Army—and Elvis—didn't really need to be there.

Elvis, he writes, commented, "Shit, I don't think Americans even want to know about this stuff. A lot of people I know back home think I'm out of my mind doin' what I'm doin'."

Taylor, writing after the fall of the USSR, declared that "Elvis and his friends . . . may have sounded naïve, but they had it right. These guys reflected the mood of America's youth, who were on a different wavelength from America's elected officials. . . . Elvis and his friends sensed that America was heading in wrong directions, that older people were not listening to their concerns, that priorities were screwed up."[10]

Another officer who served in Germany with Elvis was Colin Powell. He wrote in his 1995 autobiography, *My American Journey,* about his time with the Third Armored Division in Germany in 1958–60 and about the Cold War and the army's mission there. He had been assigned to the division in December 1958 as a twenty-one-year-old second lieutenant and was participating in the training exercises in Grafenwöhr the same time Elvis was. He understood some of the big picture. "The Army's mission in Germany was to man the GDP, the General Defense Plan line," he wrote. "The line cut north-south across the Fulda Gap, a break in the Vogelsberg mountains through which the Iron Curtain ran. Every piece of artillery, every machine gun, rifle, mortar, tank and antitank weapon in our division was intended to hit the Russians the moment they came pouring through the gap."[11]

At this point in his narrative, Colin Powell asked the crucial question: "Why would the Russians be coming?"

Hardly any Americans asked that question in 1958; indeed hardly any historians asked it subsequently. Powell's answer: "I did not know; the answer was above my pay grade. But we assumed the assault could come at any time."[12] At the time he wrote these sentences Powell had been national security adviser to the president and chairman of the Joint Chiefs of Staff, so the question wasn't above his pay grade when he wrote the book. In 1958 he didn't have an answer to the question, "Why would the Russians be coming?," and he still didn't seem to have one in 1995, when the book was published.

Powell in 1958 did know one important fact: "Our strategists assumed that we were inferior to the Russians in conventional weaponry, so we had to rely on our nuclear superiority. All Lieutenant Powell understood of this was that we were thinly deployed along the GDP, and that once the Russians started coming, we were to fight like the devil, fall back, and watch the nuclear cataclysm begin."[13]

That story is not told in the exhibits at the General George Patton Museum or Graceland.

(Powell also wrote in his autobiography about meeting Elvis: "One morning, during maneuvers, we had come upon a scout jeep from another unit parked on a narrow road near Giessen. 'Hey Lieutenant,' one of my men shouted. 'Come on over. Look who's here.' I walked over to the jeep, where a grimy, weary-looking sergeant saluted me and put out his hand. It was Elvis Presley."[14] End of story.)

The Elvis-in-the-army exhibits at the General Patton Museum at Fort Knox and at Graceland feature photos of Elvis with female fans in West Germany.[15] The captions are generic, but the photos point to the fact that Elvis was becoming a significant cultural force in the Cold War inside Germany, East as well as West. While the West German government and media regarded Elvis as acceptable and perhaps even interesting, East German leaders described him as a threat. German Democratic Republic (GDR) party leader Walter Ulbricht gave a speech in 1958 describing the "noise" of rock 'n' roll as an "expression of impetuosity" reflecting the "anarchism of capitalist society."

"Anarchism" seems wrong; Elvis is often said to have expressed American freedom—which of course was precisely the threat to the GDR. East German Defense Minister Willi Stoph upped the ante, declaring that rock 'n' roll was "a means of seduction to make the youth ripe for atomic war."[16]

In April 1959, while Elvis at his house in Bad Nauheim hosted four winners of a "Tea with Elvis" contest sponsored by a West German magazine, Ulbricht told a cultural conference that it was "not enough to reject the capitalist decadence with words, to . . . speak out against the ecstatic 'singing' of someone like Presley. We have to offer something better."[17]

What they came up with was the Lipsi. It was an officially promoted dance, offered as an alternative to Elvis's rock 'n' roll. *Time* magazine in 1959 described the Lipsi as "a sort of double-time waltz," in which "the dance steps themselves looked like a mixed-up rumba, laced with old-fashioned open steps that led to a kind of shimmying amble."[18] Historian Uta Poiger describes the Lipsi as "a compromise. Its name with the ending 'i' had a modern, American ring," and she reports that "instructional movies, public dances, and band contests for the Lipsi" all had official sponsorship.

What made the Lipsi preferable for East German officials, according to Poiger, was that it was a couples dance rather than what they termed an "open dance." In the Lipsi, the man led and the woman followed, while dancing to rock 'n' roll did not require women to follow the male lead and thus promoted more gender equality, and also permitted more sexual expressiveness by women on the dance floor. In the East German dance halls of the official youth organization, FDJ, "there were signs on the dance floor stating, "Dancing apart is forbidden." The new form of rock 'n' roll dancing with couples apart "shocked, fascinated, attracted, and repelled" East German officialdom, historian Mark Fenemore writes. Even in a country officially dedicated to working-class rule, social dancing was "dominated by mock upper-class conceptions of etiquette," and the "elasticity" of rock 'n' roll dancers "contrasted sharply with the stuffy correctness of their elders."[19] But "in spite of enormous propaganda efforts, conducted by the Ministry of Culture, the FDJ, the Association of German Composers and Musicologists, and the GDR radio stations," Poiger concludes, the Lipsi "had only limited appeal."[20]

Indeed youth protests in East Germany specifically contrasted the Lipsi to Elvis. In 1959, Poiger reports, groups of adolescents in Leipzig suburbs gathered in the streets shouting, "We want no Lipsi, we want no Ado, instead we want Elvis and his rock 'n' roll." "Ado," she explains, was a reference to "a Leipzig bandleader heavily promoted by authorities."

The rebel youth marched through downtown Leipzig with a call-and-response chant:

CALL: "Long Live Walter Ulbricht!"
RESPONSE: "Pfui, pfui, pfui!"
CALL: "Long live Elvis Presley!"
RESPONSE: "Ja, ja, ja!"

Similar demonstrations by "Presley admirers" were reported in 1959 in Dresden and thirteen other East German cities and towns.[21]

Authorities in Leipzig and elsewhere cracked down in the summer and fall of 1959. "District court in Leipzig alone sentenced fifteen demonstrators to prison sentences of six months to four and a half years," according to an Associated Press report published in the *New York Times.*[22] In Dresden fifteen of the eighty participants in the demonstrations were put in jail. In Erfurt the police arrested ten members of "a gang whose idol was Elvis Presley." A police report claimed that "the group included 46 young men and 25 young women from 15 to 20 years old. Their leader was a young man of 17 whom the others called Presley." Key evidence presented in court: in the apartments of some of the women, police found "12 pictures of Elvis Presley."[23] Poiger found that, in at least 13 East German cities and towns, "'Presley admirers,' aged 16 to 21, had formed gangs of 15 to 20, among them girls; these gangs combined demands for rock 'n' roll with 'outrageous instigation against GDR leaders.'"[24]

In West Germany, Elvis became an even more explicit weapon in the Cold War. In April 1959, in the town of Steinfurth, Elvis was enlisted by the American military "to help overcome widespread German unease over the rearmament of West Germany." Elvis posed for pictures working on the construction of a World War I Memorial dedicated (in German of course) to "Heroes 1914–1918."[25]

Why was Elvis honoring German soldiers of World War I? I'm sure he had no idea, and this photo, obviously intended for the Germans, was not part of the exhibits at the Patton Museum or Graceland. The United States believed that Europe could not be defended against a Soviet attack without West German military participation, but, as historian Maria Hohn explains, the German Social Democratic party opposed West German rearmament, and many in West Germany were not reconciled to the U.S. military presence.

The unease was widespread in West Germany, and it had several sources. Some of it, historian Frank Biess explains, was simply pacifism. But resistance to rearmament also had a nationalist basis: many veterans wanted a new army but not under American/NATO auspices. And Germans also had a less tangible sense that German soldiers would not make any difference in a potential nuclear war between the United States and the USSR and that they might simply be used as cannon fodder for the Americans.[26]

So the United States undertook a variety of projects to "convert the Germans to the American mission," and one key effort consisted of public events at which the U.S. Army honored the German armies of the past. Eisenhower himself led this effort, declaring that he had "come to know that there is a real difference between the regular German soldier and officer and Hitler and his criminal group." West Germany established an official day of mourning for the dead of two world wars, and part of the American military strategy in Germany was to publicly participate in official memorial observances and to "treat Germany's war dead with the same respect accorded to U.S. soldiers." This involved wreath laying by American officers and also American construction of new war memorials to honor German soldiers. Thus the U.S. Army sent its most famous soldier to advance the cause of winning Germans to the American Cold War project.[27]

Let us return to Elvis's question—what was going on in the world that required U.S. troops to be preparing for war in southern Germany in 1958? The Soviets feared they would be the target of renewed German aggression. Germany had joined NATO in 1955, and in December 1957, the same month Elvis was drafted, NATO authorized the use of tactical nuclear weapons against the Red Army. At the same time the Bonn government demanded nuclear weapons for West German forces, although under NATO control. The Soviets wanted the United States to sign a peace treaty that would formally end World War II, fourteen years after the fighting stopped, and officially establish the post-Hitler borders of the states of Eastern Europe. They wanted the United States to recognize the German Democratic Republic. After all, the Soviets had formally recognized the Federal Republic of Germany in 1955, and expected the West to reciprocate.

Khrushchev's proposal was a reasonable one: the United States, along with the United Kingdom and France, should join the Soviet Union in signing an agreement that would recognize the de facto border between East and West Germany. West Berlin was a special problem, because it lay one hundred miles inside the GDR, with several hundred thousand Soviet troops standing between it and the West German border. Khrushchev's proposal was to make all of Berlin a "free city"—free of occupation forces, demilitarized and self-governing, with its access to the West guaranteed by the GDR and the USSR.

Berlin in 1958 was unique, a result of the peculiarities of the Cold War. As John Lewis Gaddis explains, in Berlin the Allies had frozen in place the supposedly temporary occupation arrangements set up at the end of the war. Thus the city was separated into four sectors, American, British, French, and Soviet. West Berlin had been turned into "a permanent advertisement for the virtues of capitalism" in the middle of communist East Germany, as a result of Marshall Plan aid, big subsidies from the West German government, and CIA-funded cultural centers and media outlets.[28]

The United States objected to a treaty providing formal recognition of the existence of the German Democratic Republic and argued instead that all of Germany should be reunified and given the option of becoming part of NATO—that is, an anti-Soviet military base. And the United States rejected the idea of pulling out of West Berlin, "removing from the heart of the Soviet Empire a Western outpost, glittering in prosperity and beaming out radio waves and TV transmissions of the capitalist promise," as Martin Walker writes. Also, pulling out "would close an extremely useful intelligence listening post." And, as Tony Judt suggests, pulling out would also encourage "neutralist, anti-nuclear sentiment in West Germany to grow." Of course Americans were told by Ike that the issue was whether we would abandon our "rights and responsibilities" in Berlin. (He said we wouldn't.)[29]

Khrushchev replied that if Eisenhower rejected the proposal, the Soviet Union would sign its own separate treaty with the GDR, giving it control of access to West Berlin. That would require the West to negotiate directly with East Germany, something the United States and NATO refused to do. At least one reporter asked whether Elvis's tank unit, the fabled Third Armored Division, would "move on Berlin" if the Soviets signed a separate treaty with the GDR, and whether Elvis would be part of the move. Elvis's captain, John Mawn, replied, "As to the division moving on Berlin . . . I prefer not to comment because it would be premature. If the division did make a tactical move or operation, the first priority is the mission itself."[30]

Eisenhower knew that the NATO tank divisions, including Elvis's, were no match for the Soviets, so he announced that the United States "had no intention of fighting a ground war against the massive Soviet army in central Europe," Walter LaFeber writes. Instead Eisenhower made it clear that "the war would be nuclear."[31] The head of NATO was quoted in a page one article in the *New York Times* saying the mission of the NATO alliance—and of soldiers like Elvis on maneuvers in Grafenwöhr—was "collective defense for the preservation of Western civilization." General Lauris Norstad said NATO strategy rested on "a forward wall, or military shield with atomic capability, in Europe and the will and determination of the people of the Allied nations to use these."[32]

The Berlin Crisis of the Elvis years neatly encapsulated the dilemma of nuclear weapons. Those weapons, as Walker explains, "were, in themselves, so destructive that they were militarily useless. They could not free anything, only eradicate it." But, according to war games strategists, they could not be renounced either, because that might encourage the other side to take aggressive action. And Eisenhower and Khrushchev each had military and political constituencies at home that they had to appease. Each faced the danger that intransigents or hotheads in the military might do something provocative—like MacArthur had done in Korea. So even though there was "no sign that Eisenhower or Khrushchev was ever seriously prepared to initiate the final step toward war" over Berlin, Walker writes, each was also "reluctant to be seen to back down at any point." In this situation, "it became almost as important to save the other side's face in a crisis as to save one's own."[33]

So Eisenhower invited Khrushchev to talk, and Khrushchev came to the United States in 1959, while Elvis was still in Germany. A "spirit of Camp David" emerged from the meetings. The Soviets stepped back from their demands regarding Berlin, and the Cold War cooled off. When Elvis left Germany in March 1960, the situation was more peaceful than when he had arrived two years earlier.

Then in May the Soviets shot down Francis Gary Powers's U-2, and Khrushchev, who thought of the U-2 as a plane that could drop a nuclear bomb on Moscow, set off a new Berlin crisis, renewing his threat to sign a separate peace treaty with East Germany. Soon Kennedy was president, and soon the Cuban Missile Crisis would lead Kennedy to conclude—erroneously, it turned out—that Khrushchev would respond to a U.S. attack on Cuba with his own move on Berlin. But of course that didn't happen either.

Was it really necessary for anyone, including Elvis, to prepare to fight a tank battle with the Russians at the Fulda Gap in 1958? That question was posed at the time not just by pacifists and old leftists, but by some of the most distinguished political thinkers of the era. A year before Elvis went to Germany, George Kennan went to England. The famed architect of the

Containment Doctrine delivered the Reith Lectures on the BBC, in which he suggested that American, British, and Russian troops should all be withdrawn from all of Germany, East and West.[34]

In a book based on those lectures, published the same year Elvis was sent to defend Germany from Russian attack, Kennan took up the question of Soviet intentions in central Europe. "The German question still stands at the center of world tensions," he declared, "and no greater contribution can be made to world peace than the removal of the present deadlock over Germany." As for the U.S. position—that Germany should be reunified and free to ally with NATO—Kennan said that "Moscow is really being asked to abandon . . . the military and political bastion in Central Europe which it won by its military effort from 1941 to 1945, and to do this without any compensatory withdrawal of American armed power from the heart of the continent. This, in my opinion, is something the Soviet Government is most unlikely to accept."[35]

As for the American belief that American tanks were required in southern Germany to defend against invasion by the Red Army, Kennan called the threat "over-rated" and said it was based on "a failure to take into account all the implications of the ballistic missile." Instead of basing American troops in West Germany, he favored demilitarization of both East and West Germany, and indeed all of Eastern and Western Europe, because it was "far more desirable on principle to get the Soviet forces out of Central and Eastern Europe than to cultivate a new German army for the purpose of opposing them while they remain there." Kennan's proposals, Brian Urquhart reports, "were as controversial as they were widely read."[36] Today they seem obviously right.

Elvis returned home from Germany in March 1960; a year later Walter Lippmann went to Moscow—to interview Nikita Khrushchev, "mostly on Berlin." Lippmann was the premier political columnist and commentator of the era, and his articles on the interviews were "required reading in foreign ministries" because of "Khrushchev's frankness on the Berlin issue." He told Lippmann there had to be an all-German peace treaty and a new status for Berlin before "Hitler's generals with their twelve NATO divisions" got atomic weapons from the United States.[37] That suggested he had a view of the West German army different from the Americans'.

Without a peace treaty recognizing the new frontiers in Eastern Europe, Khrushchev said, the West Germans would drag America into a war to recover their lost territories. Khrushchev was determined to seek a solution to the German question, Lippmann concluded, even though he "dreaded the tension" and hoped for an accommodation. Despite the "relentless determination" of the Soviets to promote revolution in the Third World, Lippmann concluded, they were definitely "not contemplating war" in Germany and were "genuinely concerned to prevent any crisis."[38]

What Khrushchev told Lippmann revealed the key to the Berlin crisis: Soviet threats were not really about gaining control over Berlin, or even winning recognition of East Germany; the Soviets' motivation was to keep West Germany from becoming too powerful, to prevent West Germany from getting nuclear weapons. A more powerful West Germany might intervene if another uprising in the East took place, as had happened in 1953. And the existence of a militarily strong West Germany would encourage rebellion in the East; that was the "war to recover lost territories" that Khrushchev was talking about. West German officials occasionally talked about that possibility openly. And Eisenhower's policy of building up the NATO allies to reduce American commitments in Europe certainly implied a nuclear-armed Germany at some point in the not too distant future.

It wasn't hard for Eisenhower and John Foster Dulles to understand why Russia feared a strong Germany. And as Marc Trachtenberg shows, by the mid-1950s both Ike and Dulles bitterly regretted the Berlin occupation arrangements that the Allies had made at the end of the war. They had never intended to support a city one hundred miles behind enemy lines for a decade. Eisenhower and Dulles now agreed it had been a mistake, an "error," "wholly illogical."[39] They looked for some way to bring in the United Nations to replace the Allied occupation.

And while the West Germans were unalterably opposed to East Germany controlling access to West Berlin, instead of the Soviets, the United States didn't necessarily feel the same way. Would it really mean accepting the legitimacy of the GDR to deal with East German officials over transit to West Berlin? Dulles himself, Trachtenberg reports, "doubted the practicality of total non-recognition of the existence of something which is a fact." And one fact was that "East and West Germany were not going to be reunified for a long time."[40]

Dulles himself, Trachtenberg shows, "did think there was a real problem of German power" and that the United States and the USSR "had a common interest in keeping Germany under 'some measure of external control.'" He insisted that the Germans could not be allowed to do "a third time what they had done in 1914 and 1939."[41] Thus some sort of acknowledgment of Soviet fears was justified and reasonable. But the solution for Dulles—and for the United States—was to keep Germany divided and to keep U.S. troops in West Germany.

The official line at both the Patton Museum and Graceland was that Elvis in the army proved he was a regular guy, an ordinary soldier, willing to do his duty and not ask for special treatment. Neither museum makes the argument that Germany in the late 1950s was a crucial front in the defense of freedom. So let us return to Elvis's question. What was going on in the world that required U.S. troops to be preparing for war in southern Germany in 1958? Colin Powell at the same point asked the same thing: "Why would the Russians be coming?"

The striking fact is that the European borders agreed to by Stalin and FDR at Yalta in 1945 remained unchanged for the next forty-five years. The world underwent immense changes between 1945 and 1990—the Chinese revolution, the independence of India and the rest of the colonial world, wars in Korea, Vietnam, and many other places—but the European borders, including the line dividing Germany, and Berlin, in two, did not change at all.

Change seemed possible at a couple of moments, when it seemed like the Soviets might seize control of Berlin—during the 1948 Berlin Airlift and then in the "Berlin Crisis" of 1958–60. And at the time of the Cuban Missile Crisis in 1962, Kennedy and his advisers were obsessed with Berlin and saw Khrushchev's moving missiles to Cuba as a disguised threat to seize Berlin. But as Judt shows, Khrushchev never had any intention of risking nuclear war over Germany—during the Missile Crisis, or at any other time.[42] It's not hard to conclude, as Chalmers Johnson does, that the danger of a Soviet-U.S. war in Germany never really existed.

Evidence for this view can be found in a surprising source: a National Security Statement issued by President George W. Bush and Condoleeza Rice, at the time his national security adviser. Released on September 17, 2002—just a year after the 9/11 attacks—the statement declared, "In the Cold War . . . we faced a generally status quo, risk-averse adversary." Chalmers Johnson comments, "These are words that could not have been uttered by the White House prior to the fall of the Berlin Wall in 1989."[43]

The words uttered when the Berlin Wall went up were of course quite different. Kennedy in Berlin said, "Freedom is indivisible, and when one man is enslaved, all are not free"—noble words that sounded to some like a rationale for war. William J. Taylor, Elvis's lieutenant, recalled telling Elvis that they might have to fight the Soviets in Germany because Kennedy was "sounding tough."

Elvis replied, "Well, he can sound tough if he wants to, but I'm tellin' you that most people I know don't want any more Korean War kind of stuff. I mean goin' around the world and gettin' killed because some politician wants to show how tough he is."[44]

Finally Elvis asked, "What the hell are we doin' this for anyway?"[45]

The answer he got was the conventional one: deterrence. But it's not the answer here that's significant; it's the question—posed by Elvis about the American troop presence in Germany. Sometimes the hardest thing is not to know the "right" answer but to ask the right question. Elvis did. It's too bad that skeptical American voice is missing from the museum exhibits about Cold War Elvis.

PART FOUR

The 1960s and After

THIRTEEN

The Graceland of Cold War Tourism

THE GREENBRIER BUNKER

"All wars end in tourism," Tom Vanderbilt writes—even the Cold War.[1] The most extravagant of all Cold War tourist sites, and the most expensive to visit ($30), is the Greenbrier Bunker, underneath the legendary Greenbrier Resort in White Sulphur Springs, West Virginia. Here, a five-hour drive southwest of Washington, D.C., behind a blast door that weighs twenty-five tons, all 100 senators and 435 representatives were supposed to take refuge during a nuclear attack. Here they could live for sixty days, continuing the work of governing the country: debating the issues, passing laws, and addressing the public—or whatever was left of the public. And here the public can now see how the government prepared to preserve representative democracy after a nuclear war.[2]

You check in for the Bunker tour at the concierge desk in the north lobby of the Greenbrier. The concierge can also help with arranging hunting (for pheasant and quail in the private wing shooting preserve), fly fishing (in a private trout stream), horseback riding (English saddle only), and of course golfing at the four eighteen-hole world-class courses. There's also falconry.[3]

The tour, originally restricted to Greenbrier guests, is now open to the public, and it's hugely popular: in 2007, 33,000 people took the tour, I was told by Linda Walls, manager of Bunker tours, who has been leading the tours since they began in 1995.[4] At the start of the tour visitors learn a little history: construction of the Bunker was begun by the Eisenhower administration in 1957 and completed just in time for the Cuban Missile Crisis in 1962. The Greenbrier staff kept its existence secret from hotel guests, and it remained a military secret until 1992, when the *Washington Post* revealed its existence and location. The hotel started offering a tour in 1995, and the lesson visitors are supposed to take home has two parts: the Greenbrier Bunker demonstrates the conservatives' belief that the United States could survive a nuclear war; and it conveys the message that our leaders were committed, even after a nuclear war, to keep representative democracy functioning.

On the tour, however, some skeptics inevitably speak out. One of them was Bill Geerhart, editor and cofounder of conelrad.com, a website devoted to Cold War popular culture. He's the one who called the Greenbrier Bunker "the Graceland of Atomic Tourism."[5]

The tour starts at the twenty-five-ton blast door—12 feet high, 10 feet wide, and 18 inches thick. It looks like the door to a bank vault, which it is; but unlike a bank vault, it can be opened and closed only from the inside. When all three blast doors were closed and locked, the guide explains, the people inside were sealed off from the outside world, with enough air for seventy-two hours—three days. After that, vents would be opened and outside air circulated—after being filtered for nuclear, chemical, and biological agents.

The guide warns visitors that when the door closes the sound will be loud. Inside the group heads down a 144-yard-long tunnel, lined with freeze-dried food packages. One visitor comments that, in contrast to the opulence upstairs, this part of the Greenbrier has "all the charm of an underground parking garage."[6] Halfway down the tunnel, the blast door slams shut with a huge boom, and everybody jumps.

The first stop, for the tour and also for members of Congress arriving after a nuclear attack, is the decontamination area. It's a narrow blue-tiled room with high-pressure shower heads at two levels and tight doors at each end. Since arriving Congress members might have been contaminated by fallout, they would have been required to strip before entering the working areas of the Bunker and submit to being blasted by the showers here. Then they would be given new clothes and shoes—Geerhart calls it "bunkerwear." He imagines "Bob Dornan passing the anti-radiological soap to Strom Thurmond, then Bob Dornan and Strom Thurmond dressed like extras from *Moonraker*."[7]

After "decon," the next stop is the physical plant, with massive generators, three 25,000-gallon water storage tanks, three 14,000-gallon diesel fuel storage tanks (enough diesel fuel to run the entire Bunker for forty days); lots of air treatment equipment, including the filters for nuclear, biological, and chemical agents; pipes and gauges everywhere; and two 175-ton air-conditioners to keep the members of Congress cool. It's impressive but hardly unique; Geerhart remarks, "Scaled down, this could be the basement of my old high school."[8]

The "pathological waste incinerator" comes next—a furnace with a big door. The guide explains that it is large enough to hold a human body and that it was to be used for cremating senators and representatives who died, presumably from radiation exposure on the way out here from Washington. It's a grim moment for everyone on the tour.

Then come the dormitories, eighteen rooms with sixty beds in each, surprisingly spartan. Geerhart calls them "army barracks for people who, for the most part, avoided the draft." Thomas Mallon, who also took the tour, says, "It isn't easy to picture Sen. Everett Dirksen and Speaker John McCormack sleeping like buck privates on these bunk beds."[9] And members of Congress didn't get to pick their own bunk beds; each bed had a nameplate, and it was somebody's job for the thirty years the Bunker was operational to keep the name tags updated as new members were elected. (The nameplates are gone now, so you can't find the place your favorite senator was supposed to sleep.)

Next to the dorms are lounges where Congress members could sit on couches and read magazines or watch TV when they weren't working. Since videotape was not available for home use until the mid-1970s, it's not clear what would have been on the TV sets here after a nuclear war in the 1960s. One visitor says the lounges "look like the waiting rooms in dentists' offices."[10] Another wonders whether it would really be possible to relax, given the circumstances.

Of course the Bunker has a big cafeteria, with a black-and-white checkerboard tile floor and white walls. The corridors contain dozens of cases of freeze-dried chicken a la king, chicken stew, chicken and noodles. If the residents had had enough chicken, a great deal of freeze-dried beef and green peppers is also available. The cafeteria has no windows, of course, but Bill Geerhart says he heard the walls were hung with pastoral scenes—in 3-D.

There's a hospital, but it has only twelve beds—for a thousand people. Each bed has its own TV. There's an operating room and a pharmacy. In answer to a question, the guide says the pharmacy was well stocked with antidepressants. If they didn't work, according to Paul Lieberman of the *Los Angeles Times,* the Bunker had "a tiny jail with two boxes of straitjackets." Lieberman reports that, on his tour, the guide—Mia Decker—explained that the straitjackets were to be used "if congressmen went bonkers."[11]

The most incredible room in the Greenbrier Bunker is the TV conference room, part of a vast media center with a wide variety of communications equipment. The heart of the TV studio is a backdrop of the Capitol dome—framed by some "seasonally adjusted" foliage. The plan is clear: after the destruction of Washington, D.C., members of Congress would give speeches and hold TV "press conferences" in front of this backdrop that made it look as if nothing was wrong in America's capital. This assumes, of course, that Americans were still watching TV after a nuclear attack—that they still had houses and electric power and that they weren't dead. Bunker manager Linda Walls tells me the assumption was that "large cities would be targeted but not the small towns," so that there would still be a TV audience out there.

But Geerhart points to another problem: "How were these broadcast signals supposed to reach the survivor(s) of World War III?" Walls explains that the Bunker had telescoping antennas in concrete silos that would be raised to transmit TV signals. Geerhart remarks, "Whomever the audience, this would have been the liveliest programming in C-SPAN history."[12] This would truly be a special session of Congress.

Assuming the antennas worked, who would serve as announcer for the Greenbrier Bunker broadcasts? Geerhart tells me that Eisenhower had already lined up Arthur Godfrey and Edward R. Murrow to come with him to the presidential nuclear bunker, located underneath Mount Weather in Virginia's Blue Ridge Mountains, to serve as his announcers in the TV broadcast studio there. You might think Eisenhower himself would have been an authoritative and reassuring voice of the government in a nuclear war, but apparently Ike wanted Godfrey and Murrow to "help calm the surviving audience," according to Ted Gup, who first reported the existence of the plan in *Time* magazine in 1992.[13] Geerhart says he had been fighting for more than a decade under the Freedom of Information Act to get the official documents about the plans for Arthur Godfrey and Edward R. Murrow.[14] Whether Congress had plans for its own Arthur Godfrey or Edward R. Murrow to broadcast from its own TV studio in the Greenbrier Bunker is unknown.

At this point in the tour Geerhart has a question: "Where the hell are all the guns?" He notes that "every bomb shelter worth its salt has to have firearms, and one would expect a multimillion-dollar government facility to have really impressive ones." The answer is that the guns are in the Congressional Record Room, "a restricted area," where visitors see a single gun rack that holds five rifles, five pistols, five nightsticks, and ten helmets—very little weaponry to protect all of the House and Senate. The official explanation, from Fritz Bugas, the former on-site superintendent of the Bunker, is that "the weapons were essentially riot gear and riot control weapons used for physically safeguarding the facility."[15] Safeguarding it from whom? "In the event of war or imminent threat of war," Bugas explains, "the idea of the weapons being here was just to have them available in the event that security personnel had to perform physical safeguarding and/or any sort of riot control duties."[16]

Apparently the weapons were to be used on the guests and staff of the Greenbrier, and also the local residents. All of them might try to get into the Bunker when nuclear war threatened. Walls tells me the weapons "would have been used to protect entrances of Bunker"; she thought that the biggest problem would be "locals who would know where the doors were located" and that it was not hard to imagine "a riot outside the doors of people trying to seek safety." It's hard to picture ten staff members with rifles and pistols fighting off local people and hotel guests before the blast doors were sealed, but that is clearly what the planners had in mind. Of course those taking the tour are mostly guests in the hotel, so this realization is particularly chilling.

Next stop is the House and Senate Chambers, which look like the real rooms in the Capitol except that they are smaller—but there are seats here for all 435 representatives and 100 senators. These rooms, unlike the rest of the Bunker, are open and connected to the hotel, and were offered (and still are) as conference centers to unknowing corporate visitors, who could select the "Governor's Hall"—that is, House Chamber—if they needed 440 seats, or the "Mountaineer Room"—that is, Senate Chamber—if they needed 133.[17] And the rooms were rented out regularly: the night the Cuban Missile Crisis began, Thomas Mallon reports, the Folding Paper Box Association was meeting in one of the rooms, and the Conveyor Equipment Manufacturers Association was meeting in another.[18]

If the Bunker had been "activated," the conference rooms would have been sealed off from the rest of the hotel by closing another twenty-five-ton blast door, discreetly disguised by garish wallpaper. If those conference rooms were occupied at the time by convention groups, the five rifles, five pistols, and five nightsticks would probably have been necessary to drive the conventioneers back into the unprotected hotel before the blast door was closed and the Bunker sealed.

Geerhart tells me that he asked Fritz Bugas a couple of additional questions: Did they have "booze on the premises"? The answer was "yes—to taper off alcoholics." Did they have condoms? "He said, 'No.'"

Throughout the tour there is the proverbial elephant in the room that no one mentions, not even Bill Geerhart. The plan was for 435 representatives and

100 senators to come here—without their families. How likely was that? If the missiles were on their way, would your congressman rather be with his wife and kids or with other congressmen? How would he feel about living safely underground, while his wife and kids either were incinerated in the blast or were dying of radiation poisoning and starvation? The senators and representatives were never asked the question, because the existence of the Bunker was kept secret from all of them except for the leadership. When the time came, they would have been told: there's a shelter waiting for you, but you can't bring your wife and kids.

Bunker tour manager Linda Walls tells me, "Remember that the Bunker was built to preserve the democratic form of government. It was not built to preserve the families of congressmen." She knows the problem: "So many people say, 'I would not have left my family'—but I say, would that be your decision if you had taken an oath?"

In the *Washington Post* article that revealed the existence of the Bunker in 1992, reporter Ted Gup raised this problem. Tip O'Neill, he reported, "recalled that, as Speaker, he received an annual briefing on the facility, but says he didn't pay much attention to it. 'I kind of lost interest in it when they told me my wife would not be going with me,' O'Neill said. 'I said, "Jesus, you don't think I'm going to run away and leave my wife? That's the craziest thing I ever heard of."'"[19]

President Eisenhower expressed the same sentiment in print shortly after leaving office. If nuclear war broke out and he found himself in a shelter without his family, he said in 1962, "[I would] just walk out. I would not want to face that kind of a world and the loss of my family."[20] And what if some members of Congress showed up at the twenty-five-ton blast door with the wife and kids in tow? Would the others have reached for the five rifles and five pistols to fight them off?

Travel time was another problem nobody mentioned on the tour. War planners thought our radar would detect a Soviet missile launch about thirty minutes before the target—Washington, D.C.—would be hit. The local Greenbrier airport was expanded in 1962 to accommodate jets, but even for jets it was a one-hour flight from Washington, if congressmen could get to the airports and if planes could take off before the missiles hit. If they couldn't or didn't want to fly, they could drive. The Greenbrier is a five-hour drive (or train ride) from Washington. If members of Congress got the word to evacuate and hit the road (or got on the train) immediately, they would still have more than four hours of driving after the missiles hit Washington before they arrived at the blast door. During that four hours, the crew that maintained the Bunker would be fighting off the hotel staff and guests and the locals. Would the crew be able to hold out for five hours if locals who knew about the Bunker showed up with their own guns?

So this plan has big problems. Planners at the time concluded that the only way Congress could get to the Bunker in time to survive a nuclear war would be if they were sent there hours, or days, before Soviet missiles were launched. But the departure of all of the House and Senate from Washington to the Bunker would have been interpreted by the Russians as evidence that we were preparing to launch our own first strike—which, according to nuclear strategy, would have required them to launch their missiles before they were destroyed on the ground.[21]

It doesn't take very long for most of the people on the tour to figure out that the Greenbrier plan was absurd. "I never put much credence in it, to tell you the truth," Tip O'Neill told Ted Gup. "I just didn't think it would work."[22]

The point of the Greenbrier Bunker, as Linda Walls told me, was "to preserve the democratic form of government" during and after a nuclear war. But when Reagan became president, conservatives planning for nuclear war decided to ignore the fate of Congress and focus instead on the survival of the White House and the executive branch. The Presidential Succession Act, passed in 1947, had established who would become president if the elected president and vice president died or became incapacitated: the Speaker of the House would become president next, then the president pro tem of the Senate (usually the majority party member with the most seniority), then cabinet officers in the order in which their posts were created: first, the secretary of state, then treasury, then defense, and so on.

But as the Reagan administration began planning for war with the Soviet Union, they worried that a nuclear exchange would kill much of official Washington and could easily make it impossible to determine who was the new president who would serve as commander in chief as the nuclear war continued. They called this problem "decapitation." The Reagan strategists were planning on a "protracted" nuclear war that would last six months, "with pauses for reloading silos and firing fresh volleys of missiles."[23] So it would be crucial to have a commander in chief, who could order the military to keep fighting—and perhaps even order them to stop.

Reagan therefore created three separate leadership teams that would be sent out of Washington to three different bunkers once an attack was launched, each with a cabinet member who was prepared to become president. If the Russians took out one team, another would be ready to take command. This was not just a plan; as James Mann reported in the *Atlantic Monthly,* the Reagan administration practiced it "in concrete and elaborate detail."[24]

The most remarkable thing about this plan is that the team leaders included Dick Cheney and Donald Rumsfeld. At the time, neither was part of the Reagan administration: Cheney was a congressman from Wyoming; Rumsfeld was CEO of Searle Pharmaceuticals. The two had worked together in the Ford White House and apparently were part of the innermost circle of power, even when they were out of the White House.

The big problem planners anticipated was how to establish the legitimacy of whoever survived as president—how to convince the surviving Americans, the allies, and of course the surviving Soviet leaders, that, for example, Malcolm Baldridge, Reagan's little-known secretary of commerce, was now "President Baldridge." Their solution was "to have the new 'President' order an American submarine up from the depths to the surface of the ocean—since the power to surface a submarine would be a clear sign that he was now in full control of U.S. military forces."[25]

But what about Congress, out there in West Virginia forty feet underground in the Greenbrier Bunker? Shouldn't they be involved in decisions about fighting, and possibly ending, this war? One of the planners told James Mann that was "one of the awkward questions we faced... whether to reconstitute Congress after a nuclear attack." The Reagan conclusion: "It was decided that no, it would be easier to operate without them."[26]

Mann told me the Reagan planners believed improvements in Soviet weapons by 1981 made it more likely they could destroy bunkers like the one underneath the Greenbrier, so the new continuity-of-government plan called for shifting the three potential presidents among many hard-to-identify bunkers.[27] Even if the Greenbrier Bunker wasn't destroyed, the Reagan planners thought it might take too long to replace members of Congress who had been killed. The Constitution requires that governors appoint successors to dead senators and representatives—assuming the governors survived and were able to find out which members of Congress had survived and which had not. Then the new appointees would have to get to the Greenbrier Bunker—through the nuked American landscape—and then get the survivors inside to open the twenty-five-ton door and let them in. It's not hard to see why the Reagan people considered this a problem.

And the Reagan planners had a bigger concern: if Congress did reconvene in the Greenbrier Bunker, "it might elect a new Speaker of the House," to replace the dead one, and the new Speaker's "claim to the presidency might have greater legitimacy" than that of President Malcolm Baldridge, or whoever had taken the reins under Reagan's secret program. They feared this would "create the potential for confusion."[28]

You might think that any plan for "continuity of government" in a nuclear war was something that Congress should be involved in formulating. But Ronald Reagan established the program not with a law passed by Congress but rather with a secret executive order. Within the National Security Council, Reagan named as "action officer" for the continuity-of-government program a Marine colonel who later became famous in another context: Oliver North.

The biggest difference between the Reagan continuity-of-government program and the congressional bunker plan was that, while members of Congress were never informed about their bunker (except for the leadership), the White House ran regular exercises practicing for war. Each of the three teams had members from the CIA and the Departments of State and Defense, as well as the president-in-waiting and his chief of staff. "The exercises were designed to be stressful," Mann reported. "Participants gathered in haste[,] . . . lived in Army-base conditions, and dined on early, particularly unappetizing versions of the military's dry, mass-produced MREs (meals ready to eat). An entire exercise lasted close to two weeks. . . . [O]ne team would leave Washington, run through its drills, and then—as if it were on the verge of being 'nuked'—hand off to the next team."[29]

The only reason we know about the secret Reagan program was that CNN ran an investigative piece in 1991 reporting on allegations of waste and abuse in the secret budget, hundreds of millions of dollars a year. The waste and abuse were mostly the result of awarding contracts for advanced communications equipment (to permit the three teams to communicate with each other, and with the military). CNN also reported that the communications equipment didn't work.[30]

So Tip O'Neill wasn't the only one who thought the Greenbrier Bunker was useless; the Reagan administration came to the same conclusion. For the

Reagan people—including Cheney and Rumsfeld—continuity of government in a nuclear war didn't mean keeping representative democracy alive. It meant continuity of executive branch control of the military, what Thomas Mallon calls "continuity for those with their fingers on the button."[31] But they don't tell you that when you tour the Graceland of atomic tourism.

FOURTEEN

Ike's Emmy

MONUMENTS TO THE MILITARY-INDUSTRIAL COMPLEX

The Eisenhower Museum in Abilene has one extraordinary exhibit: a display case containing an Emmy Award, along with the wall text "Eisenhower is the only president to win any Emmy—in recognition of his extensive use of television" (figure 25).[1] Next to it in the same case is a 1950s teleprompter that displays the lines "unwarranted influence, whether sought or unsought by the military industrial complex. The potential for the disastrous rise of misplaced power exists and will persist." But visitors are given only the briefest explanation of what this is about: the wall text reads, "Teleprompter scroll of Eisenhower's farewell address, broadcast nationally on television and radio, Jan. 16, 1961. The president's 'final thoughts' including a warning against the military-industrial complex."

That's it. Nothing else anywhere in the museum tells visitors that this is Eisenhower's most famous speech, or that it introduced the phrase "military-industrial complex" into the vernacular. Nothing explains what he was talking about. And yet Ike's Emmy could be regarded as America's monument to the military-industrial complex.

In fact the speech was a key moment in the history of the Cold War: a president who had also been the nation's top military commander in World War II warning Americans about the danger posed by the military and its corporate and political supporters. Ike was prompted to give the speech because of his disputes with Congress over the military budget. Yes, at the outset he had picked the militantly anticommunist John Foster Dulles as his secretary of state. He had okayed CIA coups in Iran and Guatemala. He had established Mutual Assured Destruction as the basis of Cold War military strategy, backed up with B-52s carrying atomic bombs in the air around the clock and Polaris submarines ready to launch nuclear missiles. But by the end

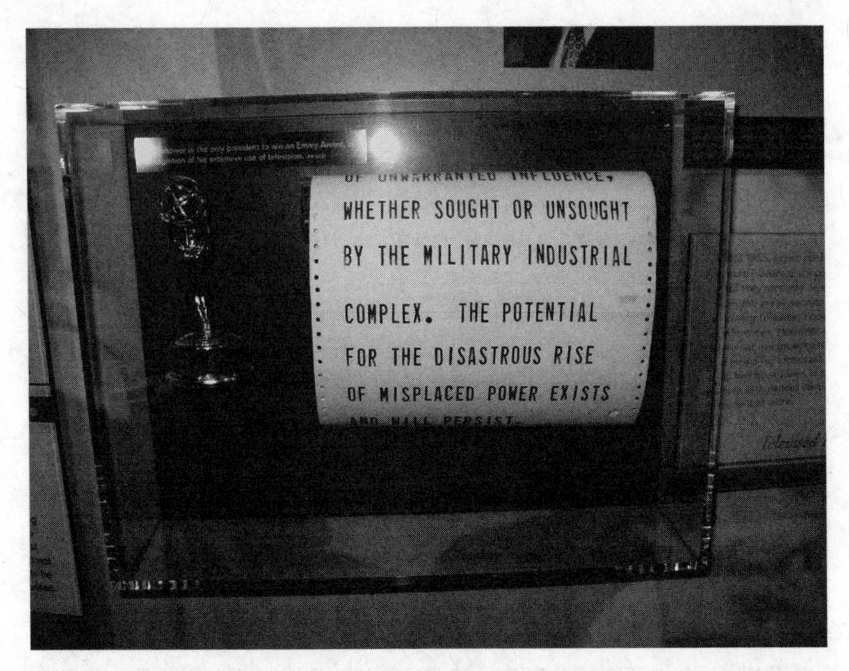

FIGURE 25. Ike's Emmy, Eisenhower Library, Abilene, Kansas. Eisenhower was awarded a special Emmy "in recognition of his extensive use of television." The library display includes the teleprompter text of his farewell speech warning Americans against the excessive power of the military industrial complex. (photo courtesy of Eisenhower Library/Nathan Myers)

of his second term, he had changed. He feared nuclear war and firmly opposed all talk that such a war could be "limited." He knew the USSR could never threaten the United States, which had invincible power. And yet his opponents in the Democratic Party, the arms industry, and even the military said he hadn't done enough—not enough weapons, not enough spending. The president-elect had won the 1960 election by frightening Americans about a "missile gap" that in fact didn't exist.

So three days before Kennedy's inauguration Eisenhower gave his Farewell Address, now regarded by many historians as the greatest since George Washington's. The warning was not just against unnecessary spending but against institutions that were threatening a crisis that would bring the end of individual liberty. "As one who knows that another war could utterly destroy this civilization," the president urged his fellow citizens to resist the military-industrial complex.[2]

Ike won the Emmy on display at his museum in Abilene because he was "the reigning master of television and politics": that's the judgment of Thomas Doherty, an authority on Cold War television. At the time Eisenhower seemed like such a natural for the new medium that the trade press referred to the TV set as the "Ike-onoscope." Doherty calls him "the first true television president, the man who provided a model for each successor." FDR of course had been a master of radio, and some of what Ike did with the new medium followed FDR's example—in particular, the direct address to the people over the airwaves. The Farewell Address is only the best known of these; some historians consider his 1954 talk, "The Multiplicity of Fears," his most memorable, in which he "played calm father to a nervous nation." Speaking from the oval office, he "leaned back casually, familiarly, against his desk, arms folded, and faced the camera nonchalantly" to caution Americans not to "fall prey to hysterical thinking."[3] The warning about the military-industrial complex continued that theme.

Not only does the Eisenhower Museum contain no wall text explaining the significance of the "military-industrial complex"; it does not display the historic TV speech on video. Nor does any other history museum in America, not even the Museum of Broadcasting in New York, which features a program on the Cold War on television. Other presidential museums display videos of other speeches; the Nixon Library in Yorba Linda, for example, runs excerpts of the 1952 Checkers speech, the 1960 Nixon-Kennedy TV debates, and the 1970 "Silent Majority" speech. But visitors to Abilene don't get to see Ike's Farewell Address. (The Eisenhower Library website has streaming video of Ike taking the oath of office; the Farewell Address is available only as audio.)

But video of Eisenhower's Farewell Address exists all over the Internet. Hundreds of thousands of people have watched it on YouTube and Google Video and elsewhere—many, many more than would have seen it in Abilene or at the Museum of Broadcasting "Cold War" exhibit. On YouTube the key two minutes have been posted at many different locations, which together have had more than a million viewings. Viewership has increased steadily over the life of YouTube.[4]

YouTube invites viewers to rate videos. More than two thousand have rated Eisenhower's Farewell Address, and virtually every one of them gave it five stars, the highest rating. YouTube also invites viewers to post comments on videos. Eisenhower's Farewell Address has received more than two thousand comments. People comment every week. A random selection: "Almost 50 years ago, and as true now as then"; "Our futures were long-ago decided in corporate board rooms. Eisenhower knew precisely where fear-corp was headed"; "He says it in plain English before the country on live TV. Yet so many stupid and foolish sheeple will deny it"; "The Last Republican with some Integrity!"[5]

And the video is not just on YouTube. One of the many other websites where you can watch Eisenhower's Farewell Address is militaryindustrial complex.com, which "exists to keep a record and tally of information that is publicly released by the United States Department of Defense." Following the theme of the Farewell Address, it lists contracts awarded by month and year; "Recent Contracts"; and, most interesting, a "leaderboard" ranking the "Top Grossing Names in the Business" since 2006. As of this writing—early 2012—Lockheed Martin holds first place with a running total of $145 billion, then comes Boeing with $100 billion and Northrup Grumman with $65 billion. After this section are buttons labeled simply "view the speech" and "read the speech."[6]

Eisenhower's Farewell Address is regarded as a classic today, but at the time it was a different story. The warning did not receive a lot of attention, in part because it was overshadowed by Kennedy's Inaugural Address three days later, with its potent "ask not" rhetoric. The *New York Times* page one story on the Farewell Address opened with Ike's warning: "President Eisenhower cautioned the nation in a farewell address from the White House tonight to be vigilant against dangers to its liberties implicit in a vast military establishment and a permanent armaments industry unparalleled in peacetime." The term *military-industrial complex* appeared only in the eighth paragraph, followed by the statement that "this warning . . . came as a surprise to many in the capital. A more sentimental leave taking had been expected from the old soldier." The paper ran the full text of the speech inside on page 22; on page 1 they ran the text of the prayer with which Eisenhower concluded his speech.[7]

The following Sunday, the paper's "News of the Week in Review" section ran a piece headed "The 'Military-Industrial Complex': An Analysis: Budget Is Key; Huge Sums Involved in Arms Contracts; Ties Are Close; Pentagon Is Friendly with Suppliers." Eisenhower, the piece said, "called attention to a problem that appears to have bothered him for many years." It concluded, "Few suggestions have been put forward to deal with the combined subtle, real but immeasurable influence of what Mr. Eisenhower described as the 'industrial-military complex.'"[8]

The day after that, *Time, Newsweek,* and *U.S. News & World Report* all came out with cover stories on JFK's inauguration. In the middle of *Time*'s long story on the inaugural events, full of photos of JFK in white tie and tux and Jackie looking beautiful, readers found a section headed "Last Days." It described how Eisenhower had spent the previous week, including the fact that he "greeted the last ambassador accredited to the U.S. during his stay in office—goateed Konan Bedie of the Ivory Coast." Only at that point did *Time* mention that "Ike also delivered his final presidential address to the nation. . . . [H]e summed up his own major disappointment in office," which was "the possible domination of Government policy by 'a permanent armaments industry of vast proportions' and an 'immense' military establishment." They did quote the phrase "military-industrial complex" but moved on quickly in the same paragraph to a longer quote about the danger to the university posed by government research contracts.[9] That was it for *Time.*

Newsweek's coverage was similar, with a section in its inauguration coverage headed "On to Gettysburg." Eisenhower's final week included, first in the story, coffee with JFK and Jackie, a "homely gesture," and, finally, taking off for his Gettysburg farm with Mamie. Only in the seventh paragraph did the magazine report on the Farewell Address: "There could be dangers to our liberties, he said, in the maintenance of a vast military establishment and armaments industry." It quoted the phrase "military-industrial complex" but moved on quickly to a section on Ike's sense of humor, headed "Lively as Ever."[10] That was it for *Newsweek.*

U.S. News & World Report provided the sharpest possible contrast. Instead of a few brief Eisenhower Farewell Address quotes inside a long JFK inauguration story, it ran a separate three-page piece devoted entirely to "Eisenhower's Farewell—a Prayer, and a Warning." The top of the page contained a highlighted box reading "President Eisenhower's parting words of warning to the nation—U.S. must guard against domination by a 'military-industrial complex.'" The full text of his Farewell Address was printed, along with a three-photo spread of Ike preparing to give the speech and then "after the address."[11] Thus whereas *Time* and *Newsweek* saw JFK as pretty much the only story, *U.S. News* judged the Farewell Address the big event. It's hard to explain the differences.

The term *military-industrial complex* did not appear in *Time, Newsweek,* or *U.S. News* for the rest of that year. But it did reappear in the *New York*

Times three months later. At the end of March, a brief piece on page 53 was headed "Drive to Expand Defense Persists; Eisenhower's Parting Advice on Undue 'Influence' Largely Forgotten." The piece reported on lobbying by the army for the Nike ICBM, and by Lockheed for a jet cargo plane, and described how widespread the benefits of the contracts would be.[12] The phrase appeared next in the *New York Times* two months later, in an AP story on page 48 under the heading "Role of Pentagon in Economy Rises: 10% of Labor Force Relies on Defense for Jobs."[13]

The fullest treatment of the concept appeared, appropriately enough, in *The Nation,* which devoted an entire issue in October 1961 to a historic article by Fred J. Cook titled "The Warfare State." The piece opened with an account of Eisenhower's Farewell Address: "He began with . . . the usual Eisenhower platitudes. Then abruptly, in midstream, he struck out on a new and decidedly uncharacteristic course. He picked this final moment of leave-taking, with the attention of the country focused upon him, to deliver a grave warning." The rest of the piece presented evidence that "events have served to invest his final words with the wisdom of accurate prophecy." Eisenhower, Cook said, had called for "a rear-guard action" to "preserve civilian, and democratic, control over the gigantic power nexus of our time, the alliance of a war-minded Military with a war-oriented Big Business."[14]

And the following year, in May 1962, the *New Yorker* ran a big piece by the now-legendary Richard Rovere on the same theme that opened, "For several years now, a bipartisan coalition that constitutes almost the entire membership of the legislative branch has been voting military budgets in excess of what has been required by the executive branch." Rovere described how the House spent exactly one minute in floor debate on a $13 billion military authorization bill, which then passed unanimously, and he reported on a half-billion dollar budget for a new bomber that the president and the Defense Department didn't want. "We may well be on the road to becoming a garrison state," Rovere declared, and then described "what is still the most memorable statement on this melancholy possibility, made by Dwight D. Eisenhower in his remarkable valedictory address to the nation. . . . With an uncharacteristic and wholly unexpected degree of emotion, he spoke of . . . the military-industry complex."[15]

During the rest of the decade, the term *military-industrial complex* appeared in the *New York Times* regularly, at least once a month. In June 1969, after Nixon took office and as the Vietnam War was peaking, the *New York Times Magazine* ran a big, six-thousand-word story by a staffer for Senator

William Fulbright, a longtime critic of the Vietnam War, that began, "Eight years have gone by since President Eisenhower opened the door on the military-industrial skeleton in the closet. Yet only recently has research started to hang some real meat on his bony, provocative phrase, 'military-industrial complex.' . . . [T]he conclusion seems inescapable that society has already suffered irreparable harm from the pressures and distortions created . . . by excessive military spending."[16] The term *military-industrial complex* introduced by Eisenhower in his Farewell Address was now part of the national language. And yet the Eisenhower Museum in Abilene has only the smallest display with the briefest explanation.

If the Eisenhower Museum doesn't really do anything with Ike's warning against the military-industrial complex, what about the other side? Is there a monument *to* the military-industrial complex?

One candidate for commemoration: Senator Henry "Scoop" Jackson, Democrat of Washington, who personified the military-industrial complex more than any other political figure. The "Senator from Boeing," as he was called, also represented the naval shipyards in Bremerton and the Hanford plutonium weapons plant. He regularly attacked Eisenhower for military weakness, even when we had the ability to destroy all of humanity a hundred times over with nuclear-armed bombers, missiles in Europe, and Polaris submarines. The idea that American military power was inferior to the Soviets' was false, and Jackson knew it; nevertheless the "missile gap" he and Senator Kennedy warned against became the Democrats' ticket to the White House in 1960.

When Eisenhower was drafting his speech about the military-industrial complex, he had at first wanted to call it the "military-industrial-congressional complex"—mostly because of Scoop Jackson and his allies in the Senate. "What Eisenhower denounced," Lars-Erik Nelson writes, "was a cabal that knowingly magnified threats, relentlessly promoted worst-case scenarios, deliberately belittled the military might of the U.S., and defamed opponents to promote spending on weapons that were costly and unneeded."[17]

You might expect a monument to Scoop Jackson at Boeing Headquarters in Seattle, but in fact the Jackson monument is located at the University of Washington Seattle Campus (figure 26).[18] It's a larger-than-life bronze bust of Jackson's head, three feet high. It was completed in 1984, a year after his death, but the university decided not to display it in public on campus

FIGURE 26. "Scoop" Jackson statue, University of Washington, Seattle. The three-foot-high bust portrays the Senate's most ardent advocate of Cold War spending, and thus provides a kind of memorial to the military-industrial complex that Eisenhower warned against. (photo courtesy of University of Washington/Mary Levin)

because of fears that it would be vandalized. The director of the School of International Relations, which had arranged for the piece, told the *Seattle Times,* "We kept it inside because the Cold War was on." According to the *New York Times,* the school feared that the statue "would become a surrogate target for protesters" who were "incensed" about Reagan's escalation of the Cold War in Central America. So the bust languished for almost twenty-five years in a campus building where students were unlikely to see it. It was moved outside only in 2006, long after the Cold War had ended.[19]

A plaque on the side of the bust says only that Scoop Jackson "gained acclaim as an expert in important regional topics such as . . . military affairs."[20] There's also a Jackson Foundation, but it doesn't mention his work on behalf of nuclear overkill. It is dedicated, not to advancing the military-industrial complex, but to human rights, the environment, and public service.[21] Apparently those in charge of the public memory of Scoop Jackson don't want to remember much about his role in provoking Eisenhower's warning.

There's another candidate for a monument to the military-industrial complex: the "boneyard" outside Tucson, where the air force has parked 4,400 surplus military planes. As "boneyard" suggests, its purpose originally was "storage and disposal" of the most gleaming and expensive products of the military-industrial complex. But now it claims a capacity for "regeneration," hence its current official name, the 309th Aerospace Maintenance and Regeneration Center (AMARC).[22] It's here because the dry hot air prevents the thousands of old planes from turning to rust. But locals don't see much "regeneration": "It's where airplanes go to die," the clerk at our hotel desk explained.

You can take a bus tour of the boneyard, courtesy of the Pima Air and Space Museum, a private organization with several hangars of old planes next to the Davis-Monthan Air Force Base, where the boneyard is located.[23] The bus has air-conditioning, a lifesaver in the summer months in Tucson. Our guide, Bill, promises that we will see "virtually every aircraft used in the Korean War and Vietnam," as well as subsequent wars—more than four thousand planes, Bill says, the cost $27 billion. A couple of people on our tour bus were Vietnam-era pilots or aircraft support personnel; they are enthusiastic and engaged. "These are the birds that I worked on during the fifties and sixties," one guy says. Bill is happy to hear it.

For us, however, the tour is at first boring, then increasingly oppressive. Here, from the Korean War, Bill says, is the F-86 Sabrejet, the famous single-seat, single-engine fighter that beat the MIG-15. Bill says it carried six half-inch Browning machine guns that fired at a rate of 1,200 rounds per minute. In Korea, Bill says, only seventy-eight F-86s were lost in combat, and they scored 792 victories over MIGs.[24] My seat-mate murmurs, "And we still lost."

Then: here's the Lockheed F-80 Shooting Star. . . . Here's the Boeing B-29 bomber. . . . Here's the Republic F-84 Thunderjet. . . . Here are the Vietnam planes, the A-4E Skyhawk, the plane John McCain was flying when he was shot down and taken as a prisoner of war and held for six years and tortured. Here are the Vietnam helicopters. Here's a B-1 bomber. The bus goes up and down aisle after aisle of abandoned warplanes; thousands of planes. For dozens of models, Bill tells us the key stats and a bit about their military glory. It takes an hour and a half.

At the halfway point, Bill explains why this place is called the boneyard: the aircraft on half of the base will never fly again. Bill says that's not just a lot of scrap metal out there; it's actually a huge outdoor warehouse of surplus parts that help keep other planes flying. This place, he says, "saves taxpayers millions of dollars every year."

When we get to the B-52, Bill tells us that it was America's greatest nuclear bomber for almost fifty years, built of course by Boeing. Up close it is immense. He says it has a wingspan of 185 feet, a length of 160 feet, and weighed nearly 220 tons at full load. He says eight Pratt and Whitney jet engines mounted in pairs gave it a top speed of 650 miles per hour, with a top altitude of 50,000 feet and a range of 8,800 miles without being refueled. Bill says it began active service in 1955, patrolling the skies for the Strategic Air Command continuously for more than a decade, ready to drop nuclear bombs on Russia in retaliation for a Soviet attack.

He doesn't say that the B-52s in Vietnam engaged in carpet bombing, the practice of targeting an entire region for complete destruction—all the inhabitants, civilian as well as military, as well as all the houses and also the animals. He doesn't talk about the most horrifying B-52 raids, the Christmas bombing of Hanoi in 1972, when B-52s flew 729 sorties over twelve days, dropping 15,237 tons of bombs—the most brutal attacks on civilian targets since Hiroshima. The Christmas bombing killed thousands of Vietnamese, but it didn't make them surrender. They won the war anyway. Bill doesn't mention that.

Bill does explain why some of the B-52s here are in three huge pieces: this is in compliance with the 1991 Strategic Arms Reduction Treaty, in which the United States agreed with Russia to reduce the total number of heavy bombers (as well as ICBMs and submarine launched missiles). "AMARC was given the awesome task of disposing of 365 of these magnificent aircraft," Bill says. They used a 13,500-pound guillotine blade to chop the wings and tail off each B-52. The parts had to be visible to Russian satellite surveillance cameras.

Thus, although Eisenhower's warning against the military-industrial complex constitutes one of the key moments in the history of the Cold War, it has received little attention in the official repositories of public memory. The video of the speech at the unofficial site YouTube, on the other hand, reveals just how widespread is the popular interest in Eisenhower's address. The Eisenhower Museum displays the teleprompter scroll from his address but doesn't explain the meaning or significance of the speech. The search for an argument for the other side, a monument to the military-industrial complex, led us to two candidates: the statue of Scoop Jackson at the University of Washington in Seattle and the "boneyard" outside Tucson, open to the public, where four square miles of desert are filled with thousands of old military jets, gone there to die. The boneyard does qualify as America's monument to the military-industrial complex. It's a memorial—albeit an unintentional one—to what Eisenhower called "the disastrous rise of misplaced power," to waste and futility—and, with the obsolete B-52s of the Vietnam War, a monument to something much worse.

FIFTEEN

The Fallout Shelters of North Dakota

North Dakota stood "on the front lines of a global Cold War" in the 1950s—that's the surprising argument made by the exhibit "The Atomic Age Arrives: North Dakota and the Cold War" at the State Historical Society Heritage Center across the street from the state capitol in Bismarck. People in North Dakota in the 1950s—the state had only 632,000 residents in 1960—apparently believed they were at the top of the Soviets' list of targets. That's because North Dakota was one of the states closest to the USSR for planes or missiles flying over the pole. And that is why the air force built two new bases for nuclear bombers as well as nuclear missile silos—150 of them—in the state.

Perhaps the exhibit exaggerates the significance of North Dakota in Cold War history, but it's not wrong to think that Soviet nuclear war strategy required a preemptive attack on the bomber bases and missile sites in the state. Indeed, the exhibit includes an incredible map, "Soviet Nuclear Weapons Targets in North Dakota," with a tiny hammer and sickle for each target, and there are at least 152.[1] So North Dakota thought it needed fallout shelters. And that's why the State Historical Society has an exhibit centered on a reconstructed North Dakota fallout shelter (figure 27).

The home fallout shelter provides the most vivid and compelling image of Cold War anxiety in postwar America. According to conservative ideology, our enemy was preparing to fight a new kind of war. They were making our civilians into targets, threatening ordinary Americans with weapons much more powerful than the bombs we dropped on Hiroshima and Nagasaki. No matter how strong the U.S. Armed Forces might be, they would be unable to stop all the Soviet bombers carrying atomic bombs. Thus Americans were told that, in the event of an attack, "some will get through to your home."[2] But the government-sponsored Civil Defense program, in partnership with

FIGURE 27. Fallout shelter in "The Atomic Age Arrives: North Dakota and the Cold War" exhibit at the State Historical Society Heritage Center in Bismarck, North Dakota. The home fallout shelter provides the most vivid and compelling image of Cold War anxiety in postwar America—although this one is spacious and well lit. (State Historical Society of North Dakota, photo by Mike Frohlich)

ordinary Americans, would prevent a Soviet victory and preserve the American way of life.

The key to victory in a nuclear war, in this view, could not be mass bomb shelters of the London-in-the-Blitz variety. Suburbia made that impossible. Instead, victory required a grassroots effort in which individual families would build their own individual fallout shelters and prepare for their own survival—a uniquely American solution that combined an entrepreneurial can-do spirit with the self-help and self-reliance that had always been hallmarks of American culture.[3] The fallout shelter demonstrated the determination of ordinary Americans to survive Soviet attack and thus constituted a key element in America's victory in the Cold War. That was the idea. You'd think it would provide a popular subject for exhibits on the 1950s. But fallout shelter exhibits are few and far between. I couldn't find any in New York or Chicago or L.A. One of the few can be found in Bismarck.[4]

Mark Halvorson of the State Historical Society explained on a local TV news broadcast that the exhibit answered the question, what was a fallout shelter like? "We have artifacts from a particular family in Jamestown, North Dakota," he said, explaining that the family kept their shelter intact, and "apparently they never cleaned it up and threw out stuff—and were kind enough to give it to us for a reconstruction based on plans that were available."[5]

I asked Genia Hesser, curator of exhibits at the State Historical Society of North Dakota, where they got their fallout shelter. She said it had been built by Francis E. Murphy, who was not exactly your average North Dakotan: he "served as the Governor's Disaster Chairman and was a Civil Defense director for the city of Jamestown and Stutsman County. He built the shelter in 1962 at a cost of $400. He gave tours of the shelter to interested people in the hope of encouraging them to build their own." His son donated the shelter's contents to the state in 2003—forty-nine items—along with a description of how it was constructed. That description is included in the exhibition text.

Visitors to the exhibit see a concrete-block basement room with two cots, a card table and two folding chairs, shelves with canned food and water, a lantern, a first aid kit, a wooden puzzle to keep the kids occupied, a radio, and a mysterious pink phone—the basics (except for the phone). Since this was in the basement of a house, there's plenty of room. The exhibit includes three panels of text, but notably absent are explanations of the larger significance of the shelter program for Cold War victory: "Groups such as the Boy Scouts, Girl Scouts, 4-H, and others encouraged people to be prepared for a communist attack. . . . These optimistic survival plans did not tell people that if a nuclear bomb exploded close by, those in fallout shelters would be incinerated or, if they survived the blast, they would die from radioactive fallout." Another panel reported that "a five-megaton blast would be 250 times more powerful than the bomb dropped on Nagasaki." You might call the exhibit text more of a critique of the conservative interpretation. Thus the exhibit in Bismarck shows what a fallout shelter was like, and explains why it was useless.

Other fallout shelter exhibits make different points. Rogers, Arkansas, had "The Life Atomic: Growing up in the Shadow of the A-Bomb." Running for six months in 2008, the exhibit at the Rogers Historical Museum (which has the motto "Real people, real stories, real history!") tells "the story of growing up in our community during the early years of the atomic age." (Rogers is in the northwest corner of Arkansas, south of Missouri and east of Oklahoma, next to Bentonville, the world headquarters of Wal-Mart.) The museum explains, "Although there were no targets for direct nuclear attack near Rogers, Arkansas, prevailing winds from a significant number of targets in Oklahoma were likely to carry fallout over much of Northwest Arkansas." The targets in Oklahoma are not specified—but Rogers is downwind from Tulsa, and Tulsa during the 1950s built B-47 Stratojets, the first generation of Cold War bombers designed to fly great distances with a nuclear payload.[6]

The Rogers museum explains that in 1962 the city "designated two downtown buildings as community fallout shelters." Question: downtown Rogers? The town's population in 1960 was 5,700.[7] It was unusual to find community shelters in a federal program that emphasized individual family shelters. Even more unusual, "the unique geology of Northwest Arkansas also provided alternatives to traditional basement fallout shelters. The profusion of limestone caves in the region led planners to designate several of these dank caverns as shelters."[8]

But the Rogers fallout shelter display is not about caves or "downtown" shelters; it portrays instead the familiar family shelter: in this case, a closet-sized, cement-block room with a single bed, a small table and chair, and a couple of shelves with the usual canned food on display, along with a bedpan on a crate and a garbage can with rolls of toilet paper. The local newspaper described the "doom and despair emanating from the museum's fallout shelter" and pointed out that tranquilizers were recommended for shelter inhabitants. Visitors were informed that families were told to stay in their shelters for two weeks after a nuclear attack; after that, apparently, they thought life in Rogers would be okay.

In an interview with the local newspaper, museum director Gaye Bland did not support the conservative interpretation. He wanted people in Rogers to know that the shelter construction program of the 1960s was not really successful. He remembered being a kid in town in the fifties, when "the government was telling everyone to take precautions, but there were a lot of people who didn't follow through." "There were only a handful of people around us who built fallout shelters, and there weren't any in my neighborhood," he said. "I can remember my mom needling my dad to build a fallout shelter. But after she saw a few movies that were put out, she was convinced nothing anyone did to prepare was going to save them anyway. There were a lot of people like that."[9]

The museum director in Rogers, Arkansas, was making a crucial point: the fallout shelter construction program was a massive failure. And not just in Rogers; Americans everywhere overwhelmingly rejected the government initiatives that urged privately constructed individual shelters. The House Military Operations Subcommittee surveyed state and local civil defense directors and came up with what historian Laura McEnaney rightly calls "a shockingly low statistic": thirty-five states and sixty-six cities reported a total of only 1,565 home shelters, "roughly one shelter for every 100,000 Americans." A second measure of fallout shelter construction can be found in the Civil Defense program's "This Home Is Prepared"—a window sticker distributed to housewives who certified that they had implemented the twenty items on a preparedness checklist. Only 40,000 people in the entire United States—of a total population of 180 million—had earned the "This Home Is Prepared" window sticker by 1960. Civil Defense officials came up with their own estimate: one million family shelters. But even that would protect less than one percent of the population.[10]

What explains the failure of Americans to build fallout shelters? McEnaney argues that Eisenhower's policies and persona were a key factor: his "peace and prosperity" message, along with his reassurances that a policy of American nuclear retaliation would prevent a Soviet nuclear attack, created confidence that undercut the anxiety necessary for people to build their own shelters. Whatever the explanation, the failure of the fallout shelter program provides a powerful refutation of the conservative interpretation emphasizing its contribution to Cold War victory.

In addition to the exhibits in North Dakota and Arkansas, there have been a couple of fallout shelter exhibits that made significant points, if only briefly. In Madison, Wisconsin, the State Historical Museum featured a fallout shelter display for six months in 1997. The exhibit, "Living under a Mushroom Cloud: Fear and Hope in the Atomic Age," was centered on a re-creation of one particular home fallout shelter built in Racine, Wisconsin, in 1959: "When Paul and Edith Sobel built their home in Racine, they worried that nearby Chicago would be the target of an atomic bomb. Determining that the fallout might drift to their city, the Sobels decided to construct a fallout shelter in their house." Their shelter, built in the basement, was "a 10'-by-8' room meant to house a family of five for two weeks. It included an 18"-thick cement ceiling, walls of solid concrete block painted a cheerful color, and a second wall or baffle outside the door to protect the occupants from radiation." Their supplies "remained in the shelter until 1996, when the State Historical Society of Wisconsin added them to its collections," and displayed them in the re-created fallout shelter in the museum the following year.

This fallout shelter had a couch with a sleeping shelf above it, gas lanterns, a portable toilet, and a trash can. The supplies included gallon cans of something labeled "MPF"—"Multi-Purpose Food, protein-rich granules fortified with vitamins and minerals—precooked, ready to use," and prominently displaying the General Mills trademark. The wall text explained that "survival manuals assured people that after two weeks they could emerge from their shelters and eventually return to their normal lives. Infrastructures, such as water mains, roads, and electrical wires, were expected to remain undamaged or be easily repairable."[11] One visitor said, "Oh, you mean like Hiroshima?"

Another fallout shelter exhibit, now closed, was featured at the University of California, Santa Barbara, art museum: "Nuclear Families: The Home Fallout Shelter Movement in California, 1950–1969," which was up for a mere two months in 2002. This one focused on the architecture of "elaborate California home fallout shelters" designed in the 1950s by two notable architects, Robert Stacy-Judd and Paul Laszlo. Laszlo, a Hungarian immigrant, designed glamorous homes for Hollywood celebrities, including Cary Grant and Barbara Stanwyck, but the curators found sketches for a planned community he called "Atomville USA," in which underground structures were connected by cable cars in tunnels. Apparently he tried to sell the idea to the Pentagon but was rejected. In the meantime, he got a more prosaic commission to build a fallout shelter for a home in suburban Woodland Hills. His design featured luxury elements and a drip coffeemaker—not because he thought it could be powered after a nuclear attack on Los Angeles but because, as he assured his clients, "If the bomb never drops, you can use the shelter as an extra room for guests . . . or another entertaining area!"[12]

There's one more notable bomb shelter: outside Northampton, Massachusetts, a 40,000-square-foot bunker is buried forty feet below ground. This huge structure was built in the mid-1960s to protect one person, Julie Nixon, who at the time was a student at nearby Smith College. The aboveground part of the building today houses Chesterfield Custom, a manufacturer of "quality vinyl organizing and filing products." Frank Keefe, the company's chief executive, told the *New York Times* in 2007 about the bunker and its purpose. (Julie was at Smith when Nixon became president in January 1969.) Of course forty feet underground makes this more than a fallout shelter; it would provide protection from a nuclear blast directly overhead. Apparently Nixon believed that the Soviets would aim a missile at Julie—and that it might be accurate enough to hit Smith College. So Julie needed to be forty feet underground—while the rest of Smith College was incinerated.

The *New York Times* Travel section invited readers to "drive by 11 Bofat Hill Road, off East Street (Chesterfield Road), to judge for yourself."[13] I wrote Frank Keefe asking if it was possible for the public to visit the bunker. He did not reply. So one of America's biggest and best bomb shelters is apparently not open to the public.

Ask any guard at the National Museum of American History (NMAH) in Washington, D.C., "Where's the fallout shelter?," and they all know the answer: "That would be on the second floor." Of course they're talking about the exhibit, not an actual shelter. The most important American history museum in the country, part of the Smithsonian Institution, displays what is frankly an amazing object: a "free-standing, double-hulled steel shelter," which looks more like a tiny submarine than the usual concrete-block basement room (figure 28). It is a genuine artifact of the fifties, "installed beneath the front yard of Mr. and Mrs. Murland E. Anderson of Ft. Wayne, Indiana," who purchased it from "J. L. Haverstock, a Ft. Wayne realtor who began selling family fallout shelters as a sideline in early 1955 after reading a promotional *Life* magazine article."

The NMAH website explains that the Andersons' submarine-like steel shelter was "insufficiently anchored against Ft. Wayne's high water table when first installed." As a result, "the shelter popped to the surface of the Anderson front yard in time for the Cuban missile crisis" in 1962. What would

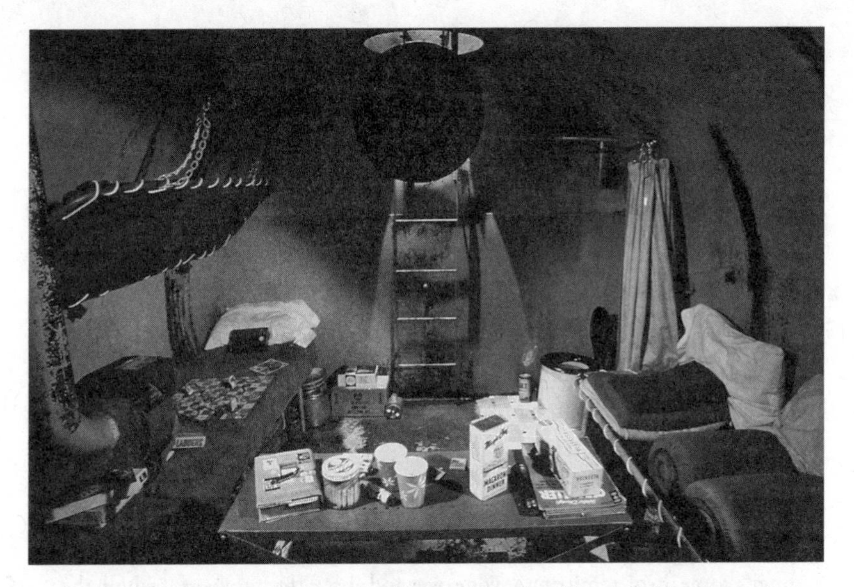

FIGURE 28. Fallout shelter exhibit, National Museum of American History, Smithsonian Institution, Washington, D.C. Originally buried in a backyard in Fort Wayne, Indiana. One visitor was overheard saying, "Why would you want to be down there when everybody else is getting killed?" (photo courtesy of Division of Political History, National Museum of American History, Smithsonian Institution)

have happened to the Andersons if the Soviet missiles had hit Fort Wayne when the water table was rising? No doubt they asked themselves the same question that October.

In 1968 another couple bought the house and the shelter and eventually dug up the shelter and donated it to the Smithsonian, where it is listed online simply as "Object ID 2005.0051.04." This shelter consists of a dismal steel gray hull with two cots, a table with a few supplies, and a portable toilet with a curtain to provide privacy. The text provides one sentence of interpretation—a good one: "The family fallout shelter represents the public policy assumptions of the atomic age, namely, that with enough preparation, the American family and with it the nation's social and political fabric would survive a nuclear attack."[14]

At the exhibit, some overheard remarks: A middle-aged man said to his wife, "Pretty crazy."

"How long were they supposed to stay down there?"

"You had to stay forever—or die of radiation poisoning."

Another older woman called it "a grim spot" and asked her companion, "Why would you want to to be down there when everybody else is getting killed?"

There's one other thing missing from every fallout shelter display: guns. The exhibits all avoid a key ethical question faced by the few who actually built fallout shelters in the 1950s: in case of a Soviet nuclear attack, who should be let in? And how do you keep out the rest of your friends and neighbors? Rick Perlstein reports that *Time* magazine ran an article titled "Gun Thy Neighbor," featuring "a suburban Chicagoan who planned to mount a machine gun on the hatch of his shelter."[15]

In *The Atomic Café,* a priest gave his opinion:

> Let's say you got your family in your shelter, the attack is on, a question might come up of admitting anyone over and above the number for whom the shelter is designed. I'd say that we should rely on the best prudential judgment that the father or the one responsible for the shelter can make in the circumstances. But I say, let him think twice before he admits the needy stranger, if admitting the needy stranger is going to cut down the chances of survival of the group that's already there.
>
> And then that final point: can a man have protective devices in order to protect his family once they are in the shelter, from, let's say, strangers that try to use a crowbar to get in? I'd say, from what I have been talking about, the matter of self defense, it would be wise for a man to at least weigh the possibility of putting some protective devices in his shelter, together with the other elements of his survival kit.[16]

That issue provided the topic for a famous episode of TV's *Twilight Zone.* As the official synopsis explains, when nuclear attack seems imminent, "several suburban friends and neighbors are reduced to selfish, conniving animals and they fight over one family's bomb shelter." The episode, aired in 1961, centers on a doctor who, alone among his friends and neighbors, has built a basement fallout shelter. But after a broadcast warning of an impending attack, the friends and neighbors panic when he locks them out. Friendliness is replaced by "the clawing desire to survive, at any cost." At the climax of the episode, the neighbors break down the door to the shelter with an improvised battering ram. Then they learn from the radio that it was a false alarm, the "attacking" objects are harmless satellites falling from orbit. In the closing narration, the host, Rod Serling, says, "No moral, no message, no prophetic tract. Just a simple statement of fact. For civilization to survive, the human race must remain civilized: tonight's very small exercise in logic—from the Twilight Zone."[17] D.J. Waldie explained it succinctly: for those with their own shelters, "the list of those who are expendable always begins with your next-door neighbor."[18]

And the fallout shelter exhibits did not raise the biggest question: what would happen after a nuclear war to those who survived in their shelters? *The Atomic Café* includes a Civil Defense instructional film, which dramatizes life in a fallout shelter during a nuclear attack. The father tells his wife and two kids, "If they're dropping an atomic bomb, it may go off any second. Whatever happens, I'll give the signal when it's all right for us to get out. If there's an explosion, we'll wait about a minute after it's all over and we'll go upstairs and take a look around, see if it's all right for us to clean up." In the next scene they are above ground, inside their damaged home. The dad says, "Children, you better clear up the broken glass and all this debris. All in all, I would say we've been very lucky around here. Nothing to do now but wait for orders from the authorities and relax."[19]

The Atomic Café also includes a TV interview with a "Los Angeles Schoolteacher" who is explaining his shelter. The interviewer says, "All right. You've been down there for eight to ten days, you come out and you find that half or three-quarters of Los Angeles has been destroyed. Well, how are you going to continue to live?"

The answer: "Well, the first thing we have to recognize is, if half of Los Angeles is destroyed, maybe eighty to ninety percent of the people will be dead, and there will be fewer mouths to feed and those of us who will survive will have more water and food to divide up."[20] The filmmakers saw no need for any comment.[21]

Some of the shelter exhibits hint at these facts, but none make explicit the expected toll in a nuclear war, despite the existence of shelters. By the early 1960s U.S. military strategists assumed that in a nuclear war the Soviets would attack with two thousand one-megaton warheads—weapons with the force of 160,000 Hiroshima-sized bombs each. The United States anticipated twenty million immediate deaths from the first strike, and millions more dying in the next days and weeks from starvation, disease, and lack of medical care.[22]

Nor do any of the shelter exhibits report on officials' thinking about nuclear war. For example, Reagan's deputy secretary of defense, Thomas K. Jones, told Robert Scheer of the *L.A. Times* in 1982 that the United States could recover from an all-out Soviet attack in two to four years. What people needed to do, Jones said, was "dig a hole, cover it with a couple of doors and then throw three feet of dirt on top. It's the dirt that does it." He concluded, "If there are enough shovels around, everybody's going to make it."[23]

Another example you don't find in any of the shelter exhibits: Eugene Rostow was President Johnson's undersecretary of state for political affairs. At his confirmation hearings in 1966, Senator Claiborne Pell asked Rostow if he thought the United States could survive a nuclear war. Rostow replied that Japan "not only survived but flourished after the nuclear attack." When questioners pointed out that the Soviet Union would attack with thousands of nuclear warheads rather than two, Rostow replied, "The human race is very resilient. . . . Depending upon certain assumptions, some estimates predict that there would be ten million casualties on one side and one hundred million on another. But that is not the whole of the population." In *Dr. Strangelove,* George C. Scott's character, General Buck Turgidson, offered the same assessment: "I'm not saying we wouldn't get our hair mussed. But I do say, no more than ten to twenty million killed, tops, depending on the breaks."[24]

Back in Bismarck, the local TV news broadcast about the fallout shelter exhibit concluded, "There's an interesting twist to the exhibit. *You* can leave *your* mark—on history." Indeed visitors were invited to write and post "memories of the Cold War" on post-it notes at the exhibit. One read: "I remember the terror of nuclear war & learning the route from school to the bomb shelter. Age 58." Another: "I grew up in Grand Forks and had no idea there were so many missiles there. Scary!"

Visitors who knew their conservative ideology also posted comments: "As we now know (i.e., Venona), there were Soviet Agents working in the State Dept (and elsewhere)"; "Reagan deserves credit for confronting the Soviets"; "The Cold War was a tragic but necessary struggle."

And a few comments came from the other side of the political spectrum: "If war is the answer we are asking the wrong questions"; "Mutually Assured Destruction still frightens me. Age 59"; "Now the wars of the world are heating up. Have we learned anything? NO."[25]

But the fallout shelter exhibit is not the popular attraction in Bismarck. The popular one is the new North Dakota Cowboy Hall of Fame, which was named the "North Dakota Tourist Attraction of the Year" in 2007. The Hall of Fame has a $3 million, 15,000-square-foot facility, which honors "more than 90 individuals, ranches, events and rodeo animals." Twelve "top western artists" from North Dakota have their paintings and prints on sale at the museum, which also holds family trail rides on Saturdays in the summer, along with "a Kids Showdeo Sunday at the Medora Ranch-O-Rama Arena." The other big event at the Hall of Fame is the annual celebration, National Day of the Cowboy.[26] It makes you realize that we have no National Day of the Fallout Shelter to be celebrated in North Dakota, or anywhere else.

SIXTEEN

"It Had to Do with Cuba and Missiles"

THIRTEEN DAYS IN OCTOBER

If liberals were presenting a semiofficial alternative to the conservatives' "good war" framework for the Cold War, the JFK Library in Boston would be the place to find it. Of course liberal anticommunism was as important, if not more important, than right-wing anticommunism in creating Cold War culture in the United States. This was true from the beginning, when Truman responded to HUAC with his own Security Loyalty Boards, giving credence to the right-wing claim that communists had infiltrated the government during the New Deal. Kennedy was in many ways the supreme Cold Warrior of the era: "the enemy is the communist system itself," he declared in 1960—"implacable, insatiable, unceasing in its drive for world domination."[1] Reagan never said anything more bloodthirsty. But most Democrats disagreed with the Republicans who wanted victory over the USSR; they were committed to the camp of containment.

The greatest challenge to containment came with the Cuban Missile Crisis, the testing ground for contending liberal and conservative strategies for dealing with the Soviets. It was of course the defining moment of the Cold War, the famous "thirteen days in October" 1962 when Kennedy confronted Khrushchev over the Soviets' installation of missiles in Cuba. The history books describe it as the closest the world ever came to nuclear war.

But when George W. Bush's White House spokesperson, Dana Perino, was asked in a 2007 press conference about the Cuban Missile Crisis, she didn't know what it was. "I was panicked a bit because I really don't know about . . . the Cuban Missile Crisis," she later told NPR. "It had to do with Cuba and missiles, I'm pretty sure."[2]

Dana Perino was thirty-five at the time of that press conference and thus had been born about a decade after the event. But her ignorance was emblematic of a striking fact. Conservatives in 1962 offered an interpretation of the Cuban Missile Crisis, but it has been completely forgotten. Not even the Bush White House spokesperson could remember it. Goldwater, Reagan, and William Buckley all said that the Cuban Missile Crisis represented a capitulation to the Soviets; that Kennedy had bowed to Russian threats when he promised not to invade Cuba; that Kennedy thereby guaranteed that a communist outpost would remain, ninety miles from our shores—when he should have taken the opportunity to liberate the Cubans from their communist overlords.

But for the past thirty years historians have ignored the conservative interpretation. Instead the Kennedy liberals have been challenged by the left ("revisionists") over whether the Missile Crisis was necessary at all. The Kennedy advocates have held that the successful resolution of the crisis demonstrated Kennedy's mastery of world politics, showing how he struck the perfect balance between steely determination and strategic flexibility. As a result, they say, he prevented nuclear war while at the same time removing the threat posed by the Cuban missiles. Radicals and realists have argued for the past three decades that Kennedy's threat of nuclear war was an irresponsible and unnecessary risk and that the crisis should have been resolved by less dangerous methods involving normal diplomacy and negotiation. The Soviet missiles in Cuba did not represent an increased threat to the United States. "A missile is a missile," Kennedy himself had said, and it didn't matter whether it was coming from Siberia or Cuba. The Cuban missiles did nothing to change the strategic balance of power—that's what McNamara told Kennedy at the beginning of the crisis: "I don't think there is a military problem."[3] And the United States had already based missiles in Turkey, closer to the USSR than the Cuban missiles were to the United States, so we had set the precedent for moving missiles up to our enemy's border.

The Cuban Missile Crisis exhibit at the JFK Library in Boston, of course, celebrates Kennedy's steely resolve and tactical flexibility, and pretty much ignores his radical critics. You might think it ought to highlight this story, but the "Oval Office" permanent exhibit at the library instead features Kennedy's contributions to civil rights. Those interested in the Missile Crisis can watch a twenty-minute video in a small side theater. The Sunday I visited the library it was fairly crowded, but the official guided tour did not stop at the Cuban Missile Crisis theater. Instead we went past it, straight to the "First Lady" gallery, and at the end of the tour, after the "Legacy" presentation, we were told we could go back to the Missile Crisis if we wanted.

I wanted to, and so did eight other people from our group of twenty-four. In the film the opening text declares (in the present tense, for dramatic effect) that the missiles "pose an immediate threat to the U.S." In an interview shot after the end of the crisis, Kennedy tells a group of newsmen that if the Soviet missiles had not been removed "it would have appeared to change the balance of power, and appearances affect reality."

The only presence of the conservative position in the Kennedy Library film is a short newsreel clip of Senator Homer E. Capehart of Indiana, fat, blustering, and hysterical, telling the cameras that Kennedy should "throw Russia out of Cuba." (Capehart was known, according to Wikipedia, as "the Indiana Neanderthal.")[4] The next clips show panic buying of canned goods in supermarkets, "duck and cover" drills in schools, and "anti-American protests" around the world. Then come TV news reports about America's preparations for war: jets taking off—useless against incoming missiles—and ground-to-air missiles deployed on the beaches of Key West—also useless against incoming missiles.

The happy ending is followed by Kennedy telling newsmen that the United States and the USSR ought to "be able to live in peace," and the closing text reports that in exchange for the Soviet withdrawal of Cuban missiles the United States agreed not to invade Cuba: "In addition private assurances were given to the Soviet Union that the U.S. would remove its own missiles from Turkey. . . . The missile crisis was over."

All this was true, but something was missing: by focusing on "thirteen days in October," by starting with the discovery of the missile sites, the exhibit excluded the history of U.S. treatment of Cuba in the preceding years and thus failed to explain the big picture, the meaning and significance of what had happened, and why. It avoided asking a big question, an obvious question: why did Khrushchev move missiles to Cuba in the first place? The answer is not hard to find: the United States had sponsored an invasion of Cuba at the Bay of Pigs just two years earlier, attempting to overthrow Castro by force. The threat that the United States might invade again was precisely what motivated Khrushchev, and especially Castro; they wanted a bargaining chip to trade for a U.S. agreement not to invade again.

And the exhibit avoids two related questions about the big picture: were conservatives right in arguing that what had happened was a capitulation to Castro? Were radicals right that Kennedy had taken unnecessary risks? The implication is that because "the missile crisis was over" Kennedy did the right thing, with the right combination of fortitude and flexibility. But in terms of a clear statement of a liberal position, the JFK Library exhibit is woefully inadequate.

The library made another attempt to explain the larger significance of Kennedy's actions during the Cuban Missile Crisis, when it mounted a special exhibit for the fortieth anniversary of the crisis in 2002. Some kind of exhibit and accompanying conference was pretty much required for that anniversary, in part because it provided the opportunity for many of the surviving principal players to speak out one last time. But museum exhibits need objects to display, and the Cuban Missile Crisis presented a challenging subject: the Kennedy Library has lots of relevant documents, along with some audio recordings and photos—the aerial photos of the sites in Cuba and the White House official photos of Kennedy looking alternately concerned and determined. But documents and photos are not the stuff of a compelling museum exhibit.

The curators at the Kennedy Library opened their Cuban Missile Crisis exhibit with a much more striking object: a silver calendar for the month of October 1962 designed by Tiffany (figure 29). After the crisis, visitors learned, Kennedy gave these silver plaques as gifts "to those closest to him during the thirteen days of the crisis." The Tiffany plaques had the date for each of the thirteen days "boldly engraved," and each was personalized with "the recipient's and the president's initials." The one displayed in the exhibit was engraved "JBK-JFK." It was the one he had given to Jackie.[5]

The website for the exhibit opens with the image of the Tiffany calendar and invites users to click on specific dates to find out what happened that day. These clicks also link to documents written on that day. The chronological storytelling is strikingly devoid of interpretation, except to emphasize the danger of nuclear war. The exhibit closed after an eight-month run in mid-2003 and is not even mentioned on the "Past Exhibits" page of the Library website.[6] And today, if you go to the Kennedy Library in search of the Cuban Missile Crisis, all you find is that short video in a side gallery. It's described as "optional" in the guide.[7] But how could the story of Kennedy saving the world from nuclear holocaust be "optional"?

While the JFK Library permanent exhibit implicitly refutes Kennedy's critics on the left—"appearances affect reality"—it ignores the right-wing critique.

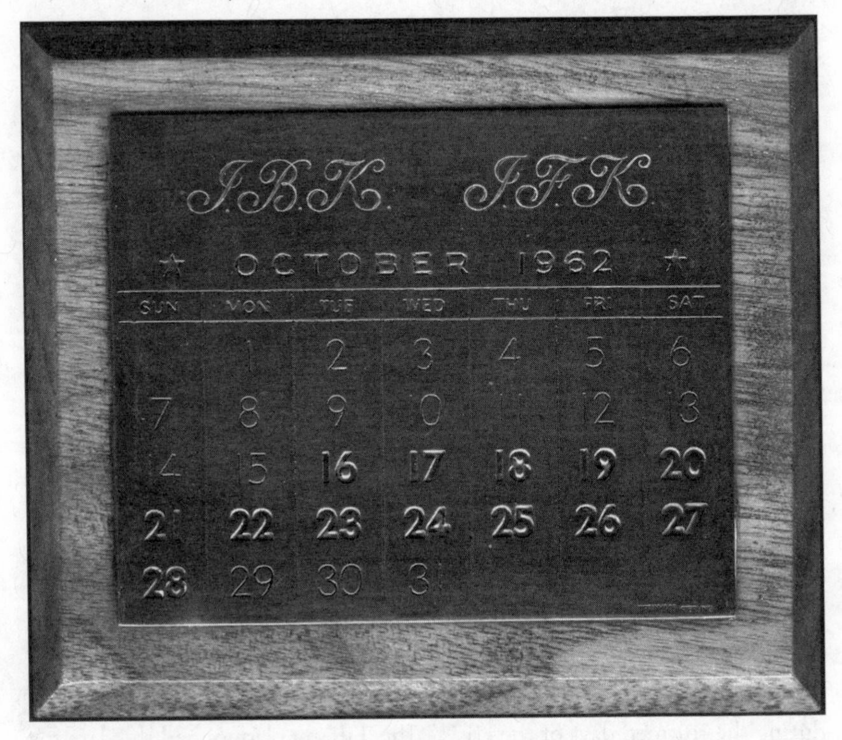

FIGURE 29. Tiffany sterling silver calendar of the Cuban Missile Crisis, a gift from JFK to Jackie (hence the initials at the top). Displayed at the JFK Library for the Cuban Missile Crisis fortieth anniversary exhibition. (image courtesy of John F. Kennedy Presidential Library and Museum)

The exhibit does not indicate that the conservatives' position had strong advocates inside the White House at the time, and also among the military as well as outside in the broader public. Conservatives afterward focused on Kennedy's promise that the United States would not invade Cuba in exchange for Khrushchev's promise to withdraw the missiles. As Rick Perlstein reports, Barry Goldwater, a senator at the time, declared he was "appalled that the president had made any sort of concession to the Soviets . . . and angry that we had forfeited our right to invade Cuba." We "locked Castro's Communism into Latin America and threw away the key to its removal," Goldwater said. There was a word for Kennedy's action: Goldwater called it "appeasement." It's the dirtiest word in the political lexicon of the West, ever since British Prime Minister Neville Chamberlain had tried appeasement on Hitler on the eve of World War II. Goldwater used a second term as well: Kennedy's actions represented "surrender"—to what Goldwater described as "blackmail."[8] Goldwater's position on Cuba didn't surprise anyone; he had published a book in 1962 titled *Why Not Victory?*

William F. Buckley and the *National Review* said the same thing as Goldwater. In Buckley's syndicated column he wrote that Kennedy "has formally given our bitterest enemy a pledge that we will enforce the non-enforcement of the Monroe Doctrine."[9] The *National Review* ran a long piece condemning Kennedy for the "weakness" of his response to the threat, saying that it "made concessions that will assist the growth of communist military power and subversion in this hemisphere"—as well as "Egypt, Laos and the Congo." The lesson of World War II was that "aggressors had to be penalized." And the installation of Soviet missiles presented Kennedy with a magnificent opportunity, "only rarely afforded by a wily and aggressive enemy—to inflict a drastic defeat upon him." We should have demanded "the departure of the Russians together with their 'offensive' weapons" and the holding of "free elections" that would have ended Castro's rule. Instead, Kennedy revealed a "morbid and doctrinaire fear of confrontation" and a "psychological paralysis in the face of modern weaponry."[10]

Ronald Reagan, who would emerge as Goldwater's greatest champion in 1964, two years after the Cuban Missile Crisis, made the same argument in the days following the crisis. Instead of pledging not to invade Cuba, Reagan said, Kennedy should have "insisted on freedom for all Cubans." The American goal, Reagan argued, should not be to coexist with communism in Cuba but rather to defeat it. On the radio he said McKinley had set a good example in 1898: "Under McKinley we freed Cuba."[11] And of course there was Richard Nixon: during the Cuban Missile Crisis he was running for governor of California against incumbent Pat Brown. At the peak of the crisis, he "advocated military action against Cuba."[12]

The conservatives, like the rest of the public at the time, did not know about the other major concession Kennedy had made to Khrushchev—an agreement to withdraw American missiles from Turkey. They were obsolete, but nevertheless their removal was something the Soviets had wanted for a long time. Goldwater, Buckley, Reagan, and the rest would have been infuriated and appalled by the secret deal.

But you won't find the conservative view of the Cuban Missile Crisis in any museum—not even the Reagan Library in Simi Valley, where the "Cold War" room displays a single panel of text informing visitors, "Kennedy took decisive action. His firm stand, based on excellent intelligence and analyses, resolved the Cuban Missile Crisis."

A few other museums contain exhibits about a different aspect of the Cuban Missile Crisis. Miami features a memorial to the flight crews that flew to the Bay of Pigs, but the exhibit—a B-26 bomber on a blue and white field representing the Cuban flag, behind a wall displaying photos of fifteen airmen killed in the failed invasion—is in the remote and little-known Kendall-Tamiami Executive Airport (figure 30).

The National Air and Space Museum in Washington, D.C., has a display about aerial reconnaissance, "The Spy Skies," featuring the aerial photos of Cuban missiles. But the only interpretation it offers emphasizes the value of aerial photos, which "verified both the presence and removal of Soviet missiles in Cuba."[13] A similar theme can be found at the National Museum of the U.S. Air Force in Dayton, Ohio, which has an exhibit declaring, "At no time in America's history has the importance of aerial reconnaissance been demonstrated more dramatically than during the Cuban Missile Crisis of 1962." Their exhibit highlights the KA-18A Stereo Strip Camera.[14] It doesn't seem to have occurred to either of them that the same aerial photos also verified the presence of communism in Cuba for the next fifty years, while Kennedy, according to the conservative interpretation, could have liberated the island in 1962.

Of course Cuba has a museum of the Missile Crisis (they call it the "October 1962 crisis"). It's located in Havana at the Parque Histórico-Militar Morro-Cabaña at a fortress, Castillo San Carlos de la Cabaña. The museum displays a collection of the missiles at issue in the crisis, featuring the Soviet FROG, one of the missiles discovered by the aerial photographs. The FROG—Free Rocket Over Ground, also known as the Luna—was an unguided missile that could carry a two-kiloton nuclear warhead over a range of twenty miles—not far enough to reach Florida. This was a tactical weapon for battlefield use. It could have decimated a U.S. invading force heading for Cuba in ships or the U.S. base in Guantánamo. The warhead would destroy everything within a thousand-yard radius of the blast and spread radiation over a considerably larger area. "Exposed American troops . . . would have been killed instantly by the heat and the pressure," Michael Dobbs of the *Washington Post* reports in his book, *One Minute to Midnight.* "Troops inside vehicles might survive a few days before dying of radiation."[15]

The exhibit in Havana also displays a surface to air missile (SAM) on a launcher. The SAMs were Cuba's "best defense against an American air attack," but they were not capable of hitting the American mainland.[16] A Soviet SAM had shot down Francis Gary Powers's U-2 spy plane in 1960. According

FIGURE 30. Bay of Pigs bomber memorial at Kendall-Tamiami Executive Airport in Miami. A Douglas B-26—the plane that was supposed to bomb the beaches before the Bay of Pigs landing—sits on the stripes of the Cuban flag, behind the faces of the pilots who died that day. (photo by Joe May/TravelForAircraft.wordpress.com)

to a guidebook, "the entire display" of missiles at the Cuban Museum of the Missile Crisis "sits in the grass behind the fortress, and lacks signage."[17]

Thus the place that ought to offer the strongest statement of a liberal alternative to the conservative position—the JFK Library in Boston—limits its exhibit to a small side gallery. What explains this "exhibition gap"? Perhaps the Cuban Missile Crisis is too grim and frightening a subject to attract visitors. It lacks the hula hoop/kitsch aura that the bomb shelter now possesses. It's one thing to display the Tiffany silver calendar for October 1962 that Jack gave Jackie, and to say, as the Kennedy Library does at the start of its online exhibit, "For thirteen days in October of 1962 the world waited—seemingly on the brink of nuclear war—and hoped for a peaceful resolution to the Cuban Missile Crisis."[18] Another kind of exhibit might explain what a nuclear war in October 1962 would have looked like.

American generals, and almost half of Kennedy's advisers at the time, favored bombing the missile sites in Cuba. An exhibit on this theme could have one display about Curtis LeMay, chief of the air force, who favored bombing a thousand sites in Cuba, followed seven days later by a ground invasion by U.S. troops.[19] LeMay had risen in power during World War II devising, and then carrying out, the strategy of firebombing Japanese cities, which killed more Japanese civilians than atomic bombs did. Rick Perlstein reports that LeMay called the naval blockade of Cuba "almost as bad as the appeasement at Munich," and said the resolution of the Cuban Missile Crisis was "the greatest defeat in our history."[20]

A historical monument to Curtis LeMay can be found in Columbus, Ohio, erected by the official Ohio Bicentennial Commission outside the Air Force ROTC building at the Ohio State campus on Woody Hayes Drive (figure 31). But it doesn't mention the Cuban Missile Crisis—or his campaign for the vice presidency in 1968 on a ticket headed by the segregationist George Wallace.[21]

The next display case might describe how the Soviets could have retaliated as the first bombers approached Cuba. Even if Khrushchev did not order the firing of missiles, a Soviet commander in charge of a missile base in Cuba could have ordered a launch. The most powerful missile in place in Cuba was the R-12. Eight were fueled and targeted and armed with nuclear warheads that October. The maximum range of the R-12 was 1,292 miles; the distance between the R-12 missile site and Manhattan was 1,290 miles. If all eight R-12s in Cuba were launched, the total payload would be eight megatons—"an explosive force equivalent to all the bombs ever dropped in the history of war."[22] Even if only a single Soviet R-12 missile reached an American city, it would have hit with one megaton of explosive force—about eighty times more powerful than the Hiroshima bomb. Even if the targeting were off, the city would probably be destroyed.[23] A museum exhibit could display a scale model of, for example, Washington, D.C., after a nuclear attack, looking like those pictures of Hiroshima.

But the Soviets might not have attacked cities on the East Coast; they might have retaliated for an American attack by shooting their short-range tactical nuclear missiles at Guantánamo, which could have killed all the Americans there. Inside the White House, they worried about that during the thirteen days; they worried that Kennedy would have to decide whether to retaliate by attacking a military base in the USSR, or a Russian city. A display could exhibit a model of the F-100 Super Sabre fighter-bomber, which at the peak of the crisis flew along the Soviet and Eastern bloc borders carrying high-yield nuclear bombs much more powerful than those the Soviets had, bombs capable of causing half a million Russian deaths. Another display could depict Kennedy's concern about control over those bombs: he

FIGURE 31. Curtis LeMay historical marker, on Woody Hayes Drive on the Ohio State University campus in Columbus. LeMay was chief of the air force during the Cuban Missile Crisis and argued for bombing a thousand sites in Cuba, followed seven days later by a D day–style invasion by U.S. troops—not mentioned on his historical marker. (photo by William E. Fischer Jr.)

worried about the lack of electronic locking systems on the bombs and about the fact that a single pilot controlled the bombs on his plane; he worried that this made it possible that a pilot would fire a nuclear weapon without authorization.[24]

And a serious exhibit would have to end with some text taking up the questions raised by the realists and the revisionists about whether the crisis was necessary at all, whether the risks Kennedy took had been unnecessary because the threat had been exaggerated. As Kennedy himself said, "a missile is a missile," and once the Soviets launched one it didn't matter whether it was coming from Siberia or Cuba.

Finally a serious exhibit would take up the question of winners and losers. The conventional wisdom is that Kennedy was the big winner and Castro the big loser. Kennedy's prestige soared while Castro was humiliated and shown to be irrelevant even to his Soviet overlords. Perhaps big photos of each circa 1962 could be displayed in this exhibit. But as Michael Dobbs argues, the conventional wisdom doesn't survive scrutiny. The Missile Crisis, he concluded, "guaranteed Castro's hold on power in Cuba for more than four decades."[25] The conservatives, who argued at the time that Kennedy's no-attack pledge guaranteed the survival of Castro's regime, turned out to be right—about that, at least.

SEVENTEEN

The Museum of the Missile Gap

ARIZONA'S TITAN MISSILE MUSEUM

In the silent, empty desert south of Tucson lies a little-known monument to the Cold War: the Titan Missile Museum, once an ICBM base, now a National Historic Landmark operated by a private organization and open to the public.[1] Here visitors descend thirty-five feet underground to see the missile launch control center, where combat crews waited twenty years for the order that never came. Here visitors stare into the 146-foot-deep silo that still contains an actual Titan II missile, the largest single nuclear weapon ever deployed by the United States, standing as it has stood since 1963, except that its fuel tank now is empty and its warhead has been removed.[2] The museum has an air of lament: our tour guide told us that "few today remember the men and women who for twenty years protected the lives and freedoms we enjoy in the United States of America."

It's hard to think of a better monument to the Cold War than this site in the middle of nowhere where for two decades soldiers worked underground around the clock, tending America's Titan—110 feet long, 10 feet wide, capable of moving upward at 15,000 miles per hour, carrying a warhead that could destroy a city. In the control room, we learn on the tour, two people sat at two control panels, each with one of the legendary launch keys. The key switches were too far apart for one person to be able to turn both simultaneously. If the two people turned their keys simultaneously, the world's largest nuclear warhead would be launched at a target inside the USSR—and after that no one could stop it.

Despite the commemorative purpose of the museum, the ideological apparatus mobilized to justify this weapon during the fifties and sixties is missing from the exhibits and tour. Hardly a word is said about the communist threat to our way of life—a threat that, Americans at the time were told, made this missile necessary. But here the brochure for the museum has a different emphasis: "Southern Arizonans and visitors alike have been drawn to the sweeping desert vistas and majestic mountains. . . . Many choose to relocate to the area because of its incredible quality of life."[3]

Instead of declaring that Americans are free today because of the weapon on display, the museum tour provides a kind of history from the bottom up, a worm's-eye view of the Cold War, from the perspective of those who were trained to fight it from their underground bunker in the Arizona desert. On the one-hour tour, offered every day of the year except for Thanksgiving and Christmas, visitors follow a day in the underground life of silo crew members, who worked a twenty-four-hour shift, followed by seventy-two hours off. Our volunteer guide was Roy, an older man wearing a pair of striking pink pants. The climax of the tour came in the subterranean launch control center, where we were invited to "have [our] picture taken launching a missile"—to sit at the launch control facilities console and follow directions: "on the countdown, push the key in, turn it to the right, and hold it for five seconds" (figure 32).

Roy counted down, and the people on our tour who had been seated at the consoles obediently did what they were told. Then, on the launch console, the "launch enable" light went on; the "silo soft" light went on (indicating the silo door above the missile has opened, that the site is no longer protected, or "hard"); then "guidance go" lit up, then "fire engine" and finally "lift off." Roy said, "Thirty minutes from now, when that missile reaches its target, that target will cease to exist." This was a moment of nervous excitement, as different folks took their turns "launching a missile" while flash cameras popped.

When the picture-taking stopped, one tour member, troubled by something she couldn't quite name, asked a question: "What were they supposed to do after firing?" Another tour member tried to help out: "Maybe they reloaded the silo with another missile."

"No," Roy said. "The site had no spare missiles. It was not intended to be reused. It would have taken ninety days to refurbish the silo. Once their missile was launched, the crew had nothing to do but kick back, pop a coke, and take it easy."

Silence fell over the group, as they realized what the guide left unsaid: when the crew emerged from underground, the "topside" world would have been destroyed.

FIGURE 32. Titan Missile Museum tour, Green Valley, Arizona. "Have your picture taken launching a missile!" Loyda Vance, eight, turns a launch key at the command console. (photo by Jeff Topping /*New York Times*/Redux)

Roy sensed the troubled silence and said, "If you had a granny in Moscow, you'd hate like hell to turn that key."

One older man blurted out, "If I had a granny in Moscow, I wouldn't do it."

Roy shot back, "Then the commander would pull his handgun and fill you full of holes."

A shadow had fallen over the tour.

Indeed, whether crews would actually launch their missile when ordered to do so was a question that worried planners and theorists of U.S. Cold War strategy. Psychological testing and continuing scrutiny of the crews attempted to weed out any who might hesitate. Incessant training and practice drills sought to make obedience to the doomsday order automatic. But the guide's answer was the correct one. Commanders had keys to the weapons locker and instructions to use their weapons on fellow crew members if necessary. The specter of an underground gun battle in the launch control room over the fate of the world must have been part of the consciousness of every Titan crew member. Each must have asked himself, if it weren't a test, if it were for real, would I be willing to turn the key—or would I face the commander's gun?

The tour that had taken that dark turn in the launch control center had started cheerfully enough in the small "topside" museum, where the people in our group were instructed to put on hard hats—blue for the gentlemen, pink for the ladies—and sit in plastic chairs in front of a TV set to watch a worn-out videotape. Roy said, "When it's over, I'll wake you up." The video explained that in the early eighties, when the Reagan administration "was planning to get rid of the Titans," some air force officers proposed a museum. That required agreement not only from our government but also from the Soviets, who had to be satisfied that the museum could not be reactivated as a missile site. The museum opened in 1986 and since that time has had more than a million visitors—fifty thousand a year. We watched film of a Titan test launch, which paid tribute to the members of the military-industrial complex responsible for the Titan system: Martin Marietta, which built the missile and the site; Aerojet General, which built the engine; and GM, which built the electronic guidance system.

Then we went outside in our hard hats, squinting in the blazing desert sun. Roy led us to view the "Mark VI reentry vehicle"—"a favorite of photographers," he said.[4] This is the missile's nose cone, which carried the nuclear warhead. The "reentry vehicle" of the Titan II, we were told, contained "the largest nuclear warhead ever deployed." This was a nine-megaton bomb, more than fifty times bigger than the Hiroshima bomb. The warhead on the Titan II would create a fireball three miles in diameter with heat intense enough to cause lethal burns to any unprotected person in a thousand-square-mile area. Within three and a half miles, "virtually all above-ground structures would be destroyed and blast effects would inflict near 100% fatalities." Within three miles, radiation would "cause a 50% to 90% casualty rate independent of thermal or blast effects at this distance."[5] After the Titan, military strategy shifted to missiles with smaller multiple warheads. The former nine-megaton bomb in front of us rested on the truck trailer that had carried it to this site; the trailer had a small sign that read, "Explosives."

At the beginning of the Cold War, no one believed you could put an atomic bomb on the tip of a missile that could travel five thousand miles and hit a target. Hitler's V-2 rockets had a short range and carried conventional explosives; that kind of weapon would be insignificant in a war between the

United States and the USSR. The Hiroshima and Nagasaki bombs weighed four tons and five tons respectively, and only the biggest bombers could get them off the ground. Thus during the first decade of the Cold War, long-range bombers were everything. "Deterrence" required bombers on round-the-clock alert, and that was the job of the Strategic Air Command, or SAC.

SAC has its own monument and used to have its own official national museum. The SAC monument can be found at the National Museum of the Air Force outside Dayton, Ohio (see introduction). There used to be a SAC museum, in Nebraska between Lincoln and Omaha, which opened in 1966 and displayed historic aircraft. With the end of SAC after the collapse of the USSR, the SAC museum took on the mission of "ensuring the American people remember the vital role SAC played in maintaining world peace" during the Cold War.[6] It displayed Cold War bombers.

But that museum is gone, replaced in 1998 by the privately run Strategic Air and Space Museum (also in Nebraska between Omaha and Lincoln) where once again the Cold War has been largely forgotten. The permanent exhibits here focus on World War II aircraft—and on space exploration.[7] The reason given for shifting the original museum's focus away from the Cold War was "reaching out to a growing audience through dynamic programming . . . that captivates the interests and imaginations of everyone." Thus the effort to commemorate and honor the long-range bombers of the Cold War with a SAC museum failed.

The other part of the "triad" of Cold War nuclear strategy—along with the Titan ICBM and the SAC bombers in the sky twenty-four hours a day—was the Polaris missile, fired underwater from submarines. The Polaris, developed starting in 1956 and first fired from a submerged submarine in 1960, was a solid fuel rocket with a range of a thousand miles that carried a six-hundred-kiloton nuclear warhead, capable of destroying "military and industrial centers of strategic importance." Because submarines were constantly moving, they were difficult for enemy forces to target. If you had a fleet of subs with Polaris missiles, you had "deterrence"—and, in contrast to the Titan or the SAC bomber fleet, you could wait longer before launching nuclear weapons, to make sure the USSR was indeed attacking the United States. Of course a Polaris is on display at the Submarine Force Museum outside the naval shipyard in Groton, Connecticut, where nuclear submarines were built. The museum features tours of the USS *Nautilus,* the first nuclear submarine, now a National Historic Landmark.[8]

In 1957 the launch of Sputnik scared Americans—what if Sputnik carried a nuclear bomb?—and missiles suddenly became the doomsday weapons of choice (even though the satellite the Soviets put into orbit weighed less than two hundred pounds). And there was one other big difference between nuclear weapons carried to their targets on long-range bombers and nuclear weapons on missiles: the missiles couldn't turn back once they had been launched, and would take only thirty minutes to reach their targets. When Eisenhower was convinced to develop rockets that could carry nuclear weapons in 1955, the Cold War became suddenly much more dangerous—especially since American military planners were determined to avoid "another Pearl Harbor," a surprise attack coming this time not from planes but from enemy missiles. The Titan Missile, with its nine-megaton warhead, was the weapon of choice in this new world, and the anxiety about its use became a central theme of Cold War military strategy.[9]

But those issues weren't raised on the Titan tour in Arizona. Next on the Titan tour we climbed onto a viewing stand and stared down into the silo through a glass cover, which provided an amazing view of the immense, silent missile, pointing directly at us. "Sort of like looking down the barrel of a gun," Roy said. This is a view no one ever had while the site was operational; when the silo cover opened—for a test—the crew was below ground at their posts.

The 750-ton silo door, designed to withstand the effects of a nuclear attack on this site, was half open, in compliance with SALT II, the treaty governing this site. The treaty, signed by Jimmy Carter in 1979, required that the United States destroy its arsenal of Titans by 1987 but permitted this base to be turned into a museum under two conditions: first, the silo cover had to be kept half open to permit a Soviet spy satellite to observe that the warhead carrier—the "reentry vehicle"—had holes cut in it that rendered it inoperable; and second, the silo cover had to be prevented from opening more than halfway by a concrete slab too gigantic to move. Although the end of the Cold War and the collapse of the Soviet Union rendered these conditions obsolete, the museum still abides by them.

The rest of the tour took us in the footsteps of the crew, starting with their arrival at the factory gates—identifying themselves with passwords, moving through the giant blast-proof locked doors, weighing six thousand pounds each, so that the Russians would never be able to force their way in. Then we arrived in the control center. Here our group came to contemplate the question of whether crew members really would have turned their launch keys and destroyed the world.

Millions of Americans learned about this problem from the 1983 film *War Games*, which starred young Matthew Broderick. The film opens at an ICBM base, where the two crew members receive an order to launch. They begin the countdown; each inserts his launch key, and the silo doors open while ominous music—electronic, of course—swells on the sound track; then the captain starts to get cold feet. "Get SAC on the phone!" he shouts.

"That's not the correct procedure, Captain," the other crew member replies.

"Screw the correct procedure! I want somebody on the phone before I kill 20 million people!"

The lieutenant tries the phone but gets nothing: "They might have been knocked out already!" he says.

When the countdown reaches zero, the captain doesn't turn his key. The lieutenant pulls his gun, points it at the captain's head, and declares, "Sir, we are at launch, turn your key, sir!"

The captain, bathed in sweat and trembling, murmurs, "I'm sorry, I'm sorry."

Cut to the NORAD Combat Operations Center, where high officials gather in their underground command post, and the actor Dabney Coleman reports that 22 percent of missile commanders failed to "launch" their missiles on this latest test. A nervous air force general says, "I have ordered a complete reevaluation of our psychological screening procedures."

Coleman shouts back, "You can't screen out human response! Those men in the silos know what it means to turn their keys, and some of them are just not up to it. It's as simple as that!"[10]

Who were the men and women on the Titan crews? The air force declared that crew members were carefully selected on the basis of several factors, including "specific aptitude levels," "security clearance eligibility," and "emotional stability."[11] In the best-selling 1962 novel *Fail-Safe,* the authors Eugene Burdick and Harvey Wheeler drew a convincing psychological portrait: "They were emotional neuters. Long ago, under the scrutiny of hard-eyed psychologists, the claustrophobic and the easily panicked men had been weeded out. The rest had been made deliberately nerveless. They were technicians of a greater terror taught to ignore the unalterable end of their work. And, in honest fact, most of them did not believe in their work. It was a gigantic child's play, a marvelous art. It had to be done perfectly each time and it was. But it came to nothing."[12]

Most of *Fail-Safe* portrayed our leaders' inability to stop an errant flight of nuclear bombers headed for Moscow, but one chapter painted a dark, compelling picture of life inside a Titan base, bringing home the issue that the Titan Missile Museum tour carefully avoids. All Titan crews, the authors wrote, "knew that the enemy, any enemy, would strike first at these bases. The cities, the seaports, the ships, the planes, these could come—or go—later." The underground command post, which provided the highlight of the tour of the Titan Missile Museum, thus constituted "an ingenious collective coffin" for those who worked there.[13]

After our tour group visited the control center, Roy led us down the cableway, a tunnel nine feet in diameter connecting the center with the missile silo, where two picture windows have been cut in the eight-foot-thick silo wall. This allows visitors to see the missile in something like the way work crews did when they performed maintenance. The silo has nine levels, each with retractable work platforms. Two mannequins on a platform on the other side of the picture window wear "Refco suits" (RFHCO, Rocket Fuel Handlers Clothing Outfits); Roy told us they were "checking for propellant leaks with a probe device attached to a Portable Vapor Detector."

He didn't tell the story of the night in 1980 when leaking vapor caused a Titan to explode in a silo just like this one in Damascus, Arkansas. *Time* called the explosion "Light on the Road to Damascus": at three o'clock in the morning, the sky north of Little Rock suddenly turned bright white, and then an immense explosion sent a gigantic red cloud into the air.[14] Chunks of concrete the size of cars fell from the sky.

"What the hell happened?" a news photographer shouted to an air force captain.

"The son of a bitch blew," he yelled back.[15]

The explosion hurtled the missile's nuclear warhead, hundreds of times more powerful than the Hiroshima bomb, two hundred yards into an empty field.

The missile crew at the Damascus silo had been struggling with a fuel leak from the Titan for almost eight hours, after a maintenance crew member working in the silo on one of those retractable platforms accidentally dropped a three-pound socket wrench; it fell seventy feet and punctured the thin skin of the missile's liquid fuel tank. When fuel began to spill, the crew evacuated the silo; then fire broke out and set off the automatic sprinkler system, which poured 100,000 gallons of water into the silo, putting out the fire. But the fuel continued to leak. The missile crew ordered an emergency evacuation of everyone within five miles of the base. The instructions: "Don't take time to close your doors—just get out."

Six hours later, as two technicians prepared to reenter the silo through an underground passageway to try to stop the leak, a stupendous explosion of liquid rocket fuel and vapor blew the 750-ton hardened concrete cover off the silo; the missile melted, the warhead was hurled two hundred yards, the silo ended up looking like a crater on the moon. One airman died of chemical pneumonia after inhaling toxic fumes; twenty-one were hurt. The air force quickly announced that the warhead lying in the field was in no danger of detonating, and it denied that any radioactive debris had been released; it also barred a visit to the site by the Arkansas governor—Bill Clinton.[16]

The residents of a town called Guy, six miles away, who had not been evacuated, reported seeing a brownish red fog drift through their town ninety minutes after the explosion; two weeks later many were complaining of nausea, dizziness, headaches, and shortness of breath. The air force of course denied that the explosion was responsible for what the residents of Guy were calling "the sickness." The mayor of Guy told *Newsweek,* "The Air Force just says it didn't happen. We know it did. We saw the fog move in, we smelled it and we breathed it." The county sheriff recalled that toxic fumes had seeped out of the Damascus silo two years earlier, in 1978; he expressed skepticism about the air force's assurances. "I've been suckered twice," he said, "and I don't want to be suckered again."

News of other Titan problems surfaced in the wake of the Damascus explosion. *Newsweek* reported that fifty-three workmen had been killed in a 1963 silo explosion in Arkansas. Seven people had been hospitalized after breathing toxic fumes at the Damascus site in 1978. *Time* reported the Titan system had "40 mishaps in ten years, two of them resulting in deaths or injuries."

The basic problem, never mentioned on the tour, was described by the *Wall Street Journal:* the Titan required "the desperate and constant attention accorded a man receiving artificial respiration." The Titans were, in the words of Bob Thompson in the *Washington Post,* "extraordinarily complex, hand-crafted machines, containing as many as 300,000 parts, each of which had to be maintained in perfect operating condition."[17] The liquid propellant was volatile and corrosive, which meant that the missile fueling process—which took hours to complete—could never be undertaken in advance. And the Damascus explosion showed what could go wrong.

The Damascus explosion provoked a wide debate over abolition of the Titan system. The press recalled that, by the time of the Damascus explosion in 1980, the liquid-fueled Titan had long since been made obsolete by the solid-fueled Minuteman. (The Minuteman has its own National Historic Site in South Dakota, where its superiority to the Titan is described in full.)[18] *Newsweek* asked, "Should the Titan II be retired?," pointing out that "plans were made to begin phasing out the missiles in the early 1970s, but Henry Kissinger ordered them kept as bargaining chips during the SALT I negotiations." Jimmy Carter's air force secretary, Hans Mark, insisted in 1980 that the Titans were "a perfectly safe system." Senator Bob Dole said he didn't believe it and called for a Senate investigation of the Titans' safety. He noted official reports of 125 fuel leaks in the preceding five years and expressed concern that the air force had concealed other such incidents.[19]

The *Bulletin of the Atomic Scientists* went further: it called the fifty-four Titans "hopelessly obsolete, pathetically first-strike vulnerable, accident-prone monstrosities." The magazine proposed that the United States "begin immediately to eliminate such dangerous and useless missiles," and that negotiations with the Soviets were not necessary: "The removal of such provocative, useless, and accident-prone missiles, irrespective of what the Russians may or may not do in exchange, can only serve to enhance the security of the U.S."[20]

President Carter asked the Pentagon for a "complete evaluation" of the safety of the fifty-three Titans that hadn't blown up in their silos, and the air force appointed a sixty-two-member study group. The group concluded only that the air force needed to upgrade its ability to evacuate nearby civilians in the event of future accidents and proposed a program to discourage the real estate developments encroaching on the Titan bases outside Tucson. Already a thousand households had moved within one mile of the closest silo. "The case for discouragement could be centered around a missile compatible use zone concept," the committee reported, suggesting that "concept" be identified by the acronym "MICUZ."[21] What belongs in a MICUZ? "Nothin' but sagebrush and rattlesnakes," they said. (The committee review endorsed the existing Reliability and Aging Surveillance Program [RASP] and Service

Life Analysis Program [SLAP] but concluded that the Refcos worn in accident recovery operations were wearing out and needed "new zippers.")

Roy's last words to us were, "It was expensive, but I guess it worked." He meant that the Titan deterred the Russians from attacking us. That one sentence was pretty much the entire justification of this site's existence. The lack of enthusiasm for claiming anything more than "I guess it worked" speaks volumes about the state of Cold War commemoration today.

Deterrence was above all an idea, based on an old psychological concept: if one's enemies fear retaliation, they will not attack. But doomsday deterrence—the idea of "mutual assured destruction"—was something no previous military power had ever realized. The simple idea of deterrence gave rise in the fifties and sixties to an immense outburst of scholarly and "scientific" energy, as Cold War academics eagerly wrote about the different ways we could threaten to use our nuclear forces.

Today hundreds of these books gather dust on the shelves of university libraries. Only one of them is remembered: *On Thermonuclear War*, the masterpiece written by Herman Kahn. He started from a simple but brilliant idea: there was no point in establishing a nuclear war capability unless we were willing to use it—because if we weren't willing to use it, the Soviets wouldn't be deterred by its existence. What made many people question the use of nuclear weapons was a simple reluctance to destroy civilization. Here Kahn made his second striking contribution: Americans would be willing to engage in a nuclear war—if they had confidence that they could survive it. He devoted his scholarly career to instilling in Americans that confidence.

"Despite a widespread belief to the contrary," he wrote in 1960, "objective studies indicate that, even though the amount of human tragedy would be greatly increased in the post [nuclear] war world, the increase would not preclude normal and happy lives for the majority of survivors and their descendants." The book argued that even if America's fifty-three largest metropolitan areas were completely destroyed, our gross national product would be set back only "a decade or two," and "much of the destroyed wealth will be a luxury." For example: "If half of our resident space is destroyed, then, even if everyone survives, these survivors will be better housed than the average Soviet citizen." Genetic defects resulting from radioactive contamination wouldn't be crippling. He titled a famous table, "Tragic but distinguishable postwar states," which indicated that 20 million dead would require ten years for economic recuperation, while 40 million required twenty years.[22]

Kahn's "objective" approach to planning to fight a nuclear war won support from pundits like Walter Lippmann and George Kennan. Many careers were built on that foundation, including Henry Kissinger's—whose first book, *Nuclear Weapons and Foreign Policy,* published in 1957, proposed that a "limited" tactical nuclear war could be fought—and won—in Europe. (Europeans were understandably unhappy with the idea of the United States fighting a war with the USSR that would leave Europe a radioactive ruin while America emerged unscathed.) Policy makers adopted Kahn's perspective; the heavy investment in civil defense provided one way our leaders tried to convince the American people we could win a nuclear war.

Not everyone objecting to the practice of nuclear deterrence came from the left. One of the most coherent arguments came from no less than President Eisenhower. In 1956, he replied to a letter urging him to establish "a crash program" of ICBM development:

> I have spent my life in the study of military strength as a deterrent to war.... [B]ut we are rapidly getting to the point that no war can be won. War implies a contest; when you get to the point that contest is no longer involved and the outlook comes close to destruction of the enemy and suicide for ourselves... then arguments as to the exact amount of available strength as compared to somebody else's are no longer the vital issues.
>
> When we get to the point... that both sides know that... destruction will be both reciprocal and complete, it is possible we will have sense enough to meet at the conference table with the understanding that the era of armaments has ended and the human race must conform its actions to this truth or die.[23]

Four years later, Democratic presidential candidate John F. Kennedy got elected after accusing Eisenhower of permitting a "missile gap" to develop.

The "missile gap" deserves its own monument. Perhaps it could include a statue of the columnist Joseph Alsop, who coined the phrase. He claimed in the late fifties that the Soviets had one hundred operational ICBMs while we had none. Of course Alsop was only one of many. Arthur Schlesinger Jr. wrote in a Kennedy campaign document that America could "drift into minor-power status and oblivion" because the it was falling "farther and farther behind the Soviet Union in ICBMs and the fight for space."[24] The liberal *Reporter* magazine declared in 1959 that the Soviet Union had "20,000 ballistic missiles with ranges from 150 to 6,000 miles."[25] And since the USSR was bent on world domination, the argument went, they were likely to launch a surprise attack on us with these weapons, to compel the capitulation of the world's democracies. Therefore we urgently needed to close the missile gap.

The truth is there was no missile gap. When Kennedy did his best in 1960 to frighten Americans about a Soviet nuclear threat, the USSR had no operational ICBMs. Their longest-range missile was 500 miles—at a time when the Titan had been successfully tested at 5,500 miles. In 1960 the United States was years ahead of the Soviet Union in virtually every area of missile and rocket technology: missile guidance, reentry systems, electronics, weight reduction of nuclear weapons, fuel technology, and miniaturization. The Soviets were ahead in only one area: the throw-weight of their rockets. But, as the historian Charles R. Morris explains, "that was an indication of the primitiveness, not the advanced character, of its technology." Because Soviet rocket engines were so inefficient, and because they had not made the progress we had in miniaturization of weapons, they had to strap many rockets together to get their heavy bombs off the ground.[26]

It would take ten years after the 1960 "missile gap" flap for the USSR to develop an ICBM force of any significance, and twenty years until they could pose a plausible first-strike threat. The only power in the world in 1960 capable of annihilating its enemies' cities with missiles was the United States.[27] Indeed the overwhelming superiority of U.S. missiles in the early sixties drove Soviet leaders to a crash program to develop their own counterparts. The resulting arms race would consume massive amounts of the world's wealth over the next three decades. The Titan was a key element accelerating that arms race.

The tragic fact is that the United States had a chance to defuse the Cold War just as the Titan system was being created. This is not the just the judgment of peacenik historians; it comes from no less a nuclear hawk than Henry Kissinger, who wrote in his memoirs that the Soviets' U.S. ambassador, Anatoly Dobrynin, remarked to him in 1972 that their countries had missed a golden opportunity to defuse the Cold War in the late fifties.[28] In fact Khrushchev wanted and needed a settlement with the West. He was committed to shifting resources from the military to consumer goods, but by 1959 his initiatives were coming apart. This was the time Khrushchev visited the United States and, after a failed trip to Disneyland, spent two days with Eisenhower at Camp David, where the two agreed to hold a summit meeting in Paris to establish a nuclear test ban treaty and begin a process of disarmament. But two weeks before the scheduled Paris summit in 1959, an

American U-2 spy plane was shot down over the Soviet Union, and Khrushchev canceled the summit. The summit would not have brought an end to the Cold War, but both leaders had hoped it would have provided a way to break the spiral of the nuclear arms race (see chapter 6).[29]

The Soviets then took the ultimate step in following the logic of deterrence: they developed a true doomsday machine, an automatic retaliatory system that would launch their missiles even if all their leaders had been killed in an American first strike. This was the work of Soviet president Leonid Brezhnev, who feared a U.S. missile attack might succeed in the "decapitation" of the entire Soviet ruling elite. They called their system "the Dead Hand." According to David E. Hoffman's award-winning book, *The Dead Hand,* the system "would leave the fate of Earth in the hands of three surviving duty officers buried deep underground in a concrete, globe-shaped bunker."[30]

The work of the "defense intellectuals" at Harvard, Yale, Princeton, and the Rand Corporation ignored the objections to waging nuclear war.[31] These questions suggest that maybe the Titan was a bad idea; maybe we never needed it at all; maybe the Titan Missile Museum is a monument to the threat to world peace posed by the United States.

What is to be done with the Titan silos now? In addition to the one that's a museum south of Tucson, there are fifty-three in Arizona, Kansas, Arkansas, and Idaho, each sixteen stories deep and forty feet in diameter. A company called Wes-Con Inc. acquired three Idaho silos and filled them with thousands of tons of hazardous waste, including agricultural pesticides, contaminated grain, heavy metals, aerosol bombs, PCBs, and hospital and electronic industry waste. Because the silos were built to withstand a nuclear attack, with walls six feet thick, Wes-Con Inc. told the locals, the walls will protect the surrounding area from toxic contamination. Once they are filled, the company promised to close and seal the two 120-ton doors on each of its silos, confident that teenage vandals will never be able to get them open. The Wes-Con Titan silos were purchased by U.S. Ecology Idaho in 2001.[32] A kind of poetic justice can be found in replacing doomsday missiles with toxic waste: at last these Titan silos are protecting us from a genuine threat.

EIGHTEEN

The Museum of Détente

THE NIXON LIBRARY IN YORBA LINDA

Liberals may still hate Nixon, but that doesn't mean conservatives like him. For those on the right celebrating Cold War victory, Nixon was part of the problem. Instead of fighting as Reagan did to roll back and eventually defeat communist totalitarianism, Nixon negotiated détente with the Russians and traveled to China to open relations with Mao. The political reversal by a lifelong anticommunist outraged conservatives, who considered it a great betrayal: Nixon went soft; he sold out.

So the Nixon Library in Yorba Linda has a problem to address. The story told there about China and détente starts in the library's Hall of World Leaders, which contains life-size bronze statues of ten heads of state with whom Nixon met. Here visitors see, and pose for pictures with, Mao and Zhou Enlai, Brezhnev and Khrushchev, portrayed not as totalitarian murderers in the mold of Hitler but rather as the equals of Churchill, de Gaulle, and Golda Meir, whose statues appear in the same display (figure 33). The wall text quotes Nixon describing all these people as leaders who "made a difference, not because they wished it, but because they willed it"—rather than, as conservatives might prefer, dividing them between defenders and enemies of freedom. For conservatives, the Nixon Library's Hall of World Leaders should be renamed the "Hall of Moral Equivalence."

But for almost twenty years, no one on the right complained about the moral equivalence on display in the Nixon Library's Hall of World Leaders. No one objected to the apparent equation of Mao with Churchill and de Gaulle—not until 2009, when the sixtieth anniversary of the Chinese communist revolution brought a Chinese man in Los Angeles to organize a protest. His protest was featured on page one of the *Los Angeles Times,* then around the world and around the Internet (figure 34).

FIGURE 33. Tourists pose with Mao in the Hall of World Leaders, Nixon Library, Yorba Linda, California. The life-sized bronze statue of Mao appears in the same room with Golda Meir, Churchill, and de Gaulle, among others. But only a few conservatives criticized this exhibit for "moral equivalence." (photo courtesy of *Orange County Register*/Bruce Chambers)

"Remove Mao-the-Man-Eater's Statue from Nixon Library"—that was the demand raised by Kai Chen at his website.[1] On the front page of the *L.A. Times,* the story about Chen's protest was headlined "The Past Haunts Richard Nixon's Library." It described Chen as "a 56-year-old Los Angeles real estate investor and former China national basketball team member" who said "relatives and friends were victims of communist purges during Mao's nearly 30 years in power." Chen was quoted as describing Mao as "the biggest mass murderer in human history.... His hands were dipped in the blood of American soldiers who fought in Korea and Vietnam. How can that image be put alongside world leaders like Winston Churchill and De Gaulle?"[2]

This is an appropriate question to be asked by someone on the right. But why was it that the only one asking was a former member of the Chinese national basketball team? Where were all the conservative pundits who had spent the previous two decades complaining about "moral equivalence" on the left? Where was Jeanne Kirkpatrick, who first made the argument in a

FIGURE 34. Anti-Mao protest at the Nixon Library, Yorba Linda, California, on the sixtieth anniversary of the Chinese revolution in 2009. For the twenty years before that, no one had complained about the library's positive display about Nixon's China diplomacy. (photo courtesy of Jebb Harris, *Orange County Register*)

famous article?[3] Where were William F. Buckley, Irving Kristol, Norman Podhoretz, and William Bennett?

The story gets stranger. The Hall of World Leaders exhibit was defended not by library director Timothy J. Naftali, who told the *L.A. Times* he was sympathetic to Chen's complaint, and who had always favored getting rid of the Mao statue. It was defended instead by the library docents, two hundred volunteers, mostly older Nixon loyalists who had been explaining the room of statues to visitors for twenty years. Georgia Mallory, a sixty-two-year-old docent with sixteen years of experience—"more than 1,850 hours" giving tours—was quoted by the *L.A. Times* as saying, "What we're being told is that what we've been doing here is insignificant and wrong, that we've been telling the story incorrectly." But "we told it that way because it was history.... We knew it was factual.... This is the *Richard Nixon library*."[4]

Mao defended against anticommunist Chinese by Nixon Library docents: who would have thought?

The story of the protest was played for laughs on local NBC-TV news: "Pinko, Commie Statues Shock, Offend at Nixon Library," their story was headed; "Red scare leaves museum visitors gasping for freedom." The report declared that "two statues of communist leaders at a local presidential library are destroying the immaculate legacy of one our nation's finest presidents: Richard M. Nixon."[5]

When the day for the protest came—the sixtieth anniversary of the Chinese Communist revolution—only a dozen protesters showed up at the Nixon Library. The protest was covered only by the *Orange County Register,* which put it on a two-minute web video following their lead piece, "Music Teacher Arrested on Suspicion of Flashing."[6]

The strongest defense of the Mao statue came from the first director of the library, John H. Taylor, at his own blog, The EpiscoNixonian. (Taylor is an Episcopalian priest as well as a former Nixon staffer.) He had "supervised the design of the display," he wrote, and the point of the display was that Nixon's "opening to Beijing was the essence of his genius as a statesman." The idea behind the statues of Mao and Zhou Enlai was "to give visitors an idea of what they looked like and illustrate RN's proposition that the U.S. could be a force for stability and constructive change by finding ways to be in dialog even with leaders of unfriendly or unsavory powers." Nixon, he concluded, should be praised rather than condemned for "being willing to shake hands with friends and foes alike in the pursuit of peace."[7]

Conservatives may have failed to complain about the Nixon Library's depiction of Mao in the Hall of World Leaders, but they did not fail to complain at the time of Nixon's trip to China. The voice of the right on this issue was no less than William F. Buckley. Buckley's *National Review* led prominent conservatives to declare a formal break with Nixon in advance of Nixon's trip in August 1971, when the magazine published a declaration signed by twelve right-wing leaders. Détente was the big issue for the group, which called itself "the Manhattan Twelve."[8]

Buckley's group was hardly alone. *Time* magazine quoted *Human Events* declaring that détente was "literally endangering the survival of the American Republic"—and William Loeb, ultraconservative publisher of the Manchester, New Hampshire, *Union Leader,* calling Nixon's diplomacy with Mao "immoral, indecent, [and] insane."[9] The Manhattan Twelve enlisted Ohio Representative John Ashbrook to speak for them on the floor of the House, where he declared that Nixon had "handed the communists a monumental victory, gratuitously, and with barely a sign of struggle."[10]

At the end of 1971, Ashbrook announced he would challenge Nixon in the upcoming Republican primaries, declaring that "the principal impact of the President's Cold War conduct has been to confirm and deepen the illusion of détente." Ashbrook's slogan, as Rick Perlstein notes in *Nixonland,* was "No Left Turns."[11] Ashbrook said Nixon had acted "in direct defiance of his statements across the years and many specific pledges made when running for the presidency three years ago and at the very same time when the Soviet Union and Red China are increasing their aggressive activities throughout the world." He concluded that Nixon's "failure to exert the necessary presidential leadership has endangered our national security."[12] Buckley endorsed Ashcroft, and so did *Human Events.*

In an effort to neutralize Buckley's opposition, White House staffer Pat Buchanan persuaded him to join the journalists on the China trip. Buckley accepted, but the effort to win him over failed: after the historic banquet where Nixon and Mao toasted each other, Buckley wrote, "It is unreasonable to suppose that anywhere in history have a few dozen men congregated who have been responsible for greater human mayhem than the hosts at this banquet and their spiritual colleagues, instruments all of Mao Tse-tung." As Perlstein noted, Buckley compared the event to the Nuremberg prosecutor "descending from the prosecutor's stand to embrace Goering and Goebbels and Doenitz and Hess, begging them to join with him in the making of a better world."[13]

At the end of the trip, when Nixon and Zhou Enlai signed the official Shanghai Communiqué pledging progress toward the ultimate normalization of relations between the two nations, Buckley wrote, "We have lost—irretrievably—any remaining sense of moral mission in the world." When Nixon toasted Mao at the concluding banquet in Peking, another conservative journalist declared, "He [Nixon] would toast Alger Hiss tonight, if he could find him."[14]

The case for the defense is made at the Nixon Library's biggest, most architecturally impressive, and most elaborate exhibit: the Structure of Peace Gallery, which follows the Hall of World Leaders and tells the story of Nixon's trip to China. Visitors are greeted by a fifteen-foot-high imitation Chinese pavilion under which stand life-size bronze figures of Nixon striding toward Zhou with his hand outstretched in friendship.[15]

But Cold War politics plays a distinctly secondary role in this gallery; what comes first is Chinese crafts. The first object on display is a large collage portraying a scholar at a desk, made, we learn, of jade, mother of pearl, ivory, and mahogany. It is an amazing thing, but it has nothing to do with Nixon's trip to China. It was a gift, the label says, of Mr. Cye Mandel from Miami, who got it on his own trip to China in 1978—six years after Nixon's. (Cye Mandel made headlines in 1993 when an Indian bingo parlor in Dade County refused to do business with his company on the grounds that he had "mob ties.")[16]

Next is a small image of a white cat on a black fabric field. The label explains that this is embroidery with silk thread and that the piece is double sided and "took a year to complete." Unlike the Cye Mandel collage, this item was presented to Nixon, by the Chinese government—but not on his 1972 trip. Instead he got it on his 1976 visit, when he was disgraced and out of office.

Then large wall text introduces Nixon's view of his China diplomacy. It begins with a ringing declaration: "President Nixon's vision for peace in the world soared beyond the constraints that hobble those who see peace as little more than the absence of war." It goes on to explain that "the great goal of his presidency" was "to secure for generations to come a world in which the U.S. and the other nations of the world worked together to attain a stable, long-lasting peace in which freedom could thrive." Of course conservatives would respond that freedom could never thrive in countries suffering under communist rule.

The wall text continues, "President Nixon's historic opening to the People's Republic of China, coupled with a new relationship with the Soviet Union, were only the visible steps on the bold road toward creating real peace for all the people of the world." Of course conservatives would respond that peace was impossible with an enemy that sought world domination. Next to this text hangs the most impressive work by Chinese craftsmen in the gallery: a gigantic image of Nixon, Mao, and Zhou—in needlepoint. Four feet long and three feet high, it reproduces the familiar photo of the three men smiling and sitting in big armchairs. The label says the item was "made expressly for the Nixon Library and presented on its first anniversary," in 1991.

Then comes another section of text, headlined simply "CHINA." "A fifth of the world's population," it says, "the People's Republic is a giant fact of modern geopolitical life." Yet "for more than 20 years . . . mainland China was not recognized by the government of the U.S. As a result, this vast and extraordinary nation became a mystery to most Americans." If it was a "mystery," that was despite bipartisan efforts to convince Americans that China was an immense prison camp, with a murderous regime responsible for the deaths of tens of millions of its own citizens.

Then comes the heart of the explanation for Nixon's move. "In the 1960s, a split between the Soviets and the Chinese brought about a change in the geopolitical balance. Richard Nixon realized it was possible—indeed imperative—to take advantage of these changes in the best interest of the U.S." So this was realpolitik, the exploitation of antagonism between China and the USSR to advance American interests—not quite the same thing as seeking peace for the entire world. It's also a lot more plausible as Nixon's motive—and Kissinger's.

After that, visitors are given a break from politics to examine more exquisite examples of Chinese crafts—jade horses, a porcelain vase. Following this display are five panels dense with small print that only the most dedicated would read (and while I was in the gallery taking notes, no one read them except me). The headings begin "China Under Mao" and "Outbreak of War in Korea." Here we get an explanation—of sorts—for Americans' opposition to China: "As their sons were being killed in Korea by Chinese Communist soldiers, Americans came to view the Communist Regime with bitter hostility."

Then Nixon enters the story: "During the 1940s, Congressman Nixon supported Chiang Kai Shek." But in the 1960s, "China came to realize it had more to fear from the Soviet Union than from the U.S." Nixon claimed to be one of the first to perceive the historic opportunity offered by the Sino-Soviet split—and his museum wants visitors to know he deserves credit. The main object on display on this wall is the cover page of a 1967 article of Nixon's published in the journal *Foreign Affairs.* This is where Nixon, already a presidential candidate, wrote, "We cannot and should not say we will never recognize the government [of the People's Republic]." The exhibit goes on to declare that "careful readers" of Nixon's 1970 interview in *Time* magazine noted that Nixon there "revealed . . . that a change was imminent" when he was quoted as saying, "If there is anything I want to do before I die, it is to go to China."

The point is that Americans shouldn't have been surprised when Nixon's China trip was announced. But surprise isn't really a big issue for visitors here. The question that needs to be answered is whether Nixon's trip to China meant he was abandoning his lifelong commitment to anticommunism. And that indeed is the next topic in this section of wall text: "While most Americans understood and applauded the President for taking this historic step, others were reacting based upon false assumptions." We know the "others" that Nixon needed to worry about: Reagan, Goldwater, Buckley, the conservatives in Congress and in his party.

But that's not where this text starts. Instead, visitors are told that "many on the left were delighted" that Nixon was going to China, "but only because of their mistaken belief that the President had finally come around to their view that the Communist Chinese were really just 'agrarian reformers.'" This is ridiculous. Some liberals and leftists had indeed called the Chinese Communists "agrarian reformers," but that was back in the 1940s. By 1972 no one on "the left" in the United States held that view. Those in the United States in 1972 who admired Mao liked the uncompromising and ruthless quality of the Cultural Revolution, which they saw as a campaign to destroy a Soviet type of Party bureaucracy and an effort to crush the "capitalist-roaders" in the Party. But again, visitors did not come here wondering, why was the left delighted with Nixon's trip to China?

Finally the wall text gets to the real issue: "Some on the right wrongly criticized the President for 'selling out' on his longstanding anti-communist position. But most Americans knew why the President was going to travel to China"; "most Americans" knew it was "a journey for peace." It's not much of an answer to the critics. The font for this wall text may be small. I didn't see anybody else reading it. But the Nixon Library probably deserves credit at least for acknowledging that some of the president's own supporters criticized him for the China trip. That kind of thing is almost unheard of in presidential libraries, which exist to celebrate the achievements of their presidents and ignore the rest.

Indeed, after that it's back to celebration. This section ends with a quotation from Nixon himself: "My most important foreign policy decision was the opening to China." Next to the quote is a snapshot-sized photo of Nixon with Mao. Finally we get out of black-and-white text to a festive collage of fifty color photos of Nixon's trip, day by day. One more panel speaks of the consequences of the trip: "graduate students increasingly chose Chinese history and politics as their field of study." Generations of peace and freedom for all the people of the world, plus new enthusiasm for Chinese studies among graduate students—what could be better?

Strangely, the Nixon Library foreign policy exhibits say almost nothing about détente with the Soviet Union. They go from the trip to China to the war in Vietnam, with a piece of the Berlin Wall standing awkwardly in the same room. But in many ways détente was equally significant, since it involved setting limits on nuclear weapons. Soviet nuclear missiles were an infinitely greater threat to the United States than anything in China. The signing of the SALT I treaty in 1972 restricted the nuclear arsenals of both powers. That same year the Anti-Ballistic Missile Treaty was also signed, and talks on SALT II began promptly. These were genuinely historic achievements, but they are barely mentioned at the Nixon Library, where the China trip gets all the attention.

Ronald Reagan had been another potential critic of détente, but Nixon succeeded in winning him over, at least in the short term. "When Nixon hosted a lavish poolside party at his estate in San Clemente for Leonid Brezhnev in June 1973," James Mann reports, Nixon "introduced the Soviet leader to Bob Hope, Frank Sinatra, Gene Autry," and other celebrities. Reagan, then governor of California, "was among the few political leaders invited to the festivities." With company like that, how could Reagan resist Nixon the diplomat? "I just think it's too bad that [Watergate] is taking people's attention away from what I think is a most brilliant accomplishment of any president of this century," Reagan told reporters a few days later, "and that is the steady progress towards peace."[17] So Nixon brought Reagan into line in 1973.

But three years later, in his 1976 challenge to Gerald Ford in the Republican primary, Reagan described détente as "a one-way street that simply gives the Soviets what they want with nothing in return." He blamed détente for "the loss of American military supremacy." Under détente, he said, the United States had acted "as if we expect the Soviets to inherit the earth." Ford's chief of staff at this time, organizing his defense, was Dick Cheney. Of course Reagan lost the nomination, but he won the Republican Party to his hard-line position, and when Reagan ran against Carter in 1980 his speeches included a line Republicans loved: "Détente—isn't that what a farmer has with his turkey—before Thanksgiving?"[18] Reagan's election, of course, brought the official repudiation of détente and the achievements celebrated in Yorba Linda at the Nixon Library.

PART FIVE

Alternative Approaches

NINETEEN

Rocky Flats

UNCOVERING THE SECRETS

The feds say the twenty-year controversy over Rocky Flats has come to an end: the former nuclear weapons plant located sixteen miles northwest of Denver has been completely demolished, and in 2007 most of the site was declared a National Wildlife Refuge.[1] There's a lot of history here—almost forty years of plutonium production, a disastrous accident that threatened Denver with a Chernobyl-like incident, and years of protests by thousands of people. But the site has no official museum, no tours, not even a historical marker. And if you want to hike, fish, or go bird-watching in the wildlife refuge, you are told, "There is no public access to Rocky Flats at this time!" (their exclamation point).[2]

But it's not over for a group of activists who want the public to know what happened here—the weapons manufacturing, the environmental disasters, and the protests demanding that nuclear weapons production be ended. They are preparing to open the Rocky Flats Cold War Museum in nearby Arvada in 2012 (figure 35).[3] They have nonprofit status, and they conducted a feasibility study that concluded that a museum "would attract between 88,000 and 110,000 visitors per year."[4] Now they're raising money and collecting oral histories and artifacts for their exhibits. Their idea of how the Cold War should be remembered: feature the history of antiwar activists who campaigned for years to close this weapons plant.

The feds apparently would like the public to forget about what happened here. That's what the federal wildlife refuge website is referring to when it says, "The ROD verifies that the CCP addresses the issues identified during the public process." Translation: the "ROD" is the Record of Decision of the U.S. Fish and Wildlife Service; "CCP" here is not the Russian abbreviation for Soviet Socialist Republic but rather refers to the Comprehensive

Rocky Flats Cold War Museum

Weapons to Wildlife

April 2011 Vol. 5 # 1 Newsletter for Friends of the Rocky Flats Cold War Museum

Board approves lease of old Arvada post office for Rocky Flats Museum

After nearly a year-long search for a building for its first museum, the Rocky Flats Cold War Museum board approved a lease of the old Arvada post office at 5608-12 Yukon St. in Olde Town Arvada beginning April 1. However, it will likely take a year or more to develop exhibits and related educational programs, hire staff and open the museum.

The one-story, 7,000 square foot property has open exhibition space, two functional kitchen areas and several classrooms and offices. Minor remodeling will be done to meet the needs of the museum.

The mission of the museum is to document the historical, social, environmental and scientific aspects of Rocky Flats, the former nuclear weapons plant in northern Jefferson County. The board is committed to telling all sides of the colorful, complex story of Rocky Flats.

"We are delighted to find a central location for our museum," said Shirley Garcia, president of the museum board. "We hope to attract many school groups and others interested in science, local history and the role Rocky Flats played in the Cold War. We have fascinating oral histories and artifacts to share for all age levels."

Garcia said the building's location, a block west of Olde Wadsworth Blvd. and north of Grandview Ave., should be convenient for tourists, school groups, former Rocky Flats workers, area residents and history buffs. The facility is one block from a future light rail stop and has street parking in front and 13 parking spaces in back.

A consultant is currently documenting the museum's artifacts in a special database with the help of volunteers who worked at Rocky Flats. A committee has been meeting for several years to plan exhibits and will soon work with an exhibit designer over the next year. The museum board created an oral history collection of more than 100 interviews of former workers, activists, community and political leaders and others. Volunteers are needed to help develop the museum. They may call 720-898-7125 or go to www.rockyflatsmuseum.org to volunteer, to donate artifacts or to sign up for this newsletter, *Weapons to Wildlife*.

Inside...	***Quote:*** "A nuclear reactor is not a macaroni factory. You can't let it slide into disrepair and then ignore it."
• *Awards presented* • *Chernobyl tourism* • *EPA inspector speaks*	Alexander Novitskas, Russian mechanic at the nuclear power plant in Smolensk quoted in the *San Francisco Chronicle*, July 19, 1997

FIGURE 35. Rocky Flats Cold War Museum newsletter. (courtesy Rocky Flats Cold War Museum, Arvada, Colorado)

Conservation Plan. As for the "issues identified during the public process," the Fish and Wildlife Service doesn't explain what they were. If you want more information—for example, about the radiation hazard here, past and present—you are invited to email them (rockyflats@fws.gov) or give them a call. (I emailed, asking if they could "provide any information about the protests that began in 1978" but got no response.)[5]

The people organizing the museum explain in their brochure and at their website why they want to do it: "Rocky Flats Is Part of History," they say, and their museum will "Explore the Cold War Role," "Maintain an Archive," and, notably, "Uncover the Secrets."[6]

None of those items are part of the mission of the federal Rocky Flats Wildlife Refuge. The refuge website doesn't report that Rocky Flats manufactured plutonium triggers for hydrogen bombs from 1952 to 1989. It doesn't report that each trigger had the power of the Hiroshima bomb and was used to detonate a weapon about a thousand times more powerful than the bomb that destroyed Nagasaki. It doesn't report that the plant was building plutonium nuclear triggers a few miles upwind from Denver, or that they were burying radioactive materials with half-lives of 24,000 years upstream from Denver. It doesn't report that when the plant ceased operations 14.2 tons of plutonium were left at Rocky Flats. It doesn't report about the fire in 1969 in the plutonium factory, which threatened Denver with a nuclear disaster—and was the most expensive industrial accident in American history up to that time. The cleanup took two years and required six hundred workers.[7]

When the Rocky Flats Cold War Museum opens its exhibit space, the displays, they say, will feature a tepee, the one that was erected in 1989 on the railroad tracks blocking rail access to the plutonium plant and serving as the center of the protests for nine months. According to LeRoy Moore, a member of the museum board, speaking at a museum event in 2006, the tepee became the "most visible symbol of that longtime civil disobedience resistance in that year, and people driving along the highway here could see that the resistance on the tracks was still going because that tepee was there." The tepee was added to the museum collection at the 2006 public event, "an afternoon of songs, speeches, and donations of money and artifacts for the museum."[8]

The museum will also feature photos and documents about how Allen Ginsberg and Daniel Ellsberg joined 3,500 demonstrators in the protests in 1978, the year before the tepee went up; they call it the "year of disobedience."

The exhibit will explain how the group laid down on the railroad tracks to stop the trains hauling nuclear materials out of the plutonium factory. The museum website features a photo of the protesters on the tracks.[9] Patrick Malone explains it at the museum website oral history section: "You could lay down, put your head on one rail, put your feet on the other. And I will tell you something, that is an experience that will change you for the rest of your life."

The museum will tell the story of how Ginsberg and Ellsberg were among the seventy-five people arrested for civil disobedience, about their trial, and about how they served a week in the Clear Creek County Jail. The exhibits will include the poem Ginsberg wrote about Rocky Flats while he was in jail for civil disobedience, "Plutonian Ode"—later published by City Lights:

> What new element before us unborn in nature? Is there
> a new thing under the Sun?
> At last inquisitive Whitman a modern epic, detonative,
> Scientific theme . . .[10]

The museum will explain how the next year, 1979, the year of the tepee, the protests were much bigger: 15,000 protesters showed up at the plant for two days of demonstrations and civil disobedience; 287 were arrested, this time on federal trespassing charges. It will describe how the year after that, 1980, the third annual Anti–Rocky Flats Rally brought 12,000 to the site, this time not for civil disobedience but for workshops in nonviolent direct action. Allen Ginsberg and Daniel Ellsberg were back; Ginsberg said, "This is the nerve center of the nation's death wish."

But the big news in 1979 was that Representative Pat Schroeder took part in the protests—the Democrat who was the first woman elected to the House from Colorado. She said the plant should be converted to peaceful use: "The whole rest of the world changes, why is this plant sacrosanct?"[11] (Republican presidential candidate John Anderson sent a message of support.) The museum will tell about the Japanese Buddhist monk, Gyoshen Sawada, who joined the protests, walking and chanting. It will tell about the two Catholic nuns, Sisters Pat Mahoney and Marie Nord, who got inside the plant in 1982 using counterfeit security badges and then raised a flag over the plutonium plant bearing the words "Death Factory." It will explain that they were arrested and that each was sentenced to five years in federal prison on felony counterfeiting and trespassing charges, sentences reduced to six months, which each served.[12] The museum will display the famous photograph from 1983 of 15,000 demonstrators encircling the seventeen-mile perimeter of the plant.

And it will have a big display about what happened on June 6, 1989, when eighty FBI and EPA agents stormed into the plant, armed with guns and a search warrant empowering them to look for evidence of criminal violations of environmental law. It will describe how they stayed for twenty days, how the Rockwell corporation then gave up operation of the plant, how plutonium production was suspended because of safety violations, and how the next year the *Denver Post* and the *New York Times* published a report that the ductwork at Rocky Flats contained more than sixty pounds of plutonium—and even a tiny amount of plutonium causes lung cancer if inhaled. Then it will describe how in 1992 Rockwell pled guilty to criminal violations and paid a fine of $18.5 million.

And then it will tell the story of Jon Lipsky, the FBI agent who led the raid in 1989, who quit the FBI in 2001 in protest against the decision to turn Rocky Flats into a wildlife refuge, and who filed a lawsuit against the Department of Justice along with the former leader of the Rocky Flats federal grand jury and a former chemical operator at the plant who suffers from radiation exposure. Their lawsuit sought to unseal testimony from the grand jury hearings documenting what they said were continuing radiation hazards at the site.

The museum may display Lipsky's open letter to Congress before the vote on turning Rocky Flats into a wildlife refuge: "I am an FBI agent. My superiors have ordered me to lie about a criminal investigation I headed in 1989. The Justice Department covered up the truth. . . . I have refused to follow the orders. . . . Some dangerous decisions are now being made based on that government cover-up." The museum could also quote Lipsky's description of the cleanup effort: he called it "woefully inadequate—a farce." They could cite his comment on the decision to make Rocky Flats a wildlife refuge open to the public: "There is nothing safe or sane about it."[13] All this is already displayed at the museum website and in its online oral history archive.

For an exhibit about the terrifying 1969 fire in the plutonium factory, the Rocky Flats Cold War Museum could do worse than install the multimedia exhibit posted online at the Rocky Flats Virtual Museum, sponsored by the Center for Environmental Journalism at the University of Colorado–Boulder and available online.[14] That exhibit uses video, audio, and photos along with text to explain how plutonium can ignite spontaneously, and how on Mother's Day in 1969 plutonium did ignite spontaneously—"in a bomb manufacturing building containing more than 7,600 pounds of plutonium, enough for 1,000 nuclear bombs."

The fire chief knew that if the fire were to burn through the building's roof, the entire Denver area could be contaminated by a Chernobyl-like release of radiation. But stopping the fire before it burned through the roof would require massive amounts of water, and water coming in contact with plutonium could set off a chain reaction. Although that would not cause a nuclear explosion with a mushroom cloud over Denver, it would dramatically increase the level of deadly radiation inside the building, threatening the firefighters: a chain reaction "would kill anyone within several feet. An eerie blue flash would be the last thing a fireman would see."

The fire chief decided to try to save Denver and take the risk of fighting the fire with water. The water did not set off a chain reaction. But forty-one firefighters, guards, and other employees who fought the fire received doses of radiation.

How close did Denver come? "If the fire had burned through the roof," the exhibit states, "thousands of pounds of deadly plutonium in the form of powdery ash would have exposed hundreds of thousands of women, men, and children living nearby to toxic radiation." The exhibit explains that an unlikely accident helped save Denver in 1969. Plutonium would have escaped into the air not only if the fire had burned through the roof but also if the filter system for the air vents had been destroyed during the fire. That almost happened, because ventilation fans in the burning plutonium factory "sucked flames into the filter system designed to prevent plutonium contamination from leaving the building. Two of the three banks of paper filters already had burned out and the third was beginning to burn." But at that point, "a fireman accidentally backed his truck into a power pole outside the building and cut off the power. The fans stopped spinning"—and the filter system that kept the plutonium inside the building wasn't destroyed by the fire. "Denver was spared."

The next section poses the question, "How could this happen?" The answer: "Government officials hid behind 'national security' in refusing to provide details of the fire. But a secret AEC investigation report from August 1969 sharply criticized both AEC and Dow management for neglecting fire safety" in the plutonium factory. The next panel is titled "The Fire Was Inevitable." It says, "From the beginning, safety took a back seat to bomb production at Rocky Flats. Dow Chemical officials had to meet quotas for the company to receive bonuses from its cost-plus federal government contract."

The final section is titled "Citizens Awaken" and describes the political protests that culminated with the FBI raid and the end of plutonium production at Rocky Flats. It's a powerful and convincing exhibit.

Of course the Rocky Flats Cold War Museum does not plan to be an exclusively antiwar, anti-nuke institution. In its fund-raising and promotional materials, it promises to document all "the historical, social, environmental and scientific aspects of Rocky Flats," fully and fairly. The official mission statement adds that the goal is "to educate the public about Rocky Flats, the Cold War, and their legacies through preservation of key artifacts and development of interpretive and educational programs." The biggest photo in the brochure, however, shows a demonstrator carrying a sign reading, "Man's Real Enemy Is Weapons Not Ideas"—and confronting a security guard.[15]

The museum board includes representatives from local government, state regulatory agencies, and former Rocky Flats employees and contractors—and also representatives from "environmental and peace groups." The artifacts they are planning to preserve include "photographs, building diagrams, respirators and protective suits, radiation measuring instruments," and, on the official list, "the tepee from anti-nuclear demonstrations." The newsletter reports the donation of other artifacts for display: a banner reading "Shut Down Rocky Flats," carried by a local group called Artists Against Nuclear War; the donor recalled that it was carried in a march from the courthouse in Boulder to the west gate of Rocky Flats "every Sunday." Another donation: a bumper sticker reading, "Save Rocky Flats—move Denver."[16]

The oral history project, which was completed in 2006, includes testimony from 151 people. In the interviews workers talk about their work; the list includes "production workers, managers, union members," and, notably, "whistleblowers"; among the topics they cover, according to the official description, are "experiencing camaraderie, fighting two fires, avoiding criticalities," and, notably, "becoming contaminated." Also listed in the official description of the oral history collection: "Peace and environmental activists who protested during the '70s," who "opposed the plant's operations," who "discuss reasons for their concerns and details of their activism."[17]

The museum has one other purpose: "Contamination will remain in some areas at the site for thousands of years. This problem requires ongoing site monitoring, stewardship and other means of institutional control to protect public health and the environment in the future."

The Rocky Flats Cold War Museum does present the official position alongside that of the antinuclear activists. In a recent newsletter, a thirty-year employee of the plant recalls his work and concludes that the weapons he worked on at Rocky Flats "won the Cold War. We bankrupted Russia by staying ahead of them." He said he hoped "we never give up that stockpile," because "12 nations now . . . can make bombs"—so "you've got to keep that as a deterrent. . . . I'm a hawk in that respect."[18] The newsletter accompanies that interview with a quote from Billy Graham: "The present insanity of the global arms race, if continued, will lead inevitably to a conflagration so great that Auschwitz will seem like a minor rehearsal."[19]

Another issue of the newsletter features Herb Bowman, who was Dow's manager of manufacturing when the fire broke out in 1969. At that time, he said, he focused on restoring plutonium production, "because we were the sole producer of plutonium parts in the country, . . . it affected Los Alamos and Livermore. . . . [T]he most serious problem was to develop a way to keep those two laboratories going . . . because there was thousands of people involved in those laboratories and at the test sites . . . depending on us being able to support them." He was asked whether the fire shook his confidence in the production of nuclear weapons: "No, not at all. In fact, it . . . reassured me, because the systems did work. There was a little contamination. . . . You had a fire . . . estimated as a $50 million fire[,] . . . and yet the safety systems to contain the contamination and the materials in the building worked."

Then he was asked about nuclear weapons in general: "I felt at the time it was absolutely necessary. To this day I am absolutely convinced that . . . if we didn't have a supreme . . . retaliatory capability, we'd have been in a big war a long time before this. . . . [B]ut God, we looked forward to the day when there would be no more need for Rocky Flats."[20]

Another issue of the newsletter features Dee Krieg, who was head of transportation for Rocky Flats and thus in charge of the rail line that the demonstrators were trying to block. She was asked what she thought about them: "They used to be a real pain, because they were always after my shipments, either rail shipments or whatever. And getting involved with them all the time was a mess." She recalled getting an anonymous call at home in the middle of the night telling her that "they were going to build a fire on the railroad tracks so that the trains couldn't come in." "So I got the Highway Patrol and the guards and everybody down there," she continued. "Well, they caught them, stopped them before they got the fire built."

She was asked whether she thought the demonstrators had a right to be there:

> I didn't care whether they were there or not.... We had ministers, we had nuns. I signed the arrest warrant for the nuns, and that didn't help too much, since I'm a Catholic. But I said I didn't give a damn, they didn't have any business out there. And then the one nun's grandfather ... lived in Colorado Springs ... [and] he wrote a very nice letter to the *Denver Post* saying that while he didn't want his granddaughter to go to jail, if that's what it took to wake her up, he didn't have any problem with it [laughs].[21]

All these oral histories will go into the museum—perhaps on video monitors. Notably, the argument that nuclear weapons won the Cold War will not be the official interpretation offered by the museum but rather the opinion of some of the employees—an interpretation challenged by others. That makes the Rocky Flats Cold War Museum project an exceptional one.

"What Happened Here?" That's the question the U.S. Fish and Wildlife Service says it will post on signs "at all trailheads." Their proposed answer is not bad:

> The land you are about to enter, Rocky Flats National Wildlife Refuge, is an historic Cold War site. Refuge lands are part of the buffer zone of the former Rocky Flats Plant that operated from 1951 until 1989, when it was closed. For nearly four decades, thousands of women and men worked here, building nuclear components for the US' deterrent weapons throughout the Cold War Period.
>
> Weapons components production at the plant involved plutonium and other radioactive and hazardous materials. The work was dangerous and secret. Over the course of decades, there were accidents. Some of these accidents and some of the waste handling practices of the early decades resulted in releases of plutonium and other contaminants into the environment.
>
> Beginning in 1995, some of the same Cold War veterans who had built weapons components at Rocky Flats, assisted with an unprecedented and enormously complex cleanup project to remediate contaminated buildings and soil on the site. They accomplished that difficult job in 2005, leaving the land as an asset for future generations of Americans.

The comes the big question: "Is there Residual Contamination?" The official answer, of course, is no: "The land is safe for public recreation.... There are hazards involved in any form of wildland recreation. Hazards at Rocky Flats include inclement or extreme weather conditions, the potential for trips, slips and falls, poisonous snakes, and unreasonable or illegal acts by other persons."[22] Watch out for snakes, and don't worry about radiation: that's the message in the proposed sign text of the U.S. Fish and Wildlife Service.

But according to news reports, "plans for 16 miles of hiking trails and a visitors center have stalled" at the Rocky Flats Wildlife Refuge.[23] As of 2012, none of the signs about "What Happened Here?" had been posted.

The Rocky Flats Cold War Museum is an inspiring one. Where the federal government is not even posting signs or historical markers, much less opening a museum, a group of citizens has decided to organize their own museum—one that will tell "both sides" of the story, in the voices of the people who worked there, and demonstrated there—the bomb makers, and the opponents of bomb making. Instead of an omniscient voice of authority instructing visitors about the one true history of this place, the museum will present a variety of voices. It's almost like democracy at work.

TWENTY

CNN's Cold War

EQUAL TIME FOR THE RUSSIANS

In response to the conservatives' "good war" framework for explaining the Cold War, CNN offered a strikingly different approach in 1998: equal time for the Russians. CNN produced and broadcast a monumental new video history of the Cold War, twenty-four one-hour programs that were widely acclaimed as the best documentary of the year. The series, which ran in prime time on Sunday nights for six months, was hailed as a landmark in the history of television. It was endorsed by the National Council for Social Studies, and the entire series was distributed on video to schools for a nominal fee. A beautiful companion volume was published, intended for use as a textbook. A state-of-the-art interactive website won awards. In 2008 each of the twenty-four hours was posted on the Internet at Google Video, available to the entire world, on demand, free. And for the twentieth anniversary of the end of the Cold War, the Paley Center for Media in Beverly Hills scheduled an exhibit about and screening of CNN's *Cold War.*[1]

Ted Turner, head of CNN, who commissioned the series, was responding to a profound weakness in the existing histories of the Cold War. Tony Judt called the problem "tunnel vision," an approach dominated by the view from Washington, D.C., and focusing almost exclusively on American politicians and statesmen and their debates about their rivals in Moscow.[2] But with the end of the USSR and the opening of Soviet archives, there was no longer an excuse for neglecting the view from Moscow.

So Turner gave instructions to his producer, Jeremy Isaacs, that were explicit: the show was to avoid an America-centered, triumphalist perspective. Instead the goal was to "tell a universal, not a partisan, story," Isaacs explained, "and to do justice to the experience, reasoning, motives and actions of both the protagonist great powers involved."[3] Thus Russian producers were hired,

Russian archives were searched, and Russian experts and witnesses were interviewed. In many episodes the Russians got half of the airtime and the Americans the other half.

Conservatives hated the whole thing. The tone was set by Charles Krauthammer, who declared in the *Washington Post* that the CNN documentary was dedicated to a "relentless attempt to find moral equivalence between the two sides."[4] Similar arguments were made by a dozen others among the right's top thinkers. They were correct about one thing: the show offered a clear challenge to the conservatives' interpretation of the Cold War as a struggle between good and evil equivalent to the Allies' World War II battle against the Nazis.

Turner, founder of CNN and still head of the network at the time *Cold War* was commissioned, "personally conceived" the series, as *Variety* reported.[5] To produce the series, Turner in 1994 commissioned the British team that had made *The World at War*, on World War II, headed by Jeremy Isaacs. Putting production in the hands of a British team was Turner's first step in avoiding an America-centered triumphalist story. The second was enlisting Russian filmmakers and historians from the start in the research, writing, and production. That meant "the other side" would explain its perspective, its understanding, its fears and hopes. And although a panel of historians was enlisted, they never appeared onscreen to explain things. The talking heads onscreen followed the convention of historical documentaries: all were "witnesses" or "key players of the time."

Turner, the conservatives pointed out, was a liberal. He had famously donated a billion dollars to the UN in 1997, the year before CNN's *Cold War* was broadcast.[6] The UN, of course, in the view of the right, was a hotbed of anti-Americanism. And as the *Washington Times* reminded readers, "This was the man who extended his hand in friendship to the Soviets with the creation of the Goodwill Games and who later married no less than Hanoi Jane Fonda."[7]

What did this series, which so outraged conservatives, actually say about the Cold War and its origins, when it gave equal time and equal treatment to the Russians? The prologue opens with film of a nuclear explosion and the narrator Kenneth Branagh in voice-over saying, "A nuclear shadow falls across the human future.... Midway through the 20th century, two superpowers prepared for a conflict which might have ended life on this planet."[8] That's quite a bit different from saying freedom confronted totalitarianism across the planet.

The prologue then takes viewers to "the underworld" beneath the "spring flowers" of the Greenbrier hotel, inside the congressional nuclear bunker. "Down here," Branagh says, "the politicians would represent the dead and the dying in the world overhead." Down here, "a handful of human beings" would "wait out the nuclear winter.... The lost world above the shelter would become only a memory—a myth. The living would come to envy the dead." Then comes film of Nagasaki in ruins, followed by a quick montage of shots of smiling Cold War leaders on both sides, and then the title of Episode 1—an ironic title: "Comrades, 1917–1945."

The next scene opens in 1945 with Berlin in ruins and with the Potsdam Conference. Right away we get perspectives from two sides: an assistant to Truman says the new president was "unprepared"; an official from the Soviet Foreign Ministry describes Stalin's first meeting with Truman and Churchill. Then comes a brief history of the Bolsheviks and Lenin's onetime hope for "world revolution." "The cold war had its origins," Branagh says, after World War I, "in a clash of ideologies: communist and capitalist." Note: *not* "slavery and freedom" or "totalitarianism and democracy." Woodrow Wilson's goal is described as a world "safe for small nations, sound for business." Viewers are told that the United States and Britain sent troops to fight the Russian Revolution and that "Churchill, fresh from victory over Germany, urged: 'Kill the Bolshie! Kiss the Hun!'... The intervention left Lenin and Stalin convinced that the West would seize any chance, embrace any ally, in order to destroy Communism."

Churchill is contrasted with an elderly veteran of the Red Army in the Revolution, who says, "We knew we were fighting for the people—the poor people." Famine in Russia is contrasted with "the good life" in Jazz Age America. But with the depression, "American politics shifted to the left"; FDR promised "to regulate capitalism for the public good" and recognized the Soviet Union—George Kennan explains why (the USSR had been in existence for sixteen years, and "realism" required opening diplomatic relations).

Then we get to Stalin—introduced by Branagh as "a tyrant" who "tolerated no criticism." "The cost of collectivization was the murder of millions of peasants—and renewed famine," he reports. The same Red Army vet says,

"It was a regime of terror." Kennan describes the show trials, and Branagh says they showed the outside world that "Stalin's Soviet Union" was "a police state, not a workers' paradise." But in the United States, thousands nevertheless supported the "ideals of communism" and rallied to fight fascism.

The Nazi-Soviet pact is described as Stalin's response to Munich and an attempt to gain time to prepare for inevitable war. The key moment in the origins of the Cold War, Branagh explains, was Hitler's invasion of Russia in June 1941—which would "bring Russian power into the heart of Europe only four years later." At the Teheran conference, the Allies agreed that Eastern Europe would become a Soviet zone of influence, including Poland; "the Poles were given no choice." Later, Churchill in Moscow "scribbled out a formula for carving up Europe." Here the screen shows Churchill's note, with Stalin's check mark of agreement: "Romania: Russia 90%, Others 10%; Greece: GB and US 90%, Russia 10%; Yugoslavia 50/50," and so on. The point was that "democracy" was not at issue at the end of World War II. Instead the victors divided Europe between them. In Eastern Europe, a British diplomat says, "Stalin was bound to get what he wanted, because the Red Army was in charge of the whole area."

A longer segment describes the meeting of American and Russian troops at the Elbe at the end of World World II in Europe. An American vet says, "You put an American uniform on them, they would have looked like Americans." The war, Branagh declares, "cost the Soviet Union 27 million lives—nearly 40 times American and British losses put together."

Episode 1 ends with Hiroshima: "Soon the human race would be able to destroy itself—in a day. At each cold war crisis to come, the nuclear shadow threatened." Viewers watch film of Nagasaki in ruins, followed by the first credit: "Series Concept Ted Turner."

Episode 1 displayed most of the themes of what was to come: equal treatment of the perspectives and experiences of Russia and the United States; a frank rejection of the notion that "democracy" and "freedom" were the central issues that divided the two powers; and an equally frank description of Stalin as a "tyrant" whose "reign of terror" was responsible for "the murder of millions" in the USSR. None of this would be regarded as surprising or controversial by any mainstream historian.

Mainstream TV critics lavished the series with superlatives, which provoked the conservatives further. The *Boston Globe* called it "riveting" and "illuminating" and named it the number one documentary of the year. *Time* magazine called it "documentary television at its best"—"serious, thorough, and absorbing." The *New York Times* praised it as "gripping straightforward history[;] . . . more intense than a John le Carré thriller."[9]

The conservative critique of CNN's *Cold War* includes some of the bitterest, lengthiest, and most vituperative writing in the history of TV criticism. Krauthammer's *Washington Post* piece began with a stunning declaration: "Whoever said that history is written by the victors has not seen CNN's 24-hour epic documentary 'Cold War.'" He hastened to add that he did not mean the series was written by the Soviets; "But it was clearly written from the perspective of those who for years considered 'Cold Warrior' an epithet and reviled as reactionary warmongers those, like Ronald Reagan, who insisted on victory."[10]

The episode describing McCarthyism in the United States was particularly infuriating to Krauthammer. He blasted it as "moral equivalence with a sledgehammer." He objected to the presentation of the anticommunist crusade of the fifties, especially narrator Branagh's line "Both sides turned their fear inward against their own people. They hunted the enemy within." The problem for Krauthammer: "The gulag—a vast continental system of arrest, torture, disappearance, execution, forced labor, starvation—is juxtaposed with what? The Hollywood Ten! Jailed, we are told. But not told that the sentences ranged from four to 10 months. . . . The horror. Yes, of course, this shouldn't have happened. It is a blot on our history that these men's civil rights were trampled. But a blot is no mirror to an ocean of blood."[11]

The series producers replied that giving the same number of minutes to the Gulag and McCarthyism did not mean they were presented as equally murderous. The narrator did report that "the Gulag, the secret universe of labor camps, swallowed the lives of millions," and the filmmakers, Isaacs said, assumed viewers would be able to tell the difference between "millions" and "the ten" without experts explaining it to them.

Even worse for Krauthammer was the section on the execution of the Rosenbergs. The documentary says they were convicted of "spying for the Soviet Union," but it didn't say they gave the Soviets secrets of the atomic bomb. The companion volume came in for special condemnation because of its explanation of the Rosenbergs' motives: "Rosenberg was at the centre of a network of spies who felt uncomfortable that the United States was the sole owner of the key to atomic warfare." Krauthammer could barely contain his rage over this line, writing, "Uncomfortable. That one of the most prodigious murderers in history lacked the deadliest weapon ever devised. No doubt, treason relieved the poor man's unease."[12]

Krauthammer did not seem to be outraged that prosecutors knew Ethel Rosenberg was not guilty of espionage but nevertheless insisted on a death sentence for her to pressure Julius to cooperate and name others to save the life of the mother of his children. Krauthammer didn't mention the problem with the testimony of David Greenglass, who admitted that the testimony that sent Ethel to the electric chair was false.[13] (Ronald Radosh in his contribution to the debate over CNN's *Cold War* mentions only the execution of Julius, cleverly avoiding the problems with the case against Ethel.)[14]

Krauthammer's fury was almost equaled by Jacob Heilbrunn's, writing in the *New Republic.* He too started out from the bedrock conservative position that victory in the Cold War was the moral equivalent to victory in World War II. When the filmmaker made *World at War* about World War II, Heilbrunn wrote, "obviously he never dreamed of giving equal time, weight, and credence to both the Nazi and Allied 'viewpoints.'" The CNN documentary's "problem" was that it didn't treat the Cold War the way World War II had been treated in Isaacs's previous documentary series. The fatal flaw with the CNN series was that it presented the Cold War as "a morally unintelligible contest between two equally dangerous superpowers." Instead of condemning the Soviets, "every effort is made to draw parallels between American misdeeds, at home and abroad, and Soviet ones." And the series failed to blame the Soviets for "perpetuating the Cold War"—when the Americans were in his view ready for détente and peaceful coexistence.[15]

Heilbrunn was equally unhappy with the depiction of Cold War America, objecting especially to the statement in the documentary that "leaders of the American Communist Party were jailed, and the persecution spread. Left-wing labor organizations were banned, radical groups indicted, demonstrations broken up." What exactly was the problem here? For Heilbrunn this was an argument that J. Edgar Hoover "equals Stalin."[16]

The Hiss case continued to provide a flash point for conservatives as CNN's *Cold War* aired in 1998. Heilbrunn was outraged that the documentary reported that Hiss "firmly denied that he had betrayed his country" and that Nixon, "an ambitious young Republican, was convinced that Hiss was lying. Hiss was jailed for perjury. Nixon's name was made." Again, this seems factually flawless, but Heilbrunn objected to the absence of a clear statement by the filmmakers not just that Hiss was convicted but that he was guilty. The filmmakers, Heilbrunn argued, ought to have pointed out that Hiss received "a trial by a jury of his peers, a constitutional nicety never observed for the multitudes accused of espionage in the Soviet Union."[17]

The importance conservatives gave to countering CNN's documentary became clear when the Hoover Institution, the oldest and most august institution of right-wing intellectuals, published an entire book about the CNN series. Although the volume was advertised as a debate, the book's editor, Arnold Beichman, made his agenda clear: "I hope that our book will be read by school boards, school principals, teachers, especially high school teachers, as demonstrating that the Cold War was not merely a struggle between a pair of equally demented gorillas whose snarls and wild swings endangered world peace." He concluded by stating the thesis of the book, the idea at the heart of the conservative interpretation: "The Cold War was as much a 'just war' as was World War II."[18] The *Washington Times* agreed that the book provided "the best antidote there is to Turnerized world history" and "ought to accompany every set of Mr. Turner's 24 tapes that goes into American classrooms."[19]

Richard Pipes, the Harvard historian who had been the leading conservative historian of the Soviet Union for decades, agreed in his essay for the book that the show advanced the "moral equivalence" argument—in particular, by its "unwillingness to confront the fundamental causes of the Cold War," which, he said, could be found long before 1947–48, in "the long-term objectives and methods of the Bolsheviks, who sought world revolution starting in 1917." Indeed Pipes could quote Lenin and Trotsky even before 1917 arguing that workers of the world should unite. But that's not quite the same as the Soviets' maintenance of a defensive perimeter after losing more than 25 million people to Nazi armies. For Pipes, the program treated "Soviet aggression and Western responses to it . . . as basically identical."[20]

The Hoover anthology bills itself as a debate, but the appearance of evenhandedness in the volume is limited. For the prosecution, Richard Pipes, Robert Conquest, Charles Krauthammer, and half a dozen others; for the other side, defending CNN is . . . John Lewis Gaddis, also a conservative—perhaps the most respected and prestigious conservative historian of the Cold War.[21] He was officially a consultant to the filmmaker, and was given space by the Hoover to respond to the repeated charges that he had betrayed the cause and collaborated with liars. Gaddis did not defend the particular passages in particular episodes that received such furious attack from his colleagues; instead he limited himself to explaining the instructions they received from

Ted Turner: "that 'Cold War' tell its story from an international, not just an American perspective, and that its tone not be triumphalist."[22] And he emphasized that his role was as a consultant, not a writer or producer, so he was not responsible for the final product.

When Gaddis's defense first appeared on the op-ed page of the *New York Times,* the *Washington Times* took him to task for accepting Jeremy Isaacs's assignment, whose "fallacy is immediately apparent. Just imagine the Nazi leadership given equal time—as the Soviet leadership is given here. Just imagine producers deliberately staying clear of 'triumphalism' as Europe is freed by the Allies and the concentration camps liberated." Because the CNN production failed to participate in conservative triumphalism, the series was "singularly offensive."[23]

Gaddis's rejoinder was surprisingly un-ideological: "All I can say is, relax, guys."[24] But how is it possible to "relax" about a failure to depict accurately—for millions of viewers—a battle between good and evil?

Many of the points that conservative critics argued were missing from the documentary were in fact made onscreen, though not in statements by the narrator. The interviews with "eyewitnesses" were especially effective, particularly the Eastern Europeans testifying about their experience of Soviet domination: Berliners recalling the airlift, Czechs remembering the Soviet tanks rolling in, Hungarians reporting what fighting the Russians was like in 1956. Viewers saw a Hungarian agricultural technician who wept as he recalled how he had been tempted to leave the barricades, but when he saw the fourteen- and fifteen-year-old boys fighting beside him, he couldn't do it. "The shame kept me there," he said.[25] The conservative critics, by focusing on the text read by the narrator, forgot about the basic rule of cinema: show it, don't tell it.

Of course the CNN series did have a narrator—Kenneth Branagh—and scripts written by accomplished writers, including Ian Buruma, Germaine Greer, and William Shawcross. But each episode was carried primarily by the visual documentation from both sides, and in many cases it was extraordinary. In addition to the interviews with "eyewitnesses," the series featured archival film footage that was often amazing: perhaps the most striking is the KGB film of the arrest of Russian CIA agents who had been betrayed by Aldrich Ames.

Of the "eyewitness" interviews with leaders, the most compelling story came from Fidel Castro, who suggested that the world was even closer to nuclear war during the Cuban Missile Crisis than we had previously understood: "On the 26th of October, at a meeting with the Soviet military commander, I was informed about the state of the missiles," Castro said. "He told me: 'The air regiment is ready. The surface-to-air missiles are ready, the tactical nuclear missile unit is ready. Missiles [are] ready.'" And viewers also learned from Castro his reaction when Khrushchev agreed to remove the missiles, in exchange for Kennedy's public promise not to invade the island and his private promise to remove U.S. missiles from Turkey. More than twenty-five years later Castro was still angry. "It really was a disgraceful agreement," he told Pat Mitchell, the CNN interviewer. "It never crossed my mind they would do anything like this."

The critics were right that the documentary sought to explain Soviet perspectives on their strategy and actions rather than simply call them "evil." None of this part of the series was surprising. The Soviets had strategic concerns about military defense; they had economic needs and economic interests; their leaders made political calculations and had blind spots and misunderstandings—in these ways the USSR was not uniquely evil. Michael Dobbs, Moscow bureau chief for the *Washington Post* in 1988–93 and author of *Down with Big Brother,* a history of the collapse of communism, wrote one of the best-informed commentaries on this aspect of the film. The "most interesting contribution" made by the series, he wrote, was "the view from the other side. During the long years of superpower rivalry, Americans had a hackneyed, distorted image of Russians as communist automatons blindly fulfilling the orders of their leaders. Yet it turns out that they were very like us, people with families and ordinary, everyday concerns, including the nagging worry of being blown to smithereens in a nuclear war." Dobbs noted that "Russian pilots and submarine captains interviewed by CNN talk in terms about their role in the Cold War that are strikingly similar to the ones used by their American counterparts, albeit from the opposite ideological perspective."[26]

While the series depicted ordinary Russians and Eastern Europeans as "more intelligent and human" than most Americans realized, Dobbs went on to note that some of the communist leaders were "even less impressive than one might have imagined." CNN included interviews with the Soviet ambassador to Czechoslovakia during the Prague Spring, along with a hardline Czechoslovak ideologist who supported the 1968 Soviet invasion of his country. "Their bland, unimaginative faces," he wrote, along with "the wooden jargon coming out of their mouths," spoke volumes about the deadness of communist rule.[27]

The final episode of the series, "Conclusions, 1989–1991," opens with interviews with George H. W. Bush and Gorbachev, who says, "For the first time we said 'we no longer consider each other enemies.'" At that point Condoleezza Rice, "aide to President Bush," explains, "The world had changed dramatically . . . the Wall had come down," and Poland and Hungary were no longer communist countries. Vaclav Havel explains how nonviolent protest in Prague brought the fall of the regime. Dramatic film shows fighting in Bucharest, where, viewers learn, nearly a thousand were killed in the overthrow and execution of Ceausescu.

Then, in the Soviet Union, Gorbachev himself explains, "We rightly chose freedom, democracy, glasnost and pluralism. But we got one thing wrong: people judged the state of the country by what they could, or couldn't, buy in the markets and shops." Now the Communist Party, "which had ruled Russia since 1917, would have to share power with others," the narrator says—"a complete break with the practice of Lenin and Stalin." Communist Party leader Boris Yeltsin, we are told, "used economic discontent to weaken Gorbachev." Interviews with Soviet Foreign Minister Edward Shevardnadze and U.S. Secretary of State James Baker review the withdrawal of the Red Army from Eastern Europe. Gorbachev's agreement that a united Germany could remain within NATO, Condi Rice says, "we called VE day two—because that really was the end of the Cold War." Gorbachev asked the leading Western states for massive loans, "but they turned him down flat." Hard-line communists then attempted a putsch in Moscow, which failed, but Yeltsin emerged the victor, and Gorbachev resigned. On December 25, 1991, the Soviet Union was dissolved.

In the concluding section Branagh says, "The cold war ended, peaceably. But need it have begun? Could it have been avoided—back in 1945, when the two sides were comrades?" It's a crucial question. Gorbachev comes back onscreen to say, "We missed our chance. The West exaggerated the strength of the Soviet Union. We could not possibly have moved into Western Europe. We were a devastated country. We'd lost millions of people." The American reply comes from Paul Nitze, who had been secretary of the navy and then deputy secretary of defense in the 1960s: "I can't imagine any circumstances under which we could have worked out our problems with Russia earlier than we did, or in a different way. I've come to the conclusion that we did it pretty goddamn well."

Branagh comes back to say, "There were costs, human and material." A Russian environmentalist says, "The cold war is still going on, because the air, water and soil are polluted" by the legacy of nuclear weapons manufacture and testing. And, Branagh reminds viewers, the toll in human lives in the hot wars of the era needed to be considered. "Millions in Korea, millions in Vietnam, over a million died in Afghanistan," he says, and tells viewers that there were other conflicts as well. Some of these would have happened anyway—but "the Cold War made them more deadly." Video shows a Russian mother visiting her son's grave and an American mother at the Vietnam Veterans Memorial kissing her son's name and sobbing. A sort of moral equivalence could be found in these shots.

"The Cold War was a clash of ideologies," Branagh says, "and the big loser was Marxism-Leninism." Then Castro appears onscreen and says, "Why believe that the ideals of socialism, which are so generous, and appeal so much to solidarity and fraternity, will one day disappear? What would prevail? Selfishness? . . . [T]hat will not save the world."

Havel offers a reply: "Communism as a system went against life . . . against the need to be enterprising, to associate freely. It suppressed national identity." Once again, both sides are presented, and the viewer can choose.

Branagh declares that "Gorbachev had done as much as anyone to end the Cold War." As the red flag came down in Moscow for the last time, the episode shows Bush on TV on Christmas Eve, 1991: "For over 40 years the U.S. led the West in the struggle against communism. . . . [T]he struggle forced all nations to live under the threat of nuclear destruction. That confrontation is now over." With Bush's speech, the series ends.

The companion volume went one step further, refuting directly the argument that the United States, led by Reagan, "won the Cold War." "It was Gorbachev," the CNN book explained, "who made the moves in ending the arms race. He surrendered Communist rule in Eastern Europe[;] . . . he introduced multiparty rule in the USSR itself." For a final verdict, the program quoted a former State Department analyst, Raymond L. Garthoff, emphasizing not Reagan but Gorbachev: "What happened would not have happened without him; that cannot be said of anyone else."[28] The book concluded that the trillions spent on weapons "could have been diverted to other social needs"—the same thing that the "ban the bomb" and "no nukes" protesters had been saying for decades. The program quoted Martin Luther King Jr., who "complained that Lyndon Johnson's promise of a Great Society was lost on the battlefields of Vietnam."[29]

So in CNN's *Cold War,* the conflict was not presented as a battle between good and evil, the moral equivalent of World War II, but rather as a conflict between two great powers, both of whose people had fears and hopes and both of which acted to advance strategic interests. The fury of the conservatives provided a measure of the success CNN had in achieving its goals.

TWENTY-ONE

Harry Truman's Amazing Museum

Who started the Cold War? Did the Cold War have to be militarized, or could it have been limited to an economic and political contest? Did it have to be organized around nuclear weapons promising "mutually assured destruction"? Were there alternatives in the beginning, in 1947–48? These are questions Harry Truman faced when he ascended to the presidency after FDR's death. Truman's defenders give him credit for seeing the aggressive nature of the Soviet threat and for his firm and uncompromising response, especially the creation of NATO, a military alliance to defend Western Europe from Soviet attack. Truman's critics ever since 1947 have argued that the Soviet Union was concerned primarily with the defense of its own borders, with preventing another German invasion. In this view, the "Eastern bloc" countries were occupied by the Red Army and ruled as Soviet satellites primarily as a buffer zone between Russia and Germany—bad for the Poles, the Hungarians, and the rest but not a threat to West Germany, Italy, or France.

You might expect the Truman Library in Independence, Missouri, to make the case that Truman was right—the way the Reagan Library, the JFK Library, the LBJ Library, and all the rest make the case for their presidents. You might expect the Truman Library to instruct visitors on the significance of the Soviet threat in the late 1940s, and the wisdom of the Truman Doctrine and the creation of NATO. But the Truman Library contains a huge surprise: it tells visitors that Truman might have been wrong.

The Truman Library is unique among presidential libraries in that it informs visitors that historians are divided about the president's decisions, and still debating them. That fact is declared at the beginning of the exhibits in what the historian Benjamin Hufbauer rightly calls "a remarkable text." It is worth quoting in full because it is "so antithetical to the displays at most other presidential libraries."[1]

> The years of Harry Truman's presidency are crowded with significant and controversial events. No single, universally accepted account of this period exists. Historians and non-experts alike bring a variety of perspectives to the study of these momentous times. Sifting through the same evidence, they often reach conflicting conclusions.
>
> This exhibition presents one interpretation of the Truman presidency. There are other ways of looking at the subjects presented here. As you visit the galleries, you will encounter flipbooks that highlight some of these alternative views. These different viewpoints are reminders that the history of the Truman years is not settled. It is constantly being disputed, reviewed and revised. New research continually emerges to challenge accepted facts and alter the story. . . . . The diverse voices in this exhibition also acknowledge an important truth: History never speaks with one voice. It is always under debate—a manuscript that is continually being revised, and is never complete.[2]

The room "How the Cold War Began" features a nine-screen video documentary outlining the Cold War's origins, accompanied by wall text. The history here is the standard version, but the wall text concludes with a startling sentence for anyone who has visited other presidential libraries: In announcing the Truman Doctrine in March 1947, the president included "a broad pledge to 'support free peoples resisting attempted subjugation by armed minorities or by outside pressures.' Years later, critics argued this sweeping language helped guide the nation into a conflict in Vietnam that did not involve America's national security."[3]

This acknowledgment of critics is elaborated in a flip book of dissenting views titled "Was the Cold War Necessary?" (figure 36). (The "flip books" are three-ring binders with pages that visitors can flip through.) This collection starts with contemporaries like Henry Wallace and includes more recent comments by historians. The introductory page reads as follows: "Some historians question the wisdom of the President's actions during the early Cold War years. They argue that a less confrontational approach toward the Soviets—one which sought to understand the fears the Soviet Union had about its vulnerability to invasion from the West—might have prevented a long and costly confrontation that lasted decades." Of course not all visitors read the flip book. But as Hufbauer writes, "The very fact that it exists" has genuine significance.[4]

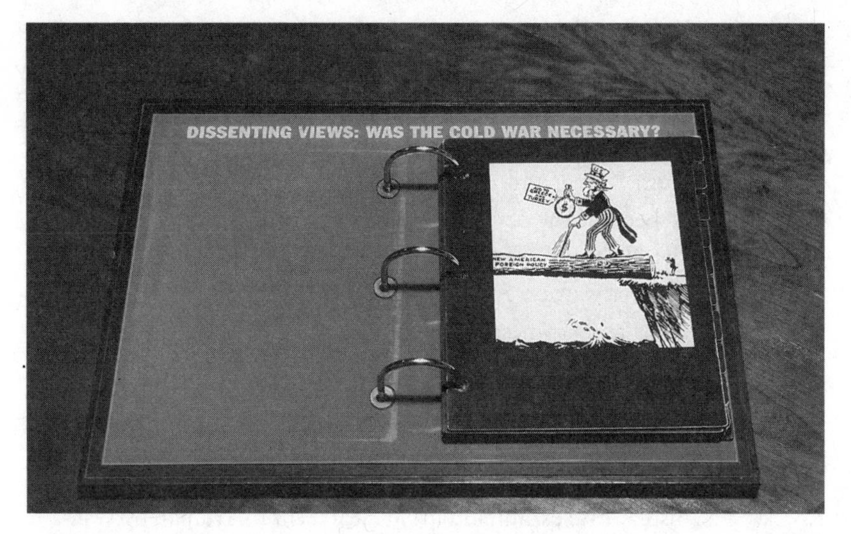

FIGURE 36. Truman Library "Dissenting Views" flip book, "Was the Cold War Necessary?" (photo by Bruce Mathews, courtesy of the Harry S. Truman Library)

In the same room with the flip book "Was the Cold War Necessary?" visitors find an exhibit titled "Architects of Containment," describing the ideas of George F. Kennan and others. The "Featured Document" here is George Kennan's Long Telegram from Moscow, written in February 1946. It provided the rationale for the policy of containment that was followed for the next forty years: Kennan described the foreign policy of the USSR as a combination of the traditional Russian fear of the West with a new fanaticism coming from "Marxist dogma." Even worse, he said, the Kremlin was "impervious to logic or reason." But Stalin was "highly sensitive to the logic of force," and he knew the USSR was far weaker than the United States. Outside the Soviet bloc, Kennan argued, communism could gain support only by feeding on what he called "diseased tissue." The solution, he concluded, was to strengthen democratic institutions everywhere, maintain U.S. military superiority, and wait for the eventual demise of the USSR.

Kennan's Long Telegram was the center of an exhibit at Princeton's Firestone Library gallery in honor of Kennan's one hundredth birthday. Kennan was Princeton class of '25. Princeton's press release declared that the Long Telegram "ranks in the annals of U.S. foreign policy documents with Washington's Farewell Address, the Monroe Doctrine and Wilson's Fourteen Points." The exhibition, Princeton proudly proclaimed, featured "the

8,000-word, 17-page telegram . . . on display for the first time in its entirety—in an 18-foot case."[5]

Next at the Truman Library comes the exhibit "10 Fateful Months," which started in fall 1949: the Soviet A-bomb blast, the Chinese revolution, the invasion of South Korea, and the rise of McCarthyism. Fears that American cities could become the next Hiroshimas are documented with the Civil Defense booklet "Just in Case Atom Bombs Fall." The Korean War exhibit reports not only that 54,000 Americans died there but also that more than a million Koreans and Chinese died. Counting the dead on the other side is profoundly significant, and is missing from the Vietnam exhibits at other presidential libraries.

Even more remarkably, the exhibit reports that "late in the war," Truman "received several bitter letters from parents of American soldiers killed in Korea." One display case exhibits a Purple Heart sent to Truman by William Banning, along with a "poignant and stinging letter" expressing the wish that the president's daughter had been killed in Korea as Mr. Banning's son had been.[6] You won't find anything remotely like that in the Nixon Library's Vietnam exhibit—even though combat medals were also returned to the White House late in that war.

The Korean War gets one entire wall, which includes a video monitor showing documentary footage and photos of the war and "soundsticks" where visitors listen to a four-minute loop of veterans recalling their experiences.[7] It's hard to convey just how traumatic the Korean War was, and the exhibit doesn't really succeed. Sarah Palin, for one, conceded that she "didn't really understand why there was a North Korea and a South Korea" when she ran for vice president in 2008.[8] Undoubtedly she wasn't the only American who didn't understand, in 2008 or indeed in 1950. Korea in 1950 was "truly obscure," as Derek Leebaert writes: "never before an American interest, never a European possession, always a byword for savagery."[9]

But after the victory of the communists in China and the Soviet A-bomb test, the invasion of South Korea by the Communist North prompted Truman to mobilize a UN defense of the South. The museum explains that part, and it suggests that, as Leebaert writes, "the war became a protracted agony"—partly because the South Koreans were led by the corrupt and unpopular government of Syngman Rhee and because U.S. troops proved to be outnumbered and unequal to fighting the Communists.[10]

The exhibits do not mention the horrifying firepower the United States unleashed on a small country. Between 1950 and 1953, the United States dropped as many bombs on Korea as it dropped in all of World War II, "leaving hardly a building standing in the northern and central parts of the country, and driving much of the population quite literally underground." The navy played its part with unprecedented shelling of coastal areas. The city of Wosun, according to Jon Halliday and Bruce Cumings, was bombarded around the clock from the sea for forty-two days and nights, "the longest sustained naval or air bombardment of a city in history," according to one admiral.[11] And yet North Korea did not give up.

General Douglas MacArthur gets a great deal of coverage at the museum. The World War II hero who was at the time heading the U.S. occupation of Japan, MacArthur was named commander in chief of the UN forces in Korea after the North invaded. When all seemed darkest for the United States, in September 1950, MacArthur made his "breathtaking" move: the amphibious Inchon landing, which placed a marine division 150 miles behind enemy lines. He then demanded "unconditional surrender" and sent U.S. forces across the 38th parallel toward the Chinese border, confident the Chinese would not intervene. He was wrong; Chinese troops crossed the Yalu River and forced the Americans into "the longest retreat in U.S. military history."[12] In 1951, American dead and wounded totaled 100,000, and most of them had been drafted. In the first year and a half of the Korean War, America suffered as many casualties as in the first twenty months of combat in World War II— and suddenly it looked like the American force could be annihilated and the entire Korean peninsula taken over by the Chinese. MacArthur had made "a mistake of apocalyptic proportions," David Halberstam wrote; he led American forces to "an epic disaster."[13] That judgment is missing from the museum.

MacArthur now made it clear that he wanted war with China: there was "no substitute for victory," he declared.[14] Truman of course wanted no war with China. MacArthur's defiance of the president in April 1951 led Truman to assert civilian control over the military and fire MacArthur. MacArthur replied that it was "a new and heretofore unknown and dangerous concept that the members of our armed forces owe primary allegiance or loyalty to those who temporarily exercise the authority of the executive branch of the government rather than to the country and its Constitution which they are sworn to defend. No proposition could be more dangerous."[15]

The general returned to immense adulation. At his first stop, Hickam Field in Hawaii, 100,000 cheered him; in San Francisco, half a million showed up for his speech. Next came Washington, where a White House staffer circulated a mock "Schedule for Welcoming General MacArthur":

12:30 wades ashore from submarine. . . .
12:40 Parade to the Capitol with General MacArthur riding on an elephant
1:00 General MacArthur addresses members of Congress
1:30–1:49 applause for General MacArthur
1:50 Burning of the Constitution
1:55 Lynching of Secretary [of State Dean] Acheson
2:00 21-atomic bomb salute.[16]

MacArthur's address to the joint session of Congress—his "old soldiers just fade away" speech—was wildly successful. Long the "darling of the far right," MacArthur had "never altered his contempt" for FDR, Stanley Weintraub writes, and "he was rigidly hard-line in his doctrinaire anti-Communism."[17] The right hoped he would be their candidate for president in 1952 against the increasingly unpopular Truman. He declined, and in the 1952 Republican primary the moderate Eisenhower faced Senator Robert A. Taft, who had been a leading opponent of the New Deal. Taft ran as a supporter of MacArthur and nearly won the nomination in one of the most bitter convention battles in Republican history. Taft was rumored to have planned to offer the vice presidential slot to MacArthur, and he did get MacArthur named keynote speaker at the 1952 Republican National Convention. But despite conservative enthusiasm for using atomic bombs to defeat world communism, the USSR's successful A-bomb test in 1949 convinced Truman that containment rather than victory should be America's policy in the Cold War.

At the Truman Library the MacArthur controversy is given its own section, which includes wall-mounted soundsticks that provide two-minute audio excerpts from Truman's national television and radio address announcing the firing of the general and another featuring MacArthur's speech to Congress. The museum displays eleven documents about MacArthur, totaling thirty-three pages, whereas the rest of the Korean War gets four documents totaling eight pages.

The museum also displays a "Dissenting Views" flip book on the MacArthur controversy, and three of the eleven documents exhibited are letters from ordinary people to Truman opposing his action. One example: "Just because the mule is symbolic of Missouri doesn't mean you have to be the biggest jackass in the history of the United States" (from Mrs. Joan Rountree, of Buffalo, New York).[18]

Finally there are the comment books. The Truman Library has a total of forty-seven volumes of comments written by visitors. MacArthur is a big topic, according to Hufbauer, who found this exchange on facing pages:

> I was a soldier in occupied Japan when Pres. Truman fired General MacArthur for trying to win the Korean war! . . . This event has stuck in my craw ever since. Howard, Washington USA.

> I disagree. I served under MacArthur in WWII. He had an excessive ego. He thought he could disobey orders of his commander in chief. And Harry did the right thing when he fired him—hey Howard, read your Constitution.[19]

The comment books also discuss the "Dissenting Views" flip books:

> What an excellent way to get the message across that there are tough questions we Americans need to ask and there are no quick answers.

> I like the different perspectives.

> I like this museum. You get to see both sides of this issues.

And of course there are the inevitable critics:

> Too much political correctness has crept into the library's exhibits, along with much Monday morning quarterbacking.[20]

MacArthur has his own memorial half a continent away, and it's considerably grander than Truman's. It has four buildings, not just one, located at "beautifully landscaped" MacArthur Square in downtown Norfolk, Virginia. The museum is housed in Norfolk's nineteenth-century city hall, a National Historic Place. As the memorial guide explains, "A monumental rotunda is the General and Mrs. MacArthur's final resting place. They lie surrounded by inscriptions, banners and flags heralding his long and glorious career. Nine separate galleries arranged in two levels circle the rotunda and tell the story of General MacArthur." Of course the museum also has a gift shop, which "displays General MacArthur's 1950 Chrysler Imperial limousine which he used from 1950 to the end of his life." A visit to the MacArthur Memorial, the website declares, can "renew your faith in those American values of

Duty-Honor-Country, values which motivated Douglas MacArthur as he served our nation through some of its greatest crises and finest hours."

All this is in Norfolk because MacArthur didn't want to be buried in Arlington National Cemetery. In 1961 he arranged to give the city of Norfolk all his "trophies, medals, prizes, decorations, uniforms, flags, swords, battle souvenirs, personal papers, documents, records and other personal memorabilia." In exchange, the city restored its historic 1850 city hall to house this collection.

The collection is big: the MacArthur archives contain two million documents, 86,000 photos, and 111 motion picture films. It also contains the general's collection of 5,000 books, "augmented by gifts and purchases of books concerning the General, his times, and his associates." In the museum, nine permanent galleries display MacArthur's "treasures" including "19th and 20th century medals, flags, paintings, weapons. . . . [P]orcelain, Jade and Cloisonne are also displayed." Of course the museum also displays "the General's trademark military cap, corncob pipe, and sunglasses." Note: the MacArthur Memorial in Norfolk has no "Dissenting Views" flip books.

There's one other thing missing: the MacArthur Memorial doesn't have an exhibit on the Truman-MacArthur controversy. Indeed it barely mentions Korea.[21] Once again, World War II is everything; the Cold War has been forgotten.

I asked Charlie Knight, curator of the MacArthur Memorial in Roanoke, where to find an exhibit presenting MacArthur's side of the controversy with Truman. He explained that you have to go to a different MacArthur memorial site: the MacArthur Museum of Arkansas Military History in Little Rock's MacArthur Park. Little Rock is MacArthur's birthplace. Here visitors can read a roomful of wall text that begins, "On April 11, 1951 President Harry S. Truman relieved General Douglas MacArthur from all his commands for publicly criticizing governmental policies in the Korean War. MacArthur received a hero's welcome home while Truman was widely scorned. The subsequent controversy created an enduring debate over the issue of civilian authority over the military, limited war versus total war and the containment of communism. The dismissal of MacArthur by Truman created a political controversy which remains today."[22] That's not bad.

Many cities in the United States and around the Pacific have MacArthur Parks, but the one with the biggest and best Cold War–era monument is Los Angeles (figure 37). The name was changed from Westlake Park in 1942 in honor of the general's World War II exploits. But the MacArthur Memorial

FIGURE 37. MacArthur Memorial, MacArthur Park, Los Angeles. The memorial was erected after President Harry Truman removed MacArthur from command in Korea. It displays his famous motto, "No substitute for victory"—a veiled criticism of Truman for accepting a stalemate in Korea rather than following MacArthur's strategy of going to war against China. (photo by David Weiner)

in the park dates from the Cold War, indeed from the period immediately after his firing by Truman in 1951: fund-raising began in 1952, and the monument was completed in 1955.

It's an amazing structure: the inevitable bronze statue is displayed against a curving wall containing quotes from the general, including his famous motto, "No substitute for victory"—a veiled criticism of Truman for accepting a stalemate in Korea rather than following MacArthur's strategy of going to war against China. But the amazing part is not the text; it's the mirror pool that lies in front of the statue: it contains "islands" representing the Philippines—"which MacArthur helped liberate," as the *Los Angeles Times* explained helpfully in 1951. Note: the pool does not contain a representation of the Korean peninsula.

Fund-raising for the MacArthur Memorial in MacArthur Park in Los Angeles was led by the conservative and Republican political forces in the city: Norman Chandler, publisher of the *L.A. Times;* David Hearst, publisher of the city's Hearst paper, the *Herald-Express;* the president of the Bank of

America; Mayor Fletcher Bowron, a onetime liberal fighting an attack by McCarthyites; and the secretary of the AFL Central Labor Council, who had been fighting the Reds in the city's CIO unions.[23] In related news, the *L.A. Times* reported that "the National Collegiate MacArthur Clubs" had unanimously endorsed the proposed memorial, on the grounds that MacArthur Park was "now taking the place of Pershing Square as a meeting place for Red-tinged soapbox orators to sell their wares. We feel such a statue will serve as a warning that America is awake." The organization claimed members on sixteen college campuses, including Pepperdine.[24]

And when the memorial was finally completed, the *L.A. Times* made the politics behind it perfectly clear in a page 1 story. "There is very good reason to believe we would not be in our present fix had MacArthur been allowed to drive the China Reds out of Korea," the editorial columnist Bill Henry wrote. Formosa was the issue of the day at that point, and MacArthur was quoted as saying, "As a matter of military urgency under no circumstances must Formosa fall under Communist control. Such an eventuality would at once threaten the freedom of the Philippines and the loss of Japan and might well force our frontier back to the coast of California, Oregon and Washington." The writer concluded, "This is a serious situation, the aftermath of the sorry muddle in Korea which cost MacArthur his job and the free nations a solid victory."[25] The monument might not refer to Korea, but its backers certainly did.

If the MacArthur Memorial in Los Angeles's MacArthur Park provided a rallying point for Republicans and anticommunists in the mid-1950s, by the 1990s it had a different meaning: a 1997 headline read "Filipino Veterans Chain Selves to Statue in Protest." Forty Filipino World War II veterans were protesting the denial of benefits they had been promised under the GI Bill at the end of the war. Explaining why he had chained himself to the statue of his former commander, seventy-five-year-old Aniceto Montaos said, "My only regret is that MacArthur has died. If he were alive today, I know that he wouldn't abandon us."[26] Once again, it was World War II that was a living thing, while the Cold War went unmentioned.

The MacArthur Memorial in Roanoke presents the sharpest possible contrast to the Truman Library in Independence. The Roanoke memorial exemplifies the history museum as celebration of heroism: visitors are invited to view the general's battle trophies and thereby "renew their faith" in his values. The Truman Library takes the opposite approach, informing visitors, "This exhibition presents one interpretation of the Truman presidency. There are other ways of looking at the subjects presented here." It's a simple idea—but, especially in the context of Cold War commemoration, a thrilling one.

Conclusion

HISTORY, MEMORY, AND THE COLD WAR

Most historians' work on memory deals with the past people can't forget—the Holocaust, the Civil War, Pearl Harbor. This book deals with a past that people seem to have trouble remembering—or don't want to remember, at least not the "good war" framework for the Cold War that they have been told about by conservatives.

An example: the "Cold War Victory Medal," proposed by the usual lineup of conservative groups, was approved by Congress in 1992 (figure 38). The medal was to commemorate military service during "the historic victory in the Cold War," and anyone who served in the military between September 2, 1945, and December 26, 1991, was eligible. The medal consists of an allegorical figure of Freedom in a landscape "suggestive of the Fulda Gap, the anticipated point of attack by Communist forces in Europe during the Cold War." It includes a sword, an eagle, a rising sun, and the inscription "Promoting Peace and Stability."[1] The medal can be purchased for $24.95 from Foxfall Medals of Madison, Virginia.

But the legislation did not require the Department of Defense to issue the medal, and it never has. Apparently the Pentagon did not consider the Cold War worth commemorating. That became official policy in 2002, when an official statement was released: "The Department of Defense will not be creating a Cold War Service medal, and commemorative medals being sold by private vendors are not authorized for wear on military uniforms."[2]

It gets worse: the same Department of Defense announcement informed interested parties that the only official Cold War service commemoration was the Cold War Recognition Certificate, established by Congress in 1998, issued by the army, and signed by Donald Rumsfeld. Those eligible, however, included not only everyone who served in the military between 1945 and

FIGURE 38. Cold War Victory Medal, for sale by Foxfall Medals of Madison, Virginia. An allegorical figure of Freedom sits in a landscape "suggestive of the Fulda Gap, the anticipated point of attack by Communist forces in Europe during the Cold War." The Pentagon in 2002 prohibited wearing it on military uniforms. (© Foxfall Medals, photo by David Weiner)

1991 but also everyone employed by the federal government anytime during those forty-six years. The Cold War Veterans Association, which had lobbied for the medal, pointed out that "this includes temporary employees of the Postal Service during the Holiday season, and thus the potential number of eligible is very large—perhaps in excess of 50 million people."[3]

Other efforts to commemorate the Cold War continue, with the same results they've always had. Twenty years after the fall of the Berlin Wall, a bill was introduced in the Senate—as it had been many times in previous years—"to require the Secretary of the Interior to conduct a theme study to identify sites and resources to commemorate and interpret the Cold War." Senator Harry Reid of Nevada told his colleagues that the United States prevailed over the USSR because of "the technological achievement, patriotism, and sacrifice of the people of the great State of Nevada." In case that sounded too parochial, he quickly added, "and of others throughout the Nation."[4]

"The time has come," Reid said, "to recognize and honor those Americans who toiled in relative obscurity to bring us victory during this most dangerous conflict in our Nation's history." He listed several "obvious Cold War sites of significance": "intercontinental ballistic missile launch sites; flight training centers; communications and command centers, such as Cheyenne Mountain, Colorado; and nuclear weapons test sites, such as the Nevada Test Site." He concluded, "A grateful Nation owes a debt of supreme gratitude to the silent heroes of the Cold War."[5]

Several months later, a Senate subcommittee held a hearing on a number of bills regarding memorials and national parks. Along with Harry Reid's Cold War memorial bill, another bill under consideration would "revise the boundary of the Martin Van Buren National Historic Site." Hillary Clinton testified in favor of that one but didn't say anything about the Cold War memorial proposal. But then she was the senator from New York, and the Cold War bill seemed to focus more on Nevada. That bill was never voted on.[6]

There is an American Cold War Museum, but as of this writing (2012), it exists only on the Internet (at www.coldwar.org) and in a mobile exhibit of artifacts related to the U-2 incident of 1960.[7] The pilot who was shot down in that incident was Francis Gary Powers, and his son is the current head of the museum. The website declares, "The Cold War Museum will lease a modest size two story building and secure storage facility at Vint Hill, located in Fauquier County, Virginia," fifteen miles southeast of Dulles airport. Two local industrial development authorities are offering the museum nine months of free storage space and putting up $100,000 "to renovate a 2000 sq ft building for museum use."[8] And its mission statement says nothing about celebrating victory or honoring those who defended freedom; it says only that the museum is "dedicated to education, preservation, and research on the global, ideological, and political confrontations between East and West."[9]

Meanwhile a bill to designate this Cold War Museum as the "National Cold War Museum" was introduced in the House in 2008 by Representative Tom Davis, in whose district the office of the Cold War Museum is found. His bill had no cosponsors, and no hearings were held to consider its merits. Since then the proposed legislation has been not been reintroduced.[10]

Why did the conservatives' "good war" framework for understanding the Cold War recede in visibility in American culture—despite massive efforts to keep it in the foreground? When Lynne Cheney, wife of the former vice president, was chair of the National Endowment for the Humanities in 1987, she offered an explanation. An official pamphlet titled *American Memory* opened with her statement, "A refusal to remember . . . is a primary characteristic of our nation."[11] That explanation, however, has been disproven by the "memory boom," by the "Greatest Generation" phenomenon, and by the survey finding that 57 percent of Americans said they had visited a history museum or historical site in the past year.[12]

Historians have been writing about memory for a while now, but Cold War memory seems to offer an exception to the approaches they have taken and the theories they have offered. In the volume *Memory and American History,* David Thelen writes that historical memory is "profoundly intertwined with the basic identities of individuals, groups and cultures."[13] One thinks, for example, of the "rebel" identity claimed by today's neo-Confederates. In the case of Cold War memory, however, people have not intertwined their identities with the official story.

David Blight's award-winning work on Civil War memory describes the successful construction of a "mythic" war, in which the public was persuaded that slavery did not underlie the conflict and that Confederate soldiers fought just as heroically as Union troops.[14] In the case of the Cold War, however, efforts at mythmaking have not met any significant popular embrace.

Emily Rosenberg's recent study of Pearl Harbor in American memory explores conflicts over how "Pearl Harbor" should be represented, and who should control remembrance. She emphasizes the significance of "memory activists" who contested the meaning of those events. In contrast, Cold War memory has exhibited neither instability nor contestation.[15] It's the persistent absence of popular battles over its meaning that needs to be explained. The memory activists engaged with the Cold War have either focused on tangential issues, like the Christian defenders of the hilltop cross in San Diego who claimed it was a Korean War monument, or emphasized the post–Cold War cleanup of weapon sites rather than the original mission of those sites. Other memory activists have been completely ineffective, like the advocates of the Cold War victory medal.

Rosenberg highlights the instability of popular memory in the case of Pearl Harbor, shifting from a call for vigilance in the 1950s to an argument for a better intelligence agency in the 1970s to a warning in the 1980s against an "economic Pearl Harbor." But in the case of Cold War museums, the only instability I found was in the shift away from the Cold War entirely to more popular topics: the Winston Churchill Memorial shifted its original focus—the Iron Curtain speech—to its current emphasis on recalling the "blood, sweat and tears" of the Battle of Britain.

Benedict Anderson wrote about the construction of "imagined communities," exploring how people have developed a sense of belonging to a group—usually a nation—for which they were willing to fight and die.[16] Cold War ideologists constructed such an imagined community; they called it "the free world." But here I have documented the apparent skepticism of the public about their past membership in it.

David Lowenthal writes in *The Past Is a Foreign Country* about "uses" for "memories of imaged idealism and heroic sacrifice." They include the way present-day ideas can be said to be valid because of their similarity to ideas in the past. Andreas Huyssen makes a related argument when he sees today's "memory culture" invoking a stable past whose qualities are absent from our present.[17] Neither of these approaches helps explain the distinctive phenomena surrounding Cold War memory.

Edward Linenthal writes in *Sacred Ground* about memorial sites "where Americans of various ideological persuasions come . . . to compete for ownership of powerful national stories and to argue about the nature of heroism [and] the meaning of war."[18] What is striking about the Cold War memorial sites is that this type of competition for ownership has not taken place.

Erika Doss documented and analyzed the "memorial mania" that has swept the country over the past few decades—"thousands of new memorials to executed witches, enslaved Africans, victims of terrorism, victims of lynching, dead astronauts, aborted fetuses. . . ." These, she argued, reveal "heightened anxieties about who and what should be remembered in America" and testify to "the fevered pitch of public feelings such as grief, gratitude, fear, shame or anger." Kirk Savage too has argued that historical monuments today "are expected to be . . . journeys of emotional discovery."[19] But the Cold War monuments and museums discussed here are an exception. They were not created as the result of "an urgent desire" to remember the emotions provoked by "tragedy and trauma"; instead they had a narrow ideological origin and a didactic intent.

Following Doss's lead in examining the feelings and emotions invoked at memorial sites, it seems the dominant emotional note in a great deal of Cold War memorialization has shifted from triumph to reassurance. At places like the Nevada Test Site, Hanford B Reactor, the Titan Missile Museum, and Missouri's radioactive mound, the message started out as a triumphant one: good defeated evil in the Cold War. But the central emotion has changed: visitors are told that the dangers at former nuclear weapons sites are not serious, and that the remaining hazards are being managed, monitored, and cleaned up by experts. But this official reassurance is not completely convincing, and in any case it's far from the more intense emotions—grief, fear, shame, anger—evoked at the more successful sites Doss examines. Perhaps that helps explain why the Cold War memorials emphasizing reassurance have aroused so little enthusiasm in comparison to the monuments she analyzes.

Alison Landsberg's work on "prosthetic memory" shows how museums can enlist media to give visitors an experience that provides "a more personal, deeply felt memory of a past event through which he or she did not live." For example, museums of slavery or the Holocaust make it possible for "these memories to be acquired by anyone, regardless of skin color [or] ethnic background." That, she argues, "creates the conditions for ethical thinking" by "encouraging people to feel connected to, while recognizing the alterity of, the 'other.'"[20] The purpose of the Victims of Communism Museum was something like that—to give visitors the experience of victims of the Gulag, of Mao's Great Leap Forward, and so on, so that they could identify with them and commit themselves to the fight to end communism in China and elsewhere. But that museum was never built, and instead the sponsors settled for a traditional memorial statue that has no power to shape the imagination or experience of visitors.

This failure of conservative Cold War commemoration is all the more remarkable in light of the continuing triumph of "the Age of Reagan." The effort to construct a public memory around the "good war" framework for the Cold War was undertaken by the same political and media forces that convinced Americans it was morning in America. It was part of the same ideological campaign that transformed a once marginal movement into a hegemonic power that dominated American life for at least three decades. It drew on half a century of political rhetoric describing a world struggle between freedom and its enemies, rhetoric that was shared by both parties and that went largely unchallenged. But we have seen that control of the mainstream media, and power over the framing of public discourse, did not bring popular acceptance of this message. The problem is to sort out the elements of popular apathy, skepticism, and resistance that led to the failure of what should have been an ideological success story, at least according to theorists of hegemony.

The simplest explanation focuses on the lack of deaths in the Cold War as the reason for popular refusal to accept the triumphalist view. The most successful memorials, Ian Gambles writes, commemorate atrocities or death on a large scale. The Cold War, he argues, "offers almost none of these . . . because it was essentially a period of peace" in the United States, because "what conflict there was tended to be limited, managed, and elsewhere."[21]

The Cold War memory activists understood that requirement and framed their projects precisely in terms of a huge death toll: the Victims of Communism Memorial has always claimed 100 million victims, which, they have always pointed out, was a larger number than any other struggle in world history. One hundred million is "surely the largest number of victims ever commemorated in one monument," Savage observes.[22] And numbers count in claims for significance: the Korean War Memorial advocates argued for decades that they deserved a monument equal to the Vietnam Veterans Memorial because their war had almost as many casualties. Even the pumpkin patch National Historic Landmark was justified on the grounds that millions of lives were at risk in the Cold War. The question is why some claims regarding the meaning and significance of massive death are embraced while others are greeted with skepticism.

Another explanation, also suggested by Gambles, lies in what he calls "the dearth of powerful symbols." He found "almost nothing to express the meaning of the Cold War in symbolic form."[23] Pearl Harbor has the battleship *Arizona,* the Civil War has Gettysburg, the Alamo has the Alamo. But this argument neglects the fact that, for the Cold War, we have an obvious and powerful symbolic object: massive segments of the Berlin Wall, its most powerful rhetorical image, from Kennedy ("Ich bin ein Berliner") to Reagan ("Mr. Gorbachev, tear down this wall!"). It may not have the emotional power of the USS *Arizona* memorial, but its display in all the presidential museums of the era, and dozens of other places, testifies to its significance, if not to its popularity, as a symbol.

But the notion that monuments require actual relics, or that they occupy "sacred ground," is an obsolete one. The Lincoln Memorial stands on a site that didn't even exist in Lincoln's lifetime: the site was dredged from the Potomac by the Army Corps of Engineers in 1914. While other Lincoln museums display actual relics—the clothes he was wearing when he was assassinated, the clock from his office, his stovepipe hat—the Lincoln Memorial contains no such objects. "It is pure representation," Savage writes: a colossal statue, and the words of the Gettysburg Address carved into one wall.[24]

Another possibility is suggested by Michael Kammen's provocative argument that "memory is more likely to be activated by contestation, and amnesia is more likely to be induced by the desire for reconciliation."[25] The lack of contestation of the conservative framing of the Cold War is significant, at least in the public sphere (again with a few notable exceptions), but "the desire for reconciliation" does not seem to be a factor here—at least not between the mainstream and the right in America. The exemplary case of reconciliation through silence came on Pearl Harbor's tenth anniversary in 1951, which coincided with the rise of Japan as a new ally against the USSR and China and a crucial base in the Korean War. But reconciliation with Russia since 1991 can hardly explain the current status of Cold War commemoration. The problem here is the opposite: not official silence but rather two decades of official noise, greeted by public indifference.

Another approach can be found in John Bodnar's argument that the federal government's interest in commemorating patriotism and national unity is often contested by local activists with different concerns. Their memorial observances often express ethnic or class consciousness or regional identity.[26] That describes some of the Rocky Flats case. But for the rest of Cold War commemoration, we do not find vernacular challenges to official ideology.

The lack of popular engagement with the conservative celebration of Cold War victory more likely stems from skepticism over its premises and resistance to its conclusions. People may not accept what Eric Hobsbawm described as the "nightmare scenario of the Muscovite super-power poised for the immediate conquest of the globe, and directing a godless 'communist world conspiracy,' ever ready to overthrow the realms of freedom." People may find implausible the notion that—Hobsbawm again—"the globe was so unstable that a world war might break out at any moment, and was held at bay only by unceasing mutual deterrence."[27] Cold War strategists insist that "deterrence worked," but the public may not find that argument convincing. As Gambles writes, "It seems uncomfortably as if it might all have been a gigantic waste of time, money, and commitment."[28]

Nobody in the mainstream media, or Congress, or the White House, ever said the Cold War was a gigantic waste. Indeed the message addressed to the public, by Democrats and Republicans alike, was always the opposite. The official message is that it was all worth it, because we won and they lost. And yet this message does not seem to have been accepted. Acceptance is the key here, as M. I. Finley suggested. Of course many official claims made about the past are inaccurate and some are completely false. That, Finley writes, is "irrelevant," as long as the claims are accepted.[29] In the case of the officially sanctioned Cold War memory, that acceptance has been refused.

The heart of the conservative argument about the Cold War is that it represented a struggle between good and evil. Here especially the public would be justified in skepticism. U.S. support for unpopular dictators around the world was well known. It isn't hard to see why Cubans might support Fidel and Che against Batista and the United States, or why Vietnamese might fight with Ho Chi Minh against the United States. And it is hard to take seriously the argument that American communists posed a fatal threat to the survival of the country. McCarthyism is seen almost universally as a blot on our history, an affront to freedom rather than a defense of it.

Although conservatives have triumphed politically for the past several decades, the Cold War is hardly the only issue where the public has refused to accept conservative arguments. The right has argued that the Environmental Protection Agency represents government bureaucracy at its worst, but opinion polls show that people overwhelmingly want more protection for the environment, not less. Ditto for OSHA and job safety. The right has argued that deficit reduction should take precedence over job creation; public opinion holds the opposite. The right wants to cut taxes on the rich; a big majority of the public would be happy to tax the rich. All of this has been true from the beginning of the Reagan administration. In this respect, public skepticism about the conservative interpretation of the Cold War is part of a broader pattern rather than an exception to it.

"The lessons of Vietnam" provide a vivid example of popular skepticism about the "good war" framework in conservative Cold War commemoration. Americans had been told that in the Vietnam War the United States was engaged in a struggle of good against evil, but the Saigon government that the United States supported didn't seem to represent "good." Americans were told that communism was innately aggressive, but the communists seemed to be winning in Vietnam because they had more popular support among the Vietnamese than we did. Americans were told the Soviet Union was implacably bent on world domination, but Vietnam seemed to be mostly a civil war among the Vietnamese. Americans were told the Soviets would attack us if we didn't threaten to destroy them, but the Soviets didn't threaten us over Vietnam. And if none of those arguments was true for Vietnam, maybe they weren't true for the rest of the Cold War either.

Critics might respond that Reagan defeated "the Vietnam syndrome." Indeed it was Reagan himself who coined the phrase "Vietnam syndrome"

FIGURE 39. Visitor at the Vietnam Veterans Memorial, Washington, D.C. More than 72 million people have visited since it opened in 1982. A monument to loss, it suggests the extent of resistance to conservative Cold War commemoration. (photo by Skyring, wikipedia.org)

when he charged during the 1980 campaign that the Carter administration was "completely oblivious" to the Soviet threat. He also said U.S. troops could have defeated the communists in Vietnam, but Nixon (and LBJ) had been "afraid to let them win."[30] Reagan's 1984 landslide was the result of an economic boom, not a response to his arguments about the "Vietnam syndrome" or his efforts to defeat the USSR around the world. In fact those efforts led to the greatest crisis of his administration, the Iran-Contra affair, when support for anticommunist forces in Nicaragua in defiance of a congressional ban nearly brought down his administration. The fact is that Reagan's revival of the Cold War never had significant popular support.[31]

Across the landscape of Cold War commemoration, there is one exception to the pattern described here of popular indifference and skepticism, one public monument that aroused passionate and widespread public enthusiasm: the Vietnam Veterans Memorial (figure 39). It provides the sharpest possible contrast to the failed Victims of Communism Memorial. More than 72 million people have visited the Vietnam Memorial since it opened in 1982, according to the National Park Service—an incredible number, equivalent to almost one in four Americans.[32] Notably, it is the one monument of the Cold War era that resolutely denies a triumphant interpretation of the conflict. With its sunken black granite walls carrying the names of all 58,000 Americans who died in the war, the memorial steadfastly refuses to celebrate heroism in a battle between good and evil. That's precisely why the design was greeted with unprecedented opposition from the right.

The design also explains why the memorial has had such a massive popular response. As Maya Lin herself declared in her often-quoted design entry, the memorial speaks only of "loss." It does so without explanatory text. Visitors descend as they walk, while the wall gets taller, until it is ten feet high; at the center, at the angle where the two walls meet, the names of the dead surround us and fill our field of vision from top to bottom, left to right. Above and on both sides, we see only the names, and our own reflections, in the black wall. The 72 million people who have visited the Vietnam Veterans Memorial suggest the depth of Americans' rejection of conservative Cold War commemoration.[33]

Epilogue

FROM THE COLD WAR TO THE WAR IN IRAQ

The conservatives failed to persuade the public to understand the Cold War as a good war, a battle between good and evil, a battle the United States won because Ronald Reagan and his allies never accepted liberal ideas about containment and coexistence and détente. Despite their best efforts, the Heritage Foundation, the *National Review,* the *Weekly Standard,* and the rest of the Republican right lost their ideological struggle, launched after the collapse of the USSR in 1991, to convince Americans to think of Reagan's victory over communism as equal to FDR's victory over fascism. The conservatives' museums weren't built, their monuments have been neglected, their ideas mostly forgotten.

But not everyone forgot about the conservative interpretation of the Cold War. Dick Cheney, Donald Rumsfeld, and a few of their cohort remembered: America should use its power to defeat and destroy its enemies, not negotiate with them to maintain the status quo or preserve the balance of power (figure 40). After the fall of the Soviet Union, they waited. Then came 9/11, which gave them the pretext they needed. The ideas they had developed during the Cold War were finally put into action—in Iraq.

The foreign policy that led to war in Iraq had been developed over the previous thirty-five years by the faction of the Republican Party that had opposed détente with the Soviet Union. As James Mann shows in *Rise of the Vulcans,* his history of Bush's war cabinet, "the bifurcation of history into Cold War and post–Cold War" for Cheney and Rumsfeld was "ultimately artificial."[1] Cheney and Rumsfeld had always favored preemptive action against enemies. They had argued for decades that a superpower could do what it wanted without the approval of allies or international organizations, and without fear of what others might call "blowback." And they repeatedly

FIGURE 40. Dick Cheney and Donald Rumsfeld in 1975, when Rumsfeld worked as White House chief of staff for President Ford and Cheney was his assistant. The two had opposed détente with the Soviet Union, arguing that the United States should use its power to defeat its enemies, not preserve the balance of power. That notion became the basis thirty-five years later for the U.S. invasion of Iraq. (AP photo/Harvey Georges)

proclaimed that these invasions and wars could be justified as benevolent actions bringing democracy to people oppressed by evil dictators.

After Gerald Ford was defeated in 1976, Cheney and Rumsfeld were out of the White House and had no place in the executive branch for the next thirty years. Cheney became a congressman from Wyoming; Rumsfeld found employment as CEO of Searle Pharmaceuticals. But once Republicans were back in the White House in 1981, Cheney and Rumsfeld were there too, at the heart of the top secret continuity-of-government exercises that would guarantee the survival of a commander in chief during a nuclear war with the Soviets. For the thirty years that they had been out of the White House, Mann writes, Cheney and Rumsfeld "were never far away. They stayed in touch with defense, military, and intelligence officials, who regularly called upon them." They were, he writes, "part of the permanent hidden national-security apparatus of the United States—inhabitants of a world in which Presidents come and go, but America keeps on fighting."[2]

The striking thing about Cheney's and Rumsfeld's work is that George W. Bush as president started out in the opposite camp. During the 2000 campaign, in the presidential debates, Bush called for a level of "humility" in American foreign policy, and said, "I just don't think it's the role of the United States to walk into a country [and] say, 'We do it this way; so should you.'" Of course that had been the policy of his father when he was president: build alliances, pursue limited but achievable goals; push Saddam out of Kuwait, but don't overthrow his regime or occupy his country.

But once the weak and inexperienced new president appointed Cheney and Rumsfeld, they quickly reeducated him in the ideology the Republican right had proclaimed since the beginning of the Cold War: Eisenhower and Nixon—and his own father, George H. W. Bush—had been wrong. Alliances and international organizations did not guarantee security; instead they restricted America's ability to pursue its interests and achieve its goals. It was not "realism" to negotiate with enemies but weakness. America was not a country like others with interests and security concerns; it was a city on a hill, a beacon of goodness. Bush could be another Jimmy Carter, who had been powerless before the Muslim students holding Americans hostage, or he could be another Reagan, triumphant in a fifty-year struggle against evil. He could be a wimp, or he could be a warrior.

The new president decided he didn't want to be a wimp.

So Saddam was cast in the same role as Stalin and Khrushchev and Brezhnev: an evil tyrant whose regime should not simply be contained. He could be overthrown and therefore should be overthrown. But Congress was incapable of decisive action, diplomacy was a distraction, arms control worthless, and "world opinion" contemptible. The American people should be told that they were in danger and that eliminating the source of danger would also liberate the suffering victims of tyranny abroad.

Rumsfeld in particular had been arguing the conservative Cold War line since the Ford years, when he served as secretary of defense. There he "did more than anyone else to block détente," Mann reports, "and to stiffen American policy toward the Soviet Union." He had always been skeptical about arms control and accommodation with the USSR. Ford and his secretary of state, Henry Kissinger, had continued the Nixonian policy of détente that had so aroused the Republican right, which mobilized in the 1976 primaries to challenge Ford's reelection—with the candidacy of Ronald Reagan.

Cheney at that point was Ford's chief of staff, but he personally opposed détente, and privately urged Ford to abandon it. Reagan fought hard in the primaries, arguing that détente had permitted the Soviets to pull ahead of the United States militarily. Reagan actually defeated Ford in the North Carolina primary—the first time a Republican incumbent president had ever lost a primary election. Ford at first defended détente as "in the best interest of the country," but, Mann reports, "Cheney turned Ford around," and the president accepted the Reaganite platform at the Republican National Convention.[3]

After Ford's defeat in 1976, Cheney went back to Wyoming and ran for Congress. In the House, he always voted for big increases in the military budget and the development of new weapons systems like the MX missile. When the *Washington Post* described him as a "moderate"—a designation many politicians yearn for—Cheney bitterly demanded a correction, stating he was a "conservative."[4]

But although Cheney and Rumsfeld understood the Iraq War in terms of their old Cold War conservative ideology, they quickly came to appreciate the ways the post-9/11 world was different. Thus there arose on the Republican right the phenomenon that became known as "Cold War nostalgia."[5] Even President Bush started saying that during the Cold War we could rely on our enemies; we knew them to be risk-averse and open to negotiation to preserve the status quo—while our new enemies were ruthless and uncompromising and bent on our destruction. Of course that's the opposite of what the same people were saying in the 1970s and 1980s. But that's the way it often is with nostalgia. Someday there will be a museum of the Iraq War, and it should open with a section on the Cold War origins of Bush's policy.

ACKNOWLEDGMENTS

This book began with *The Nation*'s "Politics of Travel" issue, edited by Victor Navasky and Katrina vanden Heuvel. They sent me to visit the Nevada Test Site and write about official hopes to develop it as a tourist destination connected to Las Vegas; after taking your chances in the casinos, you could take your chances with radioactivity. Then Harold Meyerson, at the time an editor at the old *LA Weekly*, enthusiastically published a report of mine on Hippie Day at the Reagan Library.

But it wasn't clear to me that this sort of thing could be a book until I read *A Date Which Will Live* by Emily Rosenberg. This crucial work showed how the public memory of "Pearl Harbor" has shifted dramatically from decade to decade. I realized that my book on Cold War memory could be sort of the opposite: I found no dramatic shifts in public memory of the Cold War; in fact I found hardly any memory of the Cold War at all. Emily herself has been an inspiration for this book in many big and little ways.

Several friends read the whole manuscript at different stages and provided crucial comments: Eric Foner; my University of California, Irvine (UCI), colleagues Alice Fahs and Winston James; and Ellen Shrecker and Rick Perlstein, who read drafts for UC Press. Tom Engelhardt offered indispensable advice on one key chapter, Amy Stanley and Jane Dailey commented fruitfully on another at a University of Chicago seminar, and Sara Bershtel and Sue Horton provided essential encouragement.

Among those who traveled with me to visit sites were Sean Wilentz, Reagan Library; Mike Johnson, Whittaker Chambers pumpkin patch National Historical Landmark; Sara Pearson, Victims of Communism Memorial in Washington, D.C.; Grace Barnes, Miami's Cuban sites; and Judy Fiskin, Missouri and Arizona.

Several people suggested places to visit: James Loewen told me about the Missouri mound, Clancy Sigal reminded me about blacklist exhibits, Marc Cooper gave me advice on visiting Las Vegas, and R.J. Lambrose of the *Radical History Review* discovered the Reagan monument in Grenada.

Historians need archivists. I needed Kathleen Hulser, New York Historical Society curator; Timothy Naftali, Nixon Library director; Pat Mitchell, president and CEO of the Paley Center for the Media; Tom Blanton, director of the National Security Archive; Nathan Myers, Eisenhower Library registrar; Barbara Hall, research archivist at the Academy of Motion Picture Arts and Sciences Margaret Herrick Library; Charlie Knight, curator at the MacArthur Memorial in Roanoke; Genia Hessler, curator of exhibits at the State Historical Society of North Dakota; Becky Imamoto, history bibliographer at UCI Library.

At the *New York Times* I got crucial help from both Sam Roberts and Dinitia Smith.

Don Waldie welcomed me to Memorial Day in Lakewood; Bill Geerhart of Conelrad.com provided all kinds of help. For other interviews, I thank Linda Walls, Greenbrier Bunker tour manager; James Mann on the Reagan Armageddon plan; and Peter Irons on the San Diego cross.

I needed lots of help with the photos. The single most important source of photos was the indispensable Center for Land Use Interpretation, where founder and director Matt Coolidge was extremely patient with my many requests. I also thank Debra Hashim, associate curator, Division of Political History at the Smithsonian's National Museum of American History; Conny Bogaard, project director, Rocky Flats Museum; Ljiljana Grubisic, director of collections and public programs, Wende Museum; Sharon Silengo, photo archivist, North Dakota Heritage Center Truman Library; Mary Finch, George Bush Presidential Library and Museum; Rina Luzius, Microsoft Art Collection; Denise Wagner, *Appleton* (Wisc.) *Post-Crescent;* Elisa Marquez, AP photos.

For digital photo editing as well as some photography I relied on the supremely talented David Weiner. I had a wonderful research assistant, E. B. Landesberg. I got additional help with photos from Kirk Savage, Jem Axelrod, and Eileen Luhr.

Others who helped with crucial information: Amber Black at the Rosenberg Fund for Children; Joan Miller, head archivist, Wesleyan Cinema Archives (Elia Kazan Collection); Alicia Dean at Elvis Presley Enterprises (Graceland); Yvonne Deyo, Weldon Spring site manager, S. M. Stoller Corporation; Jason Van Dyke, Supreme Council of the Scottish Rite (J. Edgar Hoover Collection); Philip Mohr, interim curator, National Churchill Museum; Jeanette Miller, director of marketing and public relations, National Atomic Museum, Albuquerque; Cameron Hardy, Hanford Site; Lynn Swann, director of public relations, the Greenbrier.

I received funding from the UCI Humanities Center, Catherine Liu, director, and the UCI Humanities Research and Travel Fund.

Friends and colleagues provided other kinds of assistance, for which I am grateful: Peter Guralnik and Greil Marcus on Cold War Elvis, Frank Biess on Cold War Germany, Jeff Kisseloff on Alger Hiss, and Laura McEnaney on fallout shelters.

Ben Pease of Pease Press made the beautiful map.

At UC Press, I thank history editor Niels Hooper, and the indispensable Kim Hogeland, as well as my superb copy editor, Sheila Berg, and our outstanding project manager, Dore Brown. Thanks also to my excellent proofreader Karen Davison and to Sharon Sweeney, who did the index.

Finally, there is Judy Fiskin, who not only traveled with me to some of the most important sites, and took some photos, but also read every chapter more than once and never hesitated to point to problems and suggest solutions. I thank her most of all.

NOTES

Most of the monuments, museums, memorials, and other sites described in this book I visited myself, but for some I relied on published sources, Internet sources, and interviews. In particular I was never able to get a seat on the Hanford tour—the very few available are taken shortly after they are posted on the web—so I relied on the accounts of others who took the tour. In other cases, exhibits I was interested in had already closed by the time I discovered them—in particular, "Private Elvis" at Graceland, which closed the week after I read about it—so I relied on the exhibit website as well as on published accounts. The notes indicate the sources I consulted and interviews I conducted. All quotations of tour guides come from my contemporaneous notes unless otherwise indicated.

INTRODUCTION

1. "Coming in from the Cold: Military Heritage in the Cold War. Report on the Department of Defense Legacy Cold War Project" (Washington, DC: GPO, 1996), 3, quoting Department of Defense Appropriations Act, 1991, P.L. No. 101–511, #8120, 104 Stat. 1905 (1990).

2. "George W. Bush's Third State of the Union Address," http://en.wikisource.org/wiki/George_W._Bush's_Third_State_of_the_Union_Address. See also Arnold Beichman, "The Cold War Was as Much a 'Just War' as World War II," in *CNN's Cold War Documentary: Issues and Controversy,* ed. Arnold Beichman (Stanford: Hoover Institution Press, 2000), xiv.

3. Ellen Schrecker, ed., *Cold War Triumphalism: The Misuses of History after the Fall of Communism* (New York: New Press, 2004). Tony Judt uses the term to

describe John Lewis Gaddis's interpretation: Judt, "A Story Still to Be Told," *New York Review,* Mar. 23, 2006. On the distinctive Cold War conception of "freedom," see Eric Foner, *The Story of American Freedom* (New York: Norton, 1999).

4. Erika Doss, *Memorial Mania: Public Feeling in America* (Chicago: University of Chicago Press, 2010); Andreas Huyssen, "Monumental Seduction," in *Acts of Memory: Cultural Recall in the Present,* ed. Mieke Bal, Jonathan Crewe, and Leo Spitzer (Hanover, NH: University Press of New England, 1999), 191; Warren Leon and Roy Rosenzweig, eds., *History Museums in the United States: A Critical Assessment* (Urbana: University of Illinois Press, 1989), xvi; Roy Rosenzweig and David Thelen, *The Presence of the Past: Popular Uses of History in American Life* (New York: Columbia University Press, 1998), 180, 234.

5. Judt, "A Story"; Leon and Rosenzweig, *History Museums,* xi–xii. Since the publication of that book, there have been a few notable exceptions. Edward Rothstein writes about history museums for the *New York Times;* the *Journal of American History* now runs half a dozen exhibition reviews twice a year.

6. For critiques, see Kirk Savage, *Monument Wars: Washington, D.C., the National Mall, and the Transformation of the Memorial Landscape* (Berkeley: University of California Press, 2005), 298–303; and Doss, *Memorial Mania,* 197–207.

7. "SAC Memorial," www.b-47.com/news/sac_memorial.htm; "Preserving Missile Heritage," www.afmissileers.org/SACBACK.jpg. See memorial park map at www.nationalmuseum.af.mil/shared/media/document/AFD-060705-004.pdf; SAC is in section B1 (accessed Apr. 25, 2011). The same monument can also be found on the grounds of the Strategic Air and Space Museum in Ashland, Nebraska.

8. Strategic Air and Space Museum, www.sasmuseum.com/about-us/history/.

9. See Philip Green, *Deadly Logic: The Theory of Nuclear Deterrence* (New York: Schocken Books, 1968), esp. 258–59. One of the architects of the Cold War, George Kennan, argued that it had not been necessary. In 1989, after the fall of the Berlin Wall, Kennan said, "I believe it would have happened earlier if we had not insisted on militarizing the rivalry." For Kennan, the USSR "posed little military threat to the West." He thought the whole thing would have been different—no threats of mutual annihilation—if the United States had relied "mostly on economic and political means to resist communist expansion"—what Kennan meant by "containment." Kennan, quoted in Mark Atwood Lawrence, "Friends, not Allies," review of *The Hawk and the Dove: Paul Nitze, George Kennan, and the History of the Cold War* by Nicholas Thompson, *New York Times Book Review,* Sept. 13, 2009, 22.

1. HIPPIE DAY AT THE REAGAN LIBRARY

1. Websites accessed Nov. 17, 2009, unless otherwise noted. Portions of this chapter were originally published in the *LA Weekly,* Sept. 20–26, 1996, 16–17.

2. John Lewis Gaddis, *The Cold War: A New History* (New York: Penguin, 2005), 226. Gaddis became a favorite historian of George W. Bush, who invited him to the White House to help prepare his second inaugural address. As the *Washington Post*

review of *The Cold War* pointed out, Gaddis became "a qualified supporter of the Bush administration's strategy in combating terrorism." James Mann, "Long Twilight Struggle; We now know why the superpowers' terrifying standoff never turned hot, argues a leading historian," Review of *The Cold War,* by John Gaddis, *Washington Post,* Jan. 29, 2006, T3, pqasb.pqarchiver.com/washingtonpost/access/977702511.html.

3. Dole, quoted in Ellen Schrecker, ed., *Cold War Triumphalism: The Misuse of History after the Fall of Communism* (New York: New Press, 2005), 4; other quotes in Dinesh D'Souza, "Russian Revolution: How Reagan Won the Cold War," *National Review,* June 6, 2004, www.nationalreview.com/flashback/dsouza200406061619.asp/.

4. Ronald Reagan, "Goldwater Speech," PBS *American Experience,* www.pbs.org/wgbh/amex/reagan/filmmore/reference/primary/choose64.html.

5. Rick Perlstein, *Before the Storm: Barry Goldwater and the Unmaking of the American Consensus* (New York: Hill & Wang, 1961), 499–504.

6. Kitty Kelly, *Nancy Reagan: The Unauthorized Biography* (New York: Simon & Schuster, 1991), 224.

7. Paul Kengor, "'That Wall': Reagan's Prodding," *National Review,* June 12, 2007, http://www.nationalreview.com/articles/221231/wall/paul-kengor. In contrast to the conservative interpretation, the leading historian of the Berlin Wall emphasizes the way it served both American and Soviet geopolitical interests: Frederick Taylor, *The Berlin Wall: A World Divided, 1961–1989* (New York: HarperCollins, 2006).

8. John Le Carré, Introduction to *The Spy Who Came in From the Cold* (New York: Pocket Books, 1991), x (introd. dated "December 1989"); Chalmers Johnson, *The Sorrows of Empire* (New York: Metropolitan, 2004), 19.

9. Robert Reinhold, "4 Presidents Join Reagan in Dedicating His Library," *New York Times,* Nov. 5, 1991. Those in attendance also included Reagan's defense secretary, Caspar W. Weinberger, his interior secretary, James G. Watt, and his attorney general, Edwin Meese III.

10. Reagan Library, "Permanent Galleries," www.reaganlibrary.com/airforceone/dtc_home.asp?gid = 7.

11. See, for example, www.flickr.com/photos/43527262@N00/451100387, www.flickr.com/photos/30501224@N05/2867879751/.

12. R.J. Lambrose, "The Abusable Past," *Radical History Review* 89 (Spring 2004): 243–47. Image at www.virtualtourist.com/travel/Caribbean_and_Central_America/Grenada/Off_the_Beaten_Path-Grenada-BR-1.html.

13. Reagan Library, "Air Force One," www.reaganlibrary.com/airforceone/.

14. Reagan Library, "Welcome to the Air Force One Pavilion," www.reaganlibrary.com/details_f.aspx?p = LM2023EAF1&h1 = 3&h2 = 7&lm = libraryandmuseum&args_a = cms&args_b = 33&argsb = N&tx = 18&sw = ex_af1. The NASCAR race looms large at the Reagan Library: in 2011 it opened a display featuring the car that won the race Reagan started from Air Force One. Michele Willer-Allred, "NASCAR Show Car Goes on Display at Reagan Library," *Ventura County Star,*

Mar. 28, 2011, www.vcstar.com/news/2011/mar/28/nascar-show-car-goes-on-display-at-reagan/ (accessed May 2, 2011).

15. Reagan Foundation, "Desk Accessories," www.reaganfoundation.org/store/prod-Berlin_Wall_Paperweight-981.aspx. On kitsch and historical memory, see Marita Sturken, *Tourists of History: Memory, Kitsch, and Consumerism from Oklahoma City to Ground Zero* (Durham: Duke University Press, 2007).

16. Michael Meyer, *The Year That Changed The World: The Untold Story behind the Fall of the Berlin Wall* (New York: Scribner, 2009). See also Michael Meyer, "Myths of 1989," *Los Angeles Times,* Jan. 3, 2010; Gerald DeGroot, "When the Iron Curtain Unraveled," *Washington Post,* Sept. 6, 2009, www.washingtonpost.com/wp-dyn/content/article/2009/09/04/AR2009090401751.html.

17. John Tirman, "How We Ended the Cold War," *The Nation,* Nov. 1, 1999, www.thenation.com/doc/19991101/tirman/1; see also Stephen F. Cohen, "The Political Tragedy of Russia," *Los Angeles Times,* Feb. 27, 2005, http://articles.latimes.com/2005/feb/27/opinion/oe-cohen27.

18. Sean Wilentz, *The Age of Reagan: A History, 1974–2008* (New York: HarperCollins, 2008), 280.

19. Ibid., 281.

20. Carol J. Williams, "Wall-Toppling Trio Honored at Berlin Reunion," *Los Angeles Times,* Nov. 9, 1999, A1, http://8.12.42.31/1999/nov/09/news/mn-31572.

21. Ronald Reagan, "Address to the Nation on Defense and National Security," Mar. 23, 1983, www.reagan.utexas.edu/archives/speeches/1983/32383d.htm.

22. Reagan to Chernenko, Feb. 11, 1984, in Jason Saltoun-Ebin, ed., *The Reagan Files: The Untold Story of Reagan's Top-Secret Efforts to Win the Cold War* (CreateSpace, 2010), www.jasonebin.com/thereaganfiles/id29.html (accessed Feb. 7, 2011).

23. For a definitive statement of the Reagan Doctrine, see Charles Krauthammer, "The Reagan Doctrine," *Time,* Apr. 1, 1985, www.time.com/time/magazine/article/0,9171,964873,00.html.

24. The main exhibit at the Carter Library features the Camp David Accords and barely mentions the Cold War: www.jimmycarterlibrary.gov/tour/ (accessed May 12, 2010).

25. Eric Hobsbawm, *The Age of Extremes: A History of the World, 1914–1991* (New York: Pantheon, 1995), 250.

26. "Berlin Wall Gallery," Newseum, www.newseum.org/exhibits-and-theaters/permanent-exhibits/berlin-wall/index.html; Wende Museum, www.wendemuseum.org/introduction.htm.

27. Tony Judt, *Postwar: A History of Europe since 1945* (New York: Penguin, 2005), 252–53.

28. Julian E. Zelizer, *Arsenal of Democracy: The Politics of National Security: From WWII to the War on Terrorism* (New York: Basic Books, 2010), 153, citing George C. Herring, *From Colony to Superpower* (New York: Oxford University Press, 2008), 710.

29. "List of Berlin Wall segments," Wikipedia, http://en.wikipedia.org/wiki/List_of_Berlin_Wall_segments.

30. George Bush Library, "The Day the Wall Came Down," http://bushlibrary.tamu.edu/museum/museum_tour/sculpture.php; Veryl Goodnight, "The Day the Wall Came Down," www.verylgoodnight.com/wall.htm. The CIA medallion is displayed online at www.verylgoodnight.com/images/wall/awardLG.jpg (accessed Apr. 28, 2011).

31. http://bushlibrary.tamu.edu/museum/museum_tour/berlinwall.php. The sculpture in the courtyard in College Station, titled *The Day the Wall Came Down,* is big: 7 tons, 12 feet high, and 18 feet wide. "The monument's composition is five horses, one stallion and four mares, running through the rubble of the collapsed Berlin Wall," http://bushlibrary.tamu.edu/museum/museum_tour/sculpture.php.

32. "Dan Quayle for President 2000" campaign brochure, www.4president.org/brochures/2000/danquayle2000brochure.htm. This claim is not made at the Dan Quayle Center and Museum in "Downtown Huntington, Indiana"—renamed Quayle Vice Presidential Learning Center in 2009, with a new motto: "Where History Educates!," www.quaylemuseum.org/.

33. Microsoft, "About the Art Collection," wwwc01vip.microsoft.com/about/artcollection/en/us/about.aspx.

34. "Microsoft's Section of the Berlin Wall," www.microsoft.com/mscorp/artcollection/exhibitions/august/story.htm.

35. Microsoft Art Collection, "Hope, Anguish, and the Berlin Wall," Aug. 2008, wwwc01vip.microsoft.com/about/artcollection/en/us/exhibitions/BerlinWall/isthis.aspx.

36. "Pee at the Berlin Wall," www.roadsideamerica.com/story/12552.

37. Cheapo Las Vegas, "Main Street Station," www.cheapovegas.com/vegas_casino_full.php?hotel_id = 1025.

38. "The Urinals of Main Street Station Hotel and Casino," www.urinal.net/main_st_sta/. The site was also featured in a *Time* magazine photo essay, "The Wall: Where Is It Now?," Nov. 5, 1999, www.time.com/time/daily/special/photo/berlin2/.

39. Diane Haithman, "Wall-to-Wall Unity Symbol," *Los Angeles Times,* Aug. 12, 2009, D1, http://8.12.42.31/2009/aug/12/entertainment/et-berlin-wall12.

40. Wende Musuem Wall Project press release, Sept. 28, 2009, www.wallproject.org/Wall%20Project%20Press%20Release_9.28.pdf.

41. Diane Haithman, "Fairey, Twitchell and Noir Brainstorm on L.A.'s Wall Project," www.latimes.com, Aug. 12, 2009; http://latimesblogs.latimes.com/culturemonster/2009/08/shepard-fairey-wall-project. html.

2. THE VICTIMS OF COMMUNISM MUSEUM

1. "About the Foundation," Victims of Communism Memorial Foundation, http://victimsofcommunism.org/about/. Accessed Jan. 30, 2012.

2. Dinitia Smith, "For the Victims of Communism," *New York Times,* Dec. 23, 1995, www.nytimes.com/1995/12/23/arts/for-the-victims-of-communism.html. All websites were accessed June 13, 2009, unless otherwise noted. The bill began as H.J.RES.237: "To authorize the construction of an international monument in the District of Columbia to honor the victims of Communism," 103rd Cong., 1st sess., H.J. RES. 237, July 23, 1993. The proposal was passed as part of the Friendship Act in 1993: H.R. 3000, Sec. 905, "Monument to Honor Victims of Communism," signed by President Clinton on Dec. 17, 1993, became P.L. No. 103–199.

3. Noam Chomsky, "Counting the Bodies," *Spectrezine,* no. 9 (Jan. 15, 2009), www.spectrezine.org/global/chomsky.htm.

4. Perry Anderson, "Two Revolutions," *New Left Review* 61 (Jan.–Feb. 2010), http://newleftreview.org/?page=article&view=2820.

5. Eric Hobsbawm, *The Age of Extremes: A History of the World, 1914–1991* (New York: Pantheon, 1995), 390–91.

6. Video of Dana Rohrabacher on "dinosaur flatulence" at http://thinkprogress.org/2007/02/10/dino-flatulence/ and http://thinkprogress.org/2007/04/24/rohrabacher-terrorists/. He was one of the leading advocates of California Prop. 187 in 1994, which denied undocumented immigrants government services, including education for their children. In 2004 he proposed legislation to deny emergency room services to undocumented people; that bill was overwhelmingly defeated.

7. http://rohrabacher.house.gov/Biography/; "Site Will Remember Communism Victims," *Washington Times,* Sept. 27, 2006, www.washingtontimes.com/metro/20060927-113701-7973r.htm.

8. Kirk Savage, *Monument Wars: Washington, D.C., the National Mall, and the Transformation of the Memorial Landscape* (Berkeley: University of California Press, 2005), 237.

9. Erika Doss, *Memorial Mania: Public Feeling in America* (Chicago: University of Chicago Press, 2010), 13.

10. Don Feder, "Communism's Victims get a Monument," *Boston Herald,* Dec. 16, 1993, 33.

11. Kevin McManus, "Memorial Ways," *Washington Post,* July 16, 1993, N7. "War Dog" memorials in fact have been erected in Holmdel, NJ, Streamwood, IL, and elsewhere. See photos in Doss, *Memorial Mania,* 223.

12. Charles Krauthammer, "Build a Cold War Memorial," *Washington Post,* Mar. 28, 1997, A29.

13. J. Michael Waller, "International Terrorism: The Communist Connection Revisited," Victims of Communism Memorial Foundation, Papers and Studies, June 1, 2002, www.iwp.edu/news_publications/detail/international-terrorism-the-communist-connection-revisited (accessed May 9, 2011).

14. Joseph A. D'Agostino, "Conservative Spotlight: Victims of Communism Memorial Foundation," *Human Events* 59 (July 14, 2003).

15. John J. Miller, "The Price of Tyranny: Communism's Victims Await Their Memorial," *Wall Street Journal,* May 26, 2004, www.opinionjournal.com/la/?id=110005127.

16. Caryle Murphy, "Anti-Communism Memorial Debated: Statue Stirs Neighborhood Concerns," *Washington Post,* Dec. 2, 2004, DZ03, www.washingtonpost.com/wp-dyn/articles/A25294–2004Dec1.html. The site was bounded by Maryland Ave., Constitution Ave., and Third Street NE.

17. "Dispute over a Potential New Memorial on Capitol Hill," *Stanton Park Neighborhood Association News* 28, no. 4 (January 2005), www.stantonpark.org/newsletter/newsletter-jan2005.pdf. See also Gary Emerling, "NE Washington Says No to Memorial Site," *Washington Times,* Feb. 11, 2005.

18. "Victims of Communism Don't Count," *Hog Haven,* Dec. 13, 2004, www.dhogberg.com/2004_12_12_dhogberg_archive.html.

19. The website is www.globalmuseumoncommunism.org/ (accessed July 6, 2010), and it includes some of the features originally promised for the museum: a "Hall of Infamy," which includes Fidel Castro alongside Pol Pot and Stalin (but leaves out Jane Fonda), and a "Gallery of Heroes," which includes Joe Lieberman and Dana Rohrabacher. See www.globalmuseumoncommunism.org/sites/all/themes/museum/flash/heroes/index.html.

20. Jennifer Lash, "Statue Moves Ahead: Memorial to Honor Communism Victims," *Roll Call,* Mar. 9, 2005.

21. Christian Toto, "Rumsfeld Offers a Tribute," *Washington Times,* Nov. 17, 2006, http://washingtontimes.com/functions/print.php?StoryID=20061116–100954–3056r. The history of the Holocaust Museum is told in Edward T. Linenthal, *Preserving Memory: The Struggle to Create America's Holocaust Museum* (New York: Columbia University Press, 1995).

22. Savage, *Monument Wars,* 263–64.

23. The full text of the Bush speech, available as text, video, and audio, can be found at "President Bush Attends Dedication of Victims of Communism Memorial," White House, Office of the Press Secretary, June 12, 2007, www.whitehouse.gov/news/releases/2007/06/20070612–2.html.

24. Omar Fekeiki, "The Toll of Communism: At Statue Dedication, Bush Draws Parallel to 'Murderous Ideology,'" *Washington Post,* June 13, 2007, C01, www.washingtonpost.com/wp-dyn/content/article/2007/06/12/AR2007061201125.html.

25. Michael Chapman, "100 Million Victims of Communism Memorial Dedication = Minimal Liberal Media Coverage," News Busters, June 13, 2007, http://newsbusters.org/node/13424.

26. Chris Kelly, "Make Your Own Bush Speech," *Huffington Post,* June 13, 2007, www.huffingtonpost.com/chris-kelly/make-your-own-bush-speech_b_51973.html.

27. Chalmers Johnson, "The Three Cold Wars," in *Cold War Triumphalism: The Misuses of History after the Fall of Communism,* ed. Ellen Schrecker (New York: New Press, 2004), 237–61.

28. Victims of Communism Memorial Foundation, "The Battle Continues," www.victimsofcommunism.org/history_communism.php. Strangely, they left Vietnam off the list of communist countries.

29. In fact, the Chinese did issue an official protest: "China Blasts Bush Tribute to Victims of Communism," Reuters, June 14, 2007, www.reuters.com/article/worldNews/idUSPEK20924820070614. On the original goddess statue, see Tsau Tsing-yuan, "The Birth of the Goddess of Democracy," in *Popular Protest and Political Culture in Modern China,* ed. Jeffrey N. Wasserstrom and Elizabeth J. Perry (Boulder, CO: Westview Press, 1994), 140–47.

30. Nicolas Werth, Karel Bartošek, Jean-Louis Panné, Jean-Louis Margolin, Andrzej Paczkowski, and Stéphane Courtois, *The Black Book of Communism: Crimes, Terror, Repression* (Cambridge, MA: Harvard University Press, 1999). Harvard University Press posted selections from positive reviews online at www.hup.harvard.edu/catalog.php?recid=26699&content=reviews.

31. Stéphane Courtois, Introduction to Werth et al., *The Black Book of Communism,* 28.

32. Richard J. Golsan, *French Writers and the Politics of Complicity* (Baltimore: Johns Hopkins University Press, 2006), 144.

33. Werth, quoted in Tom Heneghan, "'Black Book of Communism' Sparks French Debate," Reuters, Nov. 7, 1997, reprinted at http://hackvan.com/pub/stig/etext/black-book-of-communism-nazism-and-communism-have-the-same-totalitarian-roots.txt (accessed Feb. 9, 2010).

34. For the full story, see Golsan, *French Writers and the Politics of Complicity,* chap. 6; and Anson Rabinbach, "Communist Crimes and French Intellectuals," *Dissent* (Fall 1998): 61–66.

35. J. Arch Getty, "The Future Did Not Work," *Atlantic,* Mar. 2000, www.theatlantic.com/issues/2000/03/getty.htm.

36. Madhusree Mukerjee, *Churchill's Secret War: The British Empire and the Ravaging of India during World War II* (New York: Basic Books, 2011).

37. Jean Dreze and Amartya Sen, *Hunger and Public Action* (New York: Oxford University Press, 1991).

38. For example, if Russia's population from 1992 to 2006 had experienced the mortality rates recorded in the Soviet period 1986–87, there would have been a net total of 6.6 million fewer deaths. Nicholas Eberstadt, "The Enigma of Russian Mortality," American Enterprise Institute Papers, Oct. 13, 2010, www.aei.org/paper/100151 (accessed Oct. 3, 2011).

39. Tony Judt, "The Longest Road to Hell," *New York Times,* Dec. 22, 1997, www.nytimes.com/1997/12/22/opinion/the-longest-road-to-hell.html. This was an op-ed piece, not a book review.

40. Wieviorka, quoted in Golsan, *French Writers and the Politics of Complicity,* 149–50.

41. Shane J. Maddock, Review of *The Black Book, Journal of American History* 88 (Dec. 2001), www.historycooperative.org/journals/jah/88.3/br_128.html.

42. *Washington Post,* Aug. 4, 1891, quoted in Savage, *Monument Wars,* 13.

3. GETTING STARTED

1. Tom DeLay, "The Bonds of Freedom," speech delivered April 3, 2002, at the Churchill Memorial, www.churchillmemorial.org/lecture/green/Pages/TomDeLay.aspx. Websites accessed Aug. 13, 2009, unless otherwise noted.

2. Margaret Thatcher, "New Threats for Old," speech delivered Mar. 9, 1996, at the Churchill Memorial, www.churchillmemorial.org/lecture/green/Pages/NewThreatsforOld.aspx.

3. "Memorial Highlights," www.churchillmemorial.org/highlights/Pages/LivingMemorial.aspx.

4. "The Lecture Series," Churchill Memorial, www.churchillmemorial.org/lecture/Pages/default.aspx; Martin Gilbert, "Previous Lectures," www.martingilbert.com/previous.html.

5. *Bits and Pieces* (newsletter of the Churchill Memorial), Mar. 2009, www.churchillmemorial.org/newsletter/Documents/March%202009.pdf.

6. The Red Hat Society turns out to be a national organization: "fun after fifty for women in all walks of life.... We are ladies!" www.redhatsociety.com.

7. I. F. Stone, "U.S. and U.S.S.R.," *The Nation,* Mar. 16, 1946, 306–7.

8. Alexander Feinberg, "Pickets in CIO Line Taunt Churchill," *New York Times,* Mar. 16, 1946.

9. "Churchill Policy Scored: 1,700 Columbia Students Vote Disapproval of Fulton Talk," *New York Times,* Mar. 19, 1946, 4.

10. Wallace, quoted in Tony Judt, *Postwar: A History of Europe since 1945* (New York: Penguin, 2006), 110.

11. *Wall Street Journal,* quoted in Martin Gilbert, *Winston S. Churchill v. VIII, "Never Despair": 1945–1965* (Boston: Houghton-Mifflin, 1988), 205.

12. "Churchill's Call for World Domination," *Chicago Sun,* Mar. 6, 1946, quoted in Gilbert, *"Never Despair."*

13. *Boston Globe,* quoted in Patrick Wright, *Iron Curtain: From Stage to Cold War* (New York: Oxford University Press, 2007), 46.

14. "Churchill View Hit by Mrs. Roosevelt," *New York Times,* Mar. 15, 1946, 2.

15. Ronald Steel, *Walter Lippmann and the American Century* (New York: Little, Brown, 1980), 429.

16. Ibid., 430–31.

17. "Congress Splits on Churchill Plea," *New York Times,* Mar. 7, 1946, 1. The three senators were Claude Pepper of Florida, Harley Kilgore of West Virginia, and Glenn Taylor of Idaho.

18. Arthur Krock, "Washington Splits over Churchill," *New York Times,* Mar. 13, 1946, 2; "Acheson, Pleading Urgent Matters, Won't Speak at Churchill Dinner," *New York Times,* Mar. 15, 1946, 1.

19. Stone, "U.S. and U.S.S.R."

20. Eric Hobsbawm, *The Age of Extremes: A History of the World, 1914–1991* (New York: Pantheon, 1995), 231, 233.

21. Winston Churchill, "The Sinews of Peace," speech delivered Mar. 5, 1946; full text at www.nato.int/docu/speech/1946/s460305a_e.htm.

22. I. F. Stone, "Churchill Abandons the Cold War," *I. F. Stone's Weekly,* May 30, 1953; reprinted in I. F. Stone, *The Haunted Fifties: 1953–1963* (Boston: Little, Brown, 1989), 55–58. For the full story, see Gilbert, *"Never Despair,"* 829–32.

23. Legislation for an official museum failed to pass: "National Churchill Museum Act of 2007," Library of Congress, http://thomas.loc.gov/cgi-bin/query/z?c110:H.R.1242. Instead, a simple resolution was introduced in the House in 2009, which did pass that July: H.R. 390. "Recognizing the Winston Churchill Memorial," 2009, www.govtrack.us/congress/bill.xpd?bill=hr111-390.

4. SEARCHING FOR THE PUMPKIN PATCH

1. National Park Service Attendance Statistics—Ranking Report for 2007, www.nature.nps.gov/stats/viewReport.cfm. All websites accessed Sept. 19, 2009. Portions of this chapter were originally published as "Pumpkin Patch Perdu," *The Nation,* Nov. 18, 1996, 6–7.

2. Amy Goldstein, "Pumpkin Papers' Farm Designated U.S. Landmark Despite Opposition," *Washington Post,* May 18, 1988.

3. Donald P. Hodel, "The Challenge to Conservatives," speech at the Heritage Foundation, July 15, 1988, www.heritage.org/Research/PoliticalPhilosophy/HL163.cfm.

4. Presidential Medal of Freedom: http://en.wikipedia.org/wiki/List_of_Presidential_Medal_of_Freedom_recipients.

5. Whittaker Chambers, *Witness* (New York: Random House, 1952), 16.

6. Hodel, "The Challenge to Conservatives."

7. "Site in Hiss-Chambers Case Now a Landmark," *New York Times,* May 18, 1988.

8. Bruce Craig, "Politics in the Pumpkin Patch," *Public Historian 12* (Winter 1990): 15.

9. "Landmark Politics," *New York Times,* May 22, 1988, sec. 4, 38.

10. Bruce Craig, "Whittaker Chambers' Pumpkin Patch; Preservation Has Been Politicized," *Washington Post,* May 22, 1988. See also "Cold War Shrine," *The Nation,* June 4, 1988.

11. Henry Allen, "Setting Their Sites; From Pumpkin Patch to . . . ," *Washington Post,* May 19, 1988.

12. Garry Wills, *Lead Time: A Journalist's Education* (New York: Mariner, 2004), 65. (This passage appeared originally in my book *Professors, Politics, and Pop* [New York: Verso, 1991], 271–73.)

13. *Los Angeles Times,* July 17, 1990, 13.

14. Robert Sherrill, "Alger Hiss," *New York Times Book Review,* Apr. 25, 1976; Allen Weinstein, "The Alger Hiss Case Revisited," *American Scholar* 41 (Jan. 1972): 127.

15. Sherrill, "Alger Hiss."

16. "Justice Department Releases Copies of the 'Pumpkin Papers,'" *New York Times,* Aug. 1, 1975; I. F. Stone, "I. F. Stone on the Pumpkin Papers," *New York Times,* Apr. 1, 1976.

17. Ibid.

18. David Margolick, "44-Year-Old Spy Case; Russians Say Archives Clear Alger Hiss's Name," *New York Times,* Nov. 1, 1992, sec. 4, 2. Volkogonov, challenged under questioning by Herb Romerstein, formerly a staff consultant to HUAC, conceded that he could not be absolutely certain that he had searched every relevant file or that some files had not been destroyed: Serge Schmemann, "Russian General Retreats on Hiss," *New York Times,* Dec. 17, 1992, 17.

19. Eric Breindel, "Hiss's Guilt: Goodies from the Venona Files," *New Republic,* April 15, 1996, 18; see also John Corry, "Hissteria; Why Do They Insist on Distorting History?," *American Spectator,* May 1996.

20. "Washington 1822 to Moscow," in *Venona: Soviet Espionage and the American Response, 1939–1957,* ed. Robert Louis Benson and Michael Warner (Laguna Hills, CA: Aegean Park Press, 1996), 423.

21. See Eric Alterman, "Right Thinking," *The Nation,* Apr. 29, 1996.

22. Kai Bird and Svetlana Chervonnaya, "The Mystery of Ales," *American Scholar* (Summer 2007), www.theamericanscholar.org/su07/ales-bird.htm; see also Lynne Duke, "Stepping Out of the Shadows; After Nearly 60 Years, Alger Hiss's Stepson Is Finally Making His Case for the Innocence of the Notorious Alleged Spy," *Washington Post,* Apr. 5, 2007; Victor Navasky, "Hiss in History," *The Nation,* Apr. 30, 2007, www.thenation.com/doc/20070430/navasky.

23. The barn adjacent to the former pumpkin patch burned down in May 2007, and the same year the county commissioners proposed to the state that a reservoir be built on land that included the pumpkin patch, which would put the site underwater. The commissioners received a few letters of protest, including one from Mauricio Tamargo, a lawyer from Burke, Virginia, who called the farm a place "where Whittaker Chambers found sanctuary from the Communist underground and where he bravely and publicly stood his ground to challenge an enemy Communist network while hiding evidence of guilt on this farm." Penny Riordan, "Fire Causes Damage at Historic Farm," *Carroll County Times,* May 1, 2007, www.carroll countytimes.com/articles/2007/05/01/news/local_news/newsstory5.txt; Kelsey Volkmann, "Reservoir Threatens Ex-Spy Chambers' Farm," *Baltimore Examiner,* Mar. 7, 2007, www.examiner.com/printa-604138~Reservoir_threatens_ex-spy_Chambers%E2%80%99_farm.html.

5. NAMING NAMES, FROM LARAMIE TO BEVERLY HILLS

1. "One in Ten: Adrian Scott," http://digital.uwyo.edu/webarchive/scott/bio.html. See also http://rmoa.unm.edu/docviewer.php?docId=wyu-ah03238.xmlid 2616964 (accessed Apr. 24, 2011).

2. In addition to the exhibits described below, see the University of Washington Library exhibit, now online, "Anti-Communist Investigations in Seattle, 1947–1949," www.lib.washington.edu/exhibits/allpowers/Exhibit/default.htm; and Annenberg Media's online exhibit, "Writers under Fire: The 1950s," www.learner.org/interactives/cinema/screenwriting2.html.

3. Lynn Smith, "'We Behaved as Badly as Anybody,'" *Los Angeles Times,* Feb. 2, 2002.

4. "Reds and Blacklists in Hollywood" exhibit, Feb. 1–Apr. 21, 2002, Library of the Academy of Motion Picture Arts and Sciences, Beverly Hills, CA. The touring version of the show went to the Santa Fe Art Institute in 2003.

5. Audio tour script, "Reds and Blacklists in Hollywood."

6. Ibid.

7. Roy Brewer, "Hollywood Whitewash of the Cold War's Shameful Red Stain," *Los Angeles Times,* Feb. 6, 2002.

8. Quoted in Benjamin Hufbauer, *Presidential Libraries: How Memorials and Libraries Shape Public Memory* (Lawrence: University Press of Kansas, 2006), 170. The exhibit seeks to create precisely the kind of memory analyzed in Alison Landsberg, *Prosthetic Memory: The Transformation of American Remembrance in the Age of Mass Culture* (New York: Columbia University Press, 2004).

9. David Thomson, "Elia Kazan," *Guardian,* Sept. 29, 2003, www.guardian.co.uk/news/2003/sep/29/guardianobituaries.film.

10. Elia Kazan, "A Statement," *New York Times,* Apr. 12, 1952. The full text is reprinted in Navasky, *Naming Names,* 204–6.

11. Navasky, *Naming Names,* 206, 200.

12. Susan Stamberg, *Talk: NPR's Susan Stamberg Considers All Things* (New York: Perigee, 1993), 299–304.

13. Mervyn Rothstein, "Elia Kazan, Influential Director, Is Dead at 94," *New York Times,* Sept. 29, 2003, www.nytimes.com/2003/09/29/movies/elia-kazan-influential-director-is-dead-at-94.html.

14. "Celebrating the Centennial of Director Elia Kazan," http://knopf.knopfdoubleday.com/2009/09/02/celebrating-100-years-of-elia-kazan/.

15. See "Danbury Markers," www.hmdb.org/results.asp?Town = Danbury& State = Connecticut.

16. "Joe McCarthy, a Modern Tragedy," www.myhistorymuseum.org/mccarthy/menu.htm.

17. McCarthy bust photo: www.myhistorymuseum.org/mccarthy/legacy.htm; information at www.classicwisconsin.com/features/joeappleton.html. The Fox News host Greta van Susteren is from Appleton, and her father was a prominent supporter of McCarthy.

18. Ellen Schrecker, *Many Are the Crimes: McCarthyism in America* (New York: Little, Brown, 1998), chap. 6. HUAC chairman J. Parnell Thomas said in 1948, "The closest relationship exists between this committee and the FBI. . . . I think there is a very good understanding between us. It is something, however, that we cannot talk too much about." I. F. Stone, "The FBI and the Witch Hunt," Mar. 22, 1954, in Stone,

The Haunted Fifties, 1953–1963 (New York: Little, Brown, 1963), 26. "A surprisingly large number" of HUAC hearings "made public information already well known to the FBI. Often the leading witness in such committee hearings was an undercover FBI agent who had infiltrated the Communist movement. It is quite apparent that these hearings were designed to serve the purpose of publicizing information in FBI files." Robert K. Carr, *The House Committee on Un-American Activities, 1945–50,* quoted in Stone, *Haunted Fifties,* 25.

19. FBI, "About Us: FBI Tours," www.fbi.gov/aboutus/tour/tour.htm (accessed Feb. 2, 2010).

20. Bernard Rosenfield, *Let's Go to the FBI* (New York: Putnam, 1960). This was part of a series that included *Let's Go to the Supreme Court, . . . to the Capitol, . . . to the White House, . . .* etc. The FBI book was rated "not recommended" by the University of Chicago Graduate Library School the year it was published because of "pedestrian writing and cartoon-style illustrations." *Bulletin of the Center for Children's Books* 5, no. 14 (June 1961): 164.

21. FBI, "'G-Men and Journalists': D.C. Museum Features Our Famous Cases," www.fbi.gov/page2/dec08/newseum_121908.html.

22. Newseum, www.newseum.org/exhibits_th/fbi/video_blogs/video.aspx?item=HOOV080513&style=c.

23. Newseum, "G-Men and Journalists," "J. Edgar Hoover: video blog," http://www.newseum.org/news/2008/05/j-edgar-hoover.html.

24. Joseph Kennedy to J. Edgar Hoover, Oct. 11, 1955, www.newseum.org/exhibits_th/fbi_feat/images/art_hoover_letter_lrg.pdf.

25. Karl F. Cohen, *Forbidden Animation: Censored Cartoons and Blacklisted Animators in America* (Jefferson, NC: McFarland, 2004).

26. Museum of Broadcast Communications, "Lucille Ball," www.museum.tv/eotvsection.php?entrycode=balllucille.

27. Scottish Rite Supreme Council, J. Edgar Hoover Collection, www.scottishrite.org/library/hoover/general-info.htm (accessed Feb. 2, 2010).

28. Richard Hack, *Puppetmaster: The Secret Life of J. Edgar Hoover* (Chicago: Phoenix Books, 2007).

29. Patricia Ehrens, "Film Industry in the United States," in Jewish Women's Archive, *Jewish Women: A Comprehensive Encyclopedia,* http://jwa.org/encyclopedia/article/film-industry-in-united-states.

30. "J. Edgar Hoover Collection," www.scottishrite.org/web/temple-files/gallery.htm; also at www.srmason-sj.org/web/temple-files/gallery.htm (accessed Feb. 2, 2010).

31. David Halberstam, *The Fifties* (New York: Villard Books, 1993), 336–37; John Stuart Cox and Athan G. Theoharis, *The Boss: J. Edgar Hoover and the Great American Inquisition* (Philadelphia: Temple University Press, 1988), 108.

32. "Cap Presented to Illustrious Brother Hoover," www.scottishrite.org/web/temple-files/photo-gallery/40.htm (accessed Feb. 2, 2010).

33. J. Edgar Hoover Foundation, "Keeping the Legacy Alive," www.jehooverfoundation.org/ (accessed Feb. 2, 2010).

6. SECRETS ON DISPLAY

1. Peter Eisler, "True to Form, CIA Keeps Its Spy Museum Hush-Hush," *USA Today,* July 14, 2008, www.usatoday.com/tech/news/techinnovations/2008-07-13-cia-museum_N.htm.

2. CIA Museum, https://www.cia.gov/about-cia/cia-museum/cia-museum-tour/index.html (accessed Apr. 11, 2011). Other websites accessed Jan. 16, 2010, unless otherwise noted.

3. See Frances Stonor Saunders, *The Cultural Cold War: The CIA and the World of Arts and Letters* (New York: New Press, 1999).

4. Tim Weiner, *Legacy of Ashes: The History of the CIA* (New York: Doubleday, 2007), 207.

5. Monument to Martyrs, http://siris-artinventories.si.edu/ipac20/ipac.jsp?uri=full=3100001~!302194!0.

6. Ed Pilkington, "Florida's Cuban Americans Stray from the Republican Fold," *Guardian,* Jan. 28, 2008, www.guardian.co.uk/world/2008/jan/28/uselections2008.usa.

7. The official website, www.wingsovermiami.com/index.php, refers readers to "A New Monument to Flyers," http://travelforaircraft.wordpress.com/2009/10/21/a-new-monument-to-fliers-%E2%80%93-the-aviators-of-the-bay-of-pigs-invasion-%E2%80%93-the-douglas-b-26-invader/. Proposals for a big Bay of Pigs museum in downtown Miami were considered in 2008 but have not advanced as of this writing: see Daniel Chang, "Commissioners to Consider Bay of Pigs Museum," *Miami Herald,* Apr. 14, 2008, 3B.

8. National Air and Space Museum, "The Sky Spies: Lockheed U-2," www.nasm.si.edu/exhibitions/lae/script/ss_craft.htm; National Museum of the U.S. Air Force, "Cold War Gallery," www.nationalmuseum.af.mil/exhibits/coldwar/index.asp; and "Dragon Lady: The U-2," www.nationalmuseum.af.mil/factsheets/factsheet.asp?id=9166.

9. Charles R. Morris, *Iron Destinies, Lost Opportunities: The Arms Race between the United States and the Soviet Union, 1945–1987* (New York: HarperCollins, 1988), chap. 8.

10. Weiner, *Legacy of Ashes,* 227–28.

11. Ibid., 227.

12. Michael D. Gordin, *Red Cloud at Dawn: Truman, Stalin, and the End of the Atomic Monopoly* (New York: FSG, 2010), 18, 295.

13. Weiner, *Legacy of Ashes,* 500.

14. Ibid., 287.

15. Ibid., 340, 481.

16. See Myra MacPherson, *Long Time Passing* (New York: Signet, 1984), 625.

17. Weiner, *Legacy of Ashes,* 69, 70.

18. Ibid., 497.

19. "Rare Look at In-House CIA Museum," Voice of America, June 13, 2008, www.youtube.com/watch?v=hgBRvrEb_a4.

20. Weiner, *Legacy of Ashes,* 331.

21. Eisler, "True to Form, CIA Keeps Its Spy Museum Hush-Hush."

22. Ibid.

23. Since 9/11 the NSA has also engaged in massive gathering of communications between U.S. citizens—see, for example, James Bamford, "Who's in Big Brother's Database?," *New York Review,* Nov. 5, 2009, www.nybooks.com/articles/23231 (accessed Jan. 18, 2010)—but that's not a concern of this book.

24. National Cryptologic Museum, www.nsa.gov/about/cryptologic_heritage/museum/ (accessed Jan. 18, 2010).

25. National Cryptologic Museum Virtual Tour, www.nsa.gov/about/cryptologic_heritage/museum/virtual_tour/index.shtml.

26. Robert Louis Benson and Michael Warner, eds., *Venona: Soviet Espionage and the American Response, 1939–1957* (Washington, DC: NSA, CIA, 1996), doc. 67, 363.

27. The top conservative book on Venona, by John Earl Haynes and Harvey Klehr, devotes three pages to Theodore Hall in its 480 pages, even though the discovery of Hall's name is ranked as "the greatest surprise in the Venona traffic." Haynes and Klehr, *Venona* (New Haven: Yale University Press, 1999), 314, 314–17. They do concede that if the Venona information about Ted Hall had been made public, the Rosenbergs would not have been executed (16).

28. Cell phone audio guide: 240–396–4186. Venona is item 122.

29. James Bamford, "Who's in Big Brother's Database?" (accessed Mar. 21, 2010); James Bamford, *The Puzzle Palace: Inside the National Security Agency, America's Most Secret Security Organization* (New York: Penguin Books, 1982).

30. Bamford, "Who's in Big Brother's Database?"

31. Benson and Warner, *Venona.* The official volume omits from its chronology and history the fact that the Soviets turned off their code system after learning about Venona from Weisband.

32. Matthew Aid, *The Secret Sentry: The Untold History of the National Security Agency* (New York: Bloomsbury, 2009), 22–23.

33. Ibid., 23.

34. Daniel Patrick Moynihan, *Secrecy* (New Haven: Yale University Press, 1998), 70, 73.

35. Ibid., 70.

36. Aid, *Secret Sentry,* 79.

37. Ibid., 103.

38. Ibid., 121.

7. COLD WAR CLEANUP

1. Hanford Site public tours, www.hanford.gov/page.cfm/HanfordSiteTours (accessed May 11, 2010). Fluor Hanford also has started tours limited to B Reactor, which have similar requirements and restrictions and are similarly

difficult to reserve: http://manhattanprojectbreactor.hanford.gov/ (accessed May 11, 2010).

2. "DOI Designates B Reactor at DOE's Hanford Site as a National Historic Landmark," August 25, 2008, www.energy.gov/news/6489.htm. This and subsequent websites cited accessed Sept. 19, 2009, unless otherwise noted.

3. Gerber, quoted in "Nuclear Tourism: Hanford Lures Visitors," Associated Press, May 16, 2008, www.msnbc.msn.com/id/24666721/. She wrote the definitive scholarly history of Hanford, now in its third edition: Michele Gerber, *On the Home Front: The Cold War Legacy of the Hanford Nuclear Site* (Lincoln: University of Nebraska Press, 1992, 2007).

4. "Radiation Releases at Center of Trial in Spokane," *Seattle Post-Intelligencer,* Apr. 26, 2005, www.seattlepi.com/local/221657_downwinders26.html.

5. "Power of human ingenuity" is Scarlett's phrase; "serving as inspiration" is Kupfer's. See note 2.

6. "DOI Designates B Reactor at DOE's Hanford Site as a National Historic Landmark," U.S. Department of Energy, August 25, 2008, www.hanford.gov/pmm/news.cfm/DOE/B_ReactorFINAL82508.pdf.

7. Hanford Site Public Tours, www.hanford.gov/page.cfm/HanfordSiteTours (accessed May 11, 2010).

8. Volpentest HAMMER, "Welcome to HAMMER!," www.hammertraining.com/index.cfm.

9. Tonia Steed, "Boom 'n' Bust: Hanford as Nuclear Art," *The Stranger,* July 8–14, 1999, www.thestranger.com/seattle/boom-n-bust/Content?oid=1491.

10. The complete text of the script for the five-hour tour is available online at the official Hanford website: "Public Tour Script," www.hanford.gov/hanford/files/PublicTourScript08.pdf. All subsequent quotes from the tour guide are from this script.

11. James Long, "A Tour of the Hanford Reveals the Dangers of the Birthplace of the Bomb," *Oregonian,* June 28, 2008, www.oregonlive.com/travel/index.ssf/2008/06/a_tour_of_the_hanford_reveals.html. All subsequent quotes from Long are from this piece.

12. Chris Gregoire and Rob McKenna, "Washington's Lawsuit over Hanford Cleanup Is Timely and Measured Response to Delays," *Seattle Times,* Dec. 17, 2008, http://seattletimes.nwsource.com/html/opinion/2008523323_opin16gregoire.html.

13. Steed, *Stranger.*

14. John LaForge, "US Dirty Bombs," www.commondreams.org/views02/0709-07.htm (accessed May 10, 2010).

15. Steed, *Stranger.*

16. David Fishlock, "The Dirtiest Place on Earth," *New Scientist,* Feb. 19, 1994, www.newscientist.com/article/mg14119133.900-the-dirtiest-place-on-earth.html?full=true.

17. Ibid.

18. “Hanford Moves to Alleviate Safety Concerns in C-106 Tank,” Hanford News Release, Apr. 27, 1995, www.hanford.gov/communication/reporter/attachments/RL/1995/p042795a.pdf.

19. Ibid.

20. Gerber, *On the Home Front,* 233.

21. Environmental Protection News, “EPA Fines U.S. Energy Department $1.1 Million,” Mar. 1, 2007, www.eponline.com/articles/54329/.

22. Columbia River Tours promises “the areas *[sic]* best in wildlife viewing, awesome scenery and National history with the Hanford Nuclear Reservation and Hanford Reach National Monument along the shores of our major tour route!,” www.columbiariverjourneys.com/.

23. “Public Tour Script.”

24. Google search for “hanford” and “cancer” (accessed Apr. 15, 2011). See also www.doh.wa.gov/Hanford/publications/overview/overview.html.

25. John K. Wiley, “Hanford Health-Effects Trial Opens,” *Seattle Post-Intelligencer,* June 26, 2005, www.seattlepi.com/local/221657_downwinders26.html.

26. Warren Cornwall, “Hanford Likely Caused Cancer Downwind, Jury Decides,” *Seattle Times,* May 20, 2005, http://seattletimes.nwsource.com/html/localnews/2002281825_downwinder20m.html.

27. Gerber, *On the Home Front,* 220. The reference to the Cold War ending in “silence” comes from Charles Krauthammer, “The End of Heroism,” *Time*, Feb. 10, 1997, 88.

28. Gerber, *On the Home Front,* 221.

29. Ibid., 280.

30. Steed, *Stranger*.

31. Long, “A Tour of the Hanford Reveals the Dangers.”

8. TEST SITE TOURISM IN NEVADA

1. In 2010 the name Nevada Test Site was changed to Nevada National Security Site by the National Nuclear Security Administration, which said that the new name “better reflects the critical and diverse role it plays in national security.” “Nevada Nuclear Bomb Site Given New Name,” UPI, Aug. 23, 2010, www.upi.com/Top_News/US/2010/08/23/Nevada-nuclear-bomb-site-given-new-name/UPI-39551282594195/ (accessed July 25, 2011). Here I call it Nevada Test Site, or NTS, the name by which it was known for almost sixty years. The *New York Times* featured the Nevada Test Site tour in its “Escapes” section: Henry Fountain, “Strange Love,” *New York Times,* Jan. 5, 2007, http://travel.nytimes.com/2007/01/05/travel/escapes/05atomic.html. Websites accessed Sept. 29, 2009, unless otherwise noted. Portions of this chapter were previously published as “Cold War Tourism, Western Style,” *The Nation,* Oct. 6, 1997, 33–35.

2. For the schedule of tests, see *United States Nuclear Tests, July 1945 through September 1992,* U.S. Department of Energy/Nevada Operations Office, Dec. 2000; www.nv.doe.gov/library/publications/historical/DOENV_209_REV15.pdf.

3. Annie Jacobsen, *Area 51: An Uncensored History of America's Top Secret Military Base* (New York: Little, Brown, 2011), argues the air force welcomed the alien stories as a cover for the military projects actually going on there. The book presents absurd arguments that the 1947 crash in Roswell, New Mexico, of a high-altitude observation balloon was evidence that Stalin had recruited Josef Mengele to send human guinea pigs over New Mexico in a "flying saucer." For a thorough demolition of the book, see Robert S. Norris and Jeffrey T. Richelson, "Dreamland Fantasies," *Washington Decoded,* July 11, 2011, www.washingtondecoded.com/site/2011/07/area51.html (accessed Sept. 25, 2011).

4. Carole Gallagher, *American Ground Zero: The Secret Nuclear War* (Cambridge, MA: MIT Press, 1993), 73.

5. Ibid., 57.

6. Kevin Rafferty, Jayne Loader, and Pierce Rafferty, *The Atomic Café: The Book of the Film* (Toronto: Peacock Press/Bantam, 1982), 70.

7. Ibid., 70–72.

8. Gallagher, *American Ground Zero,* 35.

9. Nevada Test Site, www.nv.doe.gov/nts/tours.aspx (accessed June 23, 2010).

10. Gallagher, *American Ground Zero,* 5.

11. National Register of Historic Places, www.historicdistricts.com/NV/Nye/state.html.

12. Rebecca Solnit, *Savage Dreams: A Journey into the Landscape Wars of the American West* (Berkeley: University of California Press, 1994), 22.

13. Ibid., 30–31.

14. Jonathan Parfrey, telephone interview with author, Sept. 6, 1997; see also Helen Caldicott, *Nuclear Power Is Not the Answer* (New York: New Press, 2007), 61.

15. "Nevada Test Site Tours: General information," www.nv.doe.gov/nts/tours.htm#Tour%20Dates.

16. Gary A. Warner, "Las Vegas Museum Recalls Days of Atomic Testing," *Orange County Register,* July 6, 2008.

17. Linton F. Brooks, quoted in Edward Rothstein, "A Place to Consider Apocalypse," *New York Times,* Feb. 23, 2005, B1.

18. Rothstein, "A Place to Consider Apocalypse."

19. Ibid.

20. "Things I Love: Teller Speaks Out about His Vegas Favorites," *Las Vegas Sun,* May 16, 2010, www.lasvegassun.com/news/2010/may/16/teller-speaks-out-about-his-vegas-favorites/.

21. Sean L. McCarthy, "Dull Atomic Museum not Much of a Blast," *Boston Herald,* July 31, 2005, 56.

22. MacFrodo, "Atomic Testing Museum Is Overpriced and Lacks Heart," Trip Advisor user reviews, Atomic Testing Museum, Aug. 6, 2009, www.tripadvisor.com/

ShowUserReviews-g45963-d556066-r27470841-Atomic_Testing_Museum-Las_Vegas_Nevada.html.

23. TravellinDays, "Well Worth a Visit," TripAdvisor user reviews, Sept. 30, 2008, www.tripadvisor.com/ShowUserReviews-g45963-d556066-r27470841-Atomic_Testing_Museum-Las_Vegas_Nevada.html.

24. Sir_Cheap_a_Lot, "It BLEW Me Away!" TripAdvisor user reviews, Oct. 14, 2008, www.tripadvisor.com/ShowUserReviews-g45963-d556066-r27470841-Atomic_Testing_Museum-Las_Vegas_Nevada.html.

25. "City of Henderson Museum Study Final Report," Dec. 4, 2008, fig. 14, 33. www.cityofhenderson.com/community_development/docs/SSCandMU/Henderson%20Museum%20Study%20Final%20Report%2012–04–08.pdf.

26. "Prohibited List": www.nv.doe.gov/nts/tours.aspx#Registration (accessed June 30, 2010).

27. Ibid.

9. MEMORIAL DAY IN LAKEWOOD AND LA JOLLA

1. City of Lakewood, "Memorial Day: May 31, 1999," program in author's possession; author interview with D.J. Waldie, May 31, 1999; D. J. Waldie, *Holy Land: A Suburban Memoir* (New York: Norton, 1996).

2. Waldie, *Holy Land,* 14–15.

3. Ibid, 15.

4. Susan Sontag, *Regarding the Pain of Others* (New York: Farrar, Straus and Giroux, 2003), 35.

5. John Lewis Gaddis, *The Cold War: A New History* (New York: Penguin, 2005), 42–43.

6. The casualty figures come from the federal Korean War Memorial website, www.nps.gov/kwvm/memorial/memorial.htm. Websites accessed Sept. 19, 2009, unless otherwise noted.

7. For a history of the campaign to create a Korean War Memorial, see G. Hurt Piehler, *Remembering War the American Way* (Washington, DC: Smithsonian Institution Press, 1995), chap. 5.

8. National Park Service, "Korean War Veterans Memorial," www.nps.gov/kwvm/memorial/memorial.htm.

9. "Dear Abby," published Nov. 11, 1988, reprinted at www.koreanwar-educator.org/kwva/p_accomplish_mem_korea.htm.

10. "4 Architects Suing over War Memorial," *New York Times,* Dec. 19, 1990.

11. National Park Service, "The Korean War," www.nps.gov/kwvm/war/korea.htm.

12. The *New York Times* uses the figure "more than two million soldiers and civilians": "The Forgotten War, Remembered," *New York Times,* June 27, 2010, www.nytimes.com/2010/06/25/opinion/25KoreaIntro.html.

13. See, for example, Tom Engelhardt, *The End of Victory Culture,* rev. ed. (Amherst: University of Massachusetts Press, 2007), 65.

14. U.S. Army Corps of Engineers, "Korean War Veterans Memorial," www.nab.usace.army.mil/projects/WashingtonDC/korean.html.

15. Engelhardt, *End of Victory Culture,* 61–62, citing Jon Halliday and Bruce Cumings, *Korea: The Unknown War* (New York: Pantheon, 1988), 159–60, 194.

16. Ibid., 62–63.

17. Quoted in Engelhardt, *End of Victory Culture,* 64.

18. On Kennan, see David Allan Mayers, *George Kennan and the Dilemmas of U.S. Foreign Policy* (New York: Oxford University Press, 1988), chap. 8.

19. Lippmann, quoted in Thomas G. Patterson, *On Every Front: The Making and Unmaking of the Cold War* (New York: Norton, 1992), 72.

20. Luis Monteagudo Jr., "Korean War Vets, Bob Hope Honored on Mount Soledad," *San Diego Union Tribune,* Nov. 12, 2003, www.signonsandiego.com/news/military/20031112–9999_2m12soledad.html.

21. Ibid.

22. Allison Hoffman, "San Diego Cross May Provide National Legal Test," *San Diego Union Tribune,* July 22, 2006, www.signonsandiego.com/news/state/20060722–0842-ca-crossdispute.html. The definitive work on the San Diego cross is Peter Irons, *God on Trial: Dispatches from America's Religious Battlefields* (New York: Viking, 2007), chap. 4.

23. Bush spokesman, quoted in Irons, *God on Trial,* 115.

24. "Pretext" was the conclusion of Judge Gordon Thompson in *Murphy v. Bilbray,* 782 Federal Supplement 1420 (S.D. Cal 1991), quoted in Irons, *God on Trial,* 87.

25. American Atheists Association, July 7, 2006, www.atheists.org/flash.line/cross3.htm.

26. An image of the memorial wall can be found at http://en.wikipedia.org/wiki/Image:Memorial_Wall.jpg.

27. Author interview with Peter Irons, KPFK 90.7 FM, May 23, 2007; see also Irons, *God on Trial,* 92.

28. Irons, *God on Trial,* 92–93.

29. Ibid., 102.

30. "The Mt. Soledad Latin Cross: ACLU Program on Freedom of Religion and Belief, August 2006," www.aclu.org/pdfs/religion/mtsoledadstatement20060824.pdf.

31. "Federal Government Takes Control of a Huge Cross," *Washington Post,* Aug. 15, 2006, A02.

32. Marcia Manna, "At Cross Purposes," *San Diego Magazine,* July 2008, www.sandiegomagazine.com/media/San-Diego-Magazine/July-2008/At-Cross-Purposes/. At this point the *Washington Post* in an editorial opposed "the cross"; the *Wall Street Journal*'s editorial was in favor: "Crossing the Line; If Displaying the Ten Commandments on Federal Property Violates the Constitution, What about

a 29-Foot-High Cross?," *Washington Post,* July 21, 2006, A16; "A Cross We Want to Bear," *Wall Street Journal,* Aug. 18, 2006, W9.

33. Jia-Riu Chong, "Judge Says Cross Can Remain on San Diego's Mt. Soledad," *Los Angeles Times,* July 31, 2008, www.latimes.com/news/local/la-me-cross31-2008jul31,0,4418411.story.

34. Tony Perry and Nardine Saad, "Cross on Public Land in San Diego Is Unconstitutional, Federal Court Rules," *Los Angeles Times,* Jan. 5, 2011, latimes.com/news/local/la-me-cross-appeal-20110105,0,2450081.story (accessed Apr. 29, 2011).

35. Edwin Decker, "Monumental Debate," *San Diego CityBeat,* May 17, 2006, www.sdcitybeat.com/cms/story/detail/monumental_debate/4369/.

36. D.A. Kolodenko, "Big Star," *San Diego CityBeat,* June 21, 2006, www.sdcitybeat.com/cms/story/detail/?id = 4478.

10. CODE NAME "ETHEL"

1. Dennis Hevesi, "Ruth Greenglass, Key Witness in Trial of Rosenbergs, Dies at 83," *New York Times,* July 9, 2008, www.nytimes.com/2008/07/09/us/09greenglass.html; websites accessed Sept. 19, 2009, unless otherwise noted. Sam Roberts, *The Brother: The Untold Story of Atomic Spy David Greenglass and How He Sent His Sister, Ethel Rosenberg, to the Electric Chair* (New York: Random House, 2001), 296–98.

2. Roberts, *The Brother,* 484. If Ruth typed the notes rather than Ethel, she would have faced the death penalty instead of Ethel. A new book by Walter Schneir presents evidence that Julius never received the lens mold sketches from David Greenglass and that David and Ruth were indeed guilty of trying to steal secrets of the atomic bomb but Julius and Ethel were not. See Walter Schneir, *Final Verdict: What Really Happened in the Rosenberg Case* (Brooklyn: Melville House, 2010).

3. "The great spies of history..." www.sfgate.com/cgi-bin/article.cgi?f = /c/a/2002/07/17/MN237343.DTL.

4. See Robert D. McFadden, "Khrushchev on Rosenbergs: Stoking Old Embers," *New York Times,* Sept. 25, 1990, www.nytimes.com/1990/09/25/world/khrushchev-on-rosenbergs-stoking-old-embers.html. Khrushchev did not claim firsthand knowledge but said that this had been told to him by Soviet Foreign Minister Vyacheslav M. Molotov. He also says that "they were neither agents nor spies for the Soviet Union. Rather, they were people sympathetic with our ideals." Nikita Khrushchev, *Khrushchev Remembers: The Glasnost Tapes,* trans. and ed. Jerrold L. Schechter with Vyacheslav V. Luchkov (Boston: Little, Brown, 1992), 192–93.

5. "The Atomic Bomb Secret: 15 Years Later," Editor, *Bulletin of the Atomic Scientists,* Dec. 1966, 25.

6. Khrushchev was also challenged by Julius Rosenberg's Russian handler, Alexander Feklisov, who told the *New York Times* in 1997, "He didn't understand anything about the atomic bomb, and he couldn't help us. And still they killed them." Alessandra Stanley, "K.G.B. Agent Plays Down Atomic Role of Rosenbergs,"

New York Times, Mar. 16, 1997, www.nytimes.com/1997/03/16/world/kgb-agent-plays-down-atomic-role-of-rosenbergs.html. Feklisov died in 2007: Douglas Martin, "Aleksandr Feklisov, Spy Tied to Rosenbergs, Dies at 93," *New York Times,* Nov. 1, 2007, www.nytimes.com/2007/11/01/world/europe/01feklisov.html.

7. Sam Roberts, "Spies and Secrecy," *New York Times,* June 26, 2008, http://cityroom.blogs.nytimes.com/2008/06/26/podcast-spies-and-secrecy/#more-3235 (accessed Mar. 6, 2010).

8. See Marjorie Garber, "Jell-O," in *Secret Agents: The Rosenberg Case, McCarthyism & Fifties America,* ed. Marjorie Garber and Rebecca L. Walkowitz (New York: Routledge, 1995), 14. Garber points out that "Benny" was also the name of Jack Benny, whose popular radio program from 1934 to 1941 was called "The Jell-O Program."

9. Ibid., 14–15.

10. Rosenberg trial Jell-O box exhibit at International Spy Museum "Art and Design" section: www.spymuseum.org/programs/educate/pdfs/SPY_art_edguide.pdf.

11. International Spy Museum, "Spy for a Day: Ethel Rosenberg," www.spymuseum.org/programs/images/guide/SpyForADay_35.pdf.

12. The big conservative book on Soviet espionage in the United States, *Spies,* by John Earl Haynes, Harvey Klehr, and Alexander Vassiliev, devotes only 7 of its 550 pages to Ted Hall—even though they blame him for starting the Korean War (because Stalin's possession of the bomb gave him the "confidence" to "unleash" war in Korea). They devote more than four times as much space—31 pages—to Alger Hiss.

13. Joseph Albright and Marcia Kunstel, *Bombshell: The Secret Story of America's Unknown Atomic Spy Conspiracy* (New York: Diane Publishing Co., 1997), 282–83.

14. Ibid., 288.

15. Ibid., 6.

16. Ibid., 284, 9.

17. Ibid., 139, 127, 126.

18. Ibid., 121.

19. Ibid., 209; FBI quoted on 219.

20. Ibid., 225.

21. Ibid., 240.

22. Alan Cowell, "Theodore Hall, Prodigy and Atomic Spy, Dies at 74," *New York Times,* Nov. 10, 1999, www.nytimes.com/1999/11/10/world/theodore-hall-prodigy-and-atomic-spy-dies-at-74.html.

23. Venona "Comment" page at www.rfc.org/sites/rfc.org/files/item_10_venona_transcription_er.pdf (accessed Apr. 23, 2011).

24. Or you could say the Rosenberg defense committee was shameless in its exploitation of the boys.

25. Eisenhower later wrote to his son John, "In this instance it is the woman who is the strong and recalcitrant character, the man who is the weak one. She has obviously been the leader in everything they did in the spy ring." Ilene J. Philipson, *Ethel Rosenberg: Beyond the Myths* (New Brunswick: Rutgers University Press, 1992), 346. The museum takes a different approach.

26. "Rosenbergs Executed," *National Guardian,* June 22, 1953. The Newseum also displays black newspaper reports on the assassinations of Medgar Evers and Martin Luther King—but neither of them was executed by the government after being convicted in federal court.

27. The Newseum in this exhibit makes other striking choices: its article on the assassination of Trotsky is written by Max Schachtman; its story on the assassination of Medgar Evers comes from a black weekly in Mississippi.

28. "American Women! A Celebration of Our History," Hoover Presidential Library, http://hoover.archives.gov/exhibits/AmericanWomen/index.html.

29. "American Women! A Celebration of our History," Hoover Presidential Library, www.hoover.archives.gov/exhibits/AmericanWomen/fities-feminism/rosenberg.html.

30. Roberts, *The Brother;* Alexander Feklisov and Sergei Kostin, *The Man Behind the Rosenbergs* (New York: Enigma Books, 1991). The quotation is from Kostin: "The Rosenberg Spy Case," NYHS panel, Oct. 24, 2001, www.c-spanvideo.org/program/167111-1 (accessed July 2, 2010).

31. The 1950 *Coller's* cover is online at www.thehistoryshoppe.com/Images/ColdWar/ChapterII%28b%29.JPG.

32. Sergei Konstin, Feklisov's collaborator, said at the New York Historical Society panel discussion of the exhibit that he had asked several experts in the USSR what value the Greenglass sketches had for their bomb, and they all had the same answer: "None." NYHS panel video, Oct. 24, 2001, www.c-spanvideo.org/program/167111-1 (accessed July 2, 2010).

33. Ronald Radosh, NYHS panel video, Oct. 24, 2001, www.c-spanvideo.org/program/167111-1 (accessed July 2, 2010).

34. Daniel Patrick Moynihan, *Secrecy* (New Haven: Yale University Press, 1999), 143–44.

11. MOUND BUILDERS OF MISSOURI

1. Cahokia Mounds: http://en.wikipedia.org/wiki/Monks_Mound. The title for this chapter, and much of the underlying research, comes from Jason Krupar, "Burying Atomic History: The Mound Builders of Fernald and Weldon Spring," *Public Historian* 29, no. 1 (Winter 2007): 31–58.

2. "Weldon Spring Site: Howell Prairie and Native Plant Education Garden," www.lm.doe.gov/Weldon/Interpretive_Center/Howell_Prairie_and_Native_Plant_Education_Garden.pdf. Websites accessed Jan. 9, 2010, unless otherwise noted.

3. "Long Term Surveillance and Maintenance Plan," www.lm.doe.gov/WorkArea/linkit.aspx?LinkIdentifier=id&ItemID=1357.

4. Sara Shipley, "Radioactive Site Is Opened to Tourists," *St. Louis Post-Dispatch,* Aug. 6, 2002; reprinted at www.dnr.missouri.gov/env/hwp/ws-special/ws-slpd-080602.htm.

5. Ibid.

6. Ibid.

7. S.M. Stoller Corporation: www.stoller.com/stoller2/index.php. The company's projects include Rocky Flats and the Nevada Test Site.

8. Weldon Spring Site, Interpretive Center Online Tour, "Weldon Spring Site through the 20th Century," www.lm.doe.gov/Weldon/Interpretive_Center/Online_Tour/Weldon_Spring_Site_through_the_20th_Century.pdf (accessed Jan. 10, 2010).

9. The same information is printed on a free handout, available at the door, and posted on the website: www.lm.doe.gov/Weldon/Interpretive_Center/Online_Tour.

10. The full text is online at Weldon Spring Site Interpretive Center Online Tour, "Radiation Fundamentals," www.lm.doe.gov/Weldon/Interpretive_Center/Online_Tour/Radiation_Fundamentals.pdf.

11. See "Radiation Poisoning," http://en.wikipedia.org/wiki/Radiation_poisoning.

12. Shipley, "Radioactive Site Is Opened to Tourists"; *St. Cronan Bulletin,* Dec. 4, 2005, http://stcronan.org/bulletins/lityr0506/12-04-2005.pdf.

13. Weldon Spring Site, Interpretive Center Online Tour, "Tribute to the Mallinckrodt Uranium Workers," www.lm.doe.gov/Weldon/Interpretive_Center/Online_Tour/Tribute_to_the_Mallinckrodt_Uranium_Workers.pdf (accessed Jan. 10, 2010).

14. Destrehan Street was a uranium factory in downtown St. Louis run by Mallinckrodt, the same private company that ran the uranium factory at Weldon Spring. Radioactive waste from Destrehan Street was dumped at Weldon Spring.

15. Jeannette Batz, "The Right to Answers: Nobody Knows Why the Babies Are Dying Near Weldon Spring. But the Grownups Can't Help Asking Whether the Site's Toxic Stew Is to Blame," *Riverfront Times,* Mar. 7, 2001, www.riverfronttimes.com/2001-03-07/news/the-right-to-answers (accessed June 1, 2010). This lengthy piece provides an outstanding history of the site, the cleanup, and the protests.

16. Krupar, "Burying Atomic History," 32.

17. Shipley, "Radioactive Site Is Opened to Tourists."

12. COLD WAR ELVIS

1. "Sgt. Elvis Presley" exhibit at the General George Patton Museum, Mar. 24, 2004–Mar. 24, 2006: www.3ad.com/history/at.ease/elvis.section/elvis.exhibit.htm. Websites accessed Feb. 6, 2010, unless otherwise noted.

2. Quoted in Michael Meyer, *The Year That Changed the World: The Untold Story behind the Fall of the Berlin Wall* (New York: Scribner, 2009), 76.

3. Peter Guralnick, *Last Train to Memphis: The Rise of Elvis Presley* (New York: Little, Brown, 1994), 442–43.

4. Staff Sgt. Sean Riley, "Presley's Tour of Duty Honored," www.3ad.com/history/at.ease/elvis.section/elvis.exhibit.pages/introduction.1.htm.

5. "Secretary Norton Designates Elvis Presley's Graceland Mansion National Historic Landmark," www.interior.gov/news/06_News_Releases/060327.htm.

6. http://elvis.com/news/full_story.asp?id=1439. A video tour hosted by Priscilla was offered online for $9.99.

7. "William J. Taylor, Jr.," CSIS, http://csis.org/expert/william-j-taylor-jr.

8. William J. Taylor Jr., *Elvis in the Army: The King of Rock 'n' Roll as Seen by an Officer Who Served with Him* (Novato, CA: Presidio, 1995), 79, 80, 83.

9. Taylor, *Elvis in the Army,* 127.

10. Ibid., 128.

11. Colin Powell, *My American Journey* (New York: Ballantine, 1995), 45–46.

12. Ibid., 12.

13. Ibid.

14. Ibid., 23.

15. See, for example, www.3ad.com/history/at.ease/elvis.section/photo.pages/civies.motorbike.htm.

16. Uta G. Poiger, *Jazz, Rock, and Rebels: Cold War Politics and American Culture in a Divided Germany* (Berkeley: University of California Press, 2000), quote on 193.

17. Ibid., 195.

18. "Jukebox: Ticky, Real Ticky," *Time,* Apr. 20, 1959, www.time.com/time/magazine/article/0,9171,864588,00.html.

19. Mark Fenemore, *Sex, Thugs, and Rock 'n' Roll: Teenage Rebels in Cold War East Germany* (New York: Berghahn Books, 2007), 139–40.

20. Poiger, *Jazz,* 196.

21. Ibid.

22. "Leipzig Presley Fans Jailed," *New York Times,* Nov. 3, 1959.

23. Poiger, *Jazz,* 198.

24. Ibid., 199.

25. Maria Hohn, *GIs and Frauleins: The German-American Encounter in 1950s West Germany* (Chapel Hill: University of North Carolina Press, 2002), photo on 59. See also Andreas Schroer, *Private Presley: The Missing Years—Elvis in Germany* (New York: Harper, 1993), 68–69. The Elvis fan club 2010 trip to Germany advertises a stop in Steinfurth, "where Elvis and a work party erected a war memorial." Elvis Presley Fan Club brochure, "Elvis: August 2010," www.arenatravel.com/Brochure%20pdf%20files/Elvis%202010%20brochure.pdf.

26. Frank Biess, email to author, Mar. 25, 2010; see also Michael Geyer, "Cold War Angst," in *The Miracle Years: A Cultural History of West Germany, 1949–1968,* ed. Hanna Schissler (Princeton: Princeton University Press, 2001).

27. Hohn, *GIs and Frauleins,* 55–59.

28. John Lewis Gaddis, *The Cold War: A New History* (New York: Penguin, 2005), 112.

29. Martin Walker, *The Cold War: A History* (New York: Holt, 1993), 130–31; Tony Judt, *Postwar: A History of Europe since 1945* (New York: Penguin, 2006), 251.

30. Alan Levy, *Operation Elvis* (New York: Holt, 1960), 89. Levy does not identify the journalist making the inquiry.

31. Walter LaFeber, *The American Age: U.S. Foreign Policy at Home and Abroad,* vol. 2, *Since 1896* (New York: Norton, 1994), 571.

32. W. Granger Blair, "NATO Stepping up Switch to Missiles," *New York Times,* Nov. 4, 1958, 1.

33. Walker, *Cold War,* 129.

34. See Brian Urquhart, "A Contest in the Cold," *New York Review,* Dec. 17, 2009, 50–55.

35. George F. Kennan, *Russia, the Atom, and the West: The BBC Reith Lectures, 1957* (London: Oxford University Press, 1958), 37, 39.

36. Ibid., 46, 47; Urquhart, "A Contest in the Cold."

37. Ronald Steel, *Walter Lippmann and the American Century* (New York: Little, Brown, 1980), 528, citing Lippmann's "Today and Tomorrow" columns of Apr. 4, 18, and 19, 1961.

38. Steel, *Walter Lippmann.*

39. Marc Trachtenberg, *A Constructed Peace: The Making of the European Settlement, 1945–1993* (Princeton: Princeton University Press, 1999), 260.

40. Ibid., 261.

41. Ibid., 262.

42. Judt, *Postwar,* 253–54.

43. Chalmers Johnson, *The Sorrows of Empire: Militarism, Secrecy, and the End of the Republic* (New York: Metropolitan, 2004), 33–34.

44. Taylor, *Elvis in the Army,* 128.

45. Ibid., 144.

13. THE GRACELAND OF COLD WAR TOURISM

1. Tom Vanderbilt, *Survival City: Adventures among the Ruins of Atomic America* (Princeton: Princeton Architectural Press, 2002), 125.

2. The Greenbrier's official bunker information page is www.greenbrier.com/staying-here/the-bunker.aspx. Websites accessed Sept. 19, 2009, unless otherwise noted.

3. Greenbrier activities page at www.greenbrier.com/site/activities-list.aspx.

4. Linda Walls, telephone interview with author, Aug. 29, 2008. All subsequent quotations from Walls are from this interview.

5. Bill Geerhart, "The Greenbrier: Five-Star Fallout Shelter," www.conelrad.com/groundzero/greenbrier.html.

6. John Strausbaugh, "A West Virginia Cold War Bunker Now a Tourist Spot," *New York Times,* Nov. 12, 2006.

7. Geerhart, "The Greenbrier."

8. Ibid.

9. Thomas Mallon, "Mr. Smith Goes Underground," *American Heritage* 51, no. 5 (Sept. 2000), www.americanheritage.com/articles/magazine/ah/2000/5/2000_5_60.shtml.

10. Strausbaugh, "Cold War Bunker."

11. Paul Lieberman, "A Monument to Gentility," *Los Angeles Times*, June 18, 2000, L1, http://articles.latimes.com/2000/jun/18/travel/tr-42093. Linda Walls told me she had never seen straitjackets and that the area in question had "no bars."

12. Geerhart, "The Greenbrier."

13. Ted Gup, "The Doomsday Blueprints," *Time*, Aug. 10, 1992, 32–39, www.time.com/time/magazine/article/0,9171,976187-4,00.html.

14. Bill Geerhart, "Wanted: The Arthur Godfrey Doomsday Message!," www.conelrad.com/godfrey/.

15. PBS *American Experience*, "Interview with Paul Fritz Bugas," www.pbs.org/wgbh/amex/bomb/sfeature/interview.html#comm.

16. Ibid.

17. These rooms are still available for conferences: Governors' Hall, www.greenbrier.com/site/meeting-rooms-detail.aspx?cid=2066; Mountaineer Room, www.greenbrier.com/site/meeting-rooms-detail.aspx?cid=2066.

18. Mallon, "Mr. Smith Goes Underground."

19. Ted Gup, "The Ultimate Congressional Hideaway," *Washington Post*, May 31, 1992, W11.

20. Eisenhower, quoted in Walter Goodman, "The Truth about Fallout Shelters," *Redbook*, Jan. 1962, 34; quoted in Kenneth D. Rose, *One Nation Underground: The Fallout Shelter in American Culture* (New York: New York University Press, 2001), 20–27.

21. This scenario was outlined by Ted Gup in Mallon, "Mr. Smith Goes Underground."

22. Gup, "Ultimate Hideaway."

23. Robert Scheer, *With Enough Shovels: Reagan, Bush, and Nuclear War* (New York: Random House, 1982), 232–34; Richard Halloran, "Pentagon Draws up First Strategy for Fighting a Long Nuclear War," *New York Times*, May 30, 1982, A1; J. Peter Scoblic, *U.S. vs. Them: How a Half Century of Conservatism Has Undermined America's Security* (New York: Viking, 2008), 128.

24. James Mann, "The Armageddon Plan," *Atlantic Monthly*, Mar. 2004, www.theatlantic.com/doc/200403/mann; see also Mann, *The Vulcans: The History of Bush's War Cabinet* (New York: Penguin, 2004), 138–45.

25. Mann, "Armageddon Plan."

26. Ibid.

27. James Mann, interview with author, June 24, 2009.

28. Mann, "Armageddon Plan."

29. Ibid.

30. Ibid.

31. Mallon, "Mr. Smith Goes Underground."

14. IKE'S EMMY

1. The Academy of Television Arts and Science first voted Eisenhower an Honorary Lifetime Membership in the Academy—March 12, 1953—but declared in a letter to the White House dated August 31, 1954, that it had determined that that was "against policy" and that the board had instead created a special award for the president, an honorary Emmy. The Academy president proposed presenting the Emmy to Ike at the White House in front of cameras. Ike's secretary informed the Academy that the president accepted the award but declined the photo op. A year later, George Murphy, the actor and future Republican senator from California, wrote to the White House on MGM stationery proposing again a presentation at the White House "with a cameraman present," but Ike's press secretary again declined. In the end, the Emmy was delivered to Ike's press secretary, James Hagerty, by a board member. Ike then wrote the Academy president for the first time: "I am highly complimented by the award." Don DeFore, President, Academy of Television Arts and Sciences, letter to Thomas E. Stephens, Secretary to the President, Aug. 31, 1954; Stephens to DeFore, Sept. 8, 1954; George Murphy to James Hagerty, Sept. 14, 1955; Hagerty to Murphy, Sept. 20, 1955; Eisenhower to DeFore, Nov. 29, 1955; Eisenhower Presidential Library, copies in author's possession.

2. A good analysis of the situation is offered in Campbell Craig and Fredrik Lovevall, *America's Cold War: The Politics of Insecurity* (Cambridge, MA: Harvard University Press, 2009), chap. 5, esp. 192–96. On the significance of the Farewell Address, see Andrew Bacevich, *Washington Rules: America's Path to Permanent War* (New York: Metropolitan, 2010).

3. Thomas Doherty, *Cold War, Cool Medium: Television, McCarthyism, and American Culture* (New York: Columbia University Press, 2003), 101.

4. The total includes those who have watched it at www.youtube.com/watch?v=8y06NSBBRtY and at www.youtube.com/watch?v=rd8wwMFmCeE; it's posted on YouTube in more than 150 places. Statistics retrieved Feb. 17, 2012.

5. "Eisenhower Warns Us of the Military-Industrial Complex," www.youtube.com/watch?v=8y06NSBBRtY. Comments viewed Aug. 20, 2011.

6. "The Military Industrial Complex," http://militaryindustrialcomplex.com/contracts-leaderboard.asp (accessed Feb. 17, 2012).

7. Felix Belair Jr., "Vigilance Urged: Talk Bids 'Godspeed' to Kennedy," 1; "Text of Eisenhower's Farewell Address," *New York Times,* Jan. 18, 1961, A22.

8. Jack Raymond, "The 'Military-Industrial Complex,'" *New York Times,* Jan. 22, 1961, E4.

9. "Last Days," *Time,* Jan. 27, 1961, 27.

10. "On to Gettysburg," *Newsweek,* Jan. 30, 1961, 22.

11. "Eisenhower's Farewell," *U.S. News & World Report,* Jan. 30, 1961, 68–71.

12. "Drive to Expand Defense Persists," *New York Times,* Mar. 26, 1961, 53.

13. "Role of Pentagon in Economy Rises," *New York Times,* May 20, 1961, 48.

14. Fred J. Cook, "Juggernaut: The Warfare State," *The Nation,* Oct. 28, 1961, entire issue.

15. Richard Rovere, "Letter from Washington," *New Yorker,* May 12, 1962, 166–70.

16. Richard F. Kaufman, "'We Must Guard against Unwarranted Influence by the Military-Industrial Complex'"; "As Eisenhower was saying . . . ," *New York Times Magazine,* June 22, 1969, 10.

17. Lars-Erik Nelson, "Military-Industrial Man," *New York Review of Books* 47, no. 20 (Dec. 21, 2000): 6.

18. University of Washington, Seattle, www.historylink.org/db_images/Seattle_UWCampus-HenryJacksonBustoJSIS-bronze.jpg.

19. Nick Perry, "'Scoop' out of the Shadows," *Seattle Times,* May 12, 2006; Jessica Kowal, "At Namesake of Senator, His Likeness Gets Its Due," *New York Times,* May 15, 2006.

20. University of Washington, Seattle, www.historylink.org/index.cfm?DisplayPage=output.cfm&file_id=9005.

21. Jackson Foundation, www.hmjackson.org/.

22. 309th Aerospace Maintenance and Regeneration Center, www.dm.af.mil/units/AMARC.asp.

23. Pima Air and Space and Titan Missile Museums, www.pimaair.org/.

24. Sabrejet stats from www.korean-war.com/KWAircraft/US/USAF/north_american_f86.html.

15. THE FALLOUT SHELTERS OF NORTH DAKOTA

1. North Dakota Historical Society, "Soviet Nuclear Weapons Targets in North Dakota," http://history.nd.gov/exhibits/atomicage/Cold%20War%20Vital%20Stats-web.pdf. Websites accessed Sept. 19, 2009, unless otherwise noted.

2. Department of Civil Defense film, quoted in Kevin Rafferty, Jayne Loader, and Pierce Rafferty, *The Atomic Café: The Book of the Film* (New York: Bantam Books, 1982), 53.

3. Laura McEnaney, *Civil Defense Begins at Home* (Princeton: Princeton University Press, 2000), chap. 1.

4. North Dakota Historical Society, "The Atomic Age Arrives," www.nd.gov/hist/exhibits/atomicAgeArrives.html. There is a Civil Defense Museum, but it is online only and displays one person's collection of "civil defense stuff": www.civildefensemuseum.com/index.html.

5. KXMB-TV Bismarck, Nov. 14, 2007, 8:00 A.M. newscast, http://video.aol.com/video-detail/cold-war-exhibit/1914096028.

6. Rogers Historical Museum, "The Life Atomic! Growing Up in the Shadow of the A-Bomb," www.rogersarkansas.com/museum/AtomicBomb.asp. (accessed May 16, 2011).

7. "A Brief History of Rogers," www.rogersarkansas.com/museum/rogershistory.asp.

8. Rogers Historical Museum, www.rogersarkansas.com/Museum/current exhibits.asp; www.imls.gov/applicants/samples/mfa/Rogers%20Historical%20 Museum.pdf.

9. Sandra Cox, "Back to the 1950s," *Northwest Arkansas Times,* May 9, 2008, www.nwanews.com/nwat/WhatsUp/65024/; Jeff Mores, "The Life Atomic," *Northwest Arkansas Times,* reprinted at www.undergroundbombshelter.com/news/life-atomic-growing-up-in-the-shadow-of-the-abomb.htm.

10. McEnaney, *Civil Defense,* 64–65, 118–19.

11. Wisconsin State Historical Museum, www.wisconsinhistory.org/museum/atomic/takecovr.asp; www.wisconsinhistory.org/museum/artifacts/archives/001080.asp.

12. Jeannine Stein, "What Lies Beneath," *Los Angeles Times,* Feb. 21, 2002, http://articles.latimes.com/2002/feb/21/news. For another small fallout shelter exhibit, see the National Museum of Nuclear Science and History in Albuquerque: www.nuclearmuseum.org/featured-exhibits/detail/cold-war-fallout-shelter (accessed Apr. 14, 2011).

13. C.J. Hughes, "When the East Coast Was a Nuclear Bull's-Eye," *New York Times,* Jan. 5, 2007, http://query.nytimes.com/gst/fullpage.html?sec = travel&res = 950DE0DF1430F936A35752C0A9619C8B63 (accessed May 5, 2010).

14. "Family Fallout Shelter," http://americanhistory.si.edu/collections/object.cfm?key = 35&objkey = 5884.

15. Rick Perlstein, *Before the Storm* (New York: Hill and Wang, 2001), 143.

16. Rafferty, Loader, and Rafferty, *The Atomic Café,* 101.

17. "The Shelter" episode of *The Twilight Zone,* Sept. 29, 1961, http://en.wikipedia.org/wiki/The_Shelter_%28The_Twilight_Zone%29; complete video at www.cbs.com/classics/the_twilight_zone/video/.

18. D.J. Waldie, "The Cold War Lives on Inside Us All," Salon.com, Feb. 24, 1997, www.salon.com/feb97/coldwar970224.html.

19. Rafferty, Loader, and Rafferty, *The Atomic Café,* 113, 117.

20. Ibid., 102.

21. See Jon Wiener, "The Omniscient Narrator and the Unreliable Narrator: The Case of *Atomic Café,*" *Film & History* 37, no. 1 (2007): 73–76.

22. J. Peter Scoblic, *U.S. vs. Them: How a Half-Century of Conservatism Has Undermined America's Security* (New York: Viking, 2008), 106.

23. Robert Scheer, *With Enough Shovels: Reagan, Bush, and Nuclear War* (New York: Random House, 1982), 18–26.

24. Scoblic notes this connection in *U.S. vs. Them,* 126.

25. Visitor comments transcribed at www.nd.gov/hist/exhibits/atomicAge Arrives_comments.html.

26. North Dakota Cowboy Hall of Fame, www.northdakotacowboy.com/article.asp?ID = 71.

16. "IT HAD TO DO WITH CUBA AND MISSILES"

1. Remarks of Senator John F. Kennedy at the Mormon Tabernacle, Salt Lake City, Utah, Sept. 23, 1960, www.jfklibrary.org/Historical+Resources/Archives/Reference+Desk/Speeches/JFK/JFK+Pre-Pres/1960/002PREPRES12SPEECHES_60SEP23e.htm.

2. Peter Baker, "Bush Knows Well the Hazards of the Trail," *Washington Post*, Dec. 10, 2007, www.washingtonpost.com/wp-dyn/content/article/2007/12/09/AR2007120901336_2.html. Websites accessed Oct. 20, 2009, unless otherwise noted.

3. Martin Walker, *The Cold War: A History* (New York: Holt, 1993), 172.

4. "Homer E. Capehart," Wikipedia, http://en.wikipedia.org/wiki/Homer_Capehart.

5. "The World on the Brink: John F. Kennedy and the Cuban Missile Crisis—An Exhibit: Wednesday, October 1, 2002 through Friday, May 15, 2003," Kennedy Library, www.jfklibrary.org/jfkl/cmc/cmc_calendar_map.html. Image also at www.pimall.com/nais/pivintage/images/cubancalandar.jpg (accessed Apr. 24, 2011).

6. Kennedy Library, "Past Exhibits," www.jfklibrary.org/JFK+Library+and+Museum/Visit+the+Library+and+Museum/Museum+Exhibits/?active=past_exhibits.

7. "John F. Kennedy Library and Museum," http://boston.travelape.com/attractions/john-f-kennedy-library-and-museum/.

8. Rick Perlstein, *Before the Storm* (New York: Hill and Wang, 2001); Goldwater, quoted in J. Peter Scoblic, *U.S. vs. Them: How a Half-Century of Conservatism Has Undermined America's Security* (New York: Viking, 2008), 39.

9. John Judis, *William F. Buckley, Jr.: Patron Saint of the Conservatives* (New York: Simon & Schuster, 1988), 206.

10. David Lowenthal, "U.S. Cuban Policy: Illusion and Reality," *National Review*, Jan. 29, 1963, 61–63.

11. Peter Schweizer, "The Cuban Missile Crisis Reconsidered," *Weekly Standard*, Oct. 21, 2002, www.weeklystandard.com/Content/Public/Articles/000/000/001/764krpev.asp; Richard Parmet, *Richard Nixon and His America* (New York: Little, Brown, 1988), 428.

12. Julian E. Zelizer, *Arsenal of Democracy: The Politics of National Security: From WWII to the War on Terrorism* (New York: Basic Books, 2010), 170.

13. "The Sky Spies: Cuban Missile Crisis," National Air and Space Museum, www.nasm.si.edu/exhibitions/lae/html/sky_cuba.htm.

14. "Reconnaissance and the Cuban Missile Crisis," National Museum of the U.S. Air Force, www.nationalmuseum.af.mil/factsheets/factsheet.asp?id=1876.

15. Moon Travel Guides, "Fortaleza de San Carlos de la Cabaña," www.moon.com/destinations/cuba/havana/sights-across-the-harbor/parque-historico-militar

-morro-cabana/fortaleza-de-san-carlos-de-la-cabana; Michael Dobbs, *One Minute to Midnight: Kennedy, Khrushchev, and Castro on the Brink of Nuclear War* (New York: Knopf, 2008), 121.

16. Dobbs, *One Minute to Midnight,* 248, 102.

17. "Hello Cuba!," www.hellocuba.ca/itineraries/304Cabana.html; "Debbie's Caribbean Resort Reviews: Cuba," www.debbiescaribbeanresortreviews.com/cuba/cuba.html.

18. JFK Library, "Cuban Missile Crisis," www.jfklibrary.org/JFK/JFK-in-History/Cuban-Missile-Crisis.aspx (accessed Apr. 25, 2011).

19. Dobbs, *One Minute to Midnight,* 266.

20. Perlstein, *Before the Storm,* 272.

21. "General Curtis LeMay Marker," www.hmdb.org/marker.asp?marker=12774; Steve Coll, "The Cabinet of Dr. Strangelove," *New York Review,* Feb. 25, 2010, 28–30.

22. Dobbs, *One Minute to Midnight,* 282–83.

23. Ibid., 266, 349–50.

24. Ibid., 250–51.

25. Ibid., 348–49.

17. THE MUSEUM OF THE MISSILE GAP

1. The Titan Missile Museum is operated by the nonprofit Arizona Aerospace Foundation: www.titanmissilemuseum.org/ (accessed Apr. 3, 2010). Portions of this chapter were previously published in a different form as "Doomsday on Display," *The Nation,* Mar. 15, 1993, 350–55.

2. Henry Fountain, "Strange Love," *New York Times,* Jan. 5, 2007, http://travel.nytimes.com/2007/01/05/travel/escapes/05atomic.html. This and subsequent websites accessed Sept. 19, 2009, unless otherwise noted.

3. "Titan Missile Museum" brochure, www.titanmissilemuseum.org/pdf/Brochure2007final.pdf.

4. See photo at http://upload.wikimedia.org/wikipedia/en/8/84/TitanMissileRentryModule.jpg.

5. "B-53 Nuclear Bomb," Wikipedia, http://en.wikipedia.org/wiki/W-53_nuclear_warhead.

6. "Strategic Air Command History," press information, undated, 1997.

7. Strategic Air and Space Museum Permanent Exhibits, www.sasmuseum.com/exhibits/permanent-exhibits/. This museum also features a model of the plant where the *Enola Gay* was built. The exhibit includes "original wooden floor bricks, tools, and an engine piston from the bomber Enola Gay." www.sasmuseum.com/exhibits/permanent-exhibits/martin-bomber-plant/.

8. Submarine Force Museum: www.ussnautilus.org/. See also www.navy.mil/navydata/cno/n87/usw/issue_22/museum.htm.

9. See Steven Coll, "The Cabinet of Dr. Strangelove," *New York Review*, Feb. 25, 2010, 28–29.

10. "War Games" (1983) script, Database of Movie Dialog, http://movie.subtitlr.com/subtitle/show/256513#line101.

11. *Aviation Week*, Feb. 9, 1981, 109.

12. Eugene Burdick and Harvey Wheeler, *Fail-Safe* (New York: McGraw-Hill, 1962), 72.

13. Ibid., 71.

14. "Light on the Road to Damascus," *Time*, Sept. 29, 1980, 28, www.time.com/time/magazine/article/0,9171,952781,00.html.

15. *Newsweek*, Sept. 29, 1980, 33.

16. "Nuclear Fudge," *The Nation*, Oct. 4, 1980, 299.

17. *Wall Street Journal*, quoted in Bob Thompson, "Rethinking the Unthinkable," *Washington Post*, July 28, 2002, W12, www.washingtonpost.com/ac2/wp-dyn/A59355-2002Jul24.

18. Minuteman Missile National Historic Site in South Dakota: www.nps.gov/mimi/index.htm. It opened to the public in 2004. See Gretchen Heefner, "Missiles and Memory: Dismantling South Dakota's Cold War," *Western Historical Quarterly* 38 (Summer 2007): 181–203; Thompson, "Rethinking the Unthinkable."

19. *U.S. News & World Report*, Sept. 29, 1980, 80.

20. Bernard T. Feld, "Titan: Dangerous and Obsolete," *Bulletin of the Atomic Scientists* 36, no. 9 (Nov. 1980): 4.

21. *Aviation Week*, Feb. 19, 1981, 119.

22. Herman Kahn, *On Thermonuclear War* (Princeton: Princeton University Press, 1960), 74–80, quoted in Philip Green, *Deadly Logic: The Theory of Nuclear Deterrence* (New York: Schocken Books, 1968), 259–60.

23. Eisenhower, quoted at Eisenhower Presidential Library and Museum, "Quotes: War and Defense," www.eisenhower.archives.gov/all_about_ike/quotes.html#war.

24. Arthur M. Schlesinger Jr., "The Big Issue," *Progressive* 24, no. 9 (Sept. 1960): 10, "originally prepared by Mr. Schlesinger as a memorandum for private circulation."

25. Thomas R. Phillps, "The Growing Missile Gap," *Reporter*, Jan. 8, 1959, 12–16, quoted in Charles R. Morris, *Iron Destinies, Lost Opportunities: The Arms Race between the United States and the Soviet Union, 1945–1987* (New York: HarperCollins, 1988), 127.

26. Morris, *Iron Destinies*, 128, 122.

27. Ibid., 143.

28. Henry Kissinger, *White House Years* (New York: Little, Brown, 1979), 113.

29. Morris, *Iron Destinies*, chap. 8.

30. David E. Hoffman, *The Dead Hand: The Untold Story of the Cold War Arms Race and Its Dangerous Legacy* (New York: Doubleday, 2009); www.thedeadhandbook.com/about.html (accessed Apr. 6, 2010).

31. Among the many critics of Kahn, I have relied primarily on Green, *Deadly Logic,* esp. 258–59.

32. Andrew Szasz, *Ecopopulism: Toxic Waste and the Movement for Environmental Justice* (Minneapolis: University of Minnesota Press, 1994), 182; U.S. Ecology Idaho, Customer Audit Handbook, www.americanecology.com/downloads/grand_view_forms/grandview_audit_handbook.pdf.

18. THE MUSEUM OF DÉTENTE

1. Kai Chen Forum, www.kaichenforum.com/forums/viewtopic.php?t = 4648. Websites accessed Oct. 1, 2009, unless otherwise noted.

2. Mike Anton, "The Past Haunts Richard Nixon's Library," *Los Angeles Times,* Oct. 1, 2009, 1, www.latimes.com/news/local/la-me-nixon-mao-protest1-2009oct01,0,6352524.story.

3. Jeanne Kirkpatrick, "The Myth of Moral Equivalence," *Imprimis* 15, no. 1 (January 1986), www.hillsdale.edu/news/imprimis/archive/issue.asp?year=1986&month=01.

4. Anton, "The Past"; Naftali, interview with author, May 25, 2012. Chen in 2009 was "the first person to launch a complaint about it," according to Sandy Quinn, of the Nixon Library and Birthplace Foundation. Jessica Terrell, "Nixon Library Will Be Target of Mao Protest," *Orange County Register,* Sept. 29, 2009, www.ocregister.com/articles/library-nixon-mao-2586329-leaders-chen#.

5. Olsen Enbright, "Pinko, Commie Statues Shock, Offend at Nixon Library," KNBC-TV Channel 4 News, Oct. 1, 2009, www.nbclosangeles.com/news/local-beat/Pinko-Commie-Statues-Shock-Offend-at-Nixon-Library-63135412.html.

6. "Music Teacher Arrested on Suspicion of Flashing," *OC in Two* (video), *Orange County Register,* Oct. 2, 2009, http://video.ocregister.com/m/26688217/oc-in-two-music-teacher-arrested-on-suspicion-of-flashing.htm?pageid = 146333.

7. John H. Taylor, http://episconixonian.blogspot.com/2009/09/mao-tied.html.

8. *National Review,* Aug. 10, 1971. Among twelve signers of the statement were Allan Ryskind, editor of *Human Events;* Randall Teague, Young Americans for Freedom; Jeffrey Bell, director of the American Conservative Union; Daniel Mahoney, New York Conservative Party; and Neil McCaffery, president of the Conservative Book Club, in addition to Buckley and William A. Rusher, publisher of the *National Review.*

9. "Politics: The Right Wing versus Nixon," *Time,* Aug. 16, 1971, www.time.com/time/magazine/article/0,9171,877188–1,00.html.

10. Congress, House of Representatives, Representative John Ashbrook, "The First 1,000 Days: One Legislator's Viewpoint," 92nd Cong., 1st sess., *Congressional Record* 117 (Dec. 15, 1971): 47, 230.

11. Rick Perlstein, *Nixonland* (New York: Scribner, 2008), 610.

12. John Ashbrook, Presidential Nomination Speech, December 29, 1971, quoted in Erik Patrik Gilliland, "Richard Nixon, Détente, and the Conservative Movement, 1969–1974" (M.A. thesis, Wright State University, 2006), http://etd.ohiolink.edu/view.cgi?acc_num=wright1166382457 (accessed May 8, 2010); Perlstein, *Nixonland,* 610. Although Buckley endorsed Ashcroft, and so did *Human Events,* Republican voters didn't go for his message; he ended up with about 10 percent of the vote in New Hampshire and California and then threw in the towel.

13. Perlstein, *Nixonland,* 627; Buckley, quoted in David R. Stokes, "Buckley, Nixon, and Mao: 1972," http://townhall.com/columnists/DavidRStokes/2008/03/02/buckley,_nixon,_and_mao_1972.

14. Buckley, quoted in "Buckley, Nixon, and Mao"; "another conservative journalist," quoted in Julian E. Zelizer, *Arsenal of Democracy: The Politics of National Security: From World War II to the War on Terrorism* (New York: Basic Books, 2010), 243.

15. Nixon Library, Museum Tour: Permanent Galleries, www.nixonlibraryfoundation.org/index.php?submenu=museum&src=gendocs&link=PermanentGalleries; photo at http://picasaweb.google.com/lh/photo/WOAzwT6O64yuSrq73dn1FA.

16. James Popkin, "Gambling with the Mob? Wise Guys Have Set Their Sights on the Booming Indian Casino Business," *U.S. News & World Report,* Aug. 15, 1993, www.usnews.com/usnews/news/articles/930823/archive_015665_4.htm.

17. James Mann, *The Rebellion of Ronald Reagan: A History of the End of the Cold War* (New York: Viking, 2009), 19.

18. Reagan, quoted in Mann, *Rebellion,* 22–23.

19. ROCKY FLATS

1. "Rocky Flats National Wildlife Refuge," www.fws.gov/rockyflats/. Websites accessed June 17, 2010, unless otherwise noted. Kristen Iversen, *Full Body Burden: Growing Up in the Nuclear Shadow of Rocky Flats* (New York: Crown, 2012), will be the definitive book on Rocky Flats for the forseeable future.

2. "Visitors" page at www.fws.gov/rockyflats/visitors.htm (accessed June 15, 2010). Rocky Flats is not a National Historic Landmark, but it was listed on the National Park Service National Register of Historic Places in 1998—a list that has 80,000 entries: http://nrhp.focus.nps.gov/natreg/docs/About.html.

3. "Rocky Flats Cold War Museum," www.rockyflatscoldwarmuseum.org/.

4. Rocky Flats Cold War Museum Feasibility Study, www.rockyflatscoldwarmuseum.org/PressRelease.pdf.

5. "Record of Decision," www.fws.gov/rockyflats/Documents/Record-of-Decision.pdf; Author's e-mail to rockyflats@fws.gov.

6. Rocky Flats Cold War Museum, www.rockyflatscoldwarmuseum.org/ (accessed May 22, 2011).

7. Some of this history is told in Patricia Buffer, "Beyond the Buildings: A Timeline of More than 50 Years of Rocky Flats History," in Department of Energy, "Rocky Flats History," pdf at www.lm.doe.gov/land/sites/co/rocky_flats/rocky.htm.

8. LeRoy Moore interview, Oct. 28, 2006, for the Maria Rogers Oral History Program and the Rocky Flats Cold War Museum. Transcript, audio, and video at Maria Rogers Oral History Program Collection, Carnegie Branch Library for Local History, Boulder, CO, www.boulderlibrary.org/oralhistory/.

9. "Protesters on railroad tracks," photo at www.rockyflatscoldwarmuseum.org/ExpressThumbnail/HistorySlideshow/i-Protesters_on_RFTES_Railroa.html. For a photo of the tepee on the tracks, see http://danielpubgroup.com/disobey/disobey.html.

10. Allen Ginsberg, *Plutonian Ode and Other Poems, 1977–1980* (San Francisco: City Lights Books, 1982).

11. AP report, "Rocky Flats Protest Is Tamer This Year," *Palm Beach Post,* Apr. 21, 1980, A6.

12. Described by Pat McCormick, a sister of Loretto, "Rocky Flats Activists" transcript, Oct. 28, 2006, www.boulderlibrary.org/oralhistory/; see also "2 Nuns to Spend Six Months in Prison for Nuclear Protest," *New York Times,* Nov. 23, 1982.

13. Jon Lipsky, July 23 and 24, 2005, interview for the Maria Rogers Oral History Program and the Rocky Flats Cold War Museum. Transcript, audio, and video at Maria Rogers Oral History Program Collection, Carnegie Branch Library for Local History, Boulder, CO, www.boulderlibrary.org/oralhistory/. See also David Kelly, "Nuclear Weapons Site Still Unsafe, Says Ex-FBI Agent; The Man Who Led the Raid on Rocky Flats Calls Plans for a National Wildlife Refuge There Irresponsible," *Los Angeles Times,* Jan. 6, 2005, A12.

14. Rocky Flats Virtual Museum, www.colorado.edu/journalism/cej/exhibit/index.html. The lead designer of the site is Len Ackland, an associate professor of journalism at the University of Colorado–Boulder and codirector of the Center for Environmental Journalism. He is the author of *Making a Real Killing: Rocky Flats and the Nuclear West* (Albuquerque: University of New Mexico Press, 1999).

15. Rocky Flats Cold War Museum, www.rockyflatscoldwarmuseum.org/.

16. "Museum Receives Artists' Banner," *Weapons to Wildlife: Rocky Flats Cold War Museum Newsletter* (Feb.–Mar. 2008): 1, www.rockyflatscoldwarmuseum.org/Newsletters/RFMuseum%20Newsletter.Feb.March.pdf; "Artifacts Donated," *Weapons to Wildlife* (Summer 2009): 4, www.rockyflatscoldwarmuseum.org/Newsletters/RFMuseum%20Newsletter.Summer.09.pdf.

17. "Rocky Flats Nuclear Weapons Plant," www.boulderlibrary.org/oralhistory/.

18. "Retiree Describes Site Selection, Cleanup after '69 Fire," Interview with Burt Kelchner, *Weapons to Wildlife* (Dec. 2009): 9, www.rockyflatscoldwarmuseum.org/Newsletters/RFMuseum%20Newsletter.Fall.12.09.pdf.

19. "Billy Graham, Sermon, Auschwitz, Poland, 1978." Quoted in *Weapons to Wildlife,* Dec. 2009, 4.

20. "Herb Bowman, Former Plant Manager, Discusses His Career," *Weapons to Wildlife* (Nov.–Dec.–Jan. 2008): 6–8, www.rockyflatscoldwarmuseum.org/Newsletters/RFMuseum%20Newsletter.Nov.Dec.Jan.08.pdf.

21. "Fiery Flats Transportation Manager Made Folks Toe the Line," *Weapons to Wildlife* (Feb.–Mar. 2008): 6, www.rockyflatscoldwarmuseum.org/Newsletters/RFMuseum%20Newsletter.Feb.March.pdf.

22. "Final Rocky Flats Sign text," www.fws.gov/rockyflats/Signage/Final%20Rocky%20Flats%20Sign%20Text%202.23.07.pdf.

23. Ellen Creager, "Once Notorious Uranium Waste Site in Fernald, Ohio, Beckons Tourists," *Detroit Free Press,* June 13, 2010, www.freep.com/article/20100613/FEATURES07/6130319/1322/Once-notorious-uranium-waste-site-in-Fernald-Ohio-beckons-tourists. Nothing has been posted at the website of the Rocky Flats National Wildlife Refuge since 2007: "Rocky Flats National Wildlife Refuge," www.fws.gov/rockyflats/ (accessed May 19, 2011).

20. CNN'S COLD WAR

1. CNN released the series on VHS as an 8-cassette set: *Cold War* [videorecording] / a Jeremy Isaacs production for Turner Original Productions; series producer, Martin Smith (Warner Home Video, Burbank, CA, 1998). The Google Video starts with http://video.google.com/videoplay?docid=-7408239438440019 63. The companion volume is Jeremy Isaacs and Taylor Downing, *Cold War: An Illustrated History, 1945–1991* (Boston: Little, Brown, 1998). The original online exhibit, at www.cnn.com/SPECIALS/cold.war/, was taken down in summer 2009; an "Educator Guide" has been posted at http://cgi.turnerlearning.com/cnn/coldwar/cw_start.html (accessed Aug. 20, 2009). See also www.wilsoncenter.org/coldwarfiles/index.cfm?fuseaction=resources.details&thisunit=0&resourceid=9 (accessed Feb. 10, 2010). One exception to the critical praise was Bruce Cumings in *The Nation,* who wrote that the series was "something to be thankful for" but that it "avoids answering the question *why.*" Bruce Cumings, "Screening the Cold War," *The Nation,* Oct. 19, 1998, 25–31. Paley Center exhibit plans: Pat Mitchell, email to author, June 26, 2010.

2. Judt was criticizing in particular John Lewis Gaddis: Tony Judt, "A Story Still to Be Told," *New York Review,* Mar. 23, 2006.

3. "Cold War: An Open Letter to Viewers by Jeremy Isaacs," www.cnn.com/SPECIALS/cold.war/guides/about.series/isaacs/. This and subsequent websites accessed Oct. 1, 2009, unless otherwise noted.

4. Charles Krauthammer, "CNN's Cold War; Twenty-Four Hours of Moral Equivalence," *Washington Post,* Oct. 30, 1998, A27.

5. John Dempsey, "CNN's 'War' Barbs: Cabler's Docu Series Assailed over Content," *Variety,* Nov. 2, 1998.

6. Some chronology: Turner commissioned *Cold War* in 1994. He sold CNN to Time-Warner in 1996 but remained as vice president. He donated $1 billion to the UN in 1997. *Cold War* premiered Sept. 27, 1998, and ran weekly for six months.

7. Helle Bering-Dale, "Cold War, Hot Debate: How Ted Turner Lost the Cold War," *Washington Times,* May 10, 2000.

8. All quotes are from the video documentary, *Cold War,* unless otherwise indicated.

9. Don Aucoin, "'Cold War'; Massive CNN Project Turns the 'Long Twilight Struggle' into a Riveting Human Story," *Boston Globe,* Sept. 27, 1998, N1; Don Aucoin, "Best Television 1998," *Boston Globe,* Dec. 29, 1998, C7; Richard Sandomir, "Khrushchev, Kennedy, Mao, Nixon . . . Can the Cast on Today's Stage Compare?," *New York Times,* Sept. 27, 1998.

10. Krauthammer, "CNN's Cold War."

11. Ibid.

12. Ibid.

13. Dennis Hevesi, "Ruth Greenglass, Key Witness in Trial of Rosenbergs, Dies at 83," *New York Times,* July 9, 2008, www.nytimes.com/2008/07/09/us/09greenglass.html?_r=1&scp=4&sq=%22david%20greenglass%22&st=cse&oref=slogin.

14. Ronald Radosh, "Finding a Moral Difference between the United States and the Soviets," in *CNN's Cold War Documentary: Issues and Controversy,* ed. Arnold Beichman (Stanford: Hoover Institution Press, 2000), 141.

15. Jacob Heilbrunn, "Viewer Discretion Advised: CNN's Tendentious 'Cold War,'" *New Republic,* Nov. 9, 1998, 23.

16. Ibid.

17. Ibid.

18. Arnold Beichman, "The Cold War Was a Just War," in Beichman, *CNN's Cold War Documentary,* xiv.

19. Bering-Dale, "Cold War, Hot Debate."

20. Richard Pipes, "The Cold War: CNN's Version," in Beichman, *CNN's Cold War Documentary,* 45–55.

21. Jeremy Isaacs's brief response to critics, Isaacs, "History in the Making," *Guardian,* Sept. 7, 1998, is also reprinted in Beichman, *CNN's Cold War Documentary,* 107–11.

22. John Lewis Gaddis, "The View from Inside: Answering Some Criticism," *New York Times,* Jan. 9, 1999. For an assessment of Gaddis's work, see Leo P. Ribuffo, "Moral Judgments and the Cold War," in *Cold War Triumphalism: The Misuse of History after the Fall of Communism,* ed. Ellen Schrecker (New York: New Press, 2004), 51–70.

23. Bering-Dale, "Cold War, Hot Debate."

24. John Lewis Gaddis, "The Cold War, Television, and the Approximation of Truth," in Beichman, *CNN's Cold War Documentary,* 43.

25. This segment is emphasized in James Collins, "The Cold War from Twilight to Dawn," *Time,* Sept. 21, 1998, www.time.com/time/magazine/article/0,9171,989129,00.html?promoid=googlep.

26. Michael Dobbs, "History's Chill Wind: Gargantuan Documentary Revisits the Cold War," *Washington Post,* Sept. 26, 1998, B1.

27. Ibid.

28. The Garthoff quote appears in the book based on the series: Isaacs and Downing, *Cold War,* 418.

29. Isaacs and Downing, *Cold War,* 420.

21. HARRY TRUMAN'S AMAZING MUSEUM

1. Benjamin Hufbauer, *Presidential Temples: How Memorials and Libraries Shape Public Memory* (Lawrence: University of Kansas Press, 2005), 151. This exhibit was opened in December 2001.

2. Quoted in Hufbauer, *Presidential Temples,* 154.

3. Quoted in Hufbauer, *Presidential Temples,* 160.

4. Quoted in Hufbauer, *Presidential Temples,* 162. The flip book is described in the online version of the exhibit at www.trumanlibrary.org/hst/g.htm but no flip-book text is presented there. Websites accessed Jan. 30, 2010, unless otherwise noted.

5. Ruth Stevens, "Exhibition Marks Centennial of Alumnus and Noted Diplomat," *Princeton Weekly Bulletin,* Nov. 3, 2003, www.princeton.edu/pr/pwb/03/1103/6a.shtml (accessed Apr. 29, 2010).

6. Truman Library, "The Cold War Turns Hot," www.trumanlibrary.org/hst/l.htm.

7. A temporary exhibit opened in 2010 on the sixtieth anniversary of the war; it also focuses mostly on veterans' memories. Truman Library, "Memories of Korea," www.trumanlibrary.org/korea/exhibit.htm. The temporary exhibit also included sections on Korean history and culture, the Japanese occupation of Korea, and "the future of Korea."

8. John Heilman and Mark Halperin, *Game Change: Obama and the Clintons, McCain and Palin, and the Race of a Lifetime* (New York: Harper, 2010).

9. Derek Leebaert, *The Fifty-Year Wound: How America's Cold War Victory Shapes Our World* (Boston: Little, Brown, 2002).

10. Ibid., 84.

11. Jon Halliday and Bruce Cumings, *Korea; The Unknown War* (New York: Pantheon, 1988), 155–57, cited in Engelhardt, *End of Victory Culture: Cold War America and the Disillusioning of a Generation* (Amherst: University of Massachusetts Press, 2007), 62–63.

12. Leebaert, *Fifty-Year Wound,* 95.

13. David Halberstam, *The Fifties* (New York: Ballantine, 1994), 106, 108.

14. Ibid., 79.

15. MacArthur, quoted in Chalmers Johnson, *The Sorrows of Empire* (New York: Holt, 2004), 53.

16. Stanley Weintraub, *MacArthur's War: Korea and the Undoing of an American Hero* (New York: Free Press, 2000), 2.

17. Ibid., 14–15.

18. Mrs. Joan Rountree to Harry S. Truman, Apr. 13, 1951, www.trumanlibrary.org/exhibit_documents/index.php?tldate=1951-04-13&groupid=3463&pagenumber=1& collectionid=firem.

19. Comments quoted in Hufbauer, *Presidential Temples,* 175. For a guide to the comment books, see "Records of the National Archives and Records Administration: Records of the Harry S. Truman Library: Museum Visitor Comment Books (Record Group 64) Dates: 2001–2010," www.trumanlibrary.org/hstpaper/rg64legacy.html.

20. Quoted in Hufbauer, *Presidential Temples,* 175.

21. One mural portrays MacArthur at the Inchon landing, and another portrays his "just fade away" speech to Congress.

22. MacArthur Museum of Arkansas Military, www.arkmilitaryheritage.com/.

23. "Final Fund Drive Begun for MacArthur Memorial," *Los Angeles Times,* Oct. 16, 1951, 14.

24. "Collegiate Group Backs MacArthur Statue Plan," *Los Angeles Times,* Oct. 31, 1951, A36.

25. Bill Henry, "By the Way," *Los Angeles Times,* Jan. 27, 1955, A1.

26. Joe Mozingo, "Filipino Veterans Chain Selves to Statue in Protest," *Los Angeles Times,* June 17, 1997. Twelve years later, after taking office in 2009, President Barack Obama settled the issue with a provision in his stimulus package that included an award of lump-sum payments of $15,000 to Filipino veterans who were American citizens and $9,000 to those who were not. By that time, only 18,000 of some 250,000 were still alive. Bernie Becker, "Filipino Veterans Benefit in Stimulus Bill," *New York Times,* Feb. 17, 2009, www.nytimes.com/2009/02/17/us/politics/17vets.html.

CONCLUSION

1. "The Cold War Victory Medal, Registered in the U.S. Patent and Trademark Office," www.foxfall.com/cwm.htm#BACKGROUND. Websites accessed Apr. 23, 2009, unless otherwise noted.

2. Official Website of the U.S. Navy, "Cold War Medals," www.navy.mil/navydata/navy_legacy_hr.asp?id=154. A Senate bill authorizing the Cold War Victory medal was reintroduced annually by Sen. Hillary Clinton.

3. U.S. Department of Defense, "Cold War Recognition Certificate Approved," Apr. 5, 1999, www.defenselink.mil/releases/release.aspx?releaseid=2031; "Cold War Recognition Certificate," Wikipedia, http://en.wikipedia.org/wiki/Cold_War_Recognition_Certificate; American Cold War Veterans, "The Certificate," www.americancoldwarvets.org/victory_medal.html.

4. Senator Reid, *Congressional Record,* Jan. 28, 2008 (Senate), p. S396–S399. The bill was S. 2561.

5. Ibid.

6. U.S. Senate, 110th Cong., 2007–8 session, Bill 2561, "Cold War Theme Study," http://thomas.loc.gov/cgi-bin/bdquery/z?d110:S2561 (accessed Oct. 25, 2011).

7. The Wende Museum in Los Angeles deals with the Cold War in Germany: www.wendemuseum.org (accessed Oct. 3, 2011).

8. Cold War Museum, www.coldwar.org/museum/physical_location.asp (accessed May 22, 2011).

9. Cold War Museum Mission Statement, www.coldwar.org/museum/index.asp.

10. H.R. 5396: introduced in the House, Feb. 12, 2008, by Tom Davis of Virginia: www.govtrack.us/congress/bill.xpd?bill=h110–5396 (accessed Sept. 19, 2009).

11. Lynne V. Cheney, *American Memory: A Report on Humanities in the Nation's Public Schools* (Washington, DC: National Endowment for the Humanities, n.d. [published Sept. 1987]), 5, quoted in Roy Rosenzweig and David Thelen, *The Presence of the Past: Popular Uses of History in American Life* (New York: Columbia University Press, 2000), 3.

12. Rosenzweig and Thelen, *The Presence of the Past,* 234.

13. David Thelen, *Memory and American History* (Bloomington: Indiana University Press, 1990), vii.

14. David Blight, *Race and Reunion: The Civil War in American Memory* (Cambridge, MA: Harvard University Press, 2002).

15. Emily Rosenberg, *A Date Which Will Live: Pearl Harbor in American Memory* (Durham: Duke University Press, 2004).

16. Benedict Anderson, *Imagined Communities: Reflections on the Origin and Spread of Nationalism* (New York: Verso, 2006).

17. David Lowenthal, *The Past Is a Foreign Country* (New York: Cambridge University Press, 1985), 40–44; Andreas Huyssen, *Twilight Memories: Marking Time in a Culture of Amnesia* (New York: Routledge, 1995).

18. Edward Linenthal, *Sacred Ground: Americans and Their Battlefields* (Urbana: University of Illinois Press, 1993), 1.

19. Erika Doss, *Memorial Mania: Public Feeling in America* (Chicago: University of Chicago Press, 2010), 1–2; Kirk Savage, *Monument Wars: Washington, D.C., the National Mall, and the Transformation of the Memorial Landscape* (Berkeley: University of California Press, 2009), 21. Doss refers briefly to the Victims of Communism Memorial—pp. 17, 56, 224—but the lack of "mania" surrounding it makes it an exception to the phenomenon she found.

20. Alison Landsberg, *Prosthetic Memory: The Transformation of American Remembrance in the Age of Mass Culture* (New York: Columbia University Press, 2004), 2, 9.

21. Ian Gambles, "Lost Time: The Forgetting of the Cold War," *National Interest,* no. 41 (Fall 1995).

22. Savage, *Monument Wars,* 292.

23. Gambles, "Lost Time." He declares that the Berlin Wall "hardly suffices to fill this symbolic gap" but makes no argument about that. http://nationalinterest.org/article/lost-time-the-forgetting-of-the-cold-war-678.

24. Savage, *Monument Wars,* 5.

25. Michael Kammen, *Mystic Chords of Memory: The Transformation of Tradition in American Culture* (New York: Vintage, 1993), 13.

26. John Bodnar, *Remaking America: Public Memory, Commemoration, and Patriotism in the Twentieth Century* (Princeton: Princeton University Press, 1992).

27. Eric Hobsbawm, *The Age of Extremes: A History of the World, 1914–1991* (New York: Pantheon Books, 1994), 231, 230.

28. Gambles, "Lost Time." The argument is explicit, and extended, in Andrew Alexander, "The Soviet Threat Was Bogus," *Spectator,* Apr. 20, 2002, www.spectator.co.uk/the-magazine/cartoons/9924/the-soviet-threat-was-bogus.thtml. Alexander is a conservative columnist for the *Daily Mail.*

29. M. I. Finley, *The Use and Abuse of History: From the Myths of the Greeks to Lévi-Strauss, the Past Alive and the Present Illumined* (New York: Puffin, 1987), 26–27.

30. Ronald Reagan, "Peace: Restoring the Margin of Safety," speech to the Veterans of Foreign Wars, Aug. 18, 1980, www.reagan.utexas.edu/archives/reference/8.18.80.html.

31. See Sean Wilentz, *The Age of Reagan: A History, 1974–2008* (New York: HarperCollins, 2008), passim.

32. National Park Service Stats, Vietnam Veterans Memorial, www.nature.nps.gov/stats/viewReport.cfm.

33. Doss, *Memorial Mania,* 130. See also G. Kurt Piehler, *Remembering War the American Way* (Washington, DC: Smithsonian Institution Press, 1995), 5: The Vietnam Veterans Memorial reflects "Americans' deep misgivings and ambiguity regarding the nature of the conflict."

EPILOGUE

1. James Mann, *Rise of the Vulcans: The History of Bush's War Cabinet* (New York: Penguin, 2004), xiv. Mann includes Condoleeza Rice and Colin Powell among the "vulcans," but their ideological trajectories were different from Cheney's and Rumsfeld's.

2. Ibid., 145.

3. Ibid., 68, 72.

4. Ibid., 97.

5. For another approach to "Cold War nostalgia," see Penny von Eschen, "'God I Miss the Cold War': Memory, Nostalgia, and Global Disorder since 1989," Lecture, University of Michigan, Ann Arbor, Apr. 13, 2010, video at http://lecb.physics.lsa.umich.edu/CWIS/browser.php?ResourceId=1997.

INDEX

Page numbers in italics refer to illustrations.